FIGHTING FOR VIRTUE

Studies of the Weatherhead East Asian Institute, Columbia University

The Studies of the Weatherhead East Asian Institute of Columbia University were inaugurated in 1962 to bring to a wider public the results of significant new research on modern and contemporary East Asia.

FIGHTING FOR VIRTUE

Justice and Politics in Thailand

Duncan McCargo

CORNELL UNIVERSITY PRESS   ITHACA AND LONDON

Cornell University Press expresses its appreciation to the Schoff Fund at the University Seminars at Columbia University for their help in publication. The ideas presented in this book have benefited from discussions in the University Seminar on Southeast Asia in World Affairs.

First published 2019 by Cornell University Press

Library of Congress Cataloging-in-Publication Data
Names: McCargo, Duncan, author.
Title: Fighting for virtue : justice and politics in Thailand / Duncan McCargo.
Description: Ithaca : Cornell University Press, 2019. | Series: Studies of the
    Weatherhead East Asian Institute, Columbia University | Includes bibliographical
    references and index.
Identifiers: LCCN 2019017309 (print) | LCCN 2019018382 (ebook) |
    ISBN 9781501709586 (pdf) | ISBN 9781501712227 (epub/mobi) |
    ISBN 9780801449994 (cloth)
Subjects: LCSH: Political questions and judicial power—Thailand. | Judicial
    power—Thailand. | Judges—Thailand. | Thailand—Politics and government—
    21st century.
Classification: LCC KPT2613 (ebook) | LCC KPT2613 .M33 2019 (print) |
    DDC 347.593/013—dc23
LC record available at https://lccn.loc.gov/2019017309

Contents

Burleigh

No—she cannot stay alive—she cannot live
[Be]cause every day she does, the danger grows:
alive, she breeds rebellion from this cell
and that's the cage this case has locked the Queen in,
when every move available is wrong.
And sometimes you can see she wants to act –
but—no—the words can't pass her lips.
She's waiting for someone to take the hint.
Hoping someone saves her from this choice
of "merciful but weak" or "brutal tyrant"

—*Mary Stuart*, Act 1
   Friedrich Schiller, adapted by Robert Icke

There are people who may come along and say that me, Rama IX,
I do what I feel like doing. I have never done what I felt like doing.

—King Bhumibol, speech to Supreme Court judges, April 25, 2006

Preface

Sanam Luang, December 22, 2012. Darkness was falling as I strode across the royal grounds in the historic heart of Bangkok's Rattanakosin area. Behind me was the campus of Thammasat University, a traditional bastion of liberalism, home to the country's most prestigious law faculty, and the alma mater of many prominent judges. Before me lay the majestic Supreme Court building, constructed during the Second World War under the Phibun government. To my right were the gleaming gold chedis of the Grand Palace, catching the last rays of the sunset. On my left was Rajadamneon Avenue, the royal thoroughfare linking the old capital of Thonburi with the bustling centers of the modern capital, Bangkok. By Southeast Asian standards, the weather was mild, and all seemed right in the world.

The reality was a little different. I had just come from a long and fascinating interview with one of Thailand's most distinguished legal scholars, Thammasat's Worajet Pakeerat. In January that year I had observed a disturbing rally on the university campus, at which academics and alumni of the journalism faculty had called for Worajet to be expelled from Thammasat University, and indeed from Thailand itself. His meticulously argued criticisms of the lèse-majesté law and his calls for greater public scrutiny of the judiciary had made him an outcast among many of his own colleagues. The rally against him was held in front of a statue of Pridi Banomyong, the founder of the university and the intellectual leader of the movement that had ended Siam's absolute monarchy in June 1932.

When American president Barack Obama had paid a call on King Bhumibol Adulyadej of Thailand just a month earlier, their meeting took place not at the glittering Grand Palace—where the King met President George W. Bush in 2003—but in Thonburi's Siriraj Hospital, on the opposite bank of the river. From his sixteenth floor windows overlooking the Chao Phraya River, the ailing King could in theory have watched the January 2012 Thammasat University anti-Worajet protest through a pair of powerful binoculars. The King's lengthy absence from Bangkok's historic center was a source of growing national anxiety: how much longer could the ageing monarch remain on the throne?

Six years earlier, in April 2006, King Bhumibol had made one of the most important speeches of his reign, addressing the judges of the Supreme Court and calling on them to help resolve the country's intractable political problems. At the core of those problems was Prime Minister Thaksin Shinawatra, a former police officer turned telecommunications magnate who had proved himself electorally invincible, but had alienated the monarchy and the country's traditional elite. The final decade of Bhumibol's remarkable seventy-year reign would be overshadowed by political infighting between pro- and anti-Thaksin factions, played out in four general elections, seven prime ministers, several rounds of massive street protests, two military coups, revolving door constitutions—and numerous judicial interventions in politics.

Outwardly, the Supreme Court compound looked as imposing and enduring as ever. But as I grew closer I realized that the structure was now a hollow shell: just weeks earlier, the judges had moved to temporary quarters in the Government Complex in Chaeng Wattana, miles from the middle of the capital. Plans to replace the old Supreme Court building with a much larger one, potentially violating city zoning laws, were mired in deep controversy.

Public life during my year of fieldwork in 2012 had been punctuated by important cases in both the Criminal and Constitutional Courts, but on the surface all was orderly: no mass street protests, no change of government, no military coup. Prime Minister Yingluck Shinawatra appeared to have achieved a modus vivendi with the palace and the traditional elite. Yet, in fact, nothing around the Sanam Luang was quite what it seemed. The revered King was not in his palace, but in a hospital bed. At Thammasat University, Thailand's most progressive campus, critical professors were being harassed by their own colleagues and alumni. The Supreme Court and the judiciary were now the focus of excessive expectations and intense popular scrutiny.

The uneasy calm was not to last. In 2013, mass protests forced Yingluck to dissolve parliament; the following year she was removed from office by the Constitutional Court—the Supreme Court later sentenced her to jail—and her government was overthrown in a May 2014 military coup. In October 2016, King Bhumibol would pass away, cremated the following year in a magnificent funeral edifice erected on the Sanam Luang itself. After his funeral, the Sanam Luang would be fenced off: public space became a royal enclave.

For now, however, I was leaving Bangkok. After crossing the Sanam Luang, dodging exuberant kids flying kites, I hailed a taxi from in front of the Supreme Court. Dusk was descending, and I was heading home that night, to start working on a book about politics and justice in Thailand.

> No one would dare to send those who insult the King to jail because the King will be troubled, since people will claim that the King is not a good person, or at least is over-sensitive—sending them to jail for minor insults. Actually, the King has never told anyone to send them to jail.
>
> Under previous kings, even rebels were not sent to jail or punished. King Rama VI did not punish rebels. During the time of King Rama IX,

who were the rebels? There have never been any genuine rebels. I also followed the same approach: do not send them to jail, but let them go. If they are already in jail, release them. If they are not in custody, I will not press charges as the offended party. The person who is insulted is the one in trouble. People who insult the King and are punished are not in trouble, rather the King himself is in trouble. This is a strange business.[1]

King Bhumibol (Rama IX)'s 2005 birthday speech was understood at the time primarily as criticizing then prime minister Thaksin Shinawatra, who was suing some of his critics for defamation, for his excessive sensitivity. Thaksin dropped a number of lawsuits against his adversaries immediately following the royal speech. But other important messages of the 2005 speech were that the King did not consider himself above criticism; and he did not believe in punishing those who questioned or challenged his authority. The implication was that harsh punishments for "rebels"—jailing lèse-majesté offenders, for example—would prove counterproductive, undermining the legitimacy of the monarchy. The King insisted he did not believe there were any real rebels during his reign.

As Michael Connors has noted, these views were nothing new: King Bhumibol had said something very similar in his birthday remarks of 2003:

> [If] they criticize correctly then thank them, if they criticize wrongly tell them, very discreetly, but the trouble, the person who is greatly troubled by this, is the king, he is troubled because no one can reproach him. ... We did not tell those who wrote the constitution that no one can criticize or contradict the king. Why this was written, I do not know. If I cannot be contradicted, how can I know if I am right or wrong?[2]

While some of the nuances of King Bhumibol's birthday speeches might delicately be termed "lost in translation," the main point was pretty clear. Those who resisted or criticized royal authority should not face criminal charges, and certainly not jail terms. Draconian laws should not be enforced in his name. Even kings could be contradicted.

In 2006, the King called on Thailand's judges to find solutions for the country's political problems. As in his 2003 and 2005 birthday speeches, a major theme was "don't drag me into this": the King reprimanded those who wanted him to appoint a new prime minister to avert the crisis caused by Thaksin's missteps and the agitations of the 2006 anti-Thaksin movement. King Bhumibol was well aware of the dangers of openly picking sides during times of intense political polarization. Like Queen Elizabeth I as depicted in Schiller's play *Mary Stuart*, he feared both showing weakness and appearing tyrannical, and apparently kept hoping that someone would take the hint and deal with Thaksin for him. This book examines how judges reacted to these twin royal injunctions: both by taking to heart the King's 2006 call to political action, and by largely ignoring his 2005 insistence that rebels or critics should be tolerated rather than punished. Over the decade that followed, politicians became increasingly demonized: Thaksin and his associates were branded as a network of traitors whose criminal schemings threatened national security and the monarchy. The King may have insisted there were no real rebels, but those around him began imagining rebels everywhere. Rebellion was to be countered by legalism.

The book argues that during the final decade of the Ninth Reign, the Thai judiciary failed on all counts: their political interventions were inept and inflammatory, while their punitive treatment of supposed dissidents was unconscionable. The main questions asked by the book are: Why did the Thai courts embark on a path of judicialization, variously defined, from 2006 onward? How did they rise to the challenge? And above all, why did they fail? My tentative answers: judges failed partly because the mission they were given by the King was an impossible one, and because the monarchical network could never decide what to do about Thaksin and his associates. Judicial crackdowns, evasions, and procrastinations reflected the inconsistent position of the palace. But judges also failed because they took their nominal role as royal servants far too literally, trying too hard to protect the fading monarchy, rather than to administer justice in the public interest.

This has been a difficult book to write: it deals with a complex and rapidly changing subject, and draws on lengthy fieldwork. Very little has been published about Thai judges, most of whom are not authorized to grant formal interviews. Even before the book project officially began, I had already done some preliminary work: I observed some court cases in Thailand's southern border provinces in 2006, as part of an earlier project on the insurgency there; I coauthored a paper on judicialization in Thailand for a 2008 workshop organized by Alex Mutebi at the National University of Singapore, after which I did a round of interviews in Bangkok; and in the summer of 2009 I conducted some follow-up observations at a provincial court, aided by a small grant from the British Academy's ASEASUK Research Committee. I wrote up that fieldwork and roughed out an article during a wonderfully productive stay at the Rockefeller Foundation's Villa Serbelloni in Bellagio during the spring of 2010. A big breakthrough came when I was awarded a 2011–14 Leverhulme Trust Major Research Fellowship, the jewel in the crown of British social science fellowships, to work on the present book about the politics of justice in Thailand. Additional funding for my justice fieldwork came from the Bernard Schwartz Book Prize monies I received from the Asia Society in 2009.

In order to research this book, I followed the same inductive immersion methods that I have used with minor variations for previous monographs, notably my *Politics and the Press in Thailand* (2000) and *Tearing Apart the Land* (2008): after only minimal background reading, I plunged myself into a year of fieldwork. Using a political ethnography approach, I spent hundreds of hours during 2012 in criminal courts undertaking participation observation; I conducted dozens of formal interviews and had many more off-the-record conversations; and I reviewed a large number of Thai-language documents, mainly primary sources. I went back to Thailand for shorter periods in 2013, 2014, and 2015 to collect missing materials and conduct additional interviews.

Transliterating the Thai language is always a thorny problem. As in my previous writings, I have used a simplified version of the Library of Congress system that does not indicate vowel length. However, I have transliterated people's names according to their own preferences, where these were known to me. Thai script has been included wherever possible for major written sources, though for simplicity I have generally omitted it for the formulaic titles of documents such as court records.

I could not have done all of this alone: this book simply would not have been written without months of research support from Pete, Ying, Niw, Ploy, and Jern, with occasional help from other assistants. Nut, Ei, Joe, and Am were constant sources of ideas and information, while Boo was always ready with translation tips and more. I am extremely grateful to all those took the time to talk to me—including judges, prosecutors, police officers, defense lawyers, defendants and their families, witnesses, academics, journalists, and campaigners.

During the past thirty years I have come to rely on numerous friends, colleagues, and former students in Thailand for advice and support. Fieldwork is teamwork, and my engagement with Thailand is part of a large and continuing collaboration. Many of my supporters have been listed in the acknowledgments pages of my earlier books, and in the interests of space I will confine myself to those who contributed most directly to this project, who include Chaiwat Satha-Anand, Chanintira na Thalang, Mark Kent, Naruemon Thabchumpon, Nattharin Kittithaweepan, Thaweeslip Subwattana, and Thirayuth Boonmi. I have also benefited greatly from conversations with some of Thailand's most insightful legal scholars, notably Khemthong Tonsakulrungruang, Sawatree Suksiri, Somchai Preechasilapakul, and Worajet Pakeerat. Among the larger scholarly community, I have learned immeasurably from Chris Baker, Sarah Bishop, Katherine Bowie, Nick Cheesman, Michael Connors, Penny Darbyshire, David Engel, Tom Ginsburg, Tyrell Haberkorn, Andrew Harding, Kevin Hewison, Kasian Tejapira, Peter Leyland, Michael Montesano, Frank Munger, Nidhi Eeoseewong, David Streckfuss, and Thongchai Winichakul—and many more besides. Some of those mentioned here generously provided detailed comments on all or part of this manuscript. Many who have supported my work in various ways cannot be named and thanked personally here—Thailand is a troubled and troubling place these days—but they know who they are, and their contributions have been greatly appreciated.

Since 2010, I have been affiliated with Columbia University's Weatherhead East Asian Institute, which has served as my scholarly second home; since 2015, I have also taught spring semesters as a visiting professor at Columbia's Department of Political Science. Thanks are due to Kay Achar, Rattana Bounsouaysana, Myron Cohen, Sheila Coronel, Tim Frye, Gerry Curtis, Carol Gluck, Waichi Ho, Eugenia Lean, Xiaobo Lu, Andy Nathan, Michael Schudson, the late Al Stepan, Madeline Zelin, and numerous other colleagues at Columbia for their unfailing support; as well as the late Robert Ferguson, whose work on political trials has been a great inspiration. Thanks also to my ever-supportive New York Southeast Asia Network cofounders Ann Marie Murphy, John Gershman, and Margaret Scott.

I was very fortunate to spend the 2015–16 academic year in the idyllic surroundings of Princeton's Institute for Advanced Study, where the first full draft of the book was assembled at the School of Social Science: I am very grateful to Didier Fassin and a wonderful circle of friends and colleagues at and around the institute, including Michael Laffan and Nigel Smith of Princeton University. Alice Goffman's insightful comments helped me develop the structure of the book; Inge Bondi's nearby suite provided the perfect housing.

The University of Leeds has been my immensely supportive academic home for the past quarter-century. I am greatly indebted to the generosity and collegiality of Jeremy Higham, Jason Ralph, Martin Seeger, Kevin Theakston, Adam Tyson, Caroline Wise, and many others at that great Yorkshire university.

This manuscript has benefited greatly from close reading by a number of those named above, notably the two Michaels: Connors and Montesano. It has been immeasurably improved by insightful comments by my old friend Steven Kennedy, and from Roger Haydon's expert editing.

Stephanie Winters has shared and endured the adventure of my writing this book from start to finish, for which I am deeply appreciative.

Nobody but me is to blame for this book's shortcomings; I only hope I am not judged too harshly.

FIGHTING FOR VIRTUE

Introduction

LEGALISM AND REVIVAL OF TREASON

Court cases are inherently contentious, troublesome, and troubling: political trials are even more so. This is especially the case when political trials form microcosms of larger conflicts that have polarized and indeed immobilized a nation. Such trials were a marked feature of public life in Thailand in the decade after 2006. This book sets out to explain why these trials took place, how they proceeded, and why they turned out as they did.

A good trial works, at least at certain moments. By bringing together contending parties in a highly ritualized format, the trial can provoke revelation or even catharsis. Victims may have their voices heard. The state can impose a sentence on a defendant that in some way reflects the collective will. Defendants may acknowledge the error of their ways. A bungled prosecution may be exposed. Both innocence and guilt may be recognized and validated. A society emerges slightly stronger from every successful trial: norms are reinforced, rights are further enshrined, and the state is subtly relegitimated.

A bad trial does not work. When the charges at hand seem unfair, the proceedings mechanical, and the protagonists are of doubtful competence, no sense of revelation or catharsis will emerge. The law is seen for what it is: an ass. When the law resembles an ass, so do courts, judges, the justice system, and indeed the state as a whole. Botched court cases based on laws that are unfit for purpose help create dysfunctional politics and highly polarized societies, fueling frustrations and promoting disorder.

Here lay the central irony of Thailand's recent political court cases. The Thai legal system is primarily dedicated to the preservation of peace and order, rather than to more liberal goals such as promoting rights-based justice, or even to the conservative, technocratic objective of promoting the rule of law. But the conduct of political trials in the final decade of King Bhumibol's reign led perversely to a decline in peace and order, as the justice system itself became a focus for discontent. Banning pro-Thaksin parties twice in just over eighteen months, while acquitting the Democrat Party on similar charges, provoked accusations of "double standards." Jailing various pro-Thaksin figures for long spells on the basis of dubious lèse-majesté or cybercrime charges that were framed as acts of treason beggared belief in a twenty-first century democracy. Conflicts between two major political factions were acted out in courtrooms that became proxy sites for much larger, more unmanageable, and unwinnable contests.

The main focus of this book is on a particular period of Thailand's judicial politics: from the contentious April 2006 general election, until the passing away of King Bhumibol Adulyadej in October 2016. This was the era of *tulakanphiwat*, most commonly translated as "judicialization": an era when the courts were apparently given a special—if rather unclear—royal mission to solve the country's intractable political problems. With the ascent of King Vajiralongkorn to the throne in late 2016, Thailand entered a new era in which earlier assumptions about the role of country's core institutions would soon have to be revised.

Thailand's recent constitutions begin with a deceptively simple-sounding injunction: "May there be virtue." At the core of the various legal and political projects that these constitutions have embodied, the overall aim remains the same: the codification of virtuous rule. Virtuous rule is the primary source of legitimacy for the Thai state:[1] a benevolent ruler, or *dhammaraja*, who embodies notions of Buddhist kingship presides over a regime based on principles of *ratchaprachasamasai*,[2] which Michael Connors has termed royal liberalism. A major problem here is that virtuous rule is inextricable from a view of kingship that belongs to the pre-1932 world of Siam's absolute monarchy. As Benedict Anderson put it: "'Royalism,' in the sense of an active quest for real power in the political system *by the royal family* . . . persists in a curiously antique form in contemporary Siam."[3] In one sense virtuous rule is no mere philosophical abstraction: many Thais take it very literally, seeing King Bhumibol as epitomizing the perfect man. Patrick Jory has argued that the persistence of popular belief in royal *barami* (merit, virtue, or charisma) means that "A superficially modernized Thai monarchy continues to carry within itself the essence of an ancient theory of political authority that is alien to modern concepts of political legitimacy."[4]

During the late twentieth century, Thailand developed a hybrid mode of rule reflecting the existence of multiple modes of legitimacy, which I have termed "network monarchy."[5] The network monarchy is an aggregation of elite royalist players, including the Privy Council, the military, the upper echelons of the civil service, prominent academics and members of civil society—and the judiciary. In theory, the network took direction primarily from King Bhumibol, although also at times from the Queen and other family members. In practice, the chain of command within the monarchical network is ambiguous, since even when he was younger and more active, Bhumibol rarely spelled out the royal will. Over the years, his public speeches, often given on his birthday, became increasingly ambiguous or even cryptic. Prominent members of the network were thus left to extemporize on royal themes, pushing agendas that may—or may not—have reflected the real wishes of the palace. As the health of the King and Queen declined following the turn of the millennium, and especially after the King took up near-permanent residence in Siriraj Hospital in 2008, the network gained in power vis-à-vis the monarchy itself.

In the decades after King Bhumibol ascended the throne in 1946, Thailand experienced remarkable economic growth and social transformation. Living standards and life expectancy increased dramatically across the board. Standards of health provision and levels of education rose exponentially. Politics, however, was an entirely different story: Thailand became one of the most unstable countries on earth, topping global charts for the highest number of military coups and new constitutions in the twentieth century—what Harding and Leyland aptly term an endless search for "constitutional nirvana."[6] The strengths of the Bhumibol era network monarchy lay in its adaptability and flexibility, enabling it to survive endless political crises, and frequent alternation between military and parliamentary rule. Network monarchy's weaknesses were lack of coherence— there was always considerable infighting—and the perennial question of agency: who exactly was responsible for addressing problems?

During the heyday of network monarchy, interventions in the political process at times of crisis were made either by the monarch himself, or by proxies. These interventions took the form of public speeches and statements, or overt indications of royal support. They included explicit moves made in October 1973 (siding with students against the military), October 1976 (including inviting former dictator Thanom to return to Thailand and enter the monkhood), April 1981 (joining General Prem in Korat to signal disapproval of an attempted coup), and most iconically in May 1992 (summoning the prime minister and a protest leader for a televised dressing-down). Yet each royal intervention was extremely risky: the King could not afford to back a loser, or to go strongly against prevailing public sentiments. As Thailand's politics grew increasingly polarized after 2001, the King became understandably more reluctant to adopt an overt stance on contentious issues that divided the population. The risks of making a mistake were rising, while King Bhumibol himself was becoming ever more frail.

A series of troublesome episodes illustrated the royal intervention problem. Faced with rising levels of violence in the country's southern border provinces—predominantly caused by separatist-inclined militants from the majority Malay Muslim community—Queen Sirikrit made an outspoken intervention in November 2004. In a provocative speech, the Queen called on all 300,000 Buddhists living in the region to learn how to shoot, and she proceeded to send military shooting instructors to teach them.[7] King Bhumibol immediately responded with a nationally broadcast speech of his own, instead calling on government officials to "access, understand and develop" the troubled region—in effect, a call for bureaucratic benevolence and paternalism, and an implicit disavowal of the Queen's apocalyptic rhetoric. Bhumibol well understood that the wrong kind of royal intervention could easily—in this case literally—fuel the flames of popular anger. In October 2008, Queen Sirikrit again made headlines when she attended the high-profile funeral of a young anti-Thaksin protester Angkhana Radubpanyawut who had been fatally injured, telling Angkhana's father that she was a "good girl" who "helped protect" the monarchy and the country.[8] In both cases, the Queen pandered to a conservative royalist Buddhist base, but alienated other societal groups. For many diehard Thaksin supporters in the North and Northeast, the Angkhana funeral was a Eureka moment that "opened their eyes" and confirmed their worst fears about the political leanings of the palace.[9] This single episode arguably did more to undermine the legitimacy of the monarchy than any other moment during Bhumibol's seventy years on the throne. Under conditions of such profound polarization, the less the palace said and did in public, the better.

In light of the King's failing health, and the looming prospect of the deeply unpopular Crown Prince Vajiralongkorn—nobody's idea of a *dhammaraja*—succeeding to the throne, the challenge of firming up Thailand's shaky political order increased. How could mechanisms be put in place that would ensure political stability in the wake of the Vajiralongkorn's succession to the throne? How could this unpredictable figure be prevented from scuppering royal legitimacy?

Network monarchy had allowed a variety of royally aligned actors to flourish and to influence public life, in a somewhat laissez-faire manner, giving the outward appearance of wide-ranging, pluralistic political participation. Yet the contrast between the broadly well-intentioned Bhumibol and his potentially dangerous son made clear that network monarchy was not a sustainable set of arrangements, let alone a consolidated form of liberalism, or even pluralism. The implicit and informal arrangements underpinning the network were entirely personalized. While Bhumibol rarely chose to exercise a veto—very few people were publicly dismissed from the network—the possibility of kingly excommunication was ever present. A more activist monarch could easily purge alternative or dissenting voices, turning the monarchical network from a team of rivals into a much cruder instrument of royal power.

How could abuse of the network monarchy best be prevented, and how could peace and order be preserved after Bhumibol's passing? The simplest answer was to rely on the powerful military to check and balance royal power in a postsuccession era. The Thai military had long enjoyed considerable influence, not least because of its central role in ending the absolute monarchy in the top-down "revolution" of 1932. Over subsequent decades, the military had frequently resorted to coups d'état, becoming both highly politicized and deeply mistrustful of other actors, especially elected politicians, whom it typically viewed as corrupt and untrustworthy. The Royal Thai Army in particular believed itself to be always on the side of the people, the most reliable guardian of the public interest. During the premiership of Field Marshal Sarit Thanarat (1957–63), the army formed a strategic alliance with the monarchy that has continued to this day. From the late 1950s onward, the young King Bhumibol, Queen Sirikit, and their four children were deployed as symbols of nationalism and anticommunist developmentalism, dispatched to the countryside to win over the Thai populace at a time when neighboring Indochina became the front line for global power struggles between the United States, the Soviet Union, and China. But by 1973 the King had turned against Sarit's authoritarian successors, field marshals Thanom Kittikachorn and Praphas Charusathian; and although the palace renewed its strong alliance with the military during the violent October 1976 crackdown on the student movement, it was no longer plausible to see soldiers simply as national saviors. The generals further blotted their copybooks in "Black May" of 1992, when coup leader turned prime minister Suchinda Kraprayoon tried to halt antigovernment protests through bloody suppression: the army shot more than fifty unarmed civilians dead. The military was now clearly part of Thailand's problem, and the answer had to lie elsewhere.

Liberal figures associated with the network monarchy, including former premier Anand Panyarachun, former palace doctor Prawase Wasi, and law professor Borwornsak Uwanno, now believed that the military could not be trusted to manage such a delicate matter as the royal succession. Prawase made clear in a 1995 speech that he was anxious to head off the possibility of succession-related violence.[10] This group of establishment reformers initially placed their faith in institutionalizing representative politics, strengthening parliament and political parties in the belief that this was the best means of averting future bloody confrontations.[11] Influenced by the international discourse of the new constitutionalism, they produced the 1997 "People's Constitution"—based on extensive public consultation—which aimed to solidify electoral politics, yet also to check and balance the power of the executive through a series of new monitoring institutions, notably a Constitutional Court, an Election Commission, a Counter-Corruption Commission, and a National Human Rights Commission. Thailand was by no means unique in Southeast Asia in adopting such innovations: Indonesia established a Constitutional Court in 2003, for example, while the Philippines created a Commission on Human Rights in 1987.[12] Regionally and globally, people were placing faith in institutional innovations designed to firm up shaky political systems in times of transition.

But the bold experiment of Thailand's People's Constitution soon ended in failure, at least in the eyes of the network monarchy. Following the 1997 Asian financial crisis, former police officer turned telecoms billionaire Thaksin Shinawatra was able to exploit the new rules of the game to create a dominant political party for the first time in Thai history.[13] That party proceeded to triumph in each successive election—in 2001, 2005, 2007, and 2011—as well as in two elections (2006 and 2014) that were later annulled by the courts. Initially broadly popular, Thaksin gradually antagonized the monarchical network, as well as the majority of middle-class Bangkokians; but he retained solid support in the populous North and Northeast regions of Thailand. Thailand entered a period of prolonged political crisis when the anti-Thaksin movement first emerged in September 2005. Thaksin was accused of abuses of power, corruption, and above all of disrespect towards the monarchy, which he had allegedly tried to upstage.

The Thaksin phenomenon laid bare the fundamental problem of Thailand's politics. An effective system of representative government produces popular politicians with whom large swathes of the population may identify. On some level, popular politicians competed with the special place of the monarchy, which could no longer monopolize public trust and admiration. As King Bhumibol's powers were waning, Thaksin was at his most energetic and influential, his very existence posing a profound threat to the discourse of hyper-royalism that pervades Thai public life, in a country where all wisdom and virtue is monopolized by members of the royal family: nonroyals almost never appear on Thai postage stamps or banknotes, for example. Thailand's experience with Thaksin Shinawatra suggested that the national elite was not prepared to embrace a politician whose popularity in any sense rivaled that of the monarchy.

The fledgling new institutions ushered in under the 1997 Constitution soon proved inadequate. A master politician, Thaksin easily found ways of subverting the aims of the constitution—ironically without changing a word of it—and concentrating power in his own hands. Awkward members of independent bodies could readily be charmed, bought off, intimidated, or simply removed at the earliest opportunity. Thaksin's 2001 and 2005 election victories had demonstrated that representative politics was a dangerous beast, one that could not easily live alongside Bhumibol's all-consuming monarchy. Nor did rules of the game, as codified in microcrafted constitutions and associated laws, offer much protection from the ruthless political will of an extremely popular elected premier.

The establishment did not trust Thaksin to handle the delicate royal succession or to keep Vajiralongkorn in line. Indeed, for several years the prime minister cultivated close connections to the heir to the throne, even predicting in a newspaper interview that Thailand would enjoy a "shining" new age in the next reign.[14] In expansive 2010 interviews with American journalist Tom Plate, the now-banished Thaksin offered to return from Dubai to assume a nonpolitical, royally appointed role related to the Crown Property Bureau or rural development.[15] Thaksin seemed to envisage a scenario under which he managed the country day-to-day on behalf of the next King, in some form of hybrid co-rule. This prospect alarmed anti-Vajiralongkorn royalists—often admirers of his well-liked sister, Princess Sirindhorn—and strengthened their conviction that Thaksin had to be removed from office and permanently barred from returning to power. When King Bhumibol finally passed away in October 2016, Thaksin summoned his aides and told them to prepare for an invitation from the new monarch to return to Thailand—an invitation that never arrived.[16]

How to deal with a politician who has lost the support of the elite but still commands votes from the majority of the electorate? This was a central problem that Thailand struggled to address in the decade after 2005. In 1992, former coup leader Suchinda Kraprayoon was appointed prime minister following a general election. After massive street protests culminating in violence carried out by the military, the King helped ensure that Suchinda resign from office, summoning both the prime minister and protest leader Chamlong Srimuang to the palace for a televised reprimand. But fourteen years later, Bhumibol—well aware of the polarization surrounding Thaksin—made clear his unwillingness to intervene directly. Instead, using two speeches delivered on the same day in April 2006, he called on the courts to solve the country's political problems. Those speeches and the events that followed have spawned numerous studies and commentary on the theme of Thailand's supposed "judicialization"—and form one of the starting points for this book.

In the wake of the April 2006 royal speeches, prominent Thammasat University sociologist Thirayuth Boonmi published first a newspaper article and then a slim book coining the term *tulakanphiwat,* which he translated rather oddly as "judicial review." Thirayuth argued that the King had given judges clear responsibility for addressing a wide range of political and social questions.[17] Thirayuth's writings helped spark a long-running debate about the proper role of the judiciary,[18] but there was no consensus on the meaning of the term *tulakanphiwat* in the Thai context. Thirayuth's original reading was highly conservative: he advocated drawing on a judicial "reserve" of virtuous people to populate independent agencies, the Senate, and even the Cabinet, as well as deploying them to address political problems in the interests of the nation. Most commentators have instead preferred the translation "judicialization," or Ran Hirschl's term "juristocracy"—both of which imply a critical view of the growing political role assumed by judges. Other Thai interpretations of the term have emphasized the idea of an activist, progressive judiciary as agents of social change. Outspoken legal scholar Pichet Maolanond argued that the best translation of tulakanphiwat was in fact "judicial activism,"[19] while Ramkhamhaeng University critical legal philosopher Jarun Koananun stressed that any such judicial activism should involve greater openness on the part of judges, including a willingness to listen to criticism and play more of a part in public life.[20] Thirayuth's introduction of the term *tulakanphiwat* may have generated more heat than light, but it also helped open up greater public debate about the role of the judiciary in the years that followed. This included increasingly critical statements by Worajet Pakeerat and his Nitirat campaign group of outspoken Thammasat University legal scholars—not to mention far more criticism of the courts by pro-Thaksin elements in Thai society.[21] In practice, tulakanphiwat has become a canvas onto which commentators from very different perspectives have projected their own readings, shaped by their political orientation and preferences.

One of the most detailed critiques of Thailand's judicialization appears in Nitirat member Piyabutr Saengkanokkul's 2017 book *Coup Court*. Piyabutr argues that judicialization only operates during elected governments, when it provided a legitimating rationale for the downfall of the Thaksin, Samak/Somchai, and Yingluck premierships.[22] For Piyabutr, judicialization is simply the flip side of what he terms the "coup court," a judicial system that finds endless fault with elected governments but has no problem at all with military regimes.[23] The courts enthusiastically enforce new "laws" that simply reflect the wishes of authoritarian rulers, and support the use of existing laws to curtail peoples' rights and support dictatorships. Ultimately, he argues, the discourse of judicialization will erode the legitimacy of the courts and fuel demands for far-reaching changes in the political order and the justice system itself.[24]

Divergent understandings of judicialization were often closely related to competing views of royalism. As Thongchai Winichakul has cogently argued, hyper-royalism is an important theme in the Thai political discourse of recent decades. He identifies the following features of hyper-royalism:[25] royal nationalism—according to which it becomes impossible to separate the monarchy from the nation; "excessive intensity" of royalism and demands for expressive loyalty; growing frequency and intensity of events at which people are supposed to express loyalty; numerous old and invented royal ceremonies and anniversaries; excessive eulogies to virtues and abilities of members of the royal family; linking of all virtue—saying no to drugs, for example—with monarchy; the use of a harsh punitive regime to maintain hyper-royalism; and the embrace of hyper-royalism by media and civil society, which creates a pervasive public culture.

The overall effect of hyper-royalism was to make the monarchy so ubiquitous that for many Thais, royalism became invisible, since it had "saturated the air" and became an all-pervasive phenomenon. Thai royalism had been a salient feature of public life since the Sarit era, but hyper-royalism grew apace in the wake of the 1997 financial crisis, and the accompanying royalist discourse of "sufficiency economy." It became even more palpable during 2006, when huge celebrations of Bhumibol's sixty years on the throne coincided with a political crisis engulfing the Thaksin administration, which culminated in the September 19 military coup.

Here was the paradox: the political reform movement of the 1990s had aimed to remove the need for royal interventions in politics, in effect to prepare for a post-Bhumibol de-mystification of the monarchy, a new normal in which Vajiralongkorn's role would be essentially ceremonial. But when political reform failed to deliver the desired results, the Thai elite began ramping up royalism, turning up the volume on the monarchy channel to drown out the alarming sounds coming from populist politicians and an increasingly vocal rural electorate. The net result of the 1990s reform process was that Thailand became more royalist and not less: the ensuing delegitimation of electoral politics sowed the seeds for an eventual reassertion of monarchical power in the new reign.

Thaksin Shinawatra, who had been reelected in February 2005 with a parliamentary landslide, soon faced accusations of abuse of power, especially after his controversial sale of the telecoms giant ShinCorp to the Singapore government investment arm Temasek at the end of the same year, in a deal that allowed him to avoid paying tax.[26] While not the main reason for growing anti-Thaksin sentiment, the ShinCorp controversy helped galvanize those who saw Thaksin as challenging royal prerogatives and popularity. As Thailand entered a period of bitter and byzantine political crisis, which persists to the present day, executive power in the form of a strong premiership was being widely questioned; the legislature had become a tool of Government House; independent agencies had been politicized; the military lacked credibility; and the palace declined to intervene. No wonder the focus of elite hopes and expectations shifted to the courts. Yet despite an explicit call for judicial intervention by King Bhumibol in April 2006, the Thaksin Shinawatra administration was ultimately ousted not by judges but by soldiers, in the September 2006 military coup led by then army commander General Sonthi Boonyaratglin. The subsequent junta, initially known as the

"Council for Democratic Reform under the Constitutional Monarchy," quickly appointed privy councilor and former army commander General Surayuth Chulanond prime minister.[27] The junta proceeded to preside over the drafting of a new constitution, a referendum on that constitution, and fresh elections—all in just fifteen months. While the junta was in power, Thaksin's Thai Rak Thai Party was abolished by the Constitutional Tribunal (an interim version of the Constitutional Court), which also banned a hundred senior party executives from holding political office for five years.

None of this made much difference: following the 2007 elections, a pro-Thaksin party was returned to power. Neither military force nor legal machinations could overturn Thailand's basic electoral landscape: crudely summarized, pro-Thaksin voters registered in the populous North and Northeast outnumbered anti-Thaksin voters in Bangkok and the South. During 2008, the courts struck again. Pro-Thaksin premier Samak Sundaravej was removed from office, ostensibly for illegally hosting a television cooking show. The Thaksin-affiliated People Power Party, which had won the December 2007 general election, was dissolved by the courts a year later, and its executive members were given a five-year ban on holding political office. Thaksin himself was convicted in absentia of a corruption-related offence and sentenced to two years in jail; prior to his conviction, the courts had permitted him to leave the country (ostensibly to attend the opening ceremony of the 2008 Beijing Olympics), and he has yet to return. Finally, the Democrat Party led by Abhisit Vejjajiva formed a government through a backroom deal, despite having lost the December 2007 election. When pro-Thaksin red-shirt groups staged massive demonstrations on the streets of Bangkok between March and May 2010, the military violently repressed the protests and more than ninety people were killed: most of them were unarmed civilians, shot dead by soldiers.[28] Apparently believing his own cheerleaders, Abhisit dissolved parliament in mid-2011, expecting to win the ensuing election.

Again, none of these developments changed the basic political equation: the majority pro-Thaksin electorate. Thaksin's sister Yingluck Shinawatra became prime minister following the landslide victory of the Pheu Thai Party in the July 3, 2011, election. Yingluck's party remained in power for almost three years, until the military coup of May 22, 2014—though Yingluck had been removed from office a couple of weeks earlier by the Constitutional Court, on the grounds that she had "abused her authority" by improperly transferring national security council chief Thawil Pliensri, who was deeply loyal to her political opponents.[29]

The National Council for Peace and Order—the rather Orwellian-named junta that seized power in 2014—was determined not to repeat the supposed mistakes of the 2006–7 coup makers. While the two previous coup leaders had appointed proxies, army commander General Prayuth Chan-ocha instead made himself prime minister, was in no hurry to call an early election, and appeared intent on stamping out the influence of the Shinawatra clan at all costs. He bypassed the civilian judiciary as needed, using military courts to try civilians who failed to comply with the junta's orders. Wielding absolute power under Article 44 of the interim constitution, he showed little regard for legal niceties. Under Prayuth's rule, Yingluck was charged with abuse of power over a massive rice subsidy scheme that cost state coffers huge sums of money during her term in office. In August 2017, the very night before the verdict in her case was announced, Yingluck was spirited out of Bangkok, joining her brother in exile. Plainly, the authorities had colluded in permitting her to flee the country. A few weeks later Yingluck was sentenced in absentia to a lengthy jail term. In effect, like her brother Thaksin, she had been expelled from Thailand.[30]

Since the onset of the crisis besetting Thaksin's government in late 2005, Thailand has seen five rounds of street massive protests, five general elections (two of them later annulled by the courts), two military coups, three full-blown constitution-drafting processes, and two referendums on new constitutions. There have also been frequent legal interventions to annul elections and dissolve political parties as well as to remove politicians from office, convict them of wrongdoing, and ensure their de facto banishment from the country—along with a host of other trials and legal changes aimed at curbing freedom of expression and criminalizing different forms of dissent. This book sets out to examine what lay behind these legal interventions, and why they have failed to lay Thailand's numerous political woes to rest.

The Justice System

Many accounts of Thai legal history begin by asserting that Siamese law was derived from the ancient Three Seals Code, a collection of Ayutthaya period legislation that was edited and codified in 1805, during the reign of Rama I. The Thammasat, part of the Three Seals Code containing guidance for judges, makes clear that magistrates who lack a deep understanding of Buddhist morality will be "mired in darkness and delusion" and so never be able to perform their duties effectively:

> All such people who are magistrates, even though they live to a hundred years old, and even though they have enough eloquence for bad people to respect them, will not be praised by learned men because their judgments will be as confused as blind elephants wandering in the forest until they meet final disaster through the wrong course of delusion.[31]

Technical knowledge or skills such as eloquence could be greatly overrated: what mattered most were virtues like compassion and an ability to avoid the "Four Wrong Courses." Judges act as a "special crystal circle" on behalf of the King their lord, to whom they should show "gratitude and loyalty."[32] The Thammasat made clear that the King himself was uniquely able to lay down laws for his subjects and in this sense was personally above the law.[33]

The Three Seals Code contains a considerable amount of Palace Law, probably dating back to the late fifteenth century. This includes the provision that the King's word was law: "If the king speaks on any government matter connected with law or custom, it is considered a ruling to be followed."[34] While other parts of the code were quite widely disseminated, there were few copies of the all-important Palace Law, which may even have been kept secret.[35] The Palace Law sets out elaborate rules of hierarchy—courtiers and officials were assigned specific levels of *sakdina* points, which entitled them to a range of different privileges and obligations—but also different punishments for any transgressions. "Improper assignations"—by implication, meetings among senior officials to plot against the authority of the monarch—could be severely punished. Serious offences by members of the royal family could be punished by exile to faraway cities such as Petchabun, Chantaburi, or Nakhon Sri Thammarat, where they would be kept under house arrest either upstairs or in a dark cellar.[36] Palace Law, like ordinary Siamese law during this period, provided for extremely severe punishments, often including beatings, mutilation, and execution. Foreign travelers reported seeing surprising numbers of people who had been maimed as a result of punishments. Imprisonment appears to have been relatively rare, perhaps because it was costly and cumbersome to carry out—though there were eight jails in Ayutthaya alone.[37]

The importance of the Three Seals Code for understanding modern Thai law has been disputed by revisionist legal scholar Somchai Preechasilapakul.[38] According to Somchai, Siamese law was almost entirely imported from Western models around the end of the nineteenth century. Neil Englehart argues that the notions of royal power codified in such documents "were not especially influential in daily practice and might be dismissed as mystifications or false consciousness," and perhaps the same applies to Palace Law.[39] Were the harsh punishments listed in the Palace Law Code systematically enforced? Even if the picture we derive of Ayutthayan punitiveness is somewhat exaggerated, the Three Seals Code nevertheless constitutes a powerful legal imaginary that continues to influence judicial thinking to this day, offering a recurrent rationalization for harsh sentences. Themes such as the special link between the monarchy and the judiciary, the blurring of legal and Buddhist doctrines, a hierarchy of punishment based on social standing, anxiety about plots against the throne, the monarch as a legal authority, and the use of banishment as a punishment, continue to resonate even in the twenty-first century.

Thailand has a national court system dating from a program of legal reforms carried out during the reign of King Chulalongkorn. The Courts of Justice in their current form date back to the establishment of the Ministry of Justice in 1891. Chulalongkorn's reforms resulted in fewer courts, with clearer lines of authority, and a much more standardized legal system across the country.[40] Oversight of the system resided with the minister of justice, who appointed all judges—though the King also deployed a number of Special Commissioners who were empowered to monitor the courts, train officials, and hear certain cases. One of the first ministers of justice was Prince Raphi Pattanasak (1896–1910), today hailed as the founding father of the Thai legal system. However, Somchai argues that King Chulalongkorn's general adviser from 1892 to 1901, former Belgian interior minister Gustave Rolin-Jacquemyns, was at least equally influential.[41] Reform and administration of the justice system required considerable input from numerous foreign experts; Belgian advisers, regarded as neutral in the regional colonial rivalry between the British and the French, were particularly favored.

Around the turn of the twentieth century, Siamese law had a number of unusual features: assault was not a crime, for example, unless the victim was surprised from behind.[42] Émile Jottrand, a Belgian legal adviser who served in Siam at the turn of the twentieth century, observed that "one uses and abuses imprisonment with an almost amusing ease, unlike the tediousness of the Belgian procedures"; for example, any witnesses or defendants who might skip a trial could just be arbitrarily detained.[43] Jottrand also noted that when Prince Raphi, then justice minister, visited the courts he would serve as a judge and try cases himself: there was no clear doctrine of separation of powers.[44] Losing parties nearly always appealed then, and they still do today.[45] Engel questions whether ordinary Siamese citizens found the reformed courts "any less menacing or complex than the old system"; the main intent behind the reforms was to increase the judicial power of the monarch, while reducing the King's day-to-day involvement in the courts.[46]

King Chulalongkorn's reforms aimed to "modernize" the new nation's legal procedures and structures, introducing notions—such as the right to a fair trial—introduced from the West, while leaving unchanged the absolute monarchy, under which all legitimate authority rested in the throne.[47] However, as Engel argues, the very same reforms "created a disequilibrium in the concept of monarchical rule, an implicit set of contradictions with regard to the king and his relationship to the law."[48] More recently, Engel has argued that contemporary frustrations with the justice system, especially among people in the North and Northeast, reflect a widespread sense that modern legal systems were unjust and exclusionary.[49] According to Riggs, reforms by Chulalongkorn and his successors brought into being "a bureaucracy which was destined to become stronger than the monarchy which created it."[50] These contradictions led inexorably to the overthrow of the absolute monarchy in 1932, the promulgation of Siam's first constitution, and the rise to power of the elite People's Party, among whose leaders was the former judge Pridi Banomyong, who had a French law doctorate. The People's Party had fifty civilian members, thirteen of whom held law degrees or other legal qualifications.[51]

Nevertheless, the "disequilibrium" persisted. Despite the formal change in the country's political system, the absolute monarchy had an afterlife that persists to this day: in theory Thailand has long enjoyed a government of the people, for the people, and by the people, yet in reality the monarchy continues to enjoy a highly privileged place in the political order, and for many remains the real fount of state legitimacy.

At the same time, the decline of monarchical power in the 1930s did not lead to more democratic modes of justice. Faced with ongoing resistance, seen most explicitly in the failed 1933 Bowaradej Rebellion during which royalist hardliners took up arms against the new government, the People's Party instituted a system of "special courts" to deal with political offenders. A penal colony for political prisoners was established on Kho Tao, an island in the Gulf of Thailand off the coast of Surat Thani.[52] After Phibun Songkram became prime minister in 1938, dozens of arrests were made; of the fifty-one defendants tried in the special courts, eighteen were executed and twenty-five sentenced to life imprisonment.[53] Phibun's manipulation of the courts illustrated how judicial processes could be abused and politicized by power holders other than monarchs. The Siamese judiciary readily acquiesced to orders from above, a pattern that continued in subsequent decades.

From the late 1940s onwards, the military has been a leading player in Thailand's politics. David Streckfuss has demonstrated how three Supreme Court cases from the early 1950s established legal precedents for the legitimacy of military coups, and for the self-amnesties proclaimed by coup makers.[54] A pattern was established, according to which the judiciary never challenged the actions of the military. When the monarchy regained much of its influence from the Sarit era onwards, judges assumed a central role as loyal supporters of the palace. The long tenure of royal favorite Sanya Thammasak as president of the Supreme Court (1963–67) epitomized the proximity of the two institutions. When military strongmen Thanom and Praphas were ousted from power following the events of October 14, 1973, King Bhumibol asked Sanya to serve as prime minister during the drafting of a new constitution. After leaving the premiership in 1975, Sanya assumed the position of president of the Privy Council for the next twenty-three years. Following the violent upheavals of October 6, 1976, the King made Supreme Court justice Thanin Kraivichien prime minister—again appointing him to the Privy Council when he was removed from office in a military coup a year later.

The rise of elected politicians during the 1980s, and the growing influence of the legislature, created challenges for the judiciary. From 1991 onwards, courts were supervised by the Ministry of Justice, presided over in turn by a cabinet minister. Controversy over alleged political interference in the judiciary broke out in 1991 during the co-called "judicial crisis," which centered on future Supreme Court president Pramarn Chansue, a larger-than-life figure, and by far the most high-profile Thai judge of recent decades. Pramarn's numerous rivals sought to block his promotion to the top Supreme Court post: in February 1992, the Judicial Commission actually dismissed Pramarn and his closest allies from the judiciary.[55] Pramarn's rivals were supported by then justice minister Prapas Uaychai; the byzantine saga proved a major headache for Prime Minister Anand Panyarachun, who was later sued for abuse of power by another member of the Pramarn clique. Eventually, Pramarn and ten colleagues were able to keep their judgeships, following a rare pardon granted by the King himself. The Anand government's attempts to subordinate the courts to the power of the executive branch precipitated a staggering episode of judicial insurrection, meltdown, and uproar.

Pramarn went on to assume the post of president of the Supreme Court in November 1992, and remained in office for nearly four years.[56] But he remained the focus of constant media attention—not least after leading architect, Rangsan Torsuwan, was charged with attempting to murder him in 1993.[57] In order to avoid any repetition, following the promulgation of the 1997 "People's Constitution," the Office of the Judiciary was separated from the Ministry of Justice, thereby protecting judges from political interference. For better or worse, these changes left the judiciary an entirely self-regulating agency, always anxious to curtail external scrutiny and interference.

Structure of the Courts

Thai criminal cases are heard at three levels: the Courts of First Instance, the Courts of Appeal, and the Supreme Court. Most criminal cases are initially heard at three main kinds of Court of First Instance: *san khwaeng* (literally district courts, roughly equivalent to English magistrate's courts) for lesser offences, juvenile and family courts (for defendants up to eighteen), and general district and provincial courts (which in Bangkok are divided into criminal and civil courts). The majority of Thai judges work in Courts of the First Instance. Any-one convicted in the lower courts and either given a custodial sentence or fined at least five hundred baht is entitled to appeal; no substantive new facts or legal arguments are needed for an appeal. As a result, huge numbers of cases are heard annually by nine regional Courts of Appeal, which have their origins in the old *monthon* system of provincial regions. Those whose convictions are upheld by the Courts of Appeal are generally entitled to submit their cases to the Supreme Court.

The Thai name for the Supreme Court—*san dika*—connotes not supremacy, but proximity to monarchy: dika was a petition to the crown, originally made directly to the King. As an English document on the Supreme Court website explains:

> The Supreme Court originates in the history and civilization of the Thai people. Appeal (Dika) was the petition that people filed before the King to request his supreme prerogative to abolish any hardship. In the era of the absolute monarchy, the King would himself adjudicate all dis-putes. Once the royal duty had increased, the Department of Appeal (Dika) Scrutiny was formed to lighten his royal burdens. Subsequently, the Court of the Supreme Commissioner and the Supreme Court were founded respectively. In this manner, the Supreme Court was to [*sic*] established with the duty to expand and strengthen the King's authority over laws and legal proceedings.[58]

The document goes on to note that the Supreme Court reported directly to the King until 1912, when it was brought under the auspices of the Ministry of Jus-tice. This change was made by Rama VI, following the abortive February 1912 coup against his rule, in an apparent attempt to improve the unpopular new King's public image.[59] Implicit in this account is a nostalgic hankering for the days of King Chulalongkorn, when the san dika served literally to lighten the royal burden. Ironically, while King Chulalongkorn made extensive efforts to extricate himself from involvement in the process of granting appeals, subse-quent decades saw continuing attempts to reinsinuate the monarchy into the making of legal decisions.

Largely as a result of the Pramarn debacle, the 1997 Constitution estab-lished an independent Office of the Judiciary, which was removed from political influence, thereby creating a more explicit separation of powers. The Minister of Justice no longer had any authority over judges, to their great relief. But the downside of these changes was the lack of clear lines of authority to oversee the work of the courts as a whole. The 1991–92 judicial crisis was not simply a cau-tionary tale about political interference: it was also a story of vicious infighting and skullduggery, perpetrated largely by judges themselves. The Pramarn fiasco was hardly a ringing endorsement for judicial self-regulation. After 1997, the president of the Supreme Court became the nominal head of the entire Courts of Justice, and senior court executives in the Courts of First Instance and Courts of Appeal deferred to his higher authority. But in practice most Supreme Court presidents were overwhelmingly preoccupied with oversight of the Supreme Court itself.

In principle, Thailand has a civil law system, based on legal codes—criminal and civil—and a professional judiciary recruited through an entrance examination. But unlike judges in many civil law systems (such as those of continental Europe), Thai judges do not play a leading, quasi-investigative role in conducting criminal cases. For the most part, evidence is presented by prosecutors and defense lawyers, in adversarial proceedings that closely resemble common law Anglo-American criminal trials. This hybrid civil–common law legal system has been influenced by the fact that many prominent twentieth-century Thai judges were trained in the United Kingdom, and in some cases even qualified as English barristers.

In the Thai context, premodern notions of loyalty and treason have become overlaid by layers of legalism that draw on recent thinking about "new constitutionalism" and appropriate the discourse of transitional justice. Advocates of transitional justice assert that a global "justice cascade" promoted by institutions such as the International Criminal Court (ICC) is helping to institutionalize new standards of elite behavior.[60] Leaders who are responsible for abusing human rights or otherwise abusing their power should be tried and ultimately punished by international, hybrid, or local courts.[61] Truth commissions should also be established to investigate episodes of political violence—especially mass killings—and promote reconciliation.[62] While Thailand has flirted with a couple of half-baked truth commissions, both involved more window-dressing than deep investigation.[63] The Thai elite has been much more enthusiastic about criminalizing and prosecuting politicians, especially Thaksin-aligned politicians and those associated with the pro-Thaksin side. While it would be unthinkable for Thailand to prosecute its royal head of state, most recent Thai prime ministers have faced serious legal proceedings; and the two most popular elected premiers have been forced into exile. The result is a justice system deeply mired in contradictory understandings of its own goals, objectives, and processes.

Thongchai's arguments about hyper-royalism have parallels in other areas of the Thai state and society. Critical students of Thai politics and society might readily agree that Thailand suffers from hypermilitarism: that there is a pervasive public culture of uncritical praise for the country's military, despite the fact that the Royal Thai Army does not fight wars and is professionally rather incompetent. In similar fashion, Thailand is arguably afflicted by hyper-Buddhism: while Buddhism is not a national religion, many Thais assume the contrary. Buddhistic ceremonies and rituals are everywhere, and dhammic discourse is all pervasive.

But the Thai air is even more saturated than that. The heady Bangkok smog, already compounded by hyper-royalism, hypermilitarism, and hyper-Buddhism, contains another somewhat malodorous element, one that very few people have identified, let alone discussed. That element is hyperlegalism. The lèse-majesté regime mentioned by Thongchai is just one element of a much larger edifice of legalism. Like royalism, militarism, and Buddhism, legalism serves to legitimate the Thai state and the monarchical network. It privileges select groups (judges and legal specialists) and credits them with knowledge and expertise, but above all with virtue.

A big difference is that whereas the monarchy, military, and Buddhism are to some degree divisive—critical views of them exist—legalism is a totalizing discourse. Even people who see themselves as progressive or liberal "believe" in legalism; they may be unhappy with the judiciary, for example, but they imagine legalism as the solution to Thailand's problems, if it could simply be "got right." If we had better laws, better recognition of human rights, a better constitution, a more activist and broad-minded judiciary, everything would be okay. The problem is not the legalism itself: it is the way Thailand does legalism. It is this belief—that legalism is not the problem, the problem is we have the wrong legalism—that this book sets out to question. Like Srimati Basu, I am concerned not with "the efficacy of particular rules or concepts."[64] Rather than pursuing a project of legal reformism, I seek to understand ethnographically how and why the justice system operates as it does in the Thai context.

Legalism typically justifies itself by reference to the rule of law. However, in the Thai context there is often a considerable discrepancy between the law and the constitution as apparently authoritative texts, and their application in practice. Many mainstream legal scholars and practitioners would argue that Thailand's main problem is simply a failure to implement the rule of law. Critics of the Thai judicial system argue that it conflates rule *of* law with rule *by* law: in other words, the law becomes not an instrument for just rule, but a means of serving the agendas of power holders. But in his incisive analysis of legal issues in neighboring Burma, Nick Cheesman argues that "rule by law" is too difficult to distinguish analytically from rule of law. At the same time, there is little shared agreement about the meaning of the apparently simple term "rule of law": "Not only might [different people] be referring to different versions of the same concept, they might be referring to different concepts, even opposing concepts."[65] Cheesman argues instead that in Burma, the prevailing legal ideology is one of "law and order" rather than rule of law. He sums up the difference as follows:

> Binding of citizens to rules of propriety is opposite to the notion that the state's power to coerce its subjects must be strictly delimited through the exercise of law. The concept of law and order cannot entertain the latter idea, because people in superordinate positions are entitled to intervene to maintain order through mechanisms to discipline others.[66]

Similar arguments could be made in the case of Thailand, where a military junta known as the National Council for Peace and Order seized power in May 2014. Law is closely associated with the maintenance of order (*khwamriaproi*), which in turn is a feature of "peace" (*khwamsangnop*) in the Thai bureaucratic sense—meaning the absence of discord and dissent. Peter Jackson has argued that Thailand is a regime of images in which the legal system functions to suppress the appearance of disruption: "When a statement or representation is regarded [as] being excessively disruptive of the 'smooth calm' (*khwam-sa-ngop-riap-roi*) of social life then it can be silenced or made invisible by the deployment of the full legal (and at times extra-judicial) power of the state."[67]

Nevertheless, law (in the sense of rules, or *kotrabiap*) is neither a necessary nor a sufficient condition for creating order. In an ideal world of virtuous rule, peace could emerge spontaneously: people would act peaceably out of respect for and deference to the monarchy-centered order. In its ultimate form, virtuous rule would require no rules, no rulings, and indeed no ruling. Yet as Cheesman observes, because peace is an ideal condition rather than a daily reality, total peace can never be achieved, and state efforts to enforce peace are inherently unending.[68]

An even more radical position than Cheesman's deft deconstruction of the term "rule of law" is to deconstruct the idea of law itself. Since laws are drafted, crafted, implemented, and abused by human beings, law is an essentially political construct. It follows that law is not necessarily an answer: more legalism may only serve to compound Thailand's political dysfunctionality. State efforts to deploy law to enforce peace may become not part of the solution, but a major part of the problem.

At times, elements of the Thai state have seemed aware of this danger. As Kevin Hewison has noted, King Bhumibol was often extremely ambivalent about constitutionalism, apparently mistrusting the codification of virtuous rule.[69] The post-2014 National Council for Peace and Order was slow to embark on a process of constitution drafting, while the initial 2015 draft was thrown out on the orders of the military. Since the early 1990s, the monarchical network has been far from unified in supporting processes of legal and constitutional change, which have been championed mainly by those Connors terms royalist liberals, but have been opposed, delayed, or thwarted in other quarters.[70] Conservative royalists fear that a growing emphasis on legal mechanisms will ultimately detract from the extralegal charisma and moral authority of the monarchy. Meanwhile, military officers remain strongly attached to the coup d'état as political weapon of last resort, firmly believing that under certain circumstances, only an illegal act of violence can restore peace and order. For adherents of monarchical authority and believers in the transformative potency of military coups, legal solutions are no solutions at all. Simply put, royalism and militarism trump legalism.

The rise of critical legal studies since the 1970s has led to a widespread questioning of the assumptions that underpin the law and the criminal justice system. Nevertheless, these studies—for all their persistent problematization of legal matters—have not mounted a specific critique of legalism as a political ideology.[71] Their focus has been on providing greater social and political context for a broader framing of what constitutes the legal. This is a somewhat different intellectual project from a head-on repudiation of the assumptions of legalism, and especially of legalism's denigration of the political. However, the perspectives advanced by Roberto Unger and others offer a useful starting point, notably Unger's insistence that "[critical legal studies] must wage perpetual war against the tendency to take the workings of a particular social world as if they defined the limits of the real and the possible in social life."[72]

Following Unger's logic, simply because legalism is so ubiquitous does not mean that legalism is the only real or possible basis for public life. Yet critical arguments about legalism are few and far between. The most compelling were first advanced more than fifty years ago by Harvard government professor Judith Shklar:

> The divorce of law from politics is, to be sure, designed to prevent arbitrariness, and that is why there is so little argument about its necessity. However, ideologically legalism does not stop there. Politics is regarded as not only something apart from law, but as inferior to law. Law aims at justice, while politics looks only to expediency. The former is neutral and objective, the latter the uncontrolled child of competing interests and ideology. Justice is thus not the policy of legalism, it is treated as a policy superior to and unlike any other.[73]

For Shklar, law has adopted the garb of justice and morality, and seeks accordingly to present itself as superior to mere politics.[74] Shklar's solution is what she terms "tribunality," a judicious, nuanced, and pragmatic approach to addressing political problems.[75] Rather than pretending to be above politics, practitioners of tribunality recognize the primacy of the political and aim to craft realistic ways forward. Unfortunately, Shklar offers few details about how tribunality could operate in practice.

In the Thai context, law, like the King, is viewed as being above politics. But many recent court cases in Thailand fit Shklar's definition of a political trial: "A trial in which the prosecuting party, usually the regime in power, aided by a cooperative judiciary, tries to eliminate its political enemies."[76] The cooperative role played by the Thai judiciary in endorsing military coups and in trying those who commit what are essentially political crimes—by no means limited to lèse-majesté (Article 112) cases—has been extensively discussed by a variety of Thai scholars, notably by prominent academics who were themselves later targeted by the military: Worajet Pakeerat (who was charged in a military court in mid-2014), Nidhi Eeoseewong (hauled off to a Pathum Thani police station in September 2014), and Somchai Preechasilapakul (charged in November 2015 with taking part in an illegal political gathering).

Nevertheless, it is hard to find many scholars who accept that legalism itself is a troubling ideological construct: that, much like war, law is simply politics by other means. The best-known critical legal scholars in Thailand during the fieldwork for this book were Thammasat University's seven-member Nitirat group, led informally by Worajet Pakeerat. Nitirat made a series of widely reported critical interventions into legal and policy debates between 2010 and 2014. Nitirat's most provocative contribution to the lèse-majesté debate came in 2012, when the group proposed a new version of the controversial Article 112 that reduced maximum jail terms from fifteen years to three.[77] This legalistic proposal, which satisfied virtually nobody, failed to address the underlying issue: that crimes of defamation are symbolic crimes that should never be punished with a custodial sentence.

Thailand has obviously endured a surfeit of constitutions: it also suffers from a surfeit of "independent agencies" designed to check and balance the power of politicians. In times of crisis—such as the contentious and later nullified elections of 2006 and 2014—agencies like the Election Commission were falling over one another to evade responsibility. This evasion of responsibility begs the question of whether recrafting legalistic documents or instruments offer any real solution? A truly radical or progressive stance would instead critique legalism, along with its assumptions of superiority over politics, and defend the political realm against constant subordination to the arbitrary strictures of the legal one. In Thailand, the sphere of law is always privileged over that of politics; the most important reason to elevate and praise the law is to find new ways of denigrating and disparaging the political. Ironically, even many progressive-minded intellectuals in Thailand have no problem with denigrating politics. Nitirat, for example, insisted that they would always confine their proposals to legal recommendations.[78]

Politics in Thailand—as in much of the world—is messy, fractious, dirty, and divisive. For legalists, whether they are conservative judges or dissident academics, this messiness needs to be reined in by crafting good laws, by enforcing them properly, and by bringing sound judgments against those who violate them. But a radical antilegalist position, drawing on Shklar's arguments, would be very different. The superior moral claims of the law are highly tendentious. Since laws are the result of political decisions—whether in a democratic or an authoritarian system—they are not inherently more legitimate than the political actors that created them. Indeed, in a rapidly changing political order where laws made in an authoritarian past are being applied to a more democratic present, the law is arguably less legitimate than politics. The ideal type of "pure" law set against corrupt politics is never an accurate description of reality, even in an advanced democracy.[79] But in a hybrid regime such as Thailand, elected politicians—deeply flawed though they may be—are arguably morally superior to the laws made by earlier military regimes, which are often used to constrain them. Similarly, the widely accepted civilian-crafted 1997 Constitution had more legitimacy than the 2007 or 2017 constitutions, which were drafted under the auspices of military juntas. Yet instead of declaring large swathes of Thai law unconstitutional, successive incarnations of the Constitutional Court have avoided challenging authoritarian laws from earlier decades, or overturning the decisions of the Supreme Court that have reified these laws. Instead, both the Supreme Court and the Constitutional Court have sought to check the power of elected politicians, from the implicit starting point that they must be morally inferior to a legal edifice built largely by military regimes and their in-house lawyers.

Since 2006, Thailand has seen numerous court cases related to wider political tensions and disputes—in short, political trials. While political trials date back many decades in Thailand, they assumed new forms after King Bhumibol's April 2006 royal speeches. In the wake of the September 2006 military coup, political trials followed thick and fast. Some of these were conducted by the Constitutional Court, including the dissolution of the former ruling party, Thai Rak Thai, and the banning of Thaksin Shinawatra and 111 other party executive members from office for electoral irregularities. Others were carried out by the Supreme Court's special court for political offenders, including the trial of Thaksin himself on corruption-related charges. In many respects, however, the most important political trials were those that did not directly focus on politicians themselves but instead involved people associated with the pro-Thaksin movement, those who had committed acts of resistance in the aftermath of the 2006 coup, or those who had been charged under laws curtailing freedom of speech. These second-tier political trials were often more illuminating than the top-tier trials of leading protagonists. They were held in normal criminal courts by ordinary judges; and although the charges were unusual, the procedures followed were standard ones that applied to all criminal cases.

The phrase "law and order" has become so ubiquitous that we rarely pause to consider its meaning. The rule of law appears, superficially at least, to go hand in hand with the maintenance of order. But Thailand's courts, like those of many countries, are known as Courts of Justice. Strictly speaking, a court of law is one in which legal principles are followed, rather than a court where justice is administered. But the close affinity between court officials and the establishment—especially the monarchy—in Thailand means that these courts could also be understood as "courts of order." In other words, like the Burmese courts examined by Cheesman, Thai courts are dedicated to the maintenance of peace and order.[80] This involves more than simply convicting and punishing those guilty of crimes against that order: it entails an active role in the process of order maintenance, by creating and upholding social norms and behaviors, which include ensuring loyalty to the monarchy and other pillars of the Thai nation.

Another meaning of the word *court* is the entourage that surrounds a reigning monarch—an appropriate second meaning in the Thai case, in which law courts may also serve as "courts of the court." A court of order does not hold trials that are primarily intended to pass judgment on defendants. It conducts trials for the purpose of maintaining the status quo. In many respects, such a model of justice predates modern notions of rights and citizenship; it is a model of justice appropriate to a system of absolute monarchy, in which the populace are subjects. As subjects, they may fall victim to the use of arbitrary power by the monarch; in such an eventuality, they may appeal to the monarch, not by invoking a liberal claim to rights, but by making a request for mercy, an appeal to royal benevolence. Royal benevolence, including the routine pardoning of offenders, may benefit numerous individuals and so create the illusion of justice. But in reality, royal benevolence is a poor substitute for a truly effective justice system.

When defendants appear in political cases in Thailand, contestation is apparent on many levels. At the most obvious level, the prosecution and the defense conduct their respective elements of the proceedings in an adversarial fashion. But more important, while judges and the prosecution are often working from the premise of a "court of law," or even a "court of order," the defense is framed within the imagined parameters of a court of justice. Part of the contestation in a Thai court concerns three ideal types of how a court should function: a court of law, a court of justice, and a court of order. In Thai political trials, the competition between these ideal types often looms extremely large.

Thai Treason

The notion that the courts can rescue the people from the evil misdeeds of politicians is a problematic and troubling one. The discourse of judicial activism privileges legal mechanisms, assuming that they operate on a higher plane than the plane of politics: that law is morally superior to politics, in short. But since law can be nothing other than a politically devised set of rules, and law can only be administered by human beings with their own political views, outlooks, and perspectives, this view is profoundly flawed. The aim of this book is to examine what can go wrong when justice is reified, when extralegal considerations, beliefs, and practices underpin the actions of the courts. Thailand's experiments with law and justice are fascinating in themselves, but they are also notable as an example of the abuses of judicialization, the politicization of court cases, and the revival of illiberal notions of treason.

While the charges in the three core criminal cases featured in this book vary, they are also remarkably similar. Lèse-majesté laws are popularly understood as defamation laws, applying to those who "defame, insult or threaten" the monarchy;[81] yet Article 112 appears in the Thai Criminal Code in a section entitled "Offences Relating to the Security of the Kingdom," which includes a chapter headed "Offences against the King, the Queen, the Heir-Apparent, and the Regent." Articles 107 to 111 all relate to acts of physical violence against the monarchy, and carry sentences ranging from death to a maximum jail sentence of twenty years. As both Streckfuss and Haberkorn have noted, there was an "epidemic" of new lèse-majesté cases in the final decade of King Bhumibol's reign, including 478 cases in 2010 alone—apparently reflecting a misguided desire to protect the ailing monarch from criticism.[82]

Defamation of people other than the monarchy is covered by Articles 326 to 333, with an important set of caveats:

Section 329: Whoever, in good faith, expresses any opinion or statement:

- By way of self-justification or defense, or for the protection of a legitimate interest;
- In the status of being an official in the exercise of his functions;
- By way of fair comment on any person or thing subjected to public criticism; or
- By way of fair report of the open proceeding of any Court or meeting, shall not be guilty of defamation.

Article 112, while also addressing a crime of defamation, is not accompanied by these same caveats: in other words, the "good faith" defense is generally held to be no defense at all. The location of Article 112 alongside crimes of violence against the throne, and the conspicuous absence of a good faith defense, means that lèse-majesté is in effect not a crime of defamation, but a crime of treason.[83]

While the 2007 Computer Crime Act (CCA) carried lower penalties than Articles 112 or 116, the wide-ranging scope of the laws also located some of the act's provisions within an insurrection spectrum, especially Article 14 sections 2 and 3: section 2 made it illegal to input false computer data "in a manner likely to cause injury to national security or public panic," while section 3 made it an offence to input data that would violate the national security or terrorism provisions of the Criminal Code. Since Article 112 formed part of the national security provisions, charging a defendant under the CCA's Article 14, section 3 was a "backdoor" form of lèse-majesté or treason charge, carrying a lower penalty (a maximum sentence of five years), and attracting far less public attention. Most developed countries have passed some form of legislation against computer crime in recent years; Thailand could argue that IT-related laws and prosecutions were in line with international norms, whereas Article 112 trials were widely criticized as a global aberration, and as violations of human rights.[84] Inverting Kathryn Sikkink's optimistic claims about a "justice cascade"—a putative global decline in rights violations, coupled with more frequent prosecutions of violators and fair trials for perpetrators—Tyrell Haberkorn has convincingly demonstrated that Thailand has experienced an "uneven and episodic *injustice* cascade," where accountability is the exception rather than the rule.[85] These arguments could be pushed further with regard to a wide range of politically related court cases in late Ninth Reign Thailand: laws on the treason spectrum were frequently invoked unjustly.

The term *treason* does not appear in the Thai criminal code. Indeed, relatively few countries have a specific offence of treason on the statutes; a notable exception is Britain, where a medieval treason law has remained in force since 1351. Even where treason remains a crime, prosecutions are extremely rare; the last trial for treason in Britain took place in 1946. Yet the treason laws in Britain remain highly instructive: the Treason Felony Act of 1848, also still in force, extended the concept of treason well beyond its original meaning. The original full name of the legislation was "An Act for the Better Security of the Crown and Government of the United Kingdom." The act's provisions closely resemble the wording of the relevant sections of the Thai Criminal Code. Whereas high treason in its purest form means plotting murder, a "treason felony" means trying to subvert the legitimate authority of the state. The crime of the Thai 112 defendant is not simply having defamed the monarchy, but having threatened the royal institution.

Virtually no Thai knows a treason felony by this technical name, but every Thai understands the phrase *lom jao*—to "bring down the monarchy." *Lom jao* was the supposed goal of the "network treason" discussed here. Chapter 4 deals with the lèse-majesté case against magazine editor Somyot Prueksakasemsuk; chapter 5 examines the Computer Crime Act case against former broker Katha Pajariyapong, who were put on trial for their alleged attempts to *lom jao*; while chapter 6 analyzes how Jon Ungpakorn and nine other NGO activists had challenged the authority of a parliament established by a military junta that had been blessed by the palace, and which was headed by former army commander and privy councilor General Surayud Chulanont. Indeed, the Computer Crime Act under which Katha was charged was passed by the very same National Assembly: along with other Surayud-era legislation such as the Internal Security Act, it formed part of the junta's attempts to modernize and extend the scope of treason felonies in Thailand.

Like the Victorian concept of treason felony, *lom jao* is a crime of "compassings, imaginations, inventions, devices, or intentions," often manifested in writing or in print. *The Guardian* newspaper brought a legal action asserting that the 1848 British legislation was incompatible with the 1998 Human Rights Act, since it effectively criminalized advocating republicanism. Although the Law Lords unanimously accepted *The Guardian*'s legal arguments, they declined to strike down the law.[86] In much the same fashion, lawyers for Somyot unsuccessfully challenged the constitutionality of Article 112, arguing that the punishment did not fit the crime: the penalties for lèse-majesté were excessive. Britain's 1848 Act sought to modernize notions of treason, detaching the crime of disloyalty from a mandatory punishment of execution. Loyalty to the crown, in other words, was not an absolute—degrees of disloyalty were now legally thinkable. Yet in practice the Treason Felony Act remained a draconian piece of legislation, under which nobody has been charged in the United Kingdom since 1883.[87]

Where they remain on the statute book at all, residual treasonous crimes that cannot be subsumed under the category of conventional felonies such as murder, conspiracy, or defamation—such as flag burning or lèse-majesté—have in most modern legal systems become "treason misdemeanors," either de jure, or through custom and practice. Such a transformation has been mooted in the Thai case. David Streckfuss quotes former deputy principal private secretary to the King, Tongnoi Tongyai as saying in 1987: "The penalty for *lèse-majesté* offences is likely to be gradually commuted and its abolition is probable if the country's democracy keeps progressing as in the United Kingdom."[88] Tongnoi made clear that treason felonies operate in the political imaginary of loyalty-based relations between the ruled and the ruler, rather than the political imaginary of a democratic nation in which citizens enjoy rights, and in which national leaders are responsible to a citizenry that elects them. Arguably, the only tolerable place for statutes of treason within a modern legal order is as quaint anachronisms that are rarely if ever invoked, and have in practice been downgraded to the level of misdemeanors. Yet during the thirty-year period following Tongnoi's statement, lèse-majesté and other treason felonies were not progressively decriminalized. Legislation passed in the wake of the 2006 coup sought to "modernize" treason felonies by introducing new categories of these crimes, notably in the area of cybercrime. Meanwhile the most troubling treason felony, Article 112, far from being allowed either to wither on the vine or quietly to morph into a treason misdemeanor, has been granted a new lease of life, one seen in the unprecedented numbers of defendants charged and prosecuted. Indeed, a Supreme Court judgment of November 2013 extended the scope of lèse-majesté beyond its earlier meaning, stating that the law applies not simply to the reigning monarch Rama IX, but to his great-grand-father Rama IV. In 2014, renowned scholar Sulak Sivaraksa was charged with lèse-majesté over remarks he made about King Naresuan, who died in 1605.[89] The Supreme Court judgment—which forms a binding precedent—effectively created a new treason felony: defaming, insulting, or threatening a deceased King.

Strikingly, the British 1848 act does not contain any detailed elaboration of the crimes that constitute treason felonies. Treason felonies are essentially thought crimes and word crimes. "Compassings"—an obsolete word meaning "contrivances or schemes"—is a collective term for these transgressions.[90] Because compassings are extremely difficult to codify in legal statutes, those on trial for treason felonies are in a profoundly ambiguous position. A court is supposedly concerned with the actions of defendants whose real crimes were often committed in their heads. As a result, their trials operate in parallel: the defendants will be tried on the basis of their actions, but convicted on the basis of their compassings; or rather convicted on their compassings as imagined, invented, or devised by those sitting in judgment. In such cases, the question of intention looms large: how far was a critical thought or statement indicative of genuine criminal intent? In principle, Article 112 of the Thai Criminal Code covers only crimes of absolute liability that involve no proof of mens rea—yet in practice the courts have often struggled to distinguish clearly between defendants' actions and intentions.

This book sets out to explain who Thai judges are, how their minds work, and how they responded to a 2006 royal injunction to help solve the country's political problems. The first chapter examines the world of Thai judges: How are they recruited, given assignments, and promoted? Who determines the outcomes of criminal court cases, and on what criteria? How could the judiciary best be reformed? Chapter 2 examines the connections between the monarchy and the courts: How do judges understand their relationships with the monarchy? How have royal visits to courts, death penalty annulments, and royal pardons helped shape those relationships? Chapter 3 looks at the ideological challenges facing Thai judges in the late Bhumibol era. What ideas have shaped their worldviews?

How have judges reacted to pressures for the greater "judicialization" of politics? What critical perspectives have emerged about the attitudes and performance of the judiciary? All three of these chapters aim to explain why Thai judges think and behave as they do when dealing with political cases.

The second half of the book deals with two kinds of political court cases. Chapters 4, 5, and 6 are concerned with charges on the treason spectrum, closely reviewing three trials linked to a purported 2010 plot to bring down the Thai monarchy, here termed "network treason." How does a Thai citizen end up in court? How do defendants conduct their cases? Are they being tried for actual crimes, or for their intentions, attitudes, and personalities? The chapters examine how Thai courts deal with messy and troublesome cases, in which defense lawyers adopt aggressive courtroom tactics that seem designed to provoke the judges. Rather than producing a satisfactory resolution, judgments in these cases have undermined public confidence in the courts and exacerbated existing political tensions. Chapter 4 deals with Somyot Prueksakasemsuk's 112 case and chapter 5 with Katha Pajariyapong's Computer Crime case. These chapters review the significance of the cases as a way of reading recent developments in Thai politics. Building on the themes and approach adopted in examining the Somyot and Katha cases, chapter 6 focuses on the trial of Jon Ungpakorn and nine other activists accused of disrupting parliamentary proceedings in 2007. How far did the defendants tell convincing narratives that helped the judges to understand and sympathize with their actions? And how far did their behavior in court run counter to their own interests? Taken together, these three chapters examine how network monarchy sought to deal with the perceived threat from network treason, and why these cases only served to fuel polarization and social conflict.

Chapter 7 deals with the various major court cases that have impacted upon Thaksin Shinawatra, his political parties, and his sister Yingluck. Have Thailand's courts been engaged, as their critics contend, in a systematic campaign to purge the Shinawatra clan from office? Or has the relationship between pro-Thaksin forces and the courts been much more messy and ambiguous than a few headlines have suggested? What does a close scrutiny of the judgments in these cases tell us about the Thai justice system more generally? Chapter 8 analyzes the Constitutional Court, which has been associated with a series of anti-Thaksin decisions. Nevertheless, close examination of the court's rulings and proceedings illustrates a tendency to go with the prevailing political winds: the court is typically reactive and tentative in its decisions, rather than a prime mover in its own right. Together, these two chapters demonstrate that despite the many shortcomings of the Constitutional Court and the Supreme Court, the relationship between the judiciary and the pro-Thaksin movement has been more nuanced and ambiguous than many analysts have suggested, largely because the monarchical network has been deeply conflicted about how to manage the challenge posed by Thaksin. A brief conclusion summarizes the main arguments of the book, arguing that legalism is at the core of Thailand's political problems, and has nothing more to offer by way of solutions.

Trials create the possibility of positive change. This change might be evident in at least two different senses. One is through liminality, or indeed luminosity: that the rituals of the trial could generate catharsis, revelation, or reconciliation of a kind that lies outside the humdrum realm of daily life. Alternatively, a chance comment by a witness or a bold question by a defense lawyer could cut to the heart of a court case and illuminate something of great significance. Such liminality or luminosity might only occur at certain moments or junctures during trial proceedings, but could serve to redeem an otherwise flawed or unsatisfactory process. A second possibility rests with the potential for tribunality. Judges could deploy their powers pragmatically, with an eye to the wider political and social context, by granting bail creatively, or by giving a token sentence that acknowledges technical guilt but spares the defendant from substantive punishment. In the discussions that follow, liminality and tribunality may often seem in short supply, but they always remain possibilities. From time to time, an otherwise dark judicial landscape is illuminated by a flash of inspiration.

PRIVILEGED CASTE?

The purpose of this chapter is to examine what it means to be a Thai judge, and why judges think and behave in the ways they do. To do this, I ask how are Thai judges recruited, trained, and socialized? How are they given assignments and promotions? Much of the recent discussion of Thai judges has focused on their roles in hearing political cases, both "ordinary" criminal trials such as those brought under the *lèse-majesté* law, and Supreme Court and Constitutional Court cases brought against prominent politicians and political parties. The chapter argues that Thai judges are not irrational actors, nor are they mere instruments of the network monarchy, the military, and conservative forces in the country's state and society. For all their shortcomings, they are trying to perform extremely difficult roles to the best of their abilities and understandings, which are often unduly limited and narrow.

Suppose you are a young Thai judge, whose parents own a small noodle shop in the provinces. During your teenage years, you always lent a hand at the stall during evenings and on weekends. You return home for a visit. Your father has to run an errand, and your mother is short-handed in the shop. Can you help her out by clearing a few tables?

The answer is no. As a judge, a royal servant responsible for the administration of justice, waiting on tables is beneath your dignity, and would undermine the sanctity of your office. Similar notions of status may apply to various professions in Thailand—such as doctors—but no other occupation can rival the closeness to royalty claimed by judges.

"Some people have the wrong idea. They think that the King's representative in this province is the provincial governor. They are not correct. As chief judge of the court here, I am the King's representative." My fascination with Thai judges began when I heard this comment, which suddenly placed my understanding of the country's legal system in a new light. On one level, Thai judges form part of an extremely legalistic culture, based on decades of dusty precedents codified in the published annual volumes of past Supreme Court decisions.[1] But on another level, they are acting, at least in their own imaginations, as guardians of morality and virtue whose legitimacy derives not from penal codes but from their proximity to the monarchical institution. Of all categories of government servants—including the military, the police, Interior Ministry officials, teachers, and doctors—judges pride themselves on serving as the greatest reflectors of the shining light of royal virtue. This status marks them out, giving them a degree of special responsibility for preserving the moral integrity of the Thai nation.

But who are Thai judges? Where do they come from? How are they recruited, trained, and socialized? How are they promoted? Who oversees their work? This chapter sets out to answer these questions, drawing on approaches used in earlier studies of careers that have foregrounded interviews with members of a profession.[2] This chapter is concerned with career judges of the Courts of Justice (the Courts of First Instance, the Appeal Courts and the Supreme Court). The Administrative Courts and the Constitutional Court established following the adoption of the 1997 Constitution have their own distinct jurisdictions, bureaucracies, and recruitment processes. The Administrative Courts deal with cases brought against the government, while the Constitutional Court adjudicates on the constitutionality of laws and important rulings. Confusingly, many of the most prominent Constitutional Court judges are former judges of the Courts of Justice.

In Thailand, judges are selected on the basis of a highly competitive entrance examination, which many applicants take for the first time at age twenty-five, the minimum permissible age. Those who pass may now look forward to a forty-five-year career—the retirement age was recently raised to seventy—during which they are supposed to remain largely sequestered from the wider world. Traditionally, judges do not hand out business cards (which are widely used in Thai society), do not socialize with nonjudges, are not allowed to take on any outside work (other than part-time lecturing),[3] and spend much of their time living quietly with their families. They are not supposed to go drinking or to consort with prostitutes;[4] and they need to be very careful about attending parties or public gatherings where known shady characters will be in attendance. In other words, men in particular forsake much of the normal social life of their peers.[5] While a sober and discreet public persona is desirable in most judiciaries, Thai judges are especially concerned with maintaining appearances of propriety.[6]

Theoretically, judges' professional and personal lives are governed by a slim blue volume of ethical strictures. The *Judicial Code of Ethics*, originally compiled in 1985 by a couple of senior judges who had previously studied in Britain, has been reissued in successive editions with minor revisions.[7] Applying to trainees, associate judges, full judges, and *datho yuthitham* (Islamic family court judges) alike, the volume contains six sections, covering principles, ethics for practicing as a judge, ethics for administrative work, ethics for other duties, ethics for personal and family behavior, and special rules for other categories. In the provinces, judges typically socialize mainly among themselves, often getting together for a shared meal on Friday nights. One senior judge argued that traditionally, judges lived like monks.[8] Though desirable, this was no longer practical; judges now needed to be more engaged with society and more open to what was happening. Another senior judge told me frankly that the ethics manual was out of date, and some of its stipulations could no longer be taken literally.[9] But even younger judges were very cautious, for example, about attending social gatherings at which unknown friends of friends might be present. One judge politely declined an invitation to an official dinner that would be attended by a member of the Nitirat group of critical legal academics.[10] Judges' attitudes to drinking vary; one book by a judge cited the supposed "father of Thai law" Prince Raphi as saying that it was fine for judges to drink "where appropriate," so long as it did not compromise their integrity.[11] Another judge claimed that alcohol-related socializing was useful to get promoted; there was less recognition for those who concentrated on doing their jobs well.[12]

Partly to compensate for their quasi-monastic lifestyle, partly to reduce the temptation to accept bribes, and partly to recognize their exalted status, judges are among the best-paid public servants in Thailand. Judges also enjoy excellent fringe benefits such as free housing in many provinces and generous car allowances. They have almost complete job security and extremely predictable career paths. While some applicants are undoubtedly drawn to the judiciary by the attractive benefits, many also see their work as a moral and social calling, a form of sacrifice to the higher cause of serving the nation.

Recruitment

Thai judges are recruited through a highly competitive process. Whereas in many common law systems, judges are appointed after substantial careers as barristers, attorneys, or prosecutors, Thailand resembles many civil law systems in

continental Europe, which also have a career judiciary recruited through examinations. While in the past Thai judges came from a wide range of socioeconomic
backgrounds, including children of ordinary villagers[13]—one judge told me
proudly that he had originally come to Bangkok as a temple boy[14]—most today
are from well-to-do families and have never earned their own living by any other
means.[15] After graduating from university law faculties (largely from Thammasat and Chulalongkorn, along with a growing contingent from Ramkhamhaeng,
plus a small number from Chiang Mai and elsewhere), would-be judges qualify
as barristers and then engage in a couple of years of intensive cramming, during
which they gain token experience of working on a number of court cases.[16]

While there are very few senior female judges in Thailand, the gender balance
has improved considerably: women have made up at least 50 percent of recent
intakes. In 2015, 1,252 of the country's 4,404 judges were female, but only one of
the six deputy Supreme Court presidents. No woman has yet served in the top
judicial post, as president of the Supreme Court.

There are three ways to become a judge: entering via the large field (*sanam
yai*), the small field (*sanam lek*), or the special field (literally the "tiny" field,
sanam jiew). The sanam yai is for those with only an undergraduate degree, while
the sanam lek is for those who have a master's degree. The sanam jiew is open
to those who those who have undertaken master's degree study abroad for two
years.[17] Overseas qualifications have to be approved by the Office of the Secretariat of the Courts: in practice, only selected degrees from a short list of developed
countries including Australia, France, Japan, Singapore, the United Kingdom,
and United States are likely to pass muster. Currently, around eight thousand
applicants annually sit for the sanam yai, three thousand for the sanam lek, and
around one hundred for the sanam jiew. The pass rate is less than 1 percent for
the sanam yai, 3 to 5 percent for the sanam lek, and currently around 20 percent
for the sanam jiew (which previously had a 70 to 80 percent pass rate).[18]

The rise of the sanam jiew has been a source of controversy within the judiciary.[19] This new category of entrance examination, first opened in 2005, may
have been intended to facilitate an application to enter the judiciary from Princess Bajrakitiyabha, a holder of two law degrees from Cornell University. In the
end, the Princess became a public prosecutor rather than a judge, but the special
channel was opened anyway. Initially virtually all sanam jiew applicants passed;
even when the pass rate declined, this was a far easier way to become a judge. The
sanam jiew was much favored by the children of judges and by wealthy elite families, who had the inside knowledge and financial resources to exploit this route.[20]

The content of the entrance examination is highly predictable, and is based
entirely on former decisions of the Supreme Court, which are summarized in
the twelve annual issues of the court's law review.[21] Faculties of law in Thailand

have an extremely conservative curriculum, which is overwhelming technical and professional in orientation. While constitutional law and administrative law are taught at top law faculties such as Chulalongkorn University—and even feature in the examinations of the Thai Bar Association—students openly neglect to study these fields seriously, because they are not part of judicial entrance examinations.[22] Subjects such as critical legal studies, sociology of law, and jurisprudence are barely taught in Thailand, while legal philosophy tends to be presented in a very unreflexive fashion, framed by ideas such as legal positivism and natural law, which are applied very crudely to the Thai context. Nevertheless, judicial exams are not simply memory tests: most candidates fail on the section that tests their understanding of the law, and their ability to apply it. Those who pass the judges' examination are given an interview; while very few applicants are rejected at this final stage, interview performance helps determine the candidates' final ranking numbers, which are crucial for their later career progression. Applicants have to submit a list of referees, but these are not usually contacted.

Competition between university law faculties to maximize their success rates in the entrance examinations for the judiciary has a significant distorting effect on the curricula, since the relative prestige of faculties is often closely tied to these success rates. Progressive and critically minded law lecturers have difficulty in promoting their agendas when faced with pressures from prospective students to prepare them effectively for these examinations, even though realistically only very small numbers of applicants are likely to pass them. Even Thammasat University has revamped its curriculum to correspond more closely to the demands of the professional entrance examinations for judges and prosecutors. For many decades the Thammasat faction remained the dominant group among the judiciary, but recently Chulalongkorn University graduates have been on the rise, while the open-entrance Ramkhamhaeng University's insurgent clique has been growing in stature.[23] In a book targeted at prospective judges, serving judge Natthaphakon urges candidates to shun drugs and stay out of trouble with the police,[24] to read at least one hundred pages a day, and to pay special attention to memorizing precedents from previous Supreme Court decisions.[25] His main argument is that becoming a judge does not require any outstanding academic ability: perseverance and a passion for the law are more important.[26] The extremely low pass rate for the sanam yai rather contradicts Natthaphakon's claims.

While in theory the three routes to enter the judiciary are equal, in practice the sanam yai is by far the most difficult, and the most prestigious: virtually all of Thailand's top judges—the presidents and vice presidents of the Supreme Court—entered this way, which is effectively the front door of the judiciary. Those who have master's degrees—entering through the side door, as it were—are ranked lower and are taken less seriously than those who hold only undergraduate degrees. Every judge in Thailand has a ranking number, based on their examination place and year of entry (*run*); these numbers are known by everybody. The first ranked in the sanam yai entrance examination will carry the number "1" throughout a long career. The same goes for the second and third ranked, right the way down to the last. The sanam lek are ranked after the sanam yai, so if you gain fifth place in the sanam lek in a year when 62 people pass through the sanam yai, your effective rank number will be 67, not 5.[27]

Some judge informants favored a minimum age for judges or thirty, thirty-five, or even forty, accompanied by reforms in the examination system.[28] Most of those in favor of a higher minimum age had themselves entered the judiciary later in life, after working as a lawyer or pursuing another career.[29] But these were minority views. A more typical senior judge argued that Thailand needed judges with good memories: if they were recruited later in life they would have forgotten too much.[30] In any case, by the age of thirty-five or so the most capable people had already made alternative careers and would not want to become judges.

How many judges are recruited annually? The simple answer is: all those who pass the entrance examination. In 2008, only 42 out of more than 5,000 applicants passed the entrance examination for the sanam yai, compared with 85 in 2000. Did this mean that fewer judges were needed in 2008? On the contrary; the serious backlog of cases meant there was an urgent need for more judges. I was told that if a thousand applicants had passed the examination, all of them would have been accepted.[31] There was no quota, no predetermined number. Nor did the dates of the examinations follow a predictable calendar. Everything hinged on the quality of the applicants. In this sense, the recruitment of judges was not based on a modern system of matching applicants to vacancies. There were no vacancies; or rather, there were as many vacancies as there were qualified applicants. The recruitment of Thai judges was based on a set notion of a *matrathan* ("standard"),[32] which those seeking to enter the judiciary had to meet. Those who lived up to the standard would be admitted; those who fell short would never pass through the hallowed portals of the Courts of Justice. Some judges expressed skepticism about the rather arbitrary "standard" argument, feeling that recruitment should better reflect the needs of the organization.[33]

The idea of a fixed "standard" was more reminiscent of an ancient mandarinate than of a modern recruitment process.[34] In theory, this was not a process of recruitment but of evaluation. What mattered were not the needs of the organization, but the qualities of those recruited. In the Chinese mandarin recruitment process, moral qualities—including sexual self-restraint and the avoidance of alcohol—were important factors that could affect the success of candidates.[35] The extremely selective nature of the recruitment process served important internal purposes for the Thai judiciary, reinforcing judges' sense of themselves as a small and exceptionally knowledgeable elite, and contributing to a distinctive combination of hubris and excessive self-confidence. Despite the mythology surrounding the idea of a *matrathan*, there was an obvious boost in recruitment following the passage of the 1997 Constitution, which specified that a full quorum of judges was required.[36] Indeed, one judge admitted owing his own appointment to this hiring bump: pass rates shot up immediately after 1997, reaching more than three hundred recruits in one year, only to fall off again later.[37] One informant recounted proudly that the son of the president of the Supreme Court had recently failed the judges' entrance examination, evidence that there was no favoritism at work in the system.[38]

Yet how capable and knowledgeable really were those who passed the examination? A widespread perception among those familiar with the process was that successful examination candidates were overwhelmingly *dek rian*, study-oriented youths, single-minded swots who had dedicated their early lives to their law books, and were primarily distinguished by their well-developed capacity for rote memorization. Many applicants were Bangkokians from middle-class Sino-Thai backgrounds, and were largely unfamiliar with the provincial-born lower-class people who typically ended up in court, and who unfortunately comprised the bulk of Thailand's prison population. Judges' narrow undergraduate education did not help. The growing numbers of judges who had studied abroad (including several past presidents of the Supreme Court) were ironically even more detached from societal realities. The late human rights lawyer Thongbai Thongpao could recount numerous stories of ordinary people who had been treated with dreadful harshness by the courts, including one concerning four men who were each paid 150 baht (around 5 dollars) to cut down some trees, and ended up being sentenced to twenty-four years in jail for illegal logging.[39] Some judges seemed unable or unwilling to distinguish between those who instigated and profited from criminal activity and the unwitting hirelings who carried it out.

Despite the fact that only a tiny proportion of law graduates will become judges, the curriculum followed by law faculties around the country is tied closely to the content of the judicial entrance examination, which constitutes a gold standard emulated by other professional bodies such as the Bar Association. In other words, by insisting on an extremely narrow form of entrance examination, the Courts of Justice distort the curricula of law faculties all over the country, closing rather than opening bright young minds. Nidhi Eoseewong has argued that judges have a purely technical knowledge of the law, devoid of political context, which does a disservice to Thai society—especially since most judges enter the profession at a very young age:

> However, in Thailand, we like to think of the judiciary as the best barbers. Just as for typists, there are the best typists, and for computer scientists, there is the best one, judges are the best barbers for legal matters. Put simply, [the court] is a meeting room for experts, who descended from who knows where, using this expertise to determine the lives of people. This idea about judges as the highest experts, external experts, is a very appealing idea in Thailand. We are taught to hate and look down on politicians, and we like to create "experts," such as a benevolent people possessing virtue or skilled people, who float down from who knows where to control the people we chose.[40]

High levels of public respect reinforce judges' self-understandings as moral arbiters blessed with specialist expertise.[41] Apart from the limited range of their knowledge, many Thai judges struggle to understand notions of proportionality and balance, which are not well taught in law schools. High levels of incarceration are the direct result of a tendency to hand down so many heavy sentences.[42]

Despite the high prestige of the judiciary, the work judges perform during the first two decades of their careers is largely mundane: presiding over often trivial criminal and civil trials, during which they act partly as note takers, summarizing the proceedings into a tape recorder; then writing up their verdicts while continuing to hear an unending stream of fresh cases. Especially in their early years, they are typically posted to the provinces, far from their homes and families, and discouraged from becoming involved in the local community. In theory, the sheer brilliance of these young judges should allow them to see through the standard tricks used by prosecutors, police officers, and defense lawyers, but experienced lawyers from both sides of the trial chamber argued that many novice judges lacked familiarity with stock legal ploys such as priming witnesses and tampering with evidence.[43] As Samson Lim has shown, Thai police procedures—with their emphasis on performative crime scene reenactments—often create highly misleading images that contribute to miscarriages of justice, as in the infamous 1986 Sherry Ann Duncan case that saw four men wrongfully convicted for murder.[44] Ironically, by the time judges reached a similar level of trial experience to that of prosecutors and defense lawyers, they were promoted to levels where they no longer had to hear testimony firsthand.

An experienced judge explained that many witnesses he heard testify were not at all credible: he had to control himself so as not to betray his skepticism.[45] The job required a great deal of patience: you could not allow yourself to feel bored or irritated. The public often wanted criminals to be sentenced harshly, but judges were well aware that long jail sentences would not help either the defendant or society. As all judges knew very well, Thai jails were full of poor people and those with mental health problems. He believed that many judges had insufficient life experience, and ideally should have an undergraduate degree in a subject other than law. But if judges had to make their decisions based on a wider set of criteria than purely technical considerations, their role would be much more difficult.

For this reason, a lot of judges were happy to take a highly mechanistic approach to their work—which meant they did not need to think too much. As one English judge lamented (about spiraling costs and delays), "There is a danger that we become habituated to . . . 'this madness', and that we admire the problem instead of eliminating it."[46] For Thai judges, the temptations of habituation were very real—as were the attendant dangers. The curious world of the Thai judiciary had all the qualities of a *habitus*. Summarizing his mentor Pierre Bourdieu, Loïc Wacquant described the *habitus* as "the way society becomes deposited in persons in the form of lasting *dispositions*, or trained capacities and structural propensities to think, feel and act in determinate ways, which then guide them in their creative responses to the constraints and solicitations of their extant milieu."[47] Simply put, the socialization process of Thai judges normalizes juggling excessive caseloads and handing out harsh sentences. Once judges have internalized such practices, they become part of their judicial dispositions. It follows that defendants, defense lawyers, and prosecutors need to make every effort to understand the dispositions of the judges who hear their cases.

Career Paths

Judges enter the profession with a very clear understanding of their likely career paths. Those with high scores in the entrance examination gain pole positions, and can expect to become Supreme Court judges in due course. If you were ranked one or two in the sanam yai entrance examinations at the age of twenty-five, you have a good chance of becoming president or vice president of the Supreme Court. If you face disciplinary or health problems, you may fall off the ladder and miss your chance of a top spot, meaning that someone just below you may climb a little higher than they first expected.[48] But unlike in the police, the Interior Ministry, or other branches of the public sector, neither pure merit nor political interference can greatly boost a judicial career: performance in the initial entrance examination largely determines a judge's entire trajectory.[49]

Everett Hughes notes the importance of positive and negative career points: every American physician is aware that "if I have not received my specialty residence in a certain kind of hospital by a certain age, certain steps are closed."[50] For

Thai judges, career lines are largely determined even before they start working. This rigid adherence to a flawed mode of hierarchy is designed to minimize conflict and competition. But, as Max Weber observed a century ago, "'Democracy' also takes an ambivalent stand in the face of specialized examinations"—like those who enter professions such as the judiciary.[51] On the one hand, a democratic order promotes these apparently egalitarian procedures, yet at the same time "democracy fears that a merit system and educational certificates will result in a privileged 'caste.' Hence, democracy fights against the special examination system." Here lies the structural contradiction at the heart of the Thai judiciary: judges' egalitarian claims to status based on merit threaten to create a new mode of elite privilege, one that is potentially inimical to more democratic understandings of justice.

Judges are supposed to be proud simply of being judges, and not attached to titles, job assignments, or positions. Salary levels are largely determined by seniority—in effect, mainly by age and years of service—rather than by the post held. There are five salary levels: while the fifth of these is reserved for the president of the Supreme Court, most judges who complete a full career can expect to reach the fourth level. Moving from level 1 to level 2 used to take around three years, but because of personnel shortages, junior judges may move up to level 2 after as little as one year, after they have heard at least a hundred cases. It might then take a further decade to move up to level 3, and another fifteen years to reach level 4. Salary levels do not correspond precisely to the level of court where the judge works: some judges in the Court of Appeal are at salary level 3, and others at level 4. Salaries are boosted by additional payments based on position: in the wake of the 2014 military coup, judges were awarded extra living cost allowances (supposedly on a temporary basis).[52] This meant that the lowest-paid, fresh-faced level 1 judge in 2018 received at least 50,000 baht per month (just over $1,500), while a judge at the top of level 2 (with perhaps eight or nine years' experience) received 81,360 baht monthly (just over $2,500). These amounts were often further boosted by car allowances, and did not include the free housing provided to many judges assigned to the provinces. By the standards of the Thai public sector, this was extremely good pay.

As of 2015, there were some 4,395 judges, most based in the Courts of First Instance. The figures were complicated by the fact that some lower court judges were assigned to assist with the work of the higher courts; and by the system of reassigning postretirement "senior judges" between sixty and seventy to work at various levels.

Newly recruited judges first serve a year as an assistant judge, during which they undertake some classroom study of procedures, observe cases, and participate in trials. After taking their oaths, newly minted judges are given their first

TABLE 1.   Numbers of judges, 2018

Supreme Court judges	147
Appeal Court judges	827
Court judges	144
First-Instance Court judges	3,163
Assistant judges (not yet sworn in)	137
Senior judges (over 60)	355
	—
Total	4,773

Source: Courts of Justice and the Office of the Judiciary, *Annual Report BE 2561, 2018* (Bangkok: Courts of Justice, 2018), 18.

court assignment, usually in a province quite distant from Bangkok. In theory they should then spend two years of further training as associate judges; but in practice, due to the shortage of judges, they begin hearing their own cases right away. Just as Howard Becker's Chicago schoolteachers were extremely concerned with the location of their schools, so for Thai judges in the early years of their careers, "vertical movement" is often what matters most.[53] The more than two hundred courts in Thailand are all ranked according to their desirability. In the past this ranking was based almost entirely on distance from Bangkok: the further away, the less desirable the posting. Provincial courts in major cities had more prestige than district courts (*san khwaeng*) or family and youth courts, but in the end location was the main determinant of desirability. The distance criterion was slightly modified by the location of royal palaces, since provinces containing royal palaces, such as Chiang Mai and Sakhon Nakhon, had more prestige. This was further complicated in the case of the thoroughly undesirable, insurgency-affected southern province of Narathiwat, which also contained a palace: "Narathiwat is included . . . so they choose from the judges assigned to the three provinces, those who are the best have to be sent to Narathiwat, because they are near the King, so even though it has a royal palace it's low ranking."[54] Postings to the insurgency-affected southern border provinces of Pattani, Yala, and Narathiwat were really in a special category: few judges wanted to be sent there, especially after the very rare 2004 murder of a judge in Pattani.[55] Normally only the lowest-ranking judges on the list would be assigned to these courts, and then usually for only one year. This resulted in very inexperienced judges trying security-related cases of national importance, an undesirable situation. In 2008, the president of the Supreme Court appealed for volunteers from Bangkok-based judges to take assignments in the southern border provinces, but there were few takers, since the work was considered demanding and risky. Latterly, judges serving in the far South have been entitled to an extra 20,000 baht per month danger money (an incentive only for those who came from lower-income families), and also to a posting of their choice after working just one year in the region.[56] The original "distance-based" ranking system was later replaced by a "demand-based" list, but in practice the two lists were very similar, since most judges wanted to be as close to Bangkok as possible.

Thai judges have an enormous amount to do: the three levels of courts took on 1,390,261 new cases in 2015—equivalent to 316 cases per judge, annually.[57] While some of these cases were very trivial, many involved at least a week's serious work. The Judicial Commission, which oversees the work of judges, was very concerned about unequal workloads across the court system. As Thanit Kaesawapitak argued:

> When we use a seniority system, a senior judge is supposed to be posted in a court that has more work and where he/she has to deal with more complicated cases. Instead he/she chooses to stay in a court that doesn't have much work to do. . . . The best solution is to tackle the root cause of the problem. That is to ensure that every court has equal work to do.[58]

The workload of petty crime cases at district courts, for example, could be relentless compared with the easier pace of the provincial courts.[59] But in practice, evening out the work of the various courts was extremely difficult, and problems such as the huge backlog of appeals in drugs cases were addressed in ad hoc fashion by bringing in small teams of able young judges who were willing to put in long hours of unpaid "overtime," rather than by assigning more experienced judges to these unwelcome tasks.[60]

Previously, a judge could expect to become chief judge of a court in the provinces after about thirteen years, or around the age of forty. At the time of research, the majority of chief judges were still in their forties—but their average age was rapidly increasing. The extension of judicial retirement ages to seventy meant that promotion became less rapid after the passage of the 2007 Constitution: one judge lamented that reaching chief judge level now required an average of twenty-three years' experience.[61] Beyond the chief judge level lay the Appeal Court and the Supreme Court, large and well-staffed by international standards, reflecting the ease with which the right to appeal was granted in the Thai system. By 2018, judges typically took twenty-five years to reach the Courts of Appeal— which meant there were very few Appeal Court judges under fifty. Before 2007 there was an automatic right to appeal in most cases. While the 2007 Constitution permitted the Supreme Court to dismiss frivolous appeals out of hand,[62] the court was very reluctant to exercise this power, and only began doing so because of the sheer volume of cases.[63] While judges liked to point out that this "generosity" in granting appeals created benefits for lawyers, it also supported a very large number of senior judicial posts.[64] In November 2015, the automatic right to appeal to the Supreme Court was removed in civil cases: parties now need to obtain leave from the Supreme Court before proceeding, and this is normally granted only when there is a substantial question of law at stake.[65] But a more radical parallel move for criminal cases has yet to be initiated.

In other judicial systems, there is a strong sense of hierarchy and intellectual gradation: elite judges are academic high flyers who inhabit a very different universe from ordinary judges working in lower courts, and are often selected through different procedures. Penny Darbyshire, who had unprecedented access to deliberations in the English courts, writes: "My key findings were that if High Court work requires graft, quick-thinking, genius and stamina, then Court of Appeal work requires these in abundance."[66] Top English judges have to be exceptionally sharp. Describing leading barristers facing the Law Lords, Darbyshire wrote: "Sitting behind elite counsel, I have often watched their silk gowns tremble, as all five brains challenge them in turn."[67] But in Thailand, judges who were by no means rapier-witted could reasonably expect to reach at least the Appeal Courts before retirement.

Appeal and Supreme Court judges had no fixed working hours; they were entitled to work from home, only attending their offices for meetings, at times agreed in advance. Like the lower courts, the Appeal Courts are organized into nine regions, spanning the whole country: many of the judges on the provincial appeals courts lived in or around Bangkok, traveling to their regions only for occasional meetings. Judges assigned to higher courts benefit from the support of "research judges," who help them to review precedents and even to draft their judgments. Most of these research judges are very able young judges in the early years of their careers.

Appeal Court judges typically have a quota of twelve cases per month, and work in a fixed three-member bench, or *ongkhana*.[68] They meet regularly, and brief each another on the cases they are writing up. For simple cases, the lead judge may draft up a judgment before the meeting; for more complex ones, they first have a preliminary discussion. The judge who is taking the lead on a given case then finalizes a judgment, which then goes to a research judge who either reviews it and sends it back to clarify any problematic legal issues, or simply submits it to the director of the court. This system is popular with senior judges, who can mainly work from home, often attending the court only for weekly meetings. In 2012, regional Appeal Courts were among the most efficient components of the justice system, turning around a lot of appeals in just two or three months. By contrast, the Central Appeal Court, which covered the whole of Bangkok and also handled all drug-related appeals nationwide, had a severe backlog of cases. Chalermkiat Charnsilp argued that some appeal judges were incapable of working effectively, were inactive, and lacked motivation to improve their knowledge—largely because their promotion was based on seniority rather than performance.[69] Sirichai Watthanayothin argued that many regional Appeal Court heads lacked the ability to secure equivalent posts in Bangkok: they were often of doubtful competence, or had inappropriate personal business connections in the regions they oversaw.[70]

Supreme Court judges also worked on a quota system: nine cases per month.[71] In effect—factoring in weekends and meeting days—this meant they had an average of just two days per judgment. While Thailand had numerous Supreme Court judges by international standards, each American Supreme Court judge had a whole team of expert clerks, while five Thai judges shared one clerk between them. Asked why the Supreme Court almost never exercises its right to hear oral testimony, a judge explained that they simply did not have time.[72] A younger judge was more critical, arguing that although the Supreme Court had reduced its backlog of cases from around 39,000 to 30,000 during the course of 2012, this had been achieved by working too quickly.[73] Declining to call new witnesses simply to make work more manageable was not a good enough reason. Reviewing the whole system, hearing fewer appeals and looking at them more closely would involve a major cultural shift, for which few judges were ready.

The creation of the Supreme Court for Political Officeholders under the 1997 Constitution was an unwelcome development for most Supreme Court judges, disrupting their longstanding habitus and challenging their dispositions. Nine judges now had to sit on the bench, often hearing extensive witness testimony; but each case they heard counted the same in workload terms as a paper appeal that required just a couple of days' work. The judgments were difficult and contentious, exposing the judges to much greater criticism and scrutiny than ordinary criminal cases.[74] The idea that Supreme Court judges relish the role of trying and punishing politicians is a caricature that bears no relation to reality.

Whereas the best and the brightest ought to be sent to border regions such as in the deep South to gain extensive courtroom experience and learn about the diversity and complexity of Thai society, instead they generally sought out "academic" posts, working under senior judges and maintaining an unblemished record to ensure their future promotion prospects.[75] This led to a lack of innovation; Supreme Court judges in particular became bogged down in routine work and lacked sufficient time or incentive to push the envelope on important issues such as bail reform.[76] Not surprisingly, Thailand's top legal minds were generally found outside the judiciary: legalists such as Borwornsak Uwanno, Vitit Muntarbhorn, Wissanu Krea-ngam, Suraphol Nitikraipot, and Worajet Pakeerat had followed academic careers in the law faculties at Chulalongkorn and Thammasat universities, while Meechai Ruchuphan had worked with the Council of State.

Judicial Oversight

Since 1997, judges have not been subject to direct political oversight; there is no minister responsible for managing judges. While the principle of a politically independent judiciary is an important and highly desirable one, especially in a highly unstable political order such as Thailand's, the absence of ministerial and parliamentary scrutiny leaves open the question "Who judges the judges?" In Thailand, judges cannot be sued. The late Thongbai Thongpao, Thailand's leading human rights lawyer, recounted his attempts to bring a legal action against a judge who had given one of his clients an excessive sentence. "So you want to stay practicing as a lawyer?" a court official asked him. "Don't you know: The King can do no wrong?"[77]

Judges are now largely self-regulating, overseen only by the Judicial Commission. In the past, the Judicial Commission was a model of democratic management that was the envy of other state institutions. It comprised thirteen members: the president of the Supreme Court (in the chair), four members elected from the Courts of the First Instance, four elected from the Courts of Appeal, and four elected from the Supreme Court. But after 2007, the Judicial Commission's composition was changed to include two members from the Courts of the First Instance, four from the Appeal Courts, and six from the Supreme Court, as well as two nonjudges elected by the Senate.[78] This change was widely criticized as reflecting the growing "dictatorial" tendencies of the Supreme Court.[79] Amnat Chotichawaranont argued that while judges were generally supportive of the Judicial Commission election system, most were unhappy with the proportions of Judicial Commission seats allocated to the different courts.[80]

When coupled with the change to a standard retirement age of seventy, the Judicial Commission reforms had the effect of empowering senior judges at the expense of junior ones. Judicial Commission members from each of the three courts were selected only by those judges from their own courts, so judges in the Courts of the First Instance—the great majority of judges—could only elect two members of the commission. This meant that competition for election to the commission was quite fierce, evidenced in posters in courtroom lifts, email circulars, and even SMS messages from would-be members running for office. In some cases, those running for the Judicial Commission used misleading campaign techniques—such as calling for judges to receive benefits matching those supposedly given to prosecutors and Administrative Court judges.[81]

Opinions on the Judicial Commission varied widely. One judge explained that he and many other judges were uneasy about the growing culture of lobbying Judicial Commission members; while he knew a couple of them, this was because he had worked with them in the past and maintained professional relations with them, not because he sought to use his connections for personal advantage.[82] By contrast, another judge insisted that nobody would dare lobby Judicial Commission members, and there was no need to do so in order to advance your career.[83]

Discipline

The extent of corruption and misbehavior among the judiciary is very difficult to measure. One judge told me about a large court of around thirty judges in which he had worked, where two judges were investigated for corruption and transferred to other posts, while a third was well known to be an unreliable heavy drinker whose work was not up to standard. In other words, at least 10 percent of the judges in that court were unfit to serve. None of these judges had been fired; instead, the authorities seemed to find ways of shuffling personnel around, and covering up their misdeeds. Many informants insisted that the great majority of judges were clean and competent; but my own observations suggest that minor visible infractions such as not maintaining a quorate bench were extremely widespread, and possibly even the norm for less serious cases. Despite the prevalence of "a few bad apples" explanations, it seemed at least equally likely that the Thai judiciary had a somewhat hypocritical institutional culture, taking immense pride in a moral, legal, and intellectual superiority that was at variance with the real position. Indeed, the excessive assertion of virtue surrounding the judiciary was on some level an act of bluster, an attempt to compensate for much messier and less laudable realities.

At the time of research in 2012, minutes of recent Judicial Commission meetings—which included verbatim quotes from commission members—were available on the open shelves of the old Supreme Court library. These minutes offer fascinating insights into internal debates about disciplinary and other issues.[84] When judicial lapses were unearthed and brought to the commission, the response was often some sort of slap on the wrist or cover-up. Occasionally, a judge would be downgraded to the status of "judicial officer," an administrative official unable to hear cases. In more serious cases, the judge was quietly forced to resign.[85] For very serious offences, errant judges could occasionally face straightforward "dismissal" (*plot ok*) or outright "expulsion" (*lai ok*, which meant losing pension benefits).[86] In theory, judges who appear to have committed criminal offences should be prosecuted following disciplinary proceedings by the Judicial Commission.[87] In practice, this never seemed to happen: judges simply judged one another.

From time to time, a serious disciplinary infraction resulted in the dismissal of one or more judges. Two such cases came to the fore in 2014. In

September, three appeal court judges from the Minburi court were dismissed for granting bail, in violation of official regulations, to a drugs case defendant who had been caught in possession of two thousand amphetamine pills. The defendant subsequently fled.[88] The previous month, four senior judges had been dismissed in a major corruption case: Ong-art Rojanasupote, senior judge of the Supreme Court and former vice president of the Supreme Court; Singpol La-ongmanee, a presiding judge of the Supreme Court; Adisak Timmas, former president of the Appeals Court; and Sitthichai Promsorn, a presiding judge of the Supreme Court. Sitthichai had apparently been accused of forcing a subordinate to sleep with him.[89] The investigation of these cases was triggered by the previous dismissal of Somsak Chanthakul, a former Appeals Court judge, for taking a bribe to grant bail. Ong-art and Singpol also were stripped of their pensions, while three other senior judges were placed on probation with their salaries frozen. In an unusually frank op-ed, former *Bangkok Post* editor Veera Prateepchaikul, who knew two of the fired judges personally, wrote:

> Many Thai judges feel that they are performing their duty on behalf of the monarchy and therefore their verdicts are above criticism. That is why the judiciary has been deprived of access to information about how strongly the public feels in regard to some of its decisions—which is regrettable. The court should be more open to criticism and not feel offended every time the institution or a verdict is criticized.[90]

Every organization faces disciplinary problems and sometimes needs to fire people. But the Thai judiciary's complete lack of transparency was perturbing; a court spokesman declared that details of the four judges' wrongdoing could not be revealed. This was a problematic stance for an institution dedicated to establishing the truth about the misdoings of others, especially since rumors of highly placed judge wrongdoers had been circulating for years. Nevertheless, a strength of the Thai system was that no formal limits were placed on the powers of the Judicial Commission to dismiss errant judges where necessary—even though these powers were rarely invoked.

The majority of serious disciplinary cases dealt with by the Judicial Commission concerned bail decisions: judges were punished for improperly granting bail. I am not aware of any case where a judge was disciplined for failing to grant bail to somebody who posed no obvious risk to society, and who was unlikely to flee. While several judges told me it was better that ten guilty people went free than that one innocent person was convicted,[91] where bail was concerned the opposite principle seemed to apply, notably to defendants accused of lèse-majesté or other crimes on the treason spectrum.

Veera's article highlighted an interesting detail: he had come to know a couple of the fired judges by taking part in a training course organized by the Judicial Training Institute, which was attended not simply by judges, but also by officials from other government agencies, and by senior executives from the private sector. The institute runs two main courses: a junior course for early-career judges, and the senior course Veera joined, the better-known Bo Yo So (here BYS) for those involved in administering the higher levels of the judicial system. BYS has close parallels with two other similar programs: the National Defense College (NDC) course offered by the military since 1955,[92] and the various certificate programs run by King Prachadipok's Institute (KPI), the research and training arm of the Thai Parliament.[93] As with its NDC and KPI counterparts, it was an open secret that many BYS participants were primarily interested in making close personal connections with judges and important figures in wider Thai society. One judge expressed distaste for the BYS culture, complaining that nonjudges involved in court cases would phone up judges who had studied in the same class (*run*) and ask them for "advice."[94] Senior judges enrolled in BYS would then sometimes call up the judges hearing these classmates' cases, asking for "help." He always refused to assist: this kind of practice ran counter to everything the Thai judiciary was meant to stand for.

Reform

Thai judges have limited opportunities to debate contentious issues, either among themselves or with outsiders. A Supreme Court office organizes academic forums and study tours on topical issues such as human trafficking, often in collaboration with the Konrad Adenauer Foundation. Some academic research is commissioned by the Office of the Judiciary and by various research institutes attached to different courts. But much of the commissioned research concerns specialist, second-order topics—consumer protection or environmental law, for example—that reflect the enthusiasms of self-styled "progressive" judges who prefer to avoid raising more sensitive political issues. The courts typically shy away from convening forums or commissioning reports on controversial questions such as security legislation, computer crime, lèse-majesté, or indeed sentencing guidelines, which are still set by the chief judges of the various courts. In general, judges are indifferent to questions concerning politics or human rights, despite the huge importance of these issues to Thai society. Only rarely do court judgments make any specific reference to people's rights, or even to the constitution itself—except in cases where politicians invoke these issues as part of their defense. Only Supreme Court judgments set precedents: decisions by lower courts or by the Administrative Court are not considered binding.

One of the most serious problems facing the courts is the huge backlog of cases awaiting judgment by the Supreme Court—more than twenty thousand in mid-2015. Thailand needed urgently to reduce the number of cases that found their way to the highest court in the land, rather than being resolved by the Court of First Instance or the Appeal Courts. While on one hand, Thailand has a harsh legal system and draconian rates of incarceration, it also had an extremely generous regime of allowing appeals, so giving judges considerable power. As one judge put it: "We can deny the request. We can permit the request. If we see you want to appeal, sometimes just for the sake of being sure, to make you feel better, since you don't seem yet to believe us, we send the request on up."[95]

Even offenders given a fine of just five hundred baht (fourteen dollars) are entitled to lodge an appeal. The large number of appeals to the Supreme Court validates a sizeable complement of top judges and perpetuates the dominance of the Supreme Court over the judicial system. But it also means that instead of trying to set the direction for Thailand's justice system by issuing landmark decisions on salient questions of the day, Supreme Court judges are bogged down in a myriad of cases, most them completely trivial. Since most Supreme Court judges are actually ill-qualified to write important rulings, many of them are ironically very comfortable being buried in routines:

> Our Supreme Court judges do not make landmark decisions, but rather carry out routine work. Supreme Court judges are no different from judges in the other courts. If you ask me whether they are smarter than judges in the other courts . . . because of their old age, their inactivity, and their unwillingness to learn new things [they are not]. . . . Of course, their age helps crystallize their thoughts, and their experience helps them understand issues more clearly. But if you ask whether more than half of them are like this, I'm not sure. This is because many of them are sick. There's a problem that starts in the lower courts and appeal courts, too: judges, regardless of which court they work in, do not update themselves. After they pass the judicial entrance examination, they do not have to learn new things, unless they are willing to do so by themselves. And very few judges do so: less than 20 percent.[96]

A core problem of the judicial system was the low quality of judgments in the Courts of First Instance and the Appeal Courts. Because so many cases ended up being reviewed by higher courts, some judges in lower courts felt they could get away with writing hasty, slapdash judgments that contained basic technical errors. Sometimes identical offences were treated very differently by different courts: for example, a number of people were prosecuted for tearing up their ballot papers during the controversial April 2006 general election, which was later annulled. A defendant in one province was jailed, while a defendant in another province was given a suspended sentence, and Chulalongkorn University political science professor Chaiyan Chayaporn was acquitted.[97] There was no mechanism to ensure consistency in such cases. By 2015 there were more than one hundred Supreme Court judges, around double the number five years earlier; while more than two hundred lower court judges had been assigned to assist the Supreme Court process a backlog of more than twenty thousand cases. One long-overdue change is the posting of all court judgments online; at present, only parties to cases are able to access judgments; many judges oppose judgments being more widely disseminated, since a lot of them are quite poorly written and argued.[98] Some judges feel embarrassed about having added their signatures on second-rate judgments out of a sense of obligation to other members of the panel: "This shows that the quality of court decisions is not even good enough for publication."

One judge admitted having referred cases to appeal simply out of sympathy: "I was not sure of the quality of the Courts of First Instance . . . I wanted to give defendants the opportunity [to appeal], although I should not have done so because it would increase the courts' work." In theory, all cases are reviewed by the chief judge of each court, but in practice most chief judges do not review cases very seriously. The 1997 Constitution had stated that judicial decisions could not be reviewed by chief judges, but the 2007 Constitution reversed this change, in response to criticism about the large numbers of flawed judgments.

Judges were rarely interested in serious innovations such as experimenting with a jury system, or creating genuine magistrates' courts for lesser cases, presided over by lay judges—both of which would increase the level of popular involvement with the legal system. The separation of the Office of the Judiciary from the Ministry of Justice after 1997 had created a power vacuum at the top of Thailand's judicial system.[99] Even though the secretary-general of the Office of the Judiciary reports directly to president of the Supreme Court,[100] who in turn chairs both the Judicial Commission and the Court Administration Commission, the Supreme Court president lacks full authority over the courts as a whole:

> Given this structure, the president of the Supreme Court is not the real executive of the courts, since any policy has to be approved by the two commissions. . . . It is rather like politics: many matters are not subject to any accountability. [We] are not interested in how the quality of judging cases can be improved, but how our salaries, interest, profits, and welfare can be enhanced.[101]

The lack of central authority over Thai courts meant nobody was tasked with reforming the system. In a research paper, Sirichai Watthanayothin argued that after the Courts of Justice were separated from the Ministry of Justice in 1997, the lines of command became rather blurred.[102] The president of the Supreme Court is Thailand's top judge, but the main administrative power lay with the secretary-general of the Office of the Judiciary. There was no such post as chief of the Courts of Justice; senior administrative positions elsewhere in the court system lacked the status and prestige of the Supreme Court, which made it difficult to implement reforms.

Article 258 of the 2017 Constitution contained an extremely interesting injunction: "Reform the ways of studying and teaching the law curriculum and legal training in order to develop jurists with strong competencies and legal perspectives who adhere to morality and lawyerly ethics."[103] The fact that such a provision was inserted into the constitution by an extremely conservative drafting committee arguably indicated a degree of disquiet about how detached judges were becoming from Thailand's rapidly changing society.

Among mid-ranking judges—such as chief judges of courts in the provinces—the need for more openness, and criticism, both internally and externally, was a recurrent theme. Nevertheless, some more junior judges were skeptical.[104] One explained that he had grown wary of new bosses who arrived, trumpeting their transparency and urging everyone to make suggestions for improving the system. As one senior judge famously quipped, "I am not biased, but I have a long memory"—people who spoke out too critically could find themselves marked down as troublemakers.

One senior judge declared that he would like to see the whole system reformed from top to bottom, given a complete rethink.[105] A lot of the time, cases were very one-sided in favor of the prosecution, which was unfair for the defendants. He believed that there had been a shift in culture in favor of more need for evidence, a higher burden of proof from material witnesses. Courts, having become much more skeptical, were now more demanding in terms of the evidence presented by prosecutors, because the quality of cases being prepared was declining and judges were having more difficulty doing their jobs than before.

Judgments

In theory, the two judges trying a criminal case are the ones who determine the verdict and sentence. In practice, the reality is more complicated. First, many junior judges lack confidence in their ability to decide even quite simple matters. In one provincial court, I observed a case where the judge had apparently given an incorrect sentence in the morning and had to reconvene in the afternoon to amend it.[106] When one of the defendants announced that he now wanted a lawyer, the judge and officials were very flustered, since he had not made his request at the initial hearing. A series of frantic phone calls were made to the chief judge before the officials decided to improvise a special procedure to deal with the situation. In a highly routinized system, any unusual ordinary development could trigger virtual panic on the part of inexperienced judges, who were heavily reliant on the advice of their superiors. This raised the question of to what extent these young judges really decided the outcomes of cases; did "advice" by the chiefs of courts influence the outcomes of trials where they had not been present for any of the witness testimony?

One senior judge explained that while a head of court is only centrally involved in deciding the outcome of certain cases as part of the *ongkhana*, in practice the head will be consulted on other cases by colleagues who ask for advice in general terms. If judges give a sentence that deviates from the standard tariff (*matrathan*), they must discuss this with the chief and it will also be referred to the regional office for comment.[107] Judges are not obliged to change their decisions based on the advice from above, but any notes of comment from the regional office are added to the case file and, since they can be accessed by the defendants and their lawyers, could form part of an appeal. Even some *khwaeng* cases are automatically referred to the head of the court and the regional office for review before judgments are made public, based on certain rule-based criteria. Those reviewed would include politically related cases, some defamation cases, and all lèse-majesté cases. Prior to 1997, directors of the nine court regions had the power to revise judgments before they were issued by the Courts of First Instance. This power was removed under the 1997 Constitution, since it was associated with interference in judicial independence. The result, however, was a sharp decline in the quality of judgments. Based on the revised 2007 Constitution, regional directors again began revising judgments before they were issued, to reduce mistakes that were having an adverse effect on the credibility of the system.[108]

A former defendant in a provincial contempt of court case argued that the case had been resolved following behind-the-scenes negotiations between lawyers, prominent outsiders, and the chief judge of the court. The judges in the courtroom were not the ones who had been centrally involved in determining the outcome.[109] One very experienced trial lawyer argued that the central role of chief judges in deciding cases under their jurisdiction was an open secret in Thailand, a standard feature of cases heard in the provinces.[110] The worst abuses took place in provincial civil cases concerning business deals, property transactions, and inheritance cases, which usually involved one side buying off other parties, and so rarely went to appeal.

One judge expressed intense distrust of politicians whom he believed were constantly trying to interfere at all levels in the outcomes of court cases.[111] His arguments nicely captured judges' sense of themselves as an endangered species, a thin judicial line trying to hold back a tide of politicization and manipulation from which they had to try and protect themselves at all costs. In a research paper, junior judge Kasem Suppasit argued that there was a significant problem concerning interference in judgments. Such interference took two forms, external and internal:

> Therefore, there might be attempts from outsiders, for example, lawyers or people close to the judges, who try to change the court ruling. The independence of judges is violated by outsiders, and this may happen because judges are willing to take bribes. It may also happen because judges were compelled or convinced by outsiders concerning the judgment of cases.
>
> I always hold to rightful principles and do not work only to make my superiors happy. Sometimes, my decisions might upset some people, but I stick to rightful principles as per my oath of allegiance sworn to the King.[112]

Internal interference was equally problematic:

> During my career, I have worked with several chief judges who had different ways of working. I was interfered with directly and indirectly to deliver judgments according to the demands of these chief judges. Sometimes, there were small notes or messages written in the case files to instruct me as to what kind of decision I should make . . . I feel sad that fellow judges try to interfere in the court trials and rulings.[113]

A report by prominent ex-judge Wicha Mahakhun found that corruption and lobbying to influence case outcomes are prevalent at all levels of the Courts of Justice, especially in the Court of First Instance, where the identities of the judges are known from the outset.[114]

Cases considered politically sensitive—including all 112, computer crime, and color-coded protest cases—have their files marked *prueksa* (advice),[115] and are reviewed by the chief judge (in provincial courts) or deputy director (in the main Bangkok criminal court), who will keep a close eye on them.[116] Sometimes the deputy director will sit on the bench as an observer for parts of the case, or exceptionally even be added to the ongkhana as a third member. At times, debates among judges themselves about how to deal with these cases can become extremely heated, something never seen by outsiders. In 2016, popular singer Tom Dundee,[117] was sentenced to seven and a half years in jail on five counts of lèse-majesté by a military court. Unusually, an apparently frustrated judge declined to read the full judgment aloud, then declared in open court that he had wanted to give the defendant a harsher sentence, but had been advised by a deputy court president to combine some of the cases to reduce the total jail term.[118] Such conversations clearly occur among judges in the civilian courts too, but are not openly discussed.

The workings of the Appeals and Supreme Courts are much more arcane than those of the Courts of the First Instance, given the lack of any public hearings except in the unique instance of the Supreme Court's Criminal Division for Political Officeholders.[119] In theory, those who appeal never even know which judges have been assigned to them; the same applies at the level of the Supreme Court. This system of anonymity is designed to militate against bribery and corruption. But how influential are the presidents of the Appeal and Supreme Court in determining the outcome of cases: who really decides? Cases are reviewed by an ongkhana of three judges, and court presidents may have an inkling about which ongkhana might acquit and which judges would tend toward a guilty verdict. Anybody trying to manipulate the outcomes of higher level cases—such another judge, perhaps acting on behalf of a prominent businessperson or politician—would need good connections with the senior officials of the Appeals and Supreme Courts, and especially the secretaries who manage most of the casework.

The Supreme Court typically has monthly half-day en banc meetings,[120] when all judges sit together to discuss a particularly complex case, or one which the president has flagged for discussion. Research judges can attend but not vote, and the morning culminates in a free lunch for everybody. These en banc cases are all written up in the *Law Review*, of which twelve issues a year are published. In the recent past the Supreme Court dealt with as many as seven thousand cases a year, more than thirty each working day. Inevitably, most of these cases received only quite cursory review by the court's president and vice presidents, who were very reliant on assistants to screen the cases and flag those of particular interest or concern.

Most Thai judges are honest, hardworking, and well intentioned, dedicated to a lifelong career in public service that provides them with financial security but offers no prospect of worldly riches or fame. They generally prefer to stay out of the limelight, toiling in obscurity; few Thais could name a single judge, other than perhaps one or two more outspoken members of the Constitution Court. The majority of judges enter the profession at an early age, marked out by their success in a fiendishly difficult entrance examination that changes the course of their lives forever. Their careers are extremely predictable and much of their work is highly routinized. Somewhat removed from mainstream society, they enjoy very high social status and considerable respect—benefits that come at a price.

Yet despite their self-image as an exceptionally talented elite, not all judges excel at the business of judging. Many court judgments are flawed: their shortcomings are ameliorated by a system of close monitoring by senior administrators. Judges tend to believe that a combination of their rigorous selection procedures and their most favored status with the palace inoculates them against temptations and human failings: in short, they become the embodiment of virtuous legalism. Given the shortcomings of elected politicians, the military, the police, prosecutors, and other state agencies, some Thai judges see themselves as a thin yellow line protecting the institution of the monarchy and redeeming the land from moral and social collapse. The reality is that all judges are human, and many of them are fallible. Especially in recent years, the discourse of judicialization has fostered unrealistic expectations of the judiciary and placed judges under impossible pressures. Thailand's faltering, often dysfunctional politics in the years since May 1992 has fostered much more widespread political awareness and opened up previously sacrosanct spheres to ever-greater public scrutiny. As a result, the structural contradictions of what Max Weber terms democracy's "ambivalence" towards a meritocratic "privileged caste"—such as the Thai judiciary—have become increasingly exposed. While not an issue in the eyes of most judges, their status as an elite class has undermined their standing in the eyes of the public.

Thai judges operate in a particular habitus, a social and professional world that is both distinct from and connected with wider Thai society. Whereas in earlier decades judges led a quasi-monastic life, socializing mainly with their colleagues and keeping nonjudges at a distance, more recently they have been encouraged to establish a wider range of connections through developments such as the Bo Yo So training program. Interacting with businesspeople and other elites is a mixed blessing for Thai judges, giving them greater insights into how the world works but also increasing their exposure to lobbying and worse. While in the past many judges came from quite ordinary backgrounds, most of those entering the profession today come from affluent Sino-Thai families and have grown up insulated from the harsh life conditions of the typical criminal defendant.

Becoming a judge involves passing a dreadfully difficult entrance examination, a rite of passage that forms the basis of immense professional pride and a strong sense of fraternity. The dark side of this rich, profound fraternity is its exclusionary and self-exalted character. Many Thai judges feel intellectually and even morally superior to others. Their high social status often makes them believe they are experts in the law, even when they do not hold advanced degrees and have no specialist knowledge of any legal field. In short, Thai judges are generally very bright people, but not necessarily as bright as they would like to believe. Even those who are extremely bright are readily blinded by their collective disposition, which can make them dangerously overconfident.

All this means that when Thai judges preside over cases brought against critics of the state, they struggle to distinguish between their formal role as neutral arbiters, and their own intimate affiliations with the monarchy and deep attachment to the status quo. Trying political cases places Thai judges in an extremely uncomfortable position. The next chapter will examine the ideological framework that shapes the world of Thai judges, forming the basis of their legal, professional, and political dispositions. At the core of those dispositions lies the close yet highly ambiguous relationship between the judiciary and the crown.

BENCH AND THRONE

Many Thai judges see themselves first and foremost as royal servants, whose duty to swear an oath of loyalty before the King has been enshrined in successive recent constitutions. Since King Bhumibol's April 2006 speeches to the judges of the Administrative and Supreme Courts, in which he urged them to play a central role in solving the country's political problems, public expectations of the judiciary have been extremely high. The King's public injunctions to judges were unprecedented, but there was nothing new about a close connection between monarchy and the judiciary. Since the 1940s, members of the royal family have been invited to preside over criminal trials during visits to the courts—despite their complete lack of legal training. The King actively exercises the right to pardon convicted criminals and to shorten sentences: every couple of years as many as thirty thousand prisoners are released from jail on this basis. The King may also remit the death penalty, which is frequently pronounced but rarely carried out: in this sense, Thai kings retain their traditional status as "lords of life." This chapter examines how judges' royal connections, real or imagined, influence the ways in which they dispense justice.

When King Ananda (Rama VIII) and his younger brother Prince Bhumibol visited the Chachoengsao Provincial Court on May 24, 1946, they heard the case of a young woman who had stolen a key ring. The woman pleaded guilty, but had a small child to take care of. The judges hearing the case gave her a six-month jail sentence, but the King declared that her sentence should be suspended, since she had no previous convictions. The woman crawled on her hands and knees and prostrated herself before the King, saying that she greatly appreciated his mercy but wished to receive her punishment, since she had misbehaved. The King gave the woman some of his own money in recognition of her loyalty to the laws of the land.[1]

This story is replete with moral messages: the devotion of the subject to the King, and her obsequious insistence that she should be properly punished; and the King's great benevolence, first in commuting her sentence and then in giving her money from his own pocket. The young Rama VIII's violent and still unexplained death from a gunshot wound just a fortnight later gave the story an added poignancy, leaving his younger brother to continue with a newly reinvented tradition of royal mercy.

This chapter examines how Thai judges understand the world around them, and their own place in it, and how judges are viewed by others in Thai society. To borrow the title of a very different book, the chapter asks how Thai judges think.[2] As the Chachoengsao court anecdote illustrates, these questions are inseparable from ideas of royal authority and kingly benevolence: how do judges locate themselves in relation to the monarchy? In the decades following the end of the absolute monarchy in 1932, commentators tended to focus on the political role of the coup-happy army, on the rise of elected politicians and the growing importance of parliament, and latterly on the growing salience of civil society and social movements, including mass protests organized by students, farmers, and other groups. From the late 1950s onwards, the monarchy began to regain some of the standing it had lost after 1932. Yet the place of the judiciary was largely occluded; little public or academic attention was paid to the functions performed by Thailand's judges.

Despite their low profile, judges consistently performed important roles and functions following the end of the absolute monarchy. No less than five judges have served as prime minister since 1932,[3] including the very first holder of the office, Phraya Manopakorn Nititada (Kon Hutasingha) (1932–33); the intellectual leader of the 1932 revolution, Pridi Banomyong (1946); former Supreme Court president Sanya Thammasak (1973–75); Thanin Kraivichien, a former Supreme Court judge (1976–77); and, very briefly, former appeal court judge Somchai Wongsawat (2008), brother-in-law of ousted premier Thaksin Shinawatra.[4] Each of the five became prime minister at a critical juncture: the end of the absolute monarchy, the end of the Second World War, in the wake of mass protests, in the aftermath of a bloody military coup, and following the judicial ouster of a predecessor. None lasted much more than a year: apart from Sanya, Thailand's judge-premiers were all controversial and commanded only limited support. Sanya and Thanin were royal favorites, while Phraya Mano, Pridi, and Somchai came from very different camps. Nevertheless, all five showed how a judicial career could help endow individuals with the requisite social capital to enter Government House at crucial moments. Judicial credentials, however, were insufficient to enable these prime ministers to remain in office for very long. Thai judges were intermittently heard, but were best not seen.

While Thai judges have not shone as national leaders, the judiciary and the monarchy have generally remained very close: partly for this reason the courts have always been ready to endorse military interventions in politics. The judiciary has never challenged any of Thailand's eleven successful coups d'état since 1932, despite the fact that all of these coups were completely illegal. The judiciary's collusion with military rule might appear passive, but has entailed active decisions that have evolved into a collective and generally consistent institutional stance, taking the side of authoritarian interventions and persistently failing to defend constitutionalism, democracy, or human rights.[5]

Ambiguity lay at the heart of Thai views of legalism. Judges reified laws and precedents, but venerated the monarchy and were willing to subordinate their authority to royal prerogatives. They adhered strictly to rules, but willingly suspended them during supposedly exceptional yet highly normalized coup regimes. They insisted that only the guilty should be punished, yet acquitted virtually nobody. They spoke the language of benevolence, while dispensing some of the world's harshest prison sentences. Most Thais were highly pragmatic and wanted political and social problems dealt with quickly and without too much mess. But legal solutions, whether they involved banning politicians or rerunning elections, were usually messy, and often created at least as many problems as they solved. This chapter examines some of the reasons behind the tortuous ambiguities of Thai legalism.

Monarchy

Central to the Thai judiciary's self-understanding is the special relationship between the crown and the courts. During the latter decades of the Ninth reign, Thai judges were wont to see themselves as royal servants, working to maintain a regime of virtuous rule centered on the person of King Bhumibol. After the end of the absolute monarchy, Rama VII disagreed with the creation of a criminal law against murder, arguing that all such cases should go to the King for adjudication as the "lord of life."[6] He was overruled by the Phraya Phahon government. Even after 1932, royalists believed that judicial powers should all be vested in the monarch.

In announcing the end of the absolute monarchy on June 24, 1932, the People's Party's initial public statement contained strongly antimonarchical language, accusing King Prajadhipok of acting "above the law" and mismanaging the country. In the same vein, the interim constitution of June 27, 1932, began with a declaration that the supreme power in the country rested with all its people and that the courts (along with the monarchy, parliament, and people's executive) exercised their power on behalf of the people.[7] Article 6 of the interim constitution shockingly declared that while the King could not be brought before the courts, he could be tried by parliament. The King had no authority to act without his orders being countersigned by a member of the People's Committee. The first of the People' Party's six core principles stated that the independence of the courts must be preserved.

Yet by the time Siam's first permanent constitution was promulgated in December 1932, the tone and the language had greatly changed. The preamble to the constitution was full of praise for the monarchy, and the crucial phrase that judges adjudicate "in the name of the King" had been added to the provisions concerning the courts.[8] The royal prerogatives included in the December 1932 Constitution were intended by the People's Party to be purely honorific, part of a compromise that allowed the King to save face while losing all real power. Nevertheless they were invested with an entirely different meaning by the royalist faction, who insisted on taking them literally. While similar forms of words were found in other monarchies, in the Siamese context they were highly charged politically, markers of resistance by the royalist ancien regime to the implications of constitutional rule.[9] Although the 1977 charter omitted the crucial phrase, every constitution since 1978 has included an article along the following lines: "The trial and adjudication of cases are the power of the Courts, which must be proceeded by justice in accordance with the Constitution and the law and *in the name of the King*" (italics added).[10] Right from the onset of Siamese constitutionalism, the role of the monarch in relation to the courts has been a bone of contention: do courts really adjudicate "in the name of the King," or is this simply a figure of speech?

In May 1946, twenty-one-year-old King Ananda, Rama VIII, the elder brother of then-Prince Bhumibol, summoned the permanent secretary of the Ministry of Justice, the chair of the committee of the Supreme Court, and the chief justice of the Phra Nakhon Provincial Court to a private meeting to discuss their work. The Ministry of Justice asked those invited to submit detailed notes on the meeting, since this royal request was of unusual importance. Later that month, Rama VIII and his younger brother Bhumibol visited the Chachoengsao Provincial Court, where both of them sat on the bench during the trial of the female key ring thief.

Just over two weeks later, Rama VIII was found dead from a mysterious gunshot wound, and Bhumibol assumed the throne as Rama IX.

A focal point of the Court Museum in Bangkok is a series of photographs of the King and other royals sitting in judgment on the bench. Whether his visit to the Chachoengsao Court was a formative experience for the eighteen-year-old Bhumibol remains unclear, but after his return from Switzerland in 1950, he and other members of the royal family made frequent visits to the courts, often ostensibly to open new buildings. The King sat in judgment on at least six occasions in Bangkok, Chiang Mai, Songkhla, and Pattani between 1952 and 1984; Crown Prince Vajiralongkorn took the bench in Fang and Bangkok three times between 1977 and 1992; while Queen Sirikrit assumed the bench after opening the new Thonburi Courts in 1982.[11] From 1969 onwards, the King presided over the award of certificates to newly minted barristers, a duty that later the Crown Prince or Princess Sirindhorn carried out annually on the King's behalf.[12]

Royal images are ubiquitous in courts: judges sit directly beneath a large, usually gilded picture of the King; some pause briefly as they enter the courtroom, bowing or wai-ing before the royal photograph.[13] In earlier decades, these photographs were black and white, and rather understated; in the early 2000s, they were changed to very formal color images in heavy, gilded frames. As with the veneration of the Imperial image that began in Meiji Japan, the omnipresence of the royal gaze in the Thai courtroom helped organize the nation around the virtue of the monarch.[14] Beginning during the reign of Rama IV in the mid-nineteenth century, judges were required to swear an oath before the King on assuming office. The 1974 Constitution—drafted by a committee established by former Supreme Court president Sanya Thammasak—first specified that swearing the royal oath was a requirement to become a fully-fledged judge. This stipulation has been included in all subsequent constitutions. During the latter part of the Bhumibol era, until new judges took the oath of loyalty to the monarch at the end of the training, they were not entitled to sign judgments. Many judges set great store by the royal oath, which includes three references to the King, and two to the kingdom.[15] Judges first swear to be loyal to the King, then to create justice for the people and uphold peace in the kingdom, preserving the prevailing political order. Justice is not the first objective of the courts: creating justice is sandwiched between serving the monarchy and maintaining order. As Foucault notes in an analysis of Greek tragedy, the precise oath sworn by any judge is of immense importance for those trials that follow: a binding oath may determine the judge's own destiny.[16] One young judge explained to me that this oath taking is the most important moment for any judge: "Like the swearing-in of an American president."[17] In the post-Bhumibol era, the royal oath was less emphasized: Article 24 of the 2017 Constitution allowed senior officials to begin performing their duties without first swearing an oath before the King, implying that new judges could start hearing cases without delay. In early 2018, a batch of judges briefly began work without having sworn the oath.[18]

Thanin Kraivichien, a former Supreme Court judge who was the King's personal choice for prime minister in 1976, and who later joined the Privy Council, is an important source for royalist claims about the relationship between the monarchy and the courts. Thanin argued that in the past, the power to judge legal cases belonged to kings. Later on, as the country became more developed and kings had other duties to perform, they delegated the task of judging cases to the courts.[19] In Thanin's view, when judges hear cases they are literally doing so "in the name of the king"; there is nothing figurative in this metaphor. A brilliant LSE graduate, called to the English bar in 1958, Thanin proved a disastrous prime minister: he presided over the burning of 45,000 books during his time as premiership and declared that it would take twelve years to restore the country to democracy.[20] Thanin was too ultra-rightist even for Thailand's military generals, who removed him after just a year in office despite his reputation as a royal favorite. From the privileged enclave of the Privy Council, Thanin became a leading conservative ideologue and champion of the monarchy, articulating views about the identity of the King and the nation that were later taken up in various forms.[21]

Prominent royal adjutant Thongthong Chandrangsu, a former deputy permanent secretary of the Ministry of Justice, declared in a 1996 interview: "The statement that judges work "in the name of the King" is neither made flippantly, like invoking a paper tiger, nor simply to comply with tradition."[22] Thongthong noted that only a small number of officeholders were constitutionally required to swear an oath before the King: privy councilors, cabinet members, and judges.[23] Neither members of parliament nor senators were required to swear this oath. According to Thongthong, the oath was not simply a matter of words on paper, but had a much deeper meaning. In other words, taking such an oath before the King was a rare privilege: more than simply a pledge designed to ensure good moral behavior, the swearing ceremony was an opportunity for judges to assert their loyalty and their special connection with the Crown. He observed that if judges sitting on the bench turn their heads, they can always see a picture of the King—which can also be seen by defendants, prosecutors, and witnesses. Thongthong asserted that this was all evidence of a close relationship between the monarchy and the courts, one that had lasted for seven hundred to eight hundred years. Thongthong's arguments about the connections between the King and the courts reflected a project of ideological construction carried out by various Thai government agencies from the 1970s onwards.[24]

King Bhumibol discussed the issue of judges "working in the name of the King" when he spoke at the judicial oath ceremony on July 9, 2003:

> When you do something in the royal name, or in other words on behalf of the King, if you act immorally, the King becomes an immoral person. Thus I have to request you very strongly to act in compliance with the vow, otherwise I shall myself be in trouble, both personally and officially. And if I am in trouble, the people will be in trouble as well, since they will not receive justice.[25]

The King's speech did nothing to disabuse judges of their sense that they were carrying out a special royal mission. In the same way, royal speeches delivered at the award of certificates to new barristers and during visits to Courts served an important function in connecting the judiciary with the King. These speeches were invariably didactic and instructional: listeners were expected to reflect on them, to learn from them, and to act on their messages. The highly personal mode of didactic address in the speech exemplified what Connors terms the intimate discourse of a "citizen King."[26] Recurrent themes of King Bhumibol's speeches were the priority of justice over law and the conduct expected of judges. On numerous occasions, the King talked about the ideologies of and intentions behind the law, and as well the shortcomings of the law and of judges themselves. In Thai books relating to law and the judiciary, King Bhumibol—who had no legal training—was often praised for his brilliant insights as a legal philosopher.

The monarchy closely monitored developments inside the judiciary; on one occasion in 1999, the palace made it known that the King had vetoed the promotions of three senior judges who were allegedly involved in corruption.[27] The King's actions were lauded by the media—yet no evidence was offered, and no formal or legal proceedings were invoked to investigate their wrongdoing. This was a rare example where an extraconstitutional intervention by the palace was deliberately brought to light. Official sources were at pains to stress that the monarchy and the courts were inextricably linked.[28]

Following the 1997 financial crisis, permanent civil service status was removed from many categories of government employment, leading to a loss of standing and dignity. Most new officials became state employees, rather than *kharatchakan* (government officials, literally slaves of the King). Judges, however, retained the special standing of *kharatchakan tulakarn*.[29] In their imaginations, many judges really saw themselves as *kharatchaboriphan*, royal servants, who were distinguished from other state officials.[30] As one judge put it: "We believe we are government officials who are working in the name of the King, this is our pride, something we are proud of."[31] This proximity to the monarchy gives judges a strong sense of moral superiority to other groups in the society but also makes them reluctant to accept any need for external regulation.

Royal Verdicts

Themes of sympathetic defendants and benevolent rulers run through a series of tales of royal participation in criminal trials in the decades that followed Rama VIII's 1946 visit to Chachoengsao with his younger brother. In 1952, King Bhumibol took part in a trial at the Courts of Justice in Bangkok. A man pleaded guilty to stealing a millstone found in his possession, although there was no witness to the actual theft. Because he admitted to theft and not simply possession, the judges decided that he was an upright citizen who should be treated mercifully. His six-month jail term was commuted to a three-month suspended sentence because of his guilty plea. The judge noted that the case was decided in front of the King. It was not entirely clear whether the King's presence influenced the final sentence, but the narrative mixed together tales of judicial benevolence and royal participation.

Echoes may be found in various cases where the Crown Prince sat on the bench.[32] In two cases he heard in 1977 at the Chiang Mai Provincial Court in Fang, the twenty-four-year-old Crown Prince was a party to court decisions that the defendants should receive suspended jail sentences. Notes on these cases displayed at the Museum of the Court Archives stress that the Crown Prince was extremely cautious in his behavior, asking the Chief Judge of the Court for instructions on how to sit down and stand up while on the bench, and checked with the judge that a suspended sentence was appropriate in the second case; the Crown Prince did not add his signature to the judgment. When the Crown Prince visited the Bangkok Civil Court and the Courts of Justice in 1987, one civil case and one criminal case were specially prepared for him to decide.[33] In another criminal case heard by the Crown Prince at the Courts of Justice in Bangkok in 1992, the defense lawyer pleaded for royal mercy on behalf of two defendants who were accused of stealing soft drinks worth 540 baht. The lawyer asked for them to be given suspended sentences so that they had a chance to become "good citizens."

A book published by the Courts of Justice in 2007 explains how by deciding legal cases on their visits to courts, the King, Queen, and Crown Prince reaffirmed the longstanding royal power to decide cases, as if they were just another judge of the court.[34] This was a power based on ancient traditions. These royal visits and judgments, the book claimed, helped to motivate judges in their determination to provide justice for the people, as well as to build up public trust in the Courts of Justice. But this explanation illustrated fundamental questions about the Thai justice system. Are cases decided on rational grounds by professionally trained judges, or are they judged on the basis of extralegal considerations? The idea that a member of the royal family can substitute for a legally trained judge on the basis of "tradition" upends the legal-rational basis of the Thai judicial system. Far from building public trust in the courts, such cases ask the public to suspend whatever trust they normally place in the judiciary, and instead put their faith in royal benevolence—a completely different source of legal legitimacy, and one that has no obvious place in a modern constitutional order.

Phuttipong Ponganekgul, an outspoken legal academic, published an online article in 2013 arguing that for the King to decide a case in court, or to change the judge's decision on the day when he attended the court, was in fact illegal.[35] Any resulting judgments were therefore null and void. By contrast, Jarunee Thana-ratapon argues that the King has legitimate authority to judge a case, as part of his "immeasurable powers," which are based on the ten royal virtues and the norms appropriate to the monarch.[36] She also emphasizes that the Courts of Justice have been under royal authority since ancient times, an argument that glosses over both the introduction of a modern legal system during the Fifth Reign, and the end of the absolute monarchy and transition to constitutional rule in 1932. Phuttipong based his arguments on legal provisions dating back to 1930, which stipulate that a case must be decided by the judges responsible in a closed-door meeting before being announced in court. If anybody other than the judges responsible for the case attends the meeting, the court's decision will be unlawful. Members of the royal family are not entitled either to attend closed judicial meetings, or to change official verdicts on the spot. In principle, anyone convicted in such a case has the right to appeal to a higher court for the annulment of an unlawfully issued judgment. In practice, however, it is difficult to imagine any defendant who received a reduced sentence on the basis of "royal mercy" bringing such an appeal; nor does it seem likely that an appeal of this kind would be upheld.

Jarunee's argument, on the other hand, implies that the 1932 revolution changed nothing, and the King continues to enjoy all the rights and privileges of an absolute monarch. If the King no longer exercises judgment in court cases—except on rare occasions, such as those documented in the book—this is not because the King is no longer entitled to judge these cases, but because he chooses to delegate this power to others. Jarunee's analysis involves overturning almost ninety years of Thai political history. By extension, the King still has every right to rule the country and to proclaim its laws, but instead simply chooses to delegate these powers to a prime minister, a cabinet and a parliament. In short, the basis of the governance of the Thai state is not a legally binding constitution, but a set of monarchical preferences—or indeed whims.

Jarunee's article followed on from a best-selling 2005 book by Pramual Ruchanaseree on royal powers,[37] which helped fuel the royalist rhetoric of the anti-Thaksin movement that later developed into the PAD.[38] It was encapsulated in the slogan "We will fight for the King," which appeared on the very first generation of yellow shirts sold at Lumpini Park in late 2005.[39] Phuttipong's contrary view comes from the same intellectual stable as the revisionist Nitirat group of legal academics, who argue that such royal privileges are incompatible with constitutionalism and the end of the absolute monarchy. On rational grounds, Phuttipong's arguments may be much stronger: but for many Thais, the status of the monarchy is essentially an emotional issue.

Of course, in theory, and for most practical purposes, royal powers may have little consequence: if the King chooses not to exercise them, his powers may appear irrelevant.[40] The problem that even when not exercised, royal powers change the basis on which Thailand is governed, and the understandings that judges and other officials have of their own duties and their own authority. Furthermore, should any future King decide to exercise these powers, it might prove impossible to prevent him from doing so. This issue grew increasingly salient as King Bhumibol's reign drew to a close, given concerns that Crown Prince Vajiralongkorn had not earned the right to assume his father's extensive extralegal privileges.

Royal Pardons

Even first-time tourists to Thailand are familiar with a common practice in popular Buddhism: the release of birds from cages. At Bangkok's Erawan Shrine and elsewhere, visitors are invited to give small birds their freedom—in exchange, of course for a small donation. In fact, the birds are usually so tame (or drugged) that they soon return to the (often Muslim) cage-owners to be reincarcerated. But in Buddhist terms, the recapture of the birds makes no odds, since the demerit associated with placing them back in the cages falls entirely on their owners. A Buddhist may make merit by releasing the same bird over and over again. Imagine how much more merit is made by releasing a human being from jail. Then imagine the merit accruing to a King who releases thirty-five thousand people from jail on a single day: an awful lot of *bunbarami* is generated.

One important royal power is still regularly exercised, with very considerable impact: the power to grant pardons. Many heads of state have the right to grant pardons to convicted criminals, though precise mechanisms vary. To date, the British Queen Elizabeth II has exercised the royal prerogative of mercy only four times during a reign lasting over sixty-seven years, always in exceptional cases, generally involving miscarriages of justice. Most pardons granted to convicted criminals are instead given by Parliament. Under the American Constitution, in powers resembling those of the English crown, American presidents are entitled to grant "reprieves and pardons"; most commonly, they simply commute sentences.[41] American presidents issued more than twenty thousand pardons and sentence commutations during the twentieth century.[42] Superficially, the Thai position may appear similar to the American one. The reality is rather different.

Chachapon argues that royal pardons reflect longstanding and continuing practice: "The right to make a complaint and to receive royal help from the monarch in Thailand has been the firm historical linkage between the monarch and his subjects. People even today need this right."[43] This notion of a right of royal appeal again conflates notions of absolute and constitutional monarchy; in a modern legal order, the King signs off on pardons on behalf of the state, not as a pure exercise of royal will. During the Ayutthaya and Thonburi periods, royal justice was based on a combination of different modes: the King was expected to use royal powers (those of the *devaraja*—the King as god, or as the embodiment of law) to punish criminals based on his standing as a "lord of life," who had the power to kill any of his subjects at will. At the same time, the *devaraja's* power of punishment was offset by *dhammaraja* (royal benevolence), though in practice force typically trumped mercy.[44] Chachapon cites an example of a conditional pardon given by King Naresuan in 1592, when a senior monk asked him to spare from execution military commanders who had failed in battle. During the Chakri dynasty, kings gradually became less involved in the business of punishment and more concerned with the dispensation of royal benevolence. Pardons were extensively used, and those pardoned were sometimes required to pay back their debt to the King by ordaining into the monkhood, or joining the army. But whereas previously mass pardons had occasionally been granted to all prisoners, in the early Bangkok period collective pardons were limited to "deserving" prisoners.

This 1837 proclamation by Rama III captured the ethos of Chakri era *dhammaraja* very nicely:

> [His Majesty] mercifully considers that those criminals were his own subjects but that their poor instruction had led them to commit crimes, rob, to smoke opium, to drink alcohol, and so forth. They were treading a path to hell indeed. His Majesty is feeling such pity for these criminals that he grants them pardons, preaching to them about self-reform. From now on, the king wants criminals to turn away from wrongdo-

ing, as the old proverb articulates: the trunk bends but the tip may be straight. If criminals reform themselves now, they may finally go to heaven. Because of the royal mercy, His Majesty commands Phra Sri Bhuriprijasrisalakshana, a royal scribe, to compose a royal sermon that rests on Buddhist doctrine and that teaches criminals to stop being recalcitrant. If these criminals can finally reform themselves, the king will receive them as swordsmen in the royal army.[45]

The administration of justice and the issuance of royal pardons were both inextricably bound up with Buddhist philosophy and with highly paternalistic notions of the relationship between ruler and subject. While Rama III's proclamation predated the legal reforms that led to the creation of a more modern judicial and penal system during the reign of King Chulalongkorn, many of the themes and assumptions it contains continue to resonate to the present day:

- Criminals are ignorant and poorly educated, hence their bad behavior.
- The King feels pity and exercises compassion towards them.
- Royal pardons are granted to criminals so that they will reform themselves.
- Buddhist doctrine combined with royal wisdom and instruction offers invaluable lessons for criminals.
- Bad people who reform themselves will then be happy to demonstrate their loyalty by serving the monarchy.

Some twenty-first century Thai judges would find little to dissent from in these points, which resonate with the paternalistic and didactic discourses pervasive in wider society. For many Thais, there is no obvious contradiction between royal paternalism, and modern ideas of crime, justice, and punishment. Because royal pardons are one area in which traditional notions of the King as "lord of life" still loom large, they offer a window into competing understandings—and indeed widespread confusions—about the basis of the Thai legal system. Apparently authoritative sources on the question of royal pardons offer sharply contrasting explanations of them.

Royal pardons in their current form were first issued in the reign of Rama VI (1910–25). Explanations of the basis on which these pardons are granted vary widely. According to Thongthong Chandrangsu, the Supreme Court's decision on any case remains the highest form of judgment: requesting a royal pardon is a request for royal mercy, and not a challenge to the decision of the court.[46] In other words, Thai royal pardons are nothing like their British counterparts: English royal pardons imply an acknowledgment that an individual has been failed or mistreated by the courts, while Thai royal pardons carry no such subtext.

A book published by the Ministry of Justice states that rather than an exercise of judicial power by the King, a royal pardon represents the use of royal power to protect the country: a power superior to the authority of the courts.[47] By contrast, privy councilor and former prime minister Thanin Kraivichien contributed to another volume published by the Ministry of Justice that gives a rather different explanation. He claims that royal pardons offer a last resort for people to obtain justice and argues that sometimes the law is not in line with moral justice, especially when sentencing rules compel judges to impose excessive punishments. In such cases, judges are forced to adhere to unjust laws: Thanin views the monarch as the ultimate arbiter of justice, who is uniquely placed to right the wrongs of the system. This is radically at odds with Thongthong's view, according to which pardons are simply an expression of royal mercy. As a long-serving member of the Privy Council, Thanin was surely closely involved in reviewing pardon requests submitted to the King, and was thus well placed to offer an interpretation of the process by which decisions were made. By contrast, Thongthong's role was to prepare applications on behalf of the Ministry of Justice, which were then forwarded by the minister to the palace. There are two kinds of Thai royal pardons: general and individual. In terms of frequency, individual pardons are broadly comparable with those issued by American presidents. Only a small number of individual pardons are granted annually, following referrals by the Ministry of Justice and review by the palace—generally in practice by members of the Privy Council, who forward their recommendations to the King.

TABLE 2. General pardons and royal amnesties

YEAR	TYPE OF PARDON	OCCASION	NUMBER
1999	General—released	King 72nd birthday	33,789
1999	General—commuted	King 72nd birthday	45,681
2003	Individual—released		3
2003	Individual—commuted		17
2004	General—released	Queen 72nd birthday	35,282
2004	General—commuted	Queen 72nd birthday	101,881
2004	Individual—released		13
2004	Individual—commuted		27
2005	Individual—released		27
2005	Individual—commuted		42
2006	General—released	60 years on throne	32,427
2006	General—commuted	60 years on throne	75,834
2006	Individual—released		6
2006	Individual—commuted		13
2007	General—released	King 80th birthday	31,149
2007	General—commuted	King 80th birthday	101,607
2011	General—released	King 84th birthday	ca. 30,000
2016	General—released	Rama 10 pardons	ca. 30,000
2016	General—commuted	Rama 10 pardons	up to 120,000

As these statistics illustrate, collective royal pardons issued on the occasion of auspicious national events have a far greater impact than individual pardons, accounting for nearly 105,000 prisoner releases and 325,000 reduced sentences between 1999 and 2007. By contrast, individual royal pardons resulted in just 49 prisoner releases and 99 reduced sentences during the same period.

Individual pardons are requested by the offender or a close relative: a lawyer is not entitled to submit a petition for a pardon. Opinions on the case are prepared by the Minister of Justice, and by members of the Privy Council. The King is under no obligation to accept the advice he receives, and sometimes asks for additional information: in lèse-majesté cases (covered by Article 112 of the Criminal Code), pardons are normally granted. The King is entitled to change the judgment in any way he wishes, awarding whatever punishment he sees fit: his decisions are considered final. Thanin provided a number of examples of individual royal pardons, which fell into three categories: excessive penalties, sympathetic defendants, and miscarriages of justice. Serious medical conditions constituted the most common grounds for receiving an individual pardon.

In some cases, royal pardons were issued because the courts had not followed the correct procedures. A drug offender sentenced to life imprisonment was sent directly to jail from the Court of First Instance, instead of being bailed out to await the decision of the Appeal Court. The King later reduced his sentence to take account of a ten-year period during which the accused had been illegally detained. In one case, the King concluded that the evidence underpinning a murder conviction was insufficiently convincing, and he pardoned the defendant—thereby overturning the decisions of three different courts.

Between 1946 and 2006, 28 royal decrees were issued granting general pardons (also known as royal amnesties): roughly one every two years. The main criteria for receiving these pardons concerned inmates' behavior during their time in jail. Those convicted of minor offences, those with disabilities or illnesses, prisoners under twenty or over sixty, and prisoners who were close to the end of their sentences were generally eligible for pardons. The range of offences covered was quite broad and typically included lèse-majesté (Article 112) and other offences against the security of the kingdom.[48] However, drug offences—the leading basis of incarceration—are typically excluded from collective pardons. General pardons are widely used around the world, but the scale of Thai pardons can be huge: the 2007 birthday pardons affected more than half of the entire prison population, for example. Those who received royal pardons in 2011 were issued with special blue uniforms bearing the words "Long Live the King," along with pink caps.

They were released in batches of several thousand, following ceremonies presided over by senior officials:

> The short ceremony at Klong Prem this morning, started with PM Yingluck paying respect to a portrait of His Majesty the King. During a speech, the prime minister urged inmates freed today to be grateful for the King's great mercy and to apply the King's self sufficiency economy philosophy to their everyday lives. This was then followed by songs praising His Majesty and then finishing with the Royal Anthem. A monk then blessed the prisoners as they left to head home.[49]

The receipt of a royal pardon was not a purely bureaucratic process: prisoners were required to perform acts of loyalty to the King before their actual release. The same applied to those who received individual pardons, as described by former lèse-majesté prisoner Thanthawut Taweewarodomkul:

> I was sent into a large hall. Preparations for a ceremony for the reading of the royal decree were underway. An official told me to light incense in front of the large Buddha in the center of the room. I closed my eyes and sat peacefully without moving for many minutes. Tears flowed continuously from my eyes: "I cannot be dreaming this, right?"
>
> Sorasit Chongcharoen, the commander (of Bangkok Remand Prison), walked into the large hall that had been prepared for the ceremony. He wore a fully decorated uniform, like the ones that MPs wear when Cabinet is sworn into office in front of Government House. The ceremony proceeded with solemnity and sacredness. I kneeled in front of a picture of the king. The commander read the royal pardon decree. The volume of the royal anthem increased. When it finished, the commander instructed and advised me on the path of my life after being released from prison. Photographs were taken to include in the report back to the Royal Household Bureau.[50]

Not only was Thanthawat required to perform his loyalty, but visual evidence of his performance was later sent to the palace. Despite the fact that Thailand officially has no state religion, the civil and legal process of accepting a pardon echoed their dispensation in the nineteenth century: it was replete with Buddhist elements, and framed by royalism. Exact figures on the numbers of individual King's pardons issued vary. According to one Justice Ministry source, there were 159 requests in 2001, 69 in 2002, 47 in 2003, 44 in 2004, 29 in 2005, and 50 in 2006. Thanin states that numbers granted were 128 in 2001, 74 in 2002, 53 in 2003, 46 in 2004 and 17 in 2005.[51] Although royal pardons were most commonly given to those convicted in the criminal courts, the King has also pardoned others who have committed various kinds of noncriminal disciplinary violations.[52] Back in 1963, King Bhumibol personally pardoned nine Chulalongkorn University engineering students who had been expelled for carrying out a violent attack against students from other faculties.[53] After Bhumibol's death in 2016, this old story was revived, as an example of shining royal mercy. Thirty years later, eleven judges who had been removed from office during the 1991–92 judicial crisis by the Judicial Commission successfully petitioned the King to be reinstated. The legal basis for this royal power of pardon is hazy: it rests on custom and practice.

Thailand's tradition of royal pardons illustrates the ambiguities at the core of the legal system. Does the King issue pardons simply in his capacity as head of state, or do royal pardons indicate the existence of a higher legal authority, above the level of the courts? Thongthong argues that although those convicted of crimes are entitled to apply for pardons, there is no "royal court" with a higher status than that of the Supreme Court.[54] However, in practice the issuance of individual royal pardons seems calculated to support popular understandings of the King as a benevolent deus ex machina, functioning as a court of last resort. General pardons, by contrast, are intended to boost the reserves of Buddhist merit enjoyed by the King and other members of the royal family, while simultaneously fostering gratitude towards the monarchy among uneducated and errant criminals.

Yet royal benevolence in granting pardons—especially general pardons—needs to be seen in the context of Thailand's extraordinarily high levels of incarceration. In May 2019, Thailand had 382,895 people in jail: the sixth largest prison population in the world (all the countries ranked higher were much larger) and the third highest percentage of its population behind bars.[55] The Thai prison population has increased considerably in recent years, and Thailand imprisons a much higher proportion of its population than any other Southeast Asian country.[56] Rather than reform practices that produce high levels of incarceration—such as jailing even very minor drug offenders, and locking up those who are unable to pay fines on the day of sentencing—Thailand has pursued a twin-track policy of draconian incarceration and generous royal amnesties. Yet even pardoning thirty thousand people at once makes little impact on a prison population of more than twelve times that number. Although in theory well-behaved prisoners can apply for parole after serving two-thirds of their sentences, in practice only a tiny percentage of prisoners are paroled. High-profile mass releases on special royal occasions create a perception—even among judges—that those given harsh sentences are unlikely to serve them in full, a sentiment that in turn fuels long jail terms.

The question of royal pardons became overtly politicized following the Supreme Court conviction of former prime minister Thaksin Shinawatra on corruption-related charges in 2008. Thaksin's case was rather curious: he was not charged with benefiting directly from a dubious land deal involving his wife Potjaman, but only with abusing his authority. Thaksin was convicted on a narrow 5–4 vote of the judges: nevertheless, he was sentenced in absentia to a two-year jail term. All charges against Potjaman were dropped, and she was not ordered to return the land in question. In mid-2009, Thaksin's supporters campaigned for him to be granted a royal pardon: 20,000 people joined a rally in his support, and a 3.5 million-signature petition was eventually submitted to the King. Thaksin himself addressed his supporters in a video-linked birthday speech on July 26, declaring if he received royal mercy, he would return to serve the nation.[57]

Responding to a request from the palace, Chulalongkorn University's Faculty of Law organized an academic seminar on royal pardons in July 2009. Wrapping up the seminar, Professor Borwornsak Uwanno—who had previously served as secretary-general during Thaksin's premiership—argued that while Thaksin was personally entitled to request a pardon, there was no legal basis for a mass petition: even 20 million signatures would count for nothing.[58] Indeed, this was not a genuine request for a royal pardon or a royal intervention: it was a politically motivated request which, if granted, could lead to a dangerous proliferation of similar mass mobilizations. Furthermore, the moves by Thaksin were an attempt to drag the monarchy into the country's ongoing political conflict, enlisting large numbers of people to promote division and polarization. Borwornsak claimed that Thaksin's royal pardon campaign was unprecedented in Thai history.

Thaksin's attempts to lobby for a royal pardon from Dubai, without spending a single day in jail, were certainly brazen. But his mass petition campaign also highlighted the ambiguities of Thailand's arcane system of royal appeals, which permit the King to pardon brawling students and errant judges, while purportedly remaining firmly above the political fray. Borwornsak and others sought to explain royal pardoning powers primarily by reference to legal provisions and terminology, despite the fact that—as Thaksin well knew—kingly authority in the Thai context was ultimately based on independent and extralegal sources of legitimacy. In short, the King could perfectly well have pardoned Thaksin if he had so wished: and this was precisely the problem. If the King was praised for exercising royal mercy in certain cases, how could he avoid criticism for not exercising it in others? Could Thaksin be held responsible for "politicizing" an inherently political system of pardons? Rightly or wrongly, Thaksin supporters saw the hostile response to his pardon request as the ultimate example of judicial double standards.

Lord of Life

> Lord of Life, or *Chao Jivit*, was the title given to their King by the T'ais
> especially in the latter part of the Paternal Monarchy of Bangkok. It was
> a colloquial, affectionate, yet awesome title; suggesting that the sover-
> eign had absolute power of life and death over his subjects and enjoyed
> complete ownership of all the land and resources of the country.[59]

Closely related to the question of royal pardons is the issue of Thailand's death
penalty. Death penalty recusal is a widespread practice: in the United States, recusal is the domain of governors in the thirty-two states that retain executions.
But in Thailand, royal recusal is more than simply a legal prerogative: Kings are
still "lords of life," exercising the power of life or death over their subjects. Even
after King Chulalongkorn's extensive reforms of the judicial system, the 1908
Criminal Code specified that the death penalty could only be applied with the
approval of the King—a continuation of the "lord of life" principle.[60] Thailand
has an extraordinary number of capital crimes: 55 in total.[61] Yet executions were
relatively rare during the ninth reign, peaking at sixteen in 1986 and 1998, but
averaging just three or four annually.[62] Paul Handley argues that "for much of
his reign King Bhumibol hesitated to sign off. Instead, he sat on the appeals, consciously staying the executions. Usually after five or ten years he commuted the
sentences officially."[63] The great majority of clemency petitions were successful:
78 out of 82 in 2004, and 98 out of 110 in 2005. As Johnson and Zimring note,
when the palace simply failed to respond to a clemency petition—as often happened—execution was repeatedly postponed.[64] Accounting for the twelve distinct
stops and starts in patterns of executions since 1945 is tricky but may reflect the
relative influence of Justice Ministry officials, or the power of particular prime
ministers who were able to shape execution policy. Executions increased during the Sarit Thanarat regime, during the turbulent 1970s, and again during the
mid-1980s; but there were also quite lengthy spells without executions, notably
from 1987 to 1994.[65] During these periods, the King apparently implemented a
temporary moratorium on the death penalty, a "de facto abolition" that international campaigners optimistically hoped could form a preliminary step towards
permanent abolition.[66] Johnson and Zimring classify Thailand's death penalty as
"symbolic," since executions are so rarely carried out.[67] Handley argues that regular interludes of suspension helped the monarchy present a merciful image; but
he also claims that after 1995 the King had another change of heart, and began
getting tough with drug dealers and murderers, a stance later reflected in apparent royal support for Thaksin Shinawatra's crackdown on crime, and his 2003

"war on drugs."[68] Since the publication of Handley's book in 2006, however, only three executions have taken place.[69] Despite the popular assumption that most of those executed are drug dealers, 81 percent of executions carried out between 1935 and 2006 were for homicide, 10 percent were for crimes against the King or the kingdom, and less than 9 percent involved drug offences.[70]

Abolishing the death penalty was mooted twice: in 1934, when abolition was examined by an ad hoc committee established by the new government following the end of the absolute monarchy; and during the drafting of the 1997 Constitution. On neither occasion was there sufficient popular support.[71] The Thai public remains conflicted about the death penalty: despite the best efforts of groups such as Amnesty International and FIDH, there is no strong local movement for abolition. A research project sponsored by the Justice Ministry in 2014 found little backing for a change in the law: more than 70 percent of those surveyed supported the death penalty.[72] Most human rights activists prefer to work on other issues—unlawful detention, torture, or wrongful arrests—perhaps partly because to criticize the death penalty is to enter the dangerous realm of challenging royal powers. The Law Society of Thailand opposes the death penalty but has made no official statement to this effect; similarly, individual members of the National Human Rights Commission favored abolition, but never proposed abolition as a collectivity.[73] As Johnson and Zimring point out: "There is both irony and poetic justice when hereditary royal authority—one of the oldest forms of concentrated power—becomes a principal means for limiting a government's power to punish."[74] One interviewee told Justice Ministry researchers that pronouncing death sentences but not carrying them out "is a Thai way, different from other countries."[75] Yet it was a "Thai way" that rested on royal discretion systematically overriding judicial sentences. Another interviewee declared: "Nobody is a lord of life who can determine who dies."[76] But by exercising his clemency powers so extensively, King Bhumibol was arguably exactly that.

In April 2018, Amnesty International issued a statement pointing out that the United Nations was close to declaring Thailand a country that had effectively abolished the death penalty, since no executions had taken place for almost ten years.[77] Two months later, Thailand carried out another execution, so demonstrating that the new King Vajiralongkorn remained a lord of life.[78]

Valorizing Royalist Judges

In recent years, a couple of judges have achieved national media recognition through accounts celebrating their rags-to-riches stories, their personal virtue, and their deep loyalty to the monarchy. Laddawan Luang-ard gained popularity through her Facebook page "Dharma and Law," where she recounted stories of her life and applied principles of the dharma to legal issues.[79] She left her poor family in the northeastern province of Loei at the age of just fifteen, working in Bangkok factories and construction sites until enrolling for a law degree at Ramkhamhaeng University. She was inspired by a judge who gave guest lectures at the university and told his students that judges did not need personal connections to get promoted, and that they needed to be calm and isolated from society. Since she lacked connections and did not enjoy associating with other people, she felt the life of a judge would suit her—and after studying hard Laddawan was able to achieve her dream. Interviewed on a Channel 5 TV show in 2013, she explained: "My proudest day was when I had an audience with the King, to swear an oath before my appointment as a trial judge. That day I felt the most pride I had felt in my life. It was beyond my expectations, far, far beyond them. . . . Since then, I have wanted to devote all of my life to working for him, to serving him, for the people."[80] The moderator responded: "I feel that being a judge is one of those positions that the entire family will take pride in, because those assuming this position needed to be appointed by the King, and all of their work is done in the name of the lord of the land." It is hard to render the Thai here into equivalent English; the moderator's second reference to the King used a very conservative formulation. The exchange illustrates how both judges themselves and other state officials (TV Channel 5 belongs to the army) take the judicial oath to the King extremely literally, rather than as a ritual formality. Wearing a yellow dress (the King's color) Judge Laddawan explained that the pride in her becoming a judge extended not only to her whole family, but also to her entire home village.

Another judge whose Facebook fame led to mainstream media acclaim was Panajpon Sanesangkhom, deputy chief judge of the Pattani Provincial Court. The judge helped an impoverished girl who was unable to pay a fine incurred by her mother and younger brother for hemp leaf possession. He advised her on how to bail her mother out and then granted the bail himself, ordering officials to open up the already-closed court. When the girl expressed her deep gratitude to him, he replied "I am a judge of the King."[81] The story was originally reported on the Facebook page of Marudi Kaka, a local man.[82] Marudi added his own rather obsequious commentary on the episode: "We Pattani people are grateful to Your Honor the Deputy Chief Judge of the Pattani Provincial Court for his steadfastness of principle; a culprit must be punished. But humanity has to be preserved, and justice can then be done. The Pattani people want this kind of government officer, Sir." Panajpong's actions were highly laudable, but why could they not be explained simply as reflecting his professionalism, his dedication to justice, or his desire to serve the public? What exactly did the King have to do with an out-of-hours bail case? The favorable media coverage generated by such stories demonstrated both judges' belief in their own special status as royal officials, and an appetite for this self-mythologizing among the wider Thai public. Thai judges consciously perform virtue, not simply for its own sake, but in emulation of the King's example.

In the later years of Bhumibol's reign, Princess Bajrakitiyabha, daughter of then Crown Prince Vajiralongkorn, became increasingly associated with justice issues. A law graduate of both Thammasat University and Cornell University, Ong Pha (as she is popularly known) has served as a public prosecutor in Udon Thani Province and in 2017 was appointed as a UN Goodwill Ambassador for the rule of law in Southeast Asia.[83] Most importantly, the Princess has been closely associated with the Thailand Institute of Justice (TIJ), a quasi-independent body initiated by a long-serving former permanent secretary of the Justice Ministry, Kittipong Kittayarak. TIJ has promoted various justice initiatives, including the so-called "Bangkok Rules," a set of guidelines for the treatment of female prisoners.[84] Thailand's success in associating the name of its capital city (where prisoners of both genders are routinely shackled, in flagrant violation of global norms) with a set of internationally recognized standards for the humane treatment of women detainees is rather ironic; and testifies to the effectiveness of royalist liberals in advancing internationally progressive criminal justice agendas that have been largely thwarted domestically. As Kittipong bluntly put it: "We need to work abroad even though we can do so little inside."[85]

Buddhism

As encapsulated by the shibboleth "Nation, Religion, King," coined by King Vajiravudh in the early twentieth century, Thai Buddhism is intimately connected with monarchy. Another strand of Thai legal thinking emphasized the parallels between Buddhism and the law. New judges take a meditation course during their initial training,[86] and in the 1970s and 1980s they were all given lectures on Buddhist morality by the great scholar-monk Buddhadasa, at the invitation of former Supreme Court President Sanya Thammasak.[87] Sanya had longstanding connections with Buddhadasa, dating back to the early 1930s.[88] Leading Buddhist scholar-activist Sulak Sivaraksa claimed that Buddhadasa's lectures to trainee judges were "all over the place and very boring"; they are certainly so abstract that it would hard to apply any direct lessons from them to actual court cases.[89] But for many working in the judicial system, Buddhism was more than simply a philosophical annex to the laws of the land: Thai Buddhism and Thai law were one and the same.

One senior prosecutor argued that the problems of Thai society were ultimately derived from desires (*kilet*) and biases (*akhati*): the solution was to counter these failings with the four sublime attitudes, *metta, karuna, mudita,* and *upekkha.* If we sympathize with those who are in trouble, we can exercise metta and karuna—not only for individuals, but also for their families. But while it was important to promote these virtues, justice also has limits. According to the prosecutors, if rowdy people and wrongdoers were allowed to assert their innocence, social harmony could not be maintained:

> I think what justice has achieved is already good enough. It is better than letting people fight, shoot, or bomb each other on the streets. . . . In terms of opinion, some people are very extreme because they do not understand what real justice is. . . . Let me ask you whether things will just stop at insulting each other? Eventually they will turn into shootings and fights, which may also harm the innocent.[90]

For this informant, there was an intimate connection between the rule of law and Buddhist laws of karma: "Concerning punishments, there are two rules. There are two rules in our lives: the law and the law of karma.[91] When you do something wrong, you may be able to escape the law, or when you did nothing wrong, you may still be punished by the law. That is the law. But what you cannot escape, is the law of karma." For this prosecutor, loyalty to parents, family, and the nation was a duty, and those who felt otherwise had no place in society: "If you can't accept it then it is not hard at all. You don't have to stay in Thailand and you can find somewhere else to stay . . . in Asian and Thai society, we uphold loyalty and treat it with the utmost importance." This Buddhistic emphasis on the preservation of harmony and order led to a belief that those who violate hierarchies of loyalty lie outside the boundaries of what society can and should tolerate. Similar arguments were made by a judge, addressing two juvenile defendants before the formal start of court proceedings.[92] Could the defendants recall the two kinds of debt they were in? Yes, replied one of them (who had clearly been asked this previously): "We are in debt to our parents, and in debt to the land."[93] The judge explained how when she was eighteen, she did nothing but study. She had to perform her duties as a citizen of the country, but would not throw away her life for anything that was not clear. She had served as a judge in the southern border provinces and had been willing to die if necessary: she loved the land, and these provinces needed to have courts in order to be part of the country. People were not all equal, but everyone had opportunities to advance themselves through education.

Speaking to another defendant—this time in a drug case—the same judge asked him if he knew why people were born unequal? What was his religion?

Muslim, he replied. The judge proceeded to give this young Muslim man a lecture on Buddhist notions of karma, before urging him to "find a good woman and be a good example to your children." She stressed the importance of education to the two other defendants, and family life to the Muslim defendant: in both cases, her mode of address was informal, yet deeply imbued with paternalism and Buddhist didacticism.

By no means all judges expressed their worldviews in explicitly Buddhist terms, either in court or in private conversation. Yet notions of karma, demerit, and defilement were ever present in Thai judicial discourse: lower-class defendants were ill placed to lead meritorious lives; criminality and jail time were fates that could readily befall them. During a provincial theft trial, I asked a policeman in attendance why the two defendants—both facing jail terms—had no lawyers.[94] "People do not need lawyers in these sorts of cases," he explained. The clear implication, repeated in many other conversations I had, was that poor people should accept their situation, plead guilty in order to receive a light sentence, and hope to be released early following a royal pardon. After another provincial case had adjourned, a defense lawyer and a prosecutor both told the family of a Malaysian facing a possible death sentence for drug smuggling that there was no point hiring their own lawyer: indeed, doing so would be counterproductive.[95] For ordinary people, fighting a criminal case would simply antagonize the authorities and could achieve nothing. Middle-class or wealthy defendants, by contrast, would not hesitate to hire lawyers and try to get themselves off.

The self-image of Thai judges as royal servants, granted special proximity to the crown, is central to any understanding of Thai justice. Do judges work on behalf of the people, the nation, or the monarch? This question was never properly resolved at the end of the absolute monarchy: the radical sentiments of the June 1932 interim constitution, which made courts responsible to the people, were toned down in the December 1932 permanent Constitution, which restored the language of royal prerogatives over the justice system. For the People's Party, this language was a pragmatic concession that allowed King Prajadhipok to save face. For royalists, the revised language restored the King to his rightful place at the apex of the justice system, where successive monarchs have remained ever since.

The results of this judicial royalism are plain for all to see. Judges sit on the bench beneath large portraits of the King, literally and figuratively embodying both his merit and his authority. They are among the few public servants to swear a personal oath of allegiance to the crown—members of parliament never have, for example—a privilege that has been written into successive constitutions. On occasion, the King, the Queen, and the Crown Prince literally became judges themselves, trying actual cases during their visits to the courts. These visits were

typically characterized by demonstrations of royal mercy. There was no mention of the inconvenient truth that such performances had no clear basis in law.
Beyond these cameo judicial roles directly assumed by members of the royal family, royal occasions such as birthdays and anniversaries provided opportunities
for large-scale royal pardons that could involve the release of more than thirty
thousand prisoners at once—spectacular performances of royal benevolence.

Yet royal judicial benevolence comes at a price. Mass prison pardons go hand
in hand with one of the world's most draconian sentencing regimes. For the King
to remain literally a "lord of life," Thailand needs to retain the death penalty—
albeit a death penalty that is only rarely enforced. To question the harshness of
the justice system is implicitly to question the privileged position of the crown.
To question the performance of the courts implies not simply contempt of court,
but also a lack of respect for the monarchy. A legal system based on notions of
loyalty to the King, rather than accountability to the public, is a legal system that
is closed to critical scrutiny and where many areas of potential debate remain off
limits. Thailand's courts are not simply dedicated to the maintenance of peace
and order: they are also centrally concerned with defending the privileged position of the monarchy within the Thai state. This concern inevitably shapes the
habitus and the dispositions of Thai judges.

Judges' belief that they enjoy a special relationship with the crown—further
evidenced by the fact that King Bhumibol personally selected two Supreme Court
judges to serve as prime minister during the turbulent 1970s—creates particular
problems for the justice system. While in theory judging legal cases "in the name
of the King" is a rhetorical conceit, a piece of high symbolism, many Thai judges
take the notion far too literally. The result is that instead of acting in the public
interest, judges are inclined to act in what they understand to be the royal interest, which they conflate with the national interest. This might entail, for example,
denying bail to those charged with *lèse-majesté* or other offences against public
order, on the unspoken grounds that treating such defendants harshly constitutes
an act of loyalty to the crown. It may also include adopting an uncritical attitude
to the testimony of police officers and government officials—however implausible—and a skeptical, even hostile attitude to the testimony of human rights
activists and critical academics. It may include giving lawyers defending those
charged with politically related offences a very hard time. The myth that judge-
liness is next to kingliness undermines laudable ideals of justice as an abstract
virtue, as a public good, or as something exercised on behalf of the people. The
next chapter examines how judges responded to a variety of challenges to their
status and authority in the late Bhumibol era.

CHALLENGES TO THE JUDICIARY

Thai judges face enormous difficulties in carrying out their duties hearing political cases. Royal approbation carries with it more than immense prestige: by arguing that responsibility for addressing Thailand's political problems rested not with the monarchy but with the judiciary, King Bhumibol shifted an enormous burden onto the shoulders of judges. Like the palace, the courts struggled to adapt themselves to changing conditions. Given the intense political, social, and regional polarization that had characterized Thailand's politics since the Thaksin era, it was not realistically possible for the judiciary to pacify the populace or to placate the country's warring factions. This chapter examines the struggles of the judiciary to come to terms with its critics after 2006. Given judges' intense loyalty to the monarchy, they were unable publicly to question the burdens that had been placed on them by the King: yet they struggled to formulate convincing answers to those who disputed their evenhandedness.

Criticism of the judiciary peaked in mid-2012, after Amphon Tangnoppakhun (colloquially known as Akong, or Uncle Kong), a sixty-four-year-old retired commercial driver, died in jail. Akong had been accused of sending a number of highly defamatory SMS messages about the Queen to the prime minister's secretary in 2010.[1] Although the chain of evidence linking the defendant to the messages was far from clear-cut, Akong was sentenced to twenty years in jail for lèse-majesté in November 2011: he died in May 2012 from stomach cancer, which had been neither diagnosed nor treated by prison doctors.[2] Akong's name became a byword for the harsh and arbitrary nature of the *lèse-majesté* law, and of the brutal treatment accorded to those convicted of these offences. The defense asserted that Akong was elderly and did not even know how to send an SMS message, claims that were rejected by the court. Despite a major domestic and international campaign for his release, Akong was repeatedly denied bail and then refused permission to leave jail for medical treatment.[3] For many observers, the Akong case illustrated the willingness of the judiciary to act in a punitive fashion, out of a misplaced desire to serve the crown. For critics of the courts, the Akong case also became a symbol of the application of "double standards" to lower-class defendants.

Asked in 2012 about the handling of such sensitive political cases, one mid-ranking judge explained that in recent months the courts had been feeling under a lot of pressure, especially over high-profile cases such as the Akong case. They had been trying to be very careful and avoid problems. He believed the atmosphere was improving and that the courts were making a special effort to behave in a more reasonable fashion. He could not explain why they never granted bail for people in 112 cases: although he had not been directly involved in any of them, it was generally understood among judges that in cases touching on the royal institution, bail was not going to be granted.[4]

Another judge argued that the refusal to grant bail in lèse-majesté cases was indefensible in most cases: since the King himself apparently did not support the law in its current form, the Supreme Court ought to send out appropriate signals on the bail issue.[5] The Akong case had a huge impact, and judges were very concerned about the damage to their reputation. There was no need to take such a hard line on bail and sentencing in such cases. He cited the example of a defendant who had stolen a hundred motorbikes, was bailed out and proceeded to steal a lot more before he was rearrested. This sort of repeat offender did not deserve bail, while people accused of lèse-majesté but unlikely to reoffend should not be automatically locked up, in a misguided attempt to defend the royal institution. Good legal reasons were always needed for such decisions. Senior judges at the Criminal Court were now pretty good and were trying to adopt a less-stringent line on Article 112. But judges also did not want to be seen as caving in to the pro-Thaksin side: it would actually be easier if there was less public pressure. In any case, the palace was usually very keen to pardon offenders once convicted. Despite his liberal views on bail, this judge's response illustrated a common fallback argument for lèse-majesté law supporters: don't worry about the harsh sentences, the defendants will just be pardoned later. These cases illustrated the ambiguity of the close relationship between the courts and the monarchy, a relationship that had been tightened by King Bhumibol's 2006 royal call to judicial arms.

Royal Injunctions

A new emphasis on the centrality of the judiciary was encapsulated in two important royal speeches of April 25, 2006, in which the King called on Thailand's
judges to solve the country's political problems. The speeches served strongly to
reinforce judges' views of themselves as royal servants, but also placed on them a
burden that was not entirely welcome. Interpreting these speeches is tricky; King
Bhumibol's speeches were generally ambiguous in their language, while their
messages were not always consistent. His first speech, delivered to the Administrative Court judges, opened with an intriguing passage:[6] "The oath you have
sworn is very important, because it is a broad one. The duties of judges and
those who are involved with administration are extremely wide-ranging. So I am
afraid that you may think the duties of an Administrative Court judge are quite
narrowly defined, but actually they are very broad."[7] The King seemed irritated
by arguments about spheres of jurisdiction; he had no patience with judicial
attempts to shirk responsibility for the country's problems.[8] The oath sworn by
Thai judges, specified in Article 252 of the 1997 Constitution (later Article 201 of
the 2007 Constitution), reads as follows:

> I, (name of the declarer) do solemnly declare that I will be loyal to His
> Majesty the King and will perform my duties in the name of the King
> honestly and without any partiality, all to bring about justice for the
> people and peace in the Kingdom. I will also preserve and adhere to the
> democratic system of government with the King as Head of State,
> the Constitution of the Kingdom of Thailand and all of its laws.

King Bhumibol focused on the most important words at the core of the
oath, declaring that the judges were swearing to uphold democracy. The thrust
of his argument was simple: the April 2006 elections had been a debacle. The
results could not be allowed to stand, and some legal maneuver was needed to
help the country move forward. The King was clearly frustrated by the failure
of the Constitutional Court to take action, claiming that the court stopped
working once the constitution was drafted.[9] His comments suggested that he
viewed the Constitutional Court as an untrustworthy institution, one that
had been captured by Thaksin and his associates. He asked the courts to work
together, under the leadership of the Supreme Court, and not to shirk responsibility. His speech thus contained some direct criticism of legalism—in effect
saying "stop coming up with reasons why you can't do anything"—before
turning full circle to advocate a legalistic solution: "The courts should solve
political problems."

The King specifically disavowed calls for him to establish a royally appointed
government under Article 7 of the constitution—as demanded by some

CHALLENGES TO THE JUDICIARY

anti-Thaksin groups—saying that this would be undemocratic. In his subsequent speech to the Supreme Court judges, he insisted that he had never acted according to his own personal wishes: "There are people who may come along and say that me, Rama IX, I do what I feel like doing. I have never done what I felt like doing."[10] He had seen numerous constitutions during his reign, and if he had tried to exert his own will, the country would by now have been ruined. He appeared to be responding directly to critics who accused him of playing an active extraconstitutional role in Thailand's politics and public life. This second speech began with another reference to the oath sworn by the judges:

> If you carry out your duties as Supreme Court judges honestly and with integrity, to ensure the safety of the people.... A short while ago I spoke to the judges of the Administrative Court, and now I have to consult with you, because it is important to have judges from all sides, especially those from the Supreme Court, because the Supreme Court President is particularly important.... At the moment there is a legal problem that is very important, which if not addressed ... if you act according to the oath that you have taken, you will enable the country to be governed in a democratic fashion.

As with the Administrative Court judges, the King made direct reference to the oath they had just sworn to him. This time he started by emphasizing a different element of the oath, their pledge to ensure the "safety of the people," though this phrase was not literally part of the oath, which mentioned ensuring justice for the people and peace in the kingdom. The idea that peace was maintained for the sake of the people could be read as a liberal royalist gloss on some rather conservative language, shifting the maintenance of security from a state agenda to a public good. Like ensuring democracy, this was a demand that went beyond mere questions of justice. Despite his statement that "there is a legal problem," this was essentially a political problem to be addressed by legal means. The King had spoken quite harshly to the Administrative Court judges, telling them at three different points in his speech to resign if they were unable to avert the country's political crisis. By contrast, he adopted a tone of flattery towards the Supreme Court, telling the judges that they had the right to tell the Constitutional and Administrative Courts what to do, and never suggesting that they might need to resign:

> Today it should all come down to the judges of the Supreme Court. It is important that the Supreme Court can instruct the other courts—the Administrative Court, the Constitutional Court, any court. No claims are made beyond the Supreme Court, because the judges of the Supreme Court have the right to speak, to decide.[11]

This implied theory of Supreme Court supremacy had little basis in law: the Supreme Court had no formal jurisdiction over administrative or political questions, other than through the Criminal Division for Political Officeholders, and certainly no legal authority to give instructions to the Constitutional Court. The King had made two Supreme Court judges prime minister in the 1970s, illustrating his sympathy for the judicial institution. As the late Chai-Anan Samudavanija explained, the appointments of Sanya and Thanin to office of prime minister were both "special cases": "But it reflects the feeling about the king and the public that the judicial system is somewhat neutral, and it's like a reservoir in need, a reserve pool of so-called good people."[12]

After some apocalyptic language suggesting that Thailand was facing "the worst crisis in the world" and was in danger of metaphorically sinking into the ocean, the King ended his speech with a rousing call to action: "May your honors be able to perform your work well, enjoy good health and strength: fight, fight, yes, fight for virtue, fight for justice in the country. Thank you."

The two royal speeches of April 25 contained a series of important messages: the recent elections had not been democratic and the results were a terrible mess; people were improperly trying to get the King to take action; the King wanted the problem resolved by constitutional means; the Supreme Court should take the lead in solving it. These messages were not entirely consistent.

A central theme of the King's speech to the Administrative Court was that he had never engaged in political meddling according to his own whims: his actions had always been constitutional: even when he had appointed the Supreme Court president Sanya Thammasak to be prime minister by royal command, the decision had been countersigned by a deputy house speaker.[13] While the King's refusal to contemplate a royally appointed prime minister and his calls for a constitutional resolution of the crisis were laudable, his analysis of the "mess" produced by the Democrat Party's election boycott was more problematic: based on this logic, any major party fearing defeat at the polls could boycott an election, label the results undemocratic, and call for the outcome to be annulled.[14] Groundhog Day took place eight years later, following the Democrat-boycotted and disrupted February 2014 election: exactly the same sequence of events. As in 2006, judicial measures did not ease the later crisis, which was finally "resolved" by a military coup. In theory, electoral, judicial, or constitutional solutions to political crises offered a more desirable alternative than extraconstitutional acts such as direct royal interventions or military coups. But in practice such solutions might do little more than delay or exacerbate matters until extraconstitutional measures were deployed.

Just as the 2000–2001 period (which saw the Election Commission at its most activist, and included the near-removal of Thaksin from office by the Constitutional Court) had illustrated the impracticalities of excessive legalism, so the post-2006 period would amply demonstrate the absurdities that resulted when legal sanctions were deployed at every twist and turn. The obvious lesson of the early Thaksin period—that draconian legal measures such as banning politicians were no real answer to political problems—was quickly forgotten. One reason for the ready recourse to legal solutions was that the alternatives were equally unpalatable: military coups, or mass protests that might well culminate in terrible violence. Nevertheless, the moral burden of the 2006 royal speeches was not entirely welcomed by the judiciary. For many career judges, there was little to gain and much to lose from becoming embroiled in political court cases. Within weeks of the royal speech the April 2006 elections were annulled by the Constitutional Court, a vindication of Democrat Party strategies to undermine the electoral process.[15] The wording of the dissolution order was rather curious; the elections followed the letter of the Constitution, but violated its spirit:

> Therefore, even though the Royal Decree Dissolving the House of Representatives B.E. 2549 (2006) was enacted pursuant to the provisions of the Constitution and the Election Commission, an organ provided by the Constitution with the powers and duties of administering elections, had conducted the elections in accordance with the Constitution and relevant laws, the facts that had occurred in the elections pursuant to the said Royal Decree had caused the election results to be unfair. Representatives of the people were not truly obtained under the democratic system. As a result, the elections were unconstitutional under the spirits of section 2, section 3 and section 144 of the Constitution of the Kingdom of Thailand B.E. 2540 (1997).[16]

This was an extraordinary turnaround for a court many of whose judges had been staunchly supportive of Thaksin less than three months earlier. Constitutional Court judge Jaran Phakdithanakun later insisted that there was no coordination between the decisions of the various courts during this period.[17] A number of developments in 2006 illustrated the shifting tide among the establishment, most notably the arrest of three members of the Election Commission who were sentenced to four years in jail, and briefly put behind bars, for breaking various laws when they organized the April elections.[18]

The two royal speeches left Thaksin in a vulnerable spot: while not named explicitly, he was surely implicated in Thailand's terrible political crisis and the looming threat of complete disaster. His crimes appeared to include failing to ensure peace in the kingdom, and meddling with constitutionally mandated agencies. Thaksin did not stand directly accused of disloyalty to the throne, but the oath to judges could be construed as suggesting that failing to ensure justice and to maintain peace was tantamount to disloyalty.

Thaksin responded by sending an unusual letter to US president George W. Bush, claiming that extralegal mechanisms were being abused to subvert Thailand's democracy:

> There has been a threat to democracy in Thailand since early this year. Key democratic institutions, such as elections and their observance of Constitutional limitation on government, have been repeatedly undermined by interest that depend on creating chaos and mounting street demonstrations in Bangkok as a means to acquire political power that they cannot gain through winning elections. Having failed to provoke violence and disorder, my opponents are now attempting various extra Constitutional tactics to co-opt the will of the people.[19]

In the end, judicial measures such as the Constitutional Court's annulment of the 2006 election were insufficient to head off Thailand's looming political crisis, while Thaksin's pleas for international support yielded only muted responses. The heads of the three courts met on April 28 to review the postelection position, disappointing anti-Thaksin groups by failing to annul the polls on the spot. But the Administrative Court did immediately order a halt to the final round of poll reruns scheduled for the following weekend, so making it much more difficult to seat the newly elected parliament. Ten days later the Constitutional Court decided by a narrow 8–6 majority that the elections were unconstitutional, having also determined in a 9–5 vote that the polls were null and void. Two rather unconvincing reasons were given: there were issues with the election date, and voting booths had been improperly positioned in polling stations.[20] New polls were now to be scheduled. Prior to this decision, the Constitutional Court had been consistently sympathetic to Thaksin's interests; indeed, the courts as a whole had been reluctant to challenge the jurisdiction of the Election Commission, following a 2003 Constitutional Court ruling implying that the EC's decisions should not be subject to judicial review.[21] There was little doubt that the King's speech turned the tide against ratifying the election. As the late former Constitutional Court judge Chai-Anan Samudavanija explained: "That was probably the most important factor as an impetus towards giving the younger judges the rationale to be more involved in politics, because they think they are doing this on the request of the King."[22]

Judges expressed a range views on judicialization. Sarawut Benjakul, who as spokesman of the Judicial Affairs Office often served as the public face of the courts, argued that there had been a rise in judicial activism: but he defined this phenomenon as judges interpreting laws in a progressive way, rather than meddling in politics.[23] Nevertheless, he insisted the role of judges was essentially passive, given that they could only decide the cases before them: unlike judges in some European countries, they were not in a position to initiate proceedings themselves. By contrast, another senior judge argued that judicialization was not exactly a new phenomenon—but reflected a major change in Thai society, the rising power of politicians. Nowadays, if you want any sort of senior position, you need to ask for support from the prime minister.[24] The judiciary was virtually the only organization not controlled by politicians and so had to serve an important function to check their power. He wished the legislature would do a better job of checking political power so that all responsibility would not be given to the judiciary. He urged me to make the same proposal in my writings. The monarchy was no longer a benevolent dictator; a better system was needed.

The assignment of cases was the prerogative of the chief judge or director of the court; sensitive political cases were generally given to experienced, senior judges. Most judges preferred not to take these political cases, since if they did not turn out well, they might have an adverse impact on a judge's reputation.[25] Again, the idea that judges were eager to try and sentence political offenders was a myth. But the only acceptable grounds for declining a case assignment would be a direct personal connection with, or prior knowledge of, a defendant. In appeal courts the identity of the judges was closely guarded; only the director knew who was assigned to which cases, and even the deputy director would only find out when judgments were actually issued.[26]

Most of his colleagues were unhappy about judicialization, explained one senior judge.[27] He did not want to spend his time sorting out political problems. Judges had to do this—especially in the case of the Supreme Court's Criminal Division for Political Officeholders—because it had been mandated by the 1997 and 2007 constitutions. But this responsibility put a lot of pressure on them, and took them into areas that were not really their job, causing judges to be criticized. Each time the Political Officeholders' Division was convened for a particular case, the Supreme Court nominated nine members to sit on the bench. Nobody ever volunteered: these assignments were decided by a vote among more than one hundred Supreme Court judges. Most of the judges assigned to these cases were reluctant to take them on.[28] It was tedious for them to go back to hearing testimony again, rather than working from documents as they normally did for appeals and Supreme Court decisions. Worse still, all nine of them had to sit there throughout. Prapan Sapsaeng, who wrote a research paper on the Political Officeholders' Division, argued that many of the judges involved in these trials did not understand that they were now performing an inquisitorial role and were supposed to take a lead in asking questions—unlike the more familiar accusatorial system used in other Thai courts, where the prosecutor and defense lawyers played a more active part.[29] Nor did the judges really grasp how to make proper use of the investigation and inquiry briefs prepared by the National Anticorruption Commission, often simply calling in witnesses to go over testimony they had already given, instead of seeking new evidence and information.

A junior judge was critical of the discourse of "judicialization": unlike in some other countries, Thai judges could not initiate cases themselves, and were obliged to deal with all cases brought before them.[30] While there were relatively few judges of a "red" (pro-Thaksin) orientation, there were some; and in various cases judges had decided in favor of the "red" side simply on the basis of the legal facts, not because of their own politics. Judges rarely discussed politics among themselves but were hardly surprised by the criticism the courts faced over issues such as party bannings and the seizure of Thaksin's assets. Another judge explained that Thaksin had a significant judicial following, especially among colleagues in the North and Northeast.[31] Thaksin was skilled in gaining support, not just by giving people money and resources, but also by providing them with the recognition or status they craved. A mid-ranking informant insisted that by no means all judges were "yellow," conservative or Democrat supporters; there had been a shift in the organizational culture, and there were red-leaning judges at all levels of the court system.[32] The position was simply not as clear-cut as it appeared from the outside: like the rest of Thai society, the judiciary was far from monolithic.

The senior judge lamented that the public did not really understand that once a judge leaves the Supreme Court and becomes a judge for the Constitutional Court, he is not really a judge any more, but has assumed a different sort of role.[33] The Administrative Court was similar—many "judges" on these courts were former provincial governors or other senior bureaucrats. They saw themselves as solving technical and administrative problems, a very different matter from deciding a legal case. What they were doing was very troubling, and their decisions were incoherent from a legal perspective. For judges in the Courts of Justice, the Administrative and Constitutional Courts were not really courts at all. As one former judge put it: "It's as though before all the business came to our company, and now two rival companies have gone into the same field."[34] For many judges, judicialization had begun not with the royal speeches of 2006, but with the 1997 Constitution and the establishment of the Constitutional and Administrative Courts. The golden era of the Thai judiciary—during and after the 1960s Supreme Court presidency of Sanya Thammasak, and the most active middle phase of the Ninth Reign—was long over.

Judicial Attitudes

The worldviews of Thai judges were challenged by growing public interest in their work after 2006. At a 2012 meeting of the Judicial Commission, Supreme Court deputy president Prateep Chalermpatarakul noted that the courts were now closely scrutinized by outsiders.[35] Even the president of the Council of State had told him that judges did not know how to work in court, he declared. The courts needed to demonstrate to the world that they were working for the benefit of the people. Despite such sentiments—quite widely shared within the judiciary—when faced with a choice between explaining themselves to the public and retreating behind closed doors, the courts tended to prefer the latter. According to a junior judge, many colleagues were concerned about the level of criticism they faced.[36] In the past, Thai cultural norms meant that the courts were hardly ever criticized, whereas more recently they had faced a lot of attacks in the media and elsewhere.

Sarawut Benjakul argued that growing criticism of the courts was normal and would help the judiciary to improve themselves.[37] He had contributed regularly to the print media since first becoming spokesman for the Courts of Justice. Although the courts as a whole remained wary of communicating with the public, the rise of new media meant that individual members of the judiciary were much more accessible than before. While only a small number of judges published opinion pieces in newspapers—for which they had to seek official permission—many began posting their views on social media such as Facebook or Twitter. Sarawut noted that this was not permitted according to Article 28 of the Code of Conduct, and in 2012 he asked the Judicial Commission to issue a circular to this effect.[38] But the Judicial Commission chair observed that it was impossible to prevent judges from posting opinions online, and the commission resolved simply that judges were advised to be careful when using social media, and not to post opinions that would affect their duties or honor as judicial officials.[39] This shift from a de facto ban on public statements by judges to an injunction that judges use social media with caution marked a subtle yet fundamental shift in the relationship between the judiciary and society.

A senior judge who had previously described those attending court to me as "customers" explained that the courts were now extremely concerned about public perceptions of how they worked, and their inability to answer the questions of the public.[40] He acknowledged that the courts were undoubtedly failing properly to answer a large and growing number of questions. He insisted that issues that seemed to be examples of double standards actually were not: for instance, it was not good to bail out those accused of serious crimes, against whom there appeared to be strong evidence, and who were creating fear and all kinds of problems in their own communities. Another judge similarly argued that most cases of so-called "double standards" were actually cases of bad judgments or ill-considered decisions.[41]

One of the biggest problems that concerned the senior judge was that those with money could try to buy justice. Often judges were unhappy with the way evidence was presented to them but had to proceed with the case based on that evidence: they had no power to order additional investigations. Another senior judge—who foreswore the term *customers* as inappropriate—suggested that the courts now had two main functions: to process cases, and to explain themselves and serve the wider society.[42] This second role was relatively new; in the past, the courts had felt that simply performing their technical duties was sufficient. Judges had to be able to answer the questions of the society and all of them are very concerned about the difficulty of doing so. He felt it was good that judges were more closely scrutinized and had to defend themselves; this pressure helped them to improve their work and organization. The same judge repeated Blackstone's formulation that it was far better to acquit ten guilty people than convict one innocent one—yet conviction rates in Thailand are well over 95 percent.[43] Both judges insisted that they wanted people to leave the courts believing that they had received justice.

Instead of accepting that Thai courts were not functioning to international standards, many judges were at pains to stress that Western notions about how the justice system should operate were out of step with Thai realities. One judge who had served in several southern provinces observed that because the area had a tradition of banditry, many ordinary people—such as rubber-tappers—routinely carried guns for protection. Judges assigned to these areas needed an appreciation of local conditions.[44] A senior judge explained: "We like foreigners and their ideas, we used lots of them to create our system, but it works in its own way and you can't expect it to operate like a Western justice system."[45] When I presented another judge with a copy of a book I had published, he politely explained that he did not really approve of Thais reading English books, which were likely to confuse them—it was better for them to know the literature in Thai first, and to have a better understanding of their own society and culture.[46]

A number of judges expressed critical views of capitalism and business people. One lamented that during the 2011 floods, water was diverted away from factories into residential areas because protecting industry was more important than people's homes.[47] His colleagues in the same court were constantly bragging about their stock market transactions. In this respect, many judges reflected social attitudes common among the Thai middle classes: mouthing

Buddhist-sounding criticisms of consumerism, despite being deeply embedded in the values of an advanced capitalist society. Such attitudes mirrored official Thai discourses that could be traced back to such rhetorical constructs as the royalist "sufficiency economy," a philosophy of rural self-reliance originally advanced by King Bhumibol in the wake of the 1997 financial crisis. A judge-created blog about Buddhism and law was critical of Nitirat for advancing arguments that "seem to smell very much like the western world. The current global situation however suggests that their countries are faring not very well."[48] Western ideas, asserted the author, should not be adopted uncritically since they were predicated on individualism rather than the holistic teachings of Buddhism and Eastern philosophies.

One judge argued that a significant difference between the judiciary and other Thai organizations was that unlike, say, police officers, judges do not "display power."[49] A central element of judicial authority is an attitude of benevolence; even when judges are engaged in exercising power—including the right to restrict liberty, or even to impose a death sentence—they should not take any pleasure in doing so, or exercise it too crudely.[50] One judge explained that it was important to maintain a degree of order in the court room, since they were sitting beneath a picture of the King: it was not permitted for those in court to cross their legs, for example.[51] In the past things were much stricter: women had to wear skirts, and shorts were banned. Nowadays people can wear more or less anything. He did not mind if people typed notes during the proceedings—but he preferred them to inform the clerk if they wanted to do so. At times the proceedings were disrupted by children in the public seating area, but he was very reluctant to send them out, since it was often hot outside. Nevertheless, some judges appeared to delight in enforcing adherence to somewhat arbitrary rules.

Military

Thailand's legal system operates under a central paradox. Overthrowing state power by force is inherently illegal. But the Thai military has staged twelve successful coups and seven coup attempts since 1932.[52] On most occasions, the coup makers immediately abrogated the constitution of the day and later initiated a new constitution-drafting process. At no point in Thai political history has the judiciary protested about the illegality of military actions, or challenged the military's right to tear up the highest law of the land. Critics, notably the Nitirat group of Thammasat University revisionist legal scholars, have argued that this pattern of weak-kneed capitulation to the military is a disturbing trend, illustrating the lack of judicial commitment to either democracy or the rule of law.

In other words, judges have never asserted any autonomous moral authority, instead blindly serving whatever regime had seized power.

Asked why the courts have not challenged coup makers throughout Thai history, despite their lack of legitimacy, Sarawut answered:

> In reality, the court cannot stop it. Let's think about: if the courts say [a coup] is illegal, then they can abolish the courts as well as the legal system. . . . We have to think realistically. In a well-established democratic country, there is a system to manage matters. But in a system where men with guns are the most powerful persons, let's try telling them that they are wrong. . . . (They will respond): So you think we are wrong, do you? Then let's abolish (you), we don't need (you). As I see it, those who fight them always have finally to admit defeat and were then dealt with by various methods, time and time again. . . . It is useless.[53]

In other words, Sarawut acknowledged that Thailand was not in any real sense governed by the rule of law, but by men with guns. The courts adopted a simple survival strategy, seeking to preserve their own position by not challenging the legitimacy of other power holders. Under such circumstances, expecting the courts to assume the role of an autonomous force on the side of rights, rules, or democratic representation was unrealistic. As such, there was a curious disconnect between the high status of judges and their complete impotence in the face of crude military seizures of state power. For all their much-vaunted proximity to monarchy and their accompanying and exalted self-regard, justices were not the true guardians of the law; they were powerless to protect the legal system from regular armed incursions by men in khaki.

Sarawut adopted a disarmingly realistic view of the judiciary that, according to Nitirat member Piyabutr Saengkanokkul, was very much in line with mainstream Thai legal thinking. Drawing on Supreme Court rulings, as well as on Yut Saenuthai's writings about the 1932 revolution, Piyabutr has argued that Thai legal practitioners view the legitimacy of coup authority as based on the exercise of "real power" rather than how that power was obtained.[54] The prevailing judicial culture was to accept the legal authority of both coup makers and coup decrees. Piyabutr referred to a 1980 Supreme Court ruling that stated that unless coup decrees were later formally invalidated, their legal status remained valid beyond the life of the juntas that had created them.[55]

At the same time, Sarawut insisted that the military did not really intervene in the work of the courts; as a matter of principle, the two institutions carried out their respective roles, and neither challenged the authority of the other. The courts did not even ask whether military rule was legitimate. If the courts ever tried to question military authority, the judiciary would be in big trouble.

However, Sarawut acknowledged that working under a military regime was troublesome: judges had to deal with hastily drafted laws that had been rushed through legislative approval, and their own freedom of expression was curtailed. He had stopped writing newspaper articles in the wake of the May 2014 coup because the situation was no longer normal.

Another judge lamented that following the coup, judges were primarily interested in increasing their salaries and extending the retirement age. The Judicial Commission asked the ruling junta, the National Council for Peace and Order (NCPO) in 2014 to increase their salaries from around 100,000 baht to 200,000 baht; instead, the junta agreed to give judges an additional 6,000 baht a month living allowance. Although judicial salaries are already high, judges want to benchmark themselves against better-paid state lawyers.[56] The 1997 and 2007 constitutions stated that judges need not retire until seventy, though they had to step down from administrative positions earlier. Some judges had asked the military to reduce the retirement age because of the problems caused by slow promotions. The military and the judiciary could talk to one another: they were both elites. This was not a simple case of judges caving in to the demands of army officers: the military were amenable to pleasing the courts as well, on the basis of a mutual nonintervention policy.

After the 2014 coup, military courts became much more powerful, encroaching into the domain of the Courts of Justice and so undermining the position of the judiciary. Most lèse-majesté defendants were now tried in military courts, which abrogated unto themselves the right to try civilians. A rare critic was redshirt poet and 112 defendant Sirapop, who questioned the legitimacy of the proceedings he faced on the grounds that the 2014 coup had been an illegal act. He challenged a military court with this bold statement in September 2016: "If judicial authorities do not serve the principles of the law under a democratic society and the people, but accept the authorities of the coup-makers, who came to power by illegal means, then the judicial system and the rule of law will be destroyed."[57]

The court responded by ordering him to amend his "disrespectful statement": Sirapop refused to do so. His trial proceeded extremely slowly, and no verdict had been announced more than eighteen months later.

Yet civilian judges had made no attempt to question, let alone to challenge, the right of the military to assume greater and greater judicial powers.[58] The topic was never discussed among judges, even internally and behind closed doors. At times, the judiciary was overly zealous in kowtowing to the junta. After the NCPO ordered that all security-related cases should be tried in military courts, the juvenile court issued a statement that juvenile cases relating to security would now be decided in the military courts.[59] The NCPO then issued a clarifying order stating that juvenile cases were not to be sent to military courts.[60] This premature announcement exemplified the desire of the judiciary to bend over backwards in accommodating the junta, rather than setting firm boundaries to secure their independence. Judges did not fight to defend their independence, not only because they lacked a tradition of activism, but also because they were often so beguiled by their proximity to the throne that they apparently failed to realize that any need to defend their autonomy.

Challengers

The most vocal challenges to the authority of the Thai judiciary after 2006 came from Nitirat, an informal group of seven academics from the prestigious Thammasat University Faculty of Law.[61] Nitirat members, most of whom studied public law in either France or Germany, questioned the principles of Thai judges, claiming that they have consistently failed to base their judgments on ideas of popular sovereignty. Nitirat's de facto leader Worajet Pakeerat has argued that the single biggest problem with the Thai justice system was the ideology of the judges who preside over cases. In the past, judicial ideology was less apparent, since judges rarely dealt with politically significant cases. More recently, it has become apparent that human rights and the constitution do not really underpin the verdicts in such cases; this is true for the Administrative Court and the Constitutional Court, as well as for the Courts of Justice. Worajet singled out the Ratchada land case—for which Thaksin received a two-year jail term—for criticism, arguing that the former premier did not commit an actual crime, despite the clear existence of a conflict of interest; the Supreme Court was influenced by the prevailing political ideology in the wake of the 2006 coup. In Worajet's view, the best example of judicial ideology informing a Constitutional Court decision was the 2012 ruling that penalties for the lèse-majesté law did not conflict with the constitution:

> But, if you read the verdict . . . you will find that absolutely no legal reasons were offered. . . . There are only arguments that glorify His Majesty, and it is like this for the entire verdict. But arguments pertaining the penalty's proportionality, the ability for anyone to file a complaint against the offender, the appropriateness of the protected position, the lack of any exception to the offense and penalty regardless of whether it is a criticism, none of these points were weighed or deliberated upon by the court. It simply concluded that the penalty is appropriate since His Majesty is respected and sacred. It does not use the principle of

proportionality to weigh their considerations, which is the most basic principle of the constitution.[62]

Worajet went on to argue that since their status was boosted under the 2007 Constitution, judges had become a distinct elite class in terms of both salaries and power, even able to propose new salaries for themselves to parliament. Judicial privileges were inextricably linked to proximity to the monarchy. Here lay a central irony: the special status of judges has been enshrined in successive constitutions, yet judges derived greater status from their extraconstitutional association with the monarchy than from their constitutional standing as arbiters of justice. Any reform had to come from the outside: the majority of judges were very happy to operate in a routine fashion, without questioning the basis on which they worked. Piyabutr Saengkanokkul went even further, suggesting that it might be impossible to reform the judiciary without firing all current judges and setting up a whole new system.[63]

Asked whether any groups other than Nitirat were critical of the judiciary, Worajet replied:

> There are none, because people are afraid. Those nurtured in the legal field are afraid of the judiciary. Why are they afraid of the judiciary? There are many reasons. In this field, there is seniority. . . . If we want to progress in your career, such as by gaining a professorship, then you must not be too bold, but rather stay composed and work within the system.[64] If you are critical and you challenge authority, you would face difficulties because of the domination of power. There is actually much that is dominated. The domination extends over assessment of academic positions, research, and research funding. So who would pursue this path? It offers no benefits.

Judicial power to suppress criticism extends beyond the immediate reach of the courts, to cover the entire legal and academic spheres. Though widely admired even by judges who disagree with their arguments, members of Nitirat faced enormous public and private pressure to desist from their campaigns on controversial issues such as the lèse-majesté law.

Piyabutr has argued that the judiciary always issues judgments in a royalist manner; rule of law has become simply a cover for royalist sentiments.[65] He claimed that once a new president of a court took office, royalists would "take control" of the president to ensure that the right judges were assigned to sensitive political cases. Piyabutr argued that the political leanings of judges were an open secret, and it was easy to select the "correct" panel to ensure a particular outcome. This was especially true for lèse-majesté cases, to which the same hardline "assassin" judges were repeatedly assigned.[66] Piyabutr had previously suggested, in a research report he had submitted to the courts, that panels should be assigned randomly or in strict rotation—a proposal that fell on deaf ears.[67]

What might be termed the "Nitirat research report," a collaborative project to propose changes in the way political cases are handled in the courts, was authored by Jantajira, Piyabutr, Thira, and another colleague on behalf of Thammasat University, and commissioned by the Courts of Justice.[68] The authors proposed the creation of new Election Courts (with both Appeal and Supreme Court levels) to decide on challenges to election results, a proposal which would entail yet another sphere of judicial intervention.[69] The team also proposed that cases for political officeholders have two levels of hearings: Appeal (heard by three judges) and Supreme Court (heard by five judges), instead of the current system where nine Supreme Court judges made a binding decision that could not be appealed. The authors proposed that judges hearing these cases should no longer be selected by en banc meetings of the entire Supreme Court. Minority opinions should also be permitted in these cases. While Sarawut Benjakul claimed the majority of court cases were in fact randomly assigned to judges, including those involving politics, one former senior judge explained that in practice important cases are assigned primarily to individual judges whose biases are usually well known; other members of the panel only rarely challenge the view of the lead judge on the case.[70]

The Nitirat report was criticized as overly theoretical by the judges who read it: the academics failed to conduct any field research or gather any new data.[71] Some of those who reviewed the paper felt that the researchers were biased against the courts, while others believed that the research was of poor quality. Although rejecting the report—which would have been an unprecedented move—was discussed, the document was finally approved with some critical feedback. But it seemed unlikely that members of Nitirat would be invited to conduct any further research for the courts.

Piyabutr went on to cite the specific example of the 2008 Preah Vihear (Khao Phra Vihan) case, involving a disputed temple complex on the Thai-Cambodian border. The Central Administrative Court issued a 2:00 a.m. injunction to prevent the signing of a UNESCO agreement, despite the fact that the Administrative Courts had no jurisdiction over international treaties.[72] When the Foreign Ministry appealed to the Supreme Administrative Court, the first panel to review the case rejected it as a political issue. The president of the Supreme Administrative Court then revoked that panel's decision and convened a second panel that upheld the original decision. The Constitutional Court promptly declared the Foreign Ministry's actions unconstitutional, and the case was subsequently referred to the National Anticorruption Commission on the grounds that the foreign minister had abused his powers.

Piyabutr argued that the intransigence of the judiciary in adhering to a very conservative political line on issues like Preah Vihear was intimately linked to the stance of the monarchy. Sanya Thammsak had regularly declared in his opening "words of wisdom" when he addressed new judges that "we are the only officials that work in the name of the King"—an idea still invoked by judges all the time:[73]

> It is difficult to destroy the court's way of thinking because it is associated with the monarchy. If the monarchy wasn't like this, the judiciary wouldn't be either. If the monarchy reformed to become democratic, the judiciary would follow. It is like a pillar that the judiciary holds on to; without the pillar, the judiciary wouldn't be so hard to change.

Piyabutr compared recent developments to a snooker game, in which the King played the opening shot (with his two April 2006 speeches) and left the judiciary to finish the match. He believed there were quite a few progressive-minded senior judges, but none of them was ready to sacrifice their careers by speaking out on these issues. The judiciary was more cohesive even than the military; junior judges were very quickly socialized into institutional culture and mores. He was convinced that only by constantly challenging the legitimacy of the judiciary could any change be achieved. He had seen how friends who passed the judges' entrance examination "ascended to the bench,"[74] and soon became "possessed by the bench ghost"—in the process changing into different people.[75]

Nitirat member Jantajira Eiamayura argued that lobbying was widespread throughout the justice system, especially by major business groups, by their law firms and by influential networks who retained advisers with close personal connections to senior judges and prosecutors. For her, judicial decision making was deeply penetrated by pre-1932 thinking. A law faculty like Thammasat's was preparing students to become barristers, prosecutors, and especially judges, based on "the inheritance of the souls and ideologies of ancestors and past generations"— a notion of the judiciary as a kind of extended family, set apart from the rest of society.[76] The ideology in which judge trainees are still inculcated lionizes royalist judges such as Sanya Thammasak and Thanin Kraivichien. Sanya's prominent role in palace circles, and the appointment of both men to the offices of prime minister and privy councilor solidified the sense of a special bond between the monarchy and the judiciary. Because they had been taught that authority rests solely with the King, in the future these judges would respond only to the monarchy and not to the people. Jantajira explained that after joining Nitirat, she had been unable to maintain her longstanding friendships with judges and prosecutors, some of whom saw her as condemning them and their institutions.

Teera argued that the decision making of judges was shaped by their "thought system" that was passed down from generation to generation and "adhered closely" to the pre-1932 system of governance.[77]

> Prior to the 1932 change in governance, judges believed that they acted on behalf of the King. After the change, there may be some changes in their thought but after the coup again in 1947, when Pridi left and *khanarat*'s [People's Party] role ceased, there was a return to the old ways of thinking—that the judges are representative of the king, exercising authority in the name of the king. This strand of thought culminated when Sanya Thammasak was the head of the Privy Council. When he offered "words of wisdom" to new judges, he would claim that "the judiciary is different from other state institutions because the judiciary is the only institution that exercises the authority of the king."[78] Over time, this indoctrination manifested itself when judges adjudicated cases weighing between democracy and state authority, when the decision would tend to lean toward this thought system: in Thai democracy under the King, the King is valued over democracy.[79]

One example of a highly partisan move was the appointment of two new election commissioners in mid-2006: the Constitutional Court had urged the remaining election commissioners to resign or face possible imprisonment, a move that had no legal basis but was justified by the court simply by reference to the April 2006 royal speeches. A couple of commissioners were indeed briefly incarcerated. When the September 2006 coup happened a few months later, the retiring president of the Supreme Court was immediately appointed Minister of Justice by the military junta.

Perhaps Nitirat's most controversial proposal was made in early 2012: any new monarch should take an oath to respect the constitution.[80] Nitirat called for a balance of power, in which the monarchy, judiciary, executive, legislature, and the military could coexist according to democratic principles. According to Teera, top judges felt threatened by this vision and were deeply resentful of criticism, believing that the Thammasat lecturers were too junior to challenge their authority and question their verdicts. Fellow Nitirat member Sawatree Suksiri took a broader view. She was reluctant to place all the blame on judges for the outcomes of political cases: mistakes by defense lawyers were another factor.[81] She also believed that judges were under pressure to improve the quality of their judgments, especially after the intense disquiet over the Akong case. The expert gaze of Nitirat was the most sustained form of scrutiny to which Thai judges had been subjected since the end of the absolute monarchy.

Dissent

The judiciary faced other kinds of disagreement besides the academic critiques of Nitirat. Starting in early 2012, a group known in English as the Declaration of Street Justice[82] began holding protests on the streets outside the main Bangkok court complex in Ratchadapisek every Sunday until October 2013. Led by Suda Rangkupan, then a lecturer in linguistics at Chulalongkorn University, the protest began as a hunger strike by lèse-majesté defendant Somyot Prueksakasemsuk's son, but later became a weekly event: a political discussion held in a small tented encampment, broadcast live on the Speedhorse internet TV channel.[83] The street protest focused on the plight of those charged with political offences and demanded changes in the criminal justice system, including reform of bail conditions. Declaration of Street Justice symbolized the extent to which the judiciary, and especially the criminal courts, had incurred the lasting enmity of the redshirt movement.

Judges viewed the protests from a variety of perspectives. One sympathetic judge admitted he had sent a court security guard to observe and report back to him what was happening. A conservative judge hearing the 2012 Jon Ungpakorn case suggested to his social activist defense lawyers that they might as well make banners and hold them up outside the court. Court spokesman Sarawut Benjakul explained that while some judges favored charging the protesters with contempt of court, the majority preferred to take no action against them, in the interests of freedom of speech. Although outwardly ineffectual, these long-running protests on Rajadapisek Road were disturbing for judges, representing a tangible challenge to the reputation and indeed to the legitimacy of the courts. Nevertheless, troubling criminal justice procedures such as automatic bail denials in lèse-majesté cases remained unchanged.

Judges who are openly critical of the dominant ideology are hard to find. One notable exception is retired judge Sathit Phairo, who served briefly as vice president of the Supreme Court. Sathit, who spoke at some Nitirat events, argued that although Section 26 of the Judges of the Courts of Justice Service Act 2000 states that judges must respect and believe in democratic principles, most judges do not understand the idea of democracy properly. In this respect, judges resemble many other leading figures in Thai society— they remain beguiled by notions of absolute monarchy and popular understandings of Buddhism that underpin royal power. Sathit also questioned Sanya Thammasak's oft-quoted claim that the courts are the last resort for the Thai people, which he saw as reifying judicial authority by linking it to the monarchy.[84] The overriding principle of the Thai judiciary was actually "Inter arma enim silent leges": military force was met with legal silence.[85]

Thai judges had long since persuaded themselves that serving authoritarianism was perfectly legitimate.

Another dissident judge argued that it was unrealistic to expect judges to be any more liberal than the society and the regime they served.[86] Changing the mindset of judges could not be achieved by reforming the courts, but only by transforming larger social attitudes. A core problem was that for judges, the constitution was not the highest law of the land. Rather, the highest laws were the civil and criminal codes, because they predated 1932 and had been created under royal direction and patronage. For this reason, many Thai judges believed that the country could be governed perfectly well using an unwritten constitution and a well-codified set of laws. Because of this belief, Thai judges had little use for the country's revolving-door constitutions, and so were unwilling to embrace the rights and liberties that went along with their promulgation.

The dissident judge claimed that most judges did not feel any great need to improve their knowledge, since at an early age they had passed a very demanding entrance examination which demonstrated their abilities: "At twenty-five years old you think you are God, nobody can change you." He explained: "When the Supreme Court has an en banc, most of the judges do not have enough knowledge to discuss the issues; they don't read much, because they are Thai people. They don't want to solve hard problems and can't face reading the whole book." For the most part, the Thai Supreme Court was an inward-looking, self-congratulatory institution rather than a locus of learning or a hotbed of intellectual debate. Most judges at all levels saw little need to change, preferring to stick with the existing system, and regarded those who criticized them as lacking in intelligence.

Thammasat law lecturer (and Nitirat member) Sawatree Suksiri recounted how one judge rejected a defense request to call her as an expert witness in a criminal case, saying: "I am also an expert in law."[87] The "expertise" of judges trumped all other modes of legal expertise and professional knowledge; it is no wonder that some ambitious lawyers have been known to pass the entrance exam and serve as judges for a matter of days before quitting, partly to impress those before whom they pleaded.[88]

The dissident judge argued that strict enforcement of the lèse-majesté law formed part of asserting the pretense that the judiciary enjoyed special royal connections. Since the great majority of judges were honest—in the sense of not engaging in corruption—they believed in their own moral superiority, which they saw as a means of solving problems. In reality, the main job of the judiciary was to protect the ancien regime, including the monarchy—but most judges failed to see the reality of their own situation. "You wear sunglasses from when you were very young, and never realize just how bright the light is."[89] He went on to argue that if the public realized that the judiciary, like politicians, generally acted in the service of its own interests, then the moral standing of the courts would be undermined. The irony was that most judges now viewed Nitirat, who were fighting for the rights of the people, as troublemakers and even criminals. Meanwhile, they saw postcoup prime minister General Prayuth Chan-ocha and the leadership of the military junta as heroes, despite the fact that they had seized power illegally. Although redshirt judges certainly existed, they remained in the minority and usually kept their opinions to themselves.

The cry of "double standards" was a familiar refrain among critics of the judiciary after 2006.[90] Claudio Sopranzetti quotes Id, a motorcycle taxi driver from the Northeast, on the subject:

> "Democracy is justice," Id began. "For the most part we don't have legal, political and educational justice. It is a matter of opportunity and double standards [song mattrathan]. Look at the case of Thaksin. Maybe he is corrupt, but who isn't in Thai politics? Why are they going after him and not all the others? Why are they trying to confiscate all of his money, even what he made before taking office? This is what double standards means."[91]

Some pro-Thaksin activists sported T-shirts emblazoned with the phrase *double standards*, which referred not simply to unequal treatment by the courts, but to structural inequalities and discrimination. The judiciary was simply unable to answer certain questions: Why did PAD leader Sondhi Limthongkul keep being bailed out, even after facing lèse-majesté charges, when redshirt leaders and lèse-majesté defendants were nearly always denied bail? Why had the PAD protesters responsible for seizing Bangkok's airports in November 2008 never come to trial, despite apparently committing serious violations of international law?[92]

A junior judge was skeptical about the claim that the courts applied double standards: the joke among judges was that since every case was different, there were far more than two standards.[93] Where judgments contained nonlegal statements, this could be grounds for appeal or even for disciplinary action. A senior judge agreed, though perhaps showing his colors by insisting that lèse-majesté defendants were all "agitators," who were likely to reoffend if bailed out:[94] "The problem is that people don't have access to the information the courts have when we make decisions; if they did they would understand that we treat everybody equally."[95]

On May 17, 2012, the House Committee on Foreign Affairs met to hear evidence on the Akong case from Sarawut Benjakul, the deputy secretary-general of the Courts of Justice. Officials from various agencies including the Corrections Department, the Courts of Justice, and the National Human Rights Commission were invited to attend the session, along with members of Akong's family and his legal team.

Sarawut was in the impossible position of defending the indefensible. He declared that the court felt uneasy about what had happened, and that he himself would like to have seen Akong temporarily released.[96] But bail was not granted in this case, because the severe penalties for lèse-majesté offences meant that defendants "had a tendency to run off." The court was unaware either of the severity of the defendant's illness, or the stage of the cancer, he claimed. Sarawut failed to mention that no proper assessment of Akong's condition could have been undertaken unless he was able to leave the prison and visit a proper hospital. Akong was in the Catch-22 situation that without leaving the jail, he could not be deemed sick enough to leave it. Sarawut claimed that the courts granted bail in 93 percent of cases—but he was apparently referring to criminal cases as a whole, rather than Article 112 cases, for which bail was rarely given. While many of Sarawut's answers were incomplete or unsatisfactory, the willingness of the Courts of Justice to send a representative to address this parliamentary committee was a positive development.

The death of lèse-majesté prisoner Akong in 2012 illustrated many of the latent contradictions in Thai judicial thinking. Deference to the monarchy and an excessive enthusiasm to protect the status quo could encourage a punitive attitude towards defendants, especially after the royal speeches of 2006 that asked the judiciary to help solve the nation's most severe political problems. The resulting perception of double standards further alienated the courts from much of the populace; at the same time, the judiciary often seemed overly defensive in the face of unfamiliar levels of public criticism. Generalizing about the worldviews of Thai judges is difficult; the Thai judiciary is a diverse group, not all judges think alike, and those with less mainstream opinions often prefer to keep those views to themselves. But a number of recurrent themes emerge from conversations with Thai judges and from the work of those who study them.

Thai judges typically have a strong sense of themselves as an elite group, with a close bond to the monarchy. This bond reflects historical understandings of judges as literally standing in for the King, who could in theory still (as the late King Bhumibol occasionally did until the 1980s) exercise his traditional right to hear cases, and to pass judgment himself. Judicial decisions are in effect subject to royal review, which is also seen both in the granting of individual pardons, and in frequent royal commutations of the death sentence. This self-understanding on the part of judges—that they are royal servants, or "judges of the King"—sits uneasily with a modern constitutional order and helps account for the lack of enthusiasm felt by most judges for constitutional niceties, or for ideas of human rights. Because judges see their legitimacy as deriving from an exalted position in the Thai social hierarchy, proximate to the throne, they are often disinclined to see themselves as dispensing justice on behalf of the nation, let alone for the people. Rather, they exercise justice in the name of the King, and for the sake of the land.

Accordingly, many judges subscribe to conservative understandings of the rule of law, which is for them primarily an instrument to preserve order, to discipline troublemakers, and to punish those who engage in acts of disloyalty. Some judges conflate notions of karma, merit, and demerit—derived from popular understandings of Buddhism—with rational-legal understandings of the world, and at times seem unable clearly to distinguish one from another. This leads some of them to adopt a highly paternalistic and simplistic view of defendants' actions and motivations. While many judges would certainly disagree with such ideas, they have not been able to insert alternative understandings of justice and the rule of law into the mainstream thinking of the institution.

As one dissident judge argued, so long as Thailand is dominated by royalist and antidemocratic ideologies, such ideologies will pervade the judiciary as well.[97] Since the courts are an instrument of the larger Thai political system, any judicial activism is bound broadly to support the existing order. It was not the role of the courts to fight for democratic change, but to protect the ancien regime. Judges cannot be blamed for this: society gets the judges it deserves. If the people were unhappy, they had to demand a complete overhaul—or even overthrow—of the existing criminal justice system. Accusations of "double standards" applied to the courts reflected structural equalities in Thai society, linked to crudely understood Buddhist notions of merit. Simply put, the elite possess more merit than ordinary people; and their superior levels of virtue make them entitled to a privileged place in society, along with special treatment by the courts. Few judges would admit to such a disposition, and many may not even recognize that they possess such attitudes, but these attitudes are there.

The conservative focus of the courts is reinforced by what might be termed the Thai judicial knowledge crisis. Thai judges believe that their abilities as jurists have been abundantly validated by their success in passing the difficult entrance examinations to enter their profession. As a result, they tend to be disdainful of other forms of legal knowledge and are disinclined to update themselves, or to debate new ideas and critical issues. Nor are most judges really aware that the extremely technical legal education they have received—with very little by way of sociolegal studies or legal philosophy, let alone classes in politics or economics— leaves them ill-prepared to understand the complexities of Thailand's rapidly changing society. As a result, even most of the senior Supreme Court judges who sit atop the legal hierarchy have nothing like the intellectual caliber, knowledge, and training that such positions require in other judicial systems: quite simply, they are not performing to international standards.

The limited worldview of Thai judges has made them ready—or even actively willing—to work with military regimes, and reluctant to adopt progressive social or political stances. Following the important royal speeches of April 2006, the judiciary regularly sought to carry out King Bhumibol's expressed will by addressing Thailand's pressing political problems. Nevertheless, Thai judges have taken on this more overt political role only reluctantly, and often with grave misgivings. With good reason, they fear that any perceived judicialization of politics will lead to greater politicization of the judiciary, and to a loss of public esteem and legitimacy.

Responding to the challenges of their enhanced role after 2006, the judiciary struggled with inadequate governance mechanisms, including an overburdened Supreme Court president and a flawed Judicial Commission. Intensely suspicious of external interference, the courts nevertheless singularly failed to reform themselves in the face of growing public skepticism about their practices, procedures, and organizational cultures. Criticism from pro-Thaksin forces about apparent "double standards" in judicial decisions provoked more defensiveness than soul searching, while the insightful critiques of the Nitirat group went largely unanswered by the courts. Rather, senior judges retreated behind protestations about their own status and dignity that provided a convenient cover for lack of accountability.[98] Rarely would representatives of the judiciary come out to defend themselves—Sarawut Benjakul's 2012 parliamentary committee testimony after Akong's death was a striking exception—and none would dare debate brilliant legal minds such as Nitirat's Worajet Pakeerat in a public setting. In short, the Thai judiciary lacked effective leadership in dealing with the crisis of collective confidence it faced in the wake of the 2006 coup. This chapter has shown how judges who had modeled their brand of opaque moralism on the ambiguous public utterances of the King himself were found wanting and seemed unable to regain earlier levels of popular trust and admiration. The next three chapters examine important court cases in which defendants were accused of crimes on the treason spectrum, cases that judges struggled to manage effectively.

4

AGAINST THE CROWN?

On April 26, 2010, in the midst of massive redshirt demonstrations that had paralyzed the central Ratchaprasong district of Bangkok, Thai military spokesman Colonel Sansern Kaewkamnert released a shocking diagram depicting network treason, a large-scale conspiracy to overthrow the monarchy (*lom jao*), implicating dozens of pro-Thaksin politicians, academics, activists, and journalists. Before long, the authorities were forced to admit that the antimonarchy plot was a fabrication—but by then some of those named in the diagram had already been charged, arrested, put on trial, or even jailed.[1] The lom jao episode showed how easily, in a highly polarized political order where dissenting thoughts could constitute criminal acts, empty charges of treason could take on a judicial life of their own.

What happens when a Thai is charged with treason? This chapter will examine a court case closely linked to the narrative of overthrowing the monarchy, and the clash of dispositions between judges, defendants, and lawyers that emerged during the *lèse-majesté* trial of Somyot Prueksakasemsuk. Magazine editor Somyot was given a ten-year jail term for *lèse-majesté* on the basis of two articles he did not write. Somyot and *Voice of Taksin* magazine were both named on Colonel Sansern's April 2010 diagram, standing accused of joining an antimonarchist conspiracy. Adapting an approach developed by Robert Ferguson and based on firsthand trial observations, the chapter examines the different participants in the trial—the judges, the defendant, the defense lawyers, the prosecutor, the defense and various witnesses—and how they performed their roles. While the discipline-obsessed judges appeared woefully out of their depth, the provocative redshirt defense lawyers specialized in antagonizing the bench and arguably contributed to Somyot's harsh sentence. The chapter offers an exposition of a landmark trial that elucidated some of the structural contradictions at the heart of Thailand's troubled society and politics. The following two chapters examine the trials of Katha Pachachirayapong and that of Jon Ungpakorn and his nine codefendants, which involved parallel but different alleged challenges to public order.

Compassings

In his study of politically important trials in the United States, Robert Ferguson argued that the aim of a trial is to move from contest to ritual. Where contest "refuses to yield to the pull of ritual," no real resolution is achieved, and the judicial process may prove not simply ineffective but actually counterproductive.[2] Drawing on the work of Victor Turner, Ferguson suggests that a successful trial needs to create the possibility of liminality. Precisely because liminality exists outside the parameters of normal daily life, it is a difficult concept to deploy. Turner's most succinct description of the liminal phase of ritual is "a time and space lodged between all times and spaces defined and governed . . . by the rules of law, politics and religion, and economic necessity."[3] At such junctures, the schema of ordinary life no longer apply. In other words, for a trial to take on wider significance, the drama played out in the courtroom needs to transcend the parameters of a criminal case: at crucial phases, the narrative of the trial can be transformed into something much larger and more salient. Ferguson views great trials as performances that can offer deep insights into public life. In their different ways, all three trials discussed here concern defendants charged with acts of treason against the Thai state. These trials were not solely or even mainly about the defendants in the dock: Turner suggests that liminality always exists in relation to the abyss. In these court cases, the abyss is the terrible harshness meted out to those who fail properly to perform their loyalty to Thai state. At moments in each trial, we are offered glimpses into that abyss. Yet all three trials also included moments of playfulness, levity, and benevolence—the possibility of a shared humanity that transcended immense political, emotional, and indeed moral divides.

Yet where trials go to the heart of profound political conflicts in their societies, the scope for liminality is narrowed and the legal process can easily exacerbate and aggravate wider conflicts, rather than assuaging them. This is especially the case in a Thai context where, as Tyrell Haberkorn puts it, "some members of the polity" are viewed as human, "and others as not fully human."[4] Where the humanity of defendants and their lawyers is not recognized by judges and other trial officials, liminality is clearly impossible. Rather than moving easily to ritual, official positions harden and trials remain sites of legalistic contestation. Ferguson argues that in an important trial the crime, the victim, and the defendant represent something far larger than themselves. For him, a trial constitutes an exercise in storytelling, with the important caveat that "most stories told in a courtroom are true only in an instrumental sense."[5] By focusing on the main actors in some prominent American trials—including judges, prosecutors, defense lawyers, and defendants themselves—Ferguson examines the ways in which important court cases can shed a much wider light on the nature of justice and power.

Ferguson has argued that in order to win a case, the defense needs to tell a story that the court can understand.[6] In the Thai context, where there is no jury system, stories that courts can understand are usually stories that judges recognize, because they have heard them before. Given that all three cases represented a microcosm of Thailand's intensely contested political order, close scrutiny of the micropolitics of the trials themselves offers an opportunity for a deeper understanding of issues, attitudes, practices, and behaviors that lie at the core of Thai national life. The adversarial nature of the trials mirrors deeply adversarial conditions in wider Thai society, in which fundamental questions remain intensely contested. As Ferguson argues:

> Courtrooms and their communities normally cooperate with each other by definition in a rule of law, but they compete for articulation in a high profile trial, and the tension between them opens the field of commentary beyond the legal issues involved. Memorable trials thus become barometers of social thought, and, as such, deserve more careful study than they have received.[7]

Ferguson explains that a great trial has three important elements: the spread of conflict beyond the technical parameters of the charges to wider questions; a dramatic twist of shock, surprise, or reversal; and the use of iconography, in which the crime, the victim, or the defendant seem to represent something far larger than themselves.[8]

This chapter looks at the crucial case of Somyot Prueksakasemsuk. Like the two chapters that follow dealing with the Katha and Jon cases, it draws on Ferguson's approach by addressing both the micropolitics of the trial and its wider national significance. The charges in all three cases were highly problematic. Thailand's lèse-majesté law, under which Somyot was charged, entailed a minimum five-year jail sentence for those convicted of defaming the King, the Queen, or the heir apparent. Calls for reform of this controversial law, including reducing the sentences involved, have been advanced from all sides of the political spectrum. Similarly, the 2007 Computer Crime Act under which Katha was charged was one of the many troubling items of legislation rushed through the military-appointed National Assembly in the final weeks of the coup regime, the very same haste against which Jon and his codefendants were protesting. The legislation was widely criticized as both shoddy and overly politicized.

It would be easy to write about these three cases from a polemical perspective. To be clear, I believe these defendants should never have been charged with any crime, and that the laws under which they were charged were not fit for purpose. In my view, nobody should face the possibility of jail time on defamation charges of any kind, nor for acts of peaceful protest. But to understand the political significance of these cases, simply criticizing the Thai justice system is not enough. The defendants and their lawyers are not above critical scrutiny, simply because their causes were essentially just.

All three cases reflected the peculiar politics of their times. The 2006 military coup, which aimed to reorganize political power in Thailand and break Thaksin Shinawatra's grip on electoral success, soon began to unravel: a pro-Thaksin party had no difficulty winning the 2007 general election. When redshirt street protests broke out in Bangkok early in 2010, the military produced an organogram locating the sources of antimonarchical resistance—in effect, a vast conspiracy against the Thai establishment, and the core values of the country. Each of the three cases discussed in this chapter can be linked to the supposed lom jao conspiracy. The anti-NLA protests led by Jon Ungpakorn were connected, at least in the confused imaginations of the prosecutors, with his brother Giles Ji Ungpakorn, a former Chulalongkorn University academic who fled Thailand in 2010 after being accused of *lèse-majesté*. Somyot worked for *Voice of Thaksin* magazine, while Katha was linked to the website of the progressive journal *Fa Diao Kan*: both publications appeared on the diagram.

The idea of a movement linked to Thaksin and dedicated to overthrowing the monarchy first saw the light of day in May 2006 when maverick conservative intellectual Pramote Nakhonthap published a series of six articles under the headline "Finland Strategy: Plan To Change Thailand's Form of Government?"[9] Pramote claimed that Thaksin and a group of former leftists from the 1970s October generation had gathered in Finland in 1999 to develop a plan to abolish the monarchy, bring in one-party rule, and elect provincial governors.[10] Pramote named a number of conspirators, including several Thaksin ministers and advisers.[11] The Finland Plot allegations coincided with the sixtieth anniversary of King Bhumibol's assuming the throne, and contributed to a sharp fall in the legitimacy of the Thaksin government, culminating in its ouster in the September 19, 2006, military junta. The coup makers cited Thaksin's alleged disloyalty to the monarchy as one of the reasons for his removal. Neither Pramote nor others who wrote about the alleged Finland plot ever produced a scrap of evidence for their assertions. In March 2009 Pramote and the editor of *Phujatkan* were each fined around US $3,000 (100,000 baht) and given two-year suspended jail terms for defamation.[12] A textbook example of "fake news," the Finland plot was a complete fabrication: but one that resonated strongly with the anti-Thaksin movement, and so was widely believed.

Similar ideas resurfaced in the form of a November 2009 book entitled *The Movement to Overthrow the Monarchy*, published by ASTV-Manager, the same company that had published the earlier articles. The book, which included a discussion of the 2006 Finland plot and was reprinted eight times, linked together a number of recent developments, including Thaksin's suspiciously warm relations with Cambodia (culminating in the 2008 Preah Vihear controversy over a disputed temple on Thai-Cambodian border) and sudden falls in the stock market in October 2009 on rumors about the King's health.[13] The book claimed that three groups were conspiring to bring down the monarchy: Thaksin, his relatives, and network; networks associated with politicians in the coalition government parties; and communist-inflected members of the 1970s generation of Octobrist radicals.

The authors argued that the current antimonarchy movement emphasized supporting a one-party political system and undermining the old bureaucratic system, for example, by reducing number of civil servants.[14] These attempts to create a one-party state had been inspired by communist ideas that are incompatible with the monarchy. According to the ASTV book, the aim of the lom jao movement was systematically to change Thailand's mode of governance from "democracy with the king as head of state" to another political system. It quoted extensively from the published writings and speeches of conservative royalists such as outspoken monk Luang Ta Maha Bua, retired police general Vasit Dejkunchorn, and Privy Councilor General Pichit Kullawanit, all of whom accused Thaksin of having insulted the monarchy.

A second book along similar lines was *Exposing the Red Anti-Monarchy Movement*, produced by T-News at the beginning of 2010 and reprinted six times: it was a compilation of materials from online news program broadcasts.[15] A major theme was "inappropriate and unlawful" redshirt demands that Thaksin be pardoned: the petitioners were not relatives of Thaksin, and he had never accepted any punishment for his crime. While the clique aiming to overthrow the monarchy formed only one component of the redshirt movement, the group posed a clear and present danger. The book included statements from a number of prominent figures, including the chairman of the Ad Hoc Parliamentary Committee on Law Enforcement and Measures for Protecting the Monarchy; Jarungjit Thikhara, lady-in-waiting to the Queen, and arch-royalist retired police general

Vasit Dejkunchorn were shown in tears expressing their alarm at the situation. The T-News book also focused on supposedly communist ideas underpinning elements of the redshirt movement, ideas the authors claimed were inimical to Buddhism. Unlike communists, the book declared, Buddhists believe that people are not equal: their status depends on karma accumulated in past lives. By implication, differential treatment—the use of what redshirts termed "double standards"—could be entirely justified. Both the ASTV and T-News books named and shamed long lists of those accused of participation in, or sympathy with, the movement to "overthrow" the monarchy. The books failed clearly to distinguish between those who supported a stronger parliamentary system, critics of the monarchy, and the small minority of true republicans: people holding a wide range of political positions were bundled into the same catchall conspiracy theory.

After tens of thousands of redshirt protesters took to the streets of Bangkok in April 2010, then prime minister Abhisit Vejjajiva remarked on his weekly TV show that everything was connected: "It's not just a coincidence that these different people are playing different roles, names like Seh Daeng [Khattiya], General Chavalit, and the protest leaders."[16] The next morning, April 26, Colonel Sansern Kaewkamnert, spokesman for the Orwellian-sounding Centre for Resolution of the Emergency Situation (CRES) and the Royal Thai Army, declared at a press conference that redshirt leaders were using false information to attack the country's highest institution, which was loved and respected by all Thai people. There was a systematic movement, Sansern insisted, involving both prominent and less well-known redshirt leaders and those who had fled Thailand to evade arrest: the movement was linked to various redshirt publications and media outlets that continually attacked the institution all Thai people love.

That same afternoon, Colonel Sansern released to the public an elaborate diagram of the antimonarchy plot, which included some thirty names of individuals, as well as eleven organizations and media outlets.[17] Eighteen of these individuals had also been named in either the ASTV or T-News books, while fourteen were listed in all three sources: Thaksin Shinawatra, Petcharawat Wattanapongsirikul, Jakrapob Penkair, Jatuporn Promphan, Giles Ji Ungpakorn, Sutham Saengprathum, Nattawut Saikua, Somyot Prueksakasemsuk, Veera Musikapong and Surachai Danwattananusorn, Weng Tojirakarn, Daranee Charnchoensilpakul and Chavalit Yongchaiyudh. Twelve of these fourteen—the exceptions were former minister Sutham, and ex-prime minister Chavalit—soon faced charges of lèse-majesté, many brought shortly after the network treason diagram was issued. But the only people to be jailed for lèse-majesté were those with the lowest social status: Somyot, Surachai, and Daranee, who had never served as MPs, or held university or civil service posts.

On April 27, Abhisit explained that the CRES diagram was a means of helping people understand the network more clearly.[18] He explained that he wanted people to realize that the antimonarchy movement really existed and planned to use legal means to deal with the problem. The government was already monitoring the media. On April 29, Deputy Prime Minister Suthep Thaugsuban ordered the Department of Special Investigation to take over all cases relating to those accused in the diagram. Colonel Wijan Jottaeng was then instructed to file charges against those named. A week later, Suthachai Yimprasert, an associate professor of history at Chulalongkorn University who was named on the diagram, sued Sansern, Abhisit, and deputy premier Suthep for defamation. When Suthachai's case finally came to court almost a year later, Colonel Sansern testified that the antimonarchy diagram had been created to counter online assertions that Thanphuying Jarungjit Tikhara, the Queen's secretary, had made numerous phone calls to CRES ordering the authorities to crack down on the demonstrators.[19] Given this slanderous attempt to make people believe that the Queen was involved in politics, explained Sansern, the CRES had compiled information gathered by several agencies into the diagram to reveal the truth to society. However, the diagram did not state that those whose names appeared were all part of the subversive movement, still less that they were coconspirators. Following this testimony, Suthachai agreed to withdraw his defamation suit. In a later statement, Sansern noted that the diagram was based on evidence, not simply on "faith": but it was up to the public to work out the relationships between the people mentioned in the diagram, because nothing about this was written there.

After Yingluck Shinawatra became prime minister in mid-2011, the antimonarchy diagram became a major embarrassment to the Department of Special Investigation (DSI), an agency under the auspices of the Ministry of Justice that sees itself as a Thai version of the FBI. The DSI launched an investigation into the diagram's origins and significance and concluded that some people had been incorrectly named in the diagram; the relationships between those named there did not constitute a criminal collaboration; CRES had a vested interest in the allegations, which undermined their credibility; and there was insufficient evidence to support the claim that those listed on the diagram had collectively violated Article 112. In 2012, DSI head Tharit Pengdit, an adept political operator who thrived under both Abhisit and Yingluck, declared that they would now suspend working on the diagram cases: he did not want to say the diagram was produced simply as a tactic to end the 2010 political "game," but he strongly implied that this was the case.[20] Tharit also claimed he did not know who had actually produced the organogram.

Yet evidence concerning the origins of the diagram was already in the public domain, in the form of an article by serving general Boonrot Sisombat about the military operation to suppress the redshirt protests, published in the army journal *Senathipat* in 2011. The article focused on the "IO" (Information Operation) conducted by CRES, of which the network treason diagram formed an important part.[21] His article made clear that the diagram was deliberately fabricated by the military themselves.

It would be simplistic to suggest that the April 2010 network treason diagram was merely lifted from the recent ASTV and T-News books; but the overlapping lists of names were hardly coincidental. Both books had popularized the discourse of lom jao and a widespread belief that the monarchy was under threat. The launch of the diagram in the aftermath of the initial bloody crackdown on redshirt protesters of April 10, 2010, was clearly an attempt to regain the political initiative and to restore the flagging legitimacy of the Abhisit government, which had assumed power in late 2008 despite his Democrat Party's decisive defeat in a general election the year before. As Kasian Tejapira has argued in his "autopsy" of the diagram, the lom jao plot was created based on suspicion and insinuation, as the result of highly politicized process of intelligence gathering.[22] This process has parallels with the ways in which eighteenth-century Parisian detectives tracked and mapped the transmission of subversive poems.[23] As Robert Darnton wrote:

> After watching the police chasing poetry in so many directions, one has the impression that their investigation dribbled off into a series of arrests that could have continued indefinitely without arriving at an ultimate author. No matter where they looked, they turned up someone singing or reciting naughty verse about the court . . . It was a dangerous game, more so than they realized, but it hardly constituted a threat to the French state. Why did the police react so strongly?[24]

As Sawatree Suksri has pointed out, there was very little media coverage of Colonel Sansern's admissions under oath that the lom jao diagram was not evidence of a criminal conspiracy. A big, bold lie, once uttered and widely reported, can never be retracted: subsequent qualifications or denials will never make the same impact as the original claim.[25] The lies of the diagram were the weblike lines linking the different elements, suggesting systematic agency and causality where none existed. Like the Finland plot, the network treason diagram was a fabrication aimed at discrediting and indeed potentially imprisoning a range of individuals; unlike the Finland plot, it was created not by a small group of ideological opponents, but by the Thai state itself.

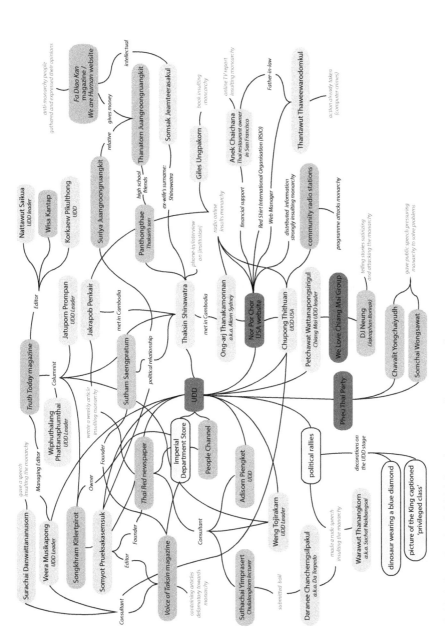

FIGURE 1. The April 2010 lom jao network treason diagram.

Source: Bangkok Pundit, "Conspiracy to Overthrow the Monarchy," April 27, 2010, https://asiancorrespondent.com/2010/04/conspiracy-against-the-monarchy/#PrPJ5tSArlWlpHF2.97. English version created for this book.

CASES

The Somyot, Katha, and Jon cases could each be reduced to a simple narrative of an oppressive state apparatus versus abused defendants who did not deserve any serious punishment. But such black-and-white readings obscure much of the nuance of these trials, and tell us little about their wider significance. Although treason felonies and associated compassings may be hard for those with a frame of reference based on modern notions of citizenship and human rights to grasp, they are familiar and readily legible for Thai judges.

In modern Thai political trials for treason felonies, contestation works on a number of levels. There is the regular adversarial relationship between the defense and prosecution, common to all criminal trials. Overlaid on top of this relationship is a fraught standoff between the judges as representatives of the crown and defendants who are accused directly or indirectly of lom jao, or seeking to undermine the monarchy. Judges are placed in the awkward position of hearing cases against defendants who allegedly challenge judicial authority. Then there is the tension between the literal facts of the case—the actions of the defendants—and the thoughts, or "compassings," which may or may not underpin those facts, and which constitute a separate crime, a more serious one in the devices of the judges.[26] Under English law, while those charged with treason felonies may be technically innocent on the literal facts, they may nevertheless be found guilty on the basis of their compassings, imaginations, or intentions. As a result, simply proposing that the powers of the monarch should be constrained constitutes a form of treason. This chapter will examine how comparable treason felony trials are conducted in Thailand, what they reveal about Thai society and politics, and how they illustrate a clash of compassings on the part of their central players. One meaning of "compassing" is plotting: something more than a private thought, yet somewhat less clear-cut than a conspiracy. The 2010 network treason diagram appears to capture this ambiguous notion perfectly, exemplifying what Streckfuss terms "traitorology" in the Thai context: "*Traitorology*'s rules and procedures were made apparent through the use of a set of defamation-based laws and their adjudication, including, crucially, their medieval focus on intent and the moral state of the alleged perpetrator—creating a taxonomy of forms and manifestations of seditious expression."[27]

Violating the law in Thailand is to transgress norms of social order, in which Thai people are supposed to behave in an orderly and peaceful fashion, demonstrating active concern for others, and to refrain from creating chaos or disharmony (*khwamwunwai*).[28] Such sentiments were expressed by King Bhumibol himself, speaking in English in a rare 1979 interview with the BBC: "We must have social order and more things of the heart—that means we must be good people, so that there won't be disorder, because people who are good don't create trouble so much."[29] For the King, orderliness was synonymous with virtue; there was no obvious place in this schema for the creative "troublemaking" often favored by political activists, writers, or artists.

During fieldwork in Bangkok police stations, I often encountered situations where victims of crime or police officers themselves accused suspects of failing to demonstrate Thai-ness: "He was not acting like a Thai" (discussion of offender, by victim of random stabbing on a crowded bus); "You would even greet a foreigner politely, so why not another Thai person?" (police investigator dealing with a dispute between neighbors).[30] Sometimes the question was posed very directly, as a form of accusation: "khon Thai ru plao?" (Are you Thai or not?). According to prescribed norms of Thai-ness, almost any legal violation may be constructed as undermining a shared sense of nationhood and collective identity; taken to its logical end point, even a traffic offence lies somewhere on the treason spectrum, since creating disorderliness on the roads would be un-Thai. Public health campaigns and promotions during Buddhist Lent implore Thais to quit smoking and to refrain from drinking alcohol, not for their own benefit or for the good of society, but "for the King." The Thai-ness discourse offers a way of measuring the compassings and imaginings of suspects and defendants: how do they locate themselves in relation to the nation? In order to be treated leniently, and especially to be acquitted, defendants need to demonstrate that they imagine themselves as loyal Thais. They are facing criminal charges simply because they themselves misunderstood, they were misunderstood, they have been misled, or they have been misrepresented—and they are anxious to be restored to a proper relationship with the nation, religion, and King at the earliest opportunity.

Somyot Prueksakasemsuk

Somyot was tried and convicted for defaming the King. But Somyot never defamed the King.[31] Two magazine articles had allegedly defamed the King, but they never mentioned the King directly, and Somyot had not written the articles. Somyot was held responsible for the articles because he was the editor of the magazine. Except that he was not legally the editor of the magazine, and magazine editors were no longer legally responsible for defamatory articles they published, in any case. Arrested in 2011, he was sentenced to a total of eleven years in jail, and eventually released in April 2018.

Somyot Prueksakasemsuk (born 1961) is a graduate of Ramkhamhaeng University's political science faculty, who took part as a high school student in the events of October 1976, the beginning of a longstanding interest in leftwing politics. He spent his early career as a trade union activist in the industrial zones of Samut Prakan, and later worked with the two NGOS, the Union of Civil Liberties and Young Christian Workers. After the 1991 coup, he helped create the Centre for Labor Information Service and Training, which he directed until the NGO folded in 2007. Somyot published a number of books on labor, social, and political issues, including a critical 2004 book on Thaksin. Later, however, like many activists and intellectuals during this period, he turned away from an anti-Thaksin position, yet without ever becoming a kneejerk Thaksin supporter.

Of the various lèse-majesté cases that surfaced in the wake of the 2006 coup, Somyot's was arguably the most troubling. Surachai Danwattanausorn and Daranee Charnchoensilpakul made speeches in front of numerous witnesses. Akong was charged over SMS messages he supposedly sent. In all three cases, the alleged statements were highly offensive. If any post-2006 lèse-majesté defendant should have been able to win the case, it was Somyot, who was in no real sense guilty: he had given no speeches, sent no text messages, and indeed written no articles. On legal grounds, the case against him was either very muddled or completely baseless.

Why did Somyot lose his case? There are a number of possible reasons: the judges were biased against him; the prosecution did an excellent job; the defense team made a hash of things; or some combination thereof. It certainly did not help that the two articles were rather obnoxious, making unsubstantiated accusations of mass murder against unnamed members of the establishment, whose identities were nevertheless easily imagined. They were written in the classic style of the anonymous Thai newspaper column, full of bile, insinuation, and not-so-cryptic metaphor.[32] The articles belong to a genre of Thai polemical journalism that pushes the boundaries of the permissible through deliberately constructing ambiguity, a genre of denunciation that resembled the pamphlets full of anti-royalist slanders and *libelles* that circulated in eighteenth-century Paris.[33] These articles operate on the premise that writers and their publishers may circumvent defamation and associated laws by creating a safe space, by anonymizing both themselves and their sources: in short, by writing in riddles. The arrest of Somyot reflected a new political climate following the launch of the network treason organogram and the May 2010 crackdown on the redshirt movement: the authorities were intent on decoding coded messages. Metaphors no longer offered any legal or customary protection. Although Somyot had not written the articles himself, his clear proximity to them undermined his claims to be a respectable journalist and social activist. Under the circumstances, nobody reading the articles could be entirely surprised that they led to criminal charges.

Ferguson argues that a defense team needs to be able to tell a convincing story about the client in the dock. For these purposes, a convincing story would be a story that Thai judges had heard before, one which resonated with them and gained their sympathy. For Somyot this was always going to be difficult. Despite his attempts to present himself as a journalist—implicitly, a "public interest" defense—Somyot had plainly dedicated his life to political activism on labor and related issues. For Thai judges, political and NGO activists are inherently suspect, people of irregular occupation, associated with protests, demonstrations, and attempts to create disorder. While most NGO activists have no interest at all in subverting the Thai state, let alone bringing down the monarchy (lom jao), for judges the imaginative leap from one form of troublemaking to another was an easy one. The presence of foreigners (myself included) on many days of Somyot's trial may have boosted the morale of the defendant, his legal team, and supporters—but in the eyes of the judges it could serve to underline his "Western" backing and his questionable intentions. When I spoke to a prosecutor familiar with the case, explaining that I was an academic and not an activist, he expressed relief. They were not supposed to talk to people from NGOs, he explained.

Somyot's profile included several strikes against him in the eyes of conservative Thais. One of these was the name of the organization he founded in 2007: 24 June for Democracy. June 24, 1932, was the day on which the absolute monarchy was overthrown; commemorations of this anniversary have been extremely muted since 1960, when Sarit Thanarat replaced it as Thailand's national day with King Bhumibol's birthday, December 5. The post-Sarit royalist revival made June 24, 1932, not to a day to remember, but a day to forget—and Somyot's valorizing this date may have struck the judges as an assertion of antimonarchism. Somyot's spell as a prominent figure in the pro-Thaksin United Front for Democracy against Dictatorship (UDD) movement was another black mark against him.[34] But most pertinent to the case were the place of Somyot's arrest and the name of his magazine.

Somyot was apprehended at the border with Cambodia, a country long viewed with suspicion for cosmological reasons: Khmers are popularly seen by many Thais as masters of black magic, who have sought to cast spells aimed at disturbing and destabilizing a rival kingdom.[35] Merit making for the Thai nation—symbolized by the King and the Buddhist religion—is aimed partly at thwarting the efforts of malicious Khmer magicians to derail the country. The burning down of the Royal Thai Embassy in Phnom Penh in 2003, along with the destruction of the Thai flag and images of the King, apparently carried out by thugs in the pay of the Cambodian government, helped cast Cambodia into outer moral darkness in the eyes of the Bangkok establishment. Nevertheless, Thaksin was able to restore strong personal relations with Cambodian premier Hun Sen, and successfully pursued a range of business activities in the country. In the wake of the 2006 coup, Thaksin was a regular visitor to Cambodia and served for a time as an economic adviser to Hun Sen. Thai royalists looked askance at neighboring Cambodia, where the long-serving King Sihanouk had abdicated in 2004 in favor of King Sihamoni, under whom the monarchy had become increasingly subordinated to the overarching power of Prime Minister Hun Sen—a potential role model for Thaksin. In April 2012, in the middle of Somyot's trial, Thaksin provocatively held a huge rally in Cambodia attended by thousands of Thai redshirts. Most importantly, various red-aligned figures who had fallen foul of the Thai authorities went into hiding in Cambodia. Among those rumored to be in Cambodia were prominent redshirts Arisman Phongruangrong, Suphorn Atthawong, and Darunee Kritboonyalai, not to mention Jakarapob Penkair himself.[36]

Somyot's repeated Cambodia trips in 2010 with members of his red-linked 24 June group must have aroused the judges' suspicions: did they ever meet Jakarapob, or other redshirt leaders? Curiously, however, no witness was asked this obvious question. For that matter, how well did Somyot know Jakarapob, and what kind of relationship did they have? It did not serve the purposes of the prosecution to focus on Jakarapob, who had authored the articles but was not facing any charges: their target was Somyot. Similarly, the defense had nothing to gain from highlighting the political subtext of Somyot's various visits to Cambodia, instead playing along with the unlikely cover story that he was simply taking tourists to Angkor Wat. Somyot's solidarity visits to Cambodia were an inconvenient truth, and the story they suggested—of a man deeply embedded in the redshirt movement, who had a strong relationship with Jakarapob—was one not told during his trial. Telling this story would have shifted the focus towards Jakarapob, yet without casting the defendant in a more positive light in the eyes of the judges.

Another problem was the magazine title: *Voice of Taksin*. The English spelling of the title actually suggested not former prime minister Thaksin Shinawatra, but King Taksin, a warrior of ethnic Chinese descent, whose murder had ushered in the present Chakri dynasty. Taksin and Thaksin were often linked by Thaksin supporters, and the two articles which formed the core of the Somyot case made direct reference to King Taksin.[37] Highlighting this comparison could be construed as a sideswipe at the legitimacy of the current Chakri line, which had arguably demonized both King Taksin and Prime Minister Thaksin. Partly for this reason, the judges in the Somyot case were very reluctant to write the English title *Voice of Taksin* into their *banthuek* (trial records). In general, Thai court documents are not supposed to contain foreign language terms: dates invariably use Thai numerals, and phrases from English or other languages are translated or transliterated into Thai. Accordingly, the lead judge in the Somyot case consistently rendered *Voice of Taksin* as *Siang Thaksin*, even when a National Library official witness protested that the English words *Voice of Taksin* were the legal name of the publication.[38] The judge's "translation" of the title had the effect of removing the ambiguity of the legal name and tightening the connection between Somyot and the deposed premier. For the chamber, Somyot the magazine editor became literally the "voice" of the former prime minister. Whereas Thai judges were normally meticulous about following legal conventions, in this case the judges spelled an important title using a nonlegal variant rather than the magazine's registered name; and this in a trial that hinged on the exact legal identity of the magazine and the defendant's relationship to that identity. This choice of magazine title told a story about the defendant which ran counter to his interests throughout the trial and continued to reflect badly on him during an appeal process that drew heavily on the same set of banthuek.

As with the Cambodia question, the defense did not try to tell a different story about Somyot's relationship with Thaksin. Royalist Thais—likely to include any judge asked to conduct a lèse-majesté trial—might tend to assume that a magazine entitled Siang Thaksin was personally backed and funded by Thaksin Shinawatra, and that Somyot was being paid by the self-exiled leader. In reality, despite representations to the contrary in conservative media, the redshirt movement was not a unified identity, wholly masterminded and funded by Thaksin personally.[39] Yet neither Somyot's consistently independent-minded stance towards the redshirt movement, nor his previous authorship of an anti-Thaksin book were issues raised during the trial.[40] Why not?

Somyot's lead lawyer Karom Polpornklang was a prominent redshirt attorney who had been nominated by the pro-Thaksin UDD movement; he had no interest in discussing divisions inside the redshirt network, even where they might have helped his client's case. Nor did the defense team seek to identify the "real" owners and financiers of the magazine. Just as the power structures of the monarchical network were an untouchable topic in the imaginations of the conservative establishment, so the power relations underpinning Thaksin's rival network were shrouded in mystery, and any attempt to elucidate them could be viewed as an act of disloyalty. Hence it was not possible for Somyot to counter charges of treasonous behavior towards the monarchy by locating his own position at the margins, rather than at the core, of the "enemy" redshirt network. To defend himself against accusations of treason would involve his engaging in a potentially treacherous disavowal of Thaksin. Thus Somyot was a remarkably isolated defendant, standing in a no-man's land between two power blocs, neither of which offered any succor. The only concession he obtained was the right to name Jakrapob as the author of the articles in question, and even then it was unclear whether he had been authorized to do so.

The initial article, "Bloodbath Plan" is a thinly disguised "fictional" story,[41] which outlines a plot to kill Thaksin either individually or as part of a mass killing, as supposedly conveyed to the writer by an insider.[42] According to the article, after an early attempt to assassinate Thaksin by placing a bomb on his plane failed, media magnate Sondi Limthongkul was deployed to attack Thaksin's reputation and prepare the public for his eventual murder.[43] Military and police officers along with professional hitmen were ordered to carry out the killing, but they repeatedly failed to accomplish their mission. Later an even more heinous plot was "sent down from the high rise of a hospital in the Rama IX neighborhood," this time in order to suppress the redshirt protests which had begun after the court seizure of 46 billion baht's ($1.4 billion) worth of Thaksin's assets. The plot involved assassinating the judges who had taken this decision one by one, blaming their deaths on Thaksin supporters—including maverick general Seh Daeng, who had stated that the judges might get killed—and using this excuse to crack down violently on the redshirts.[44] The article claims that the anti-redshirt plot resembled the intervention made by an "unidentified gigantic beast," the "invisible foot" at the time of the massacre of students and people on October 6, 1976.

The second article, which appeared two weeks later, revisits the period from 1958 to 1976.[45] It argues that figures such as Generals Prem Tinsulanond, Surayud Chulanont, and Prayut Chan-ocha were never the real enemy.[46] The real enemy "of democratic fighters like us" was "Luang Naruban" of the "Ghost Hotel," "the only vicious devil." The article goes on to discuss how "Luang Naruban" prepared the "6 October plan" in six stages: (1) creating a network of nationalists who adored the nation, religion and King, giving them funds, weapons, and moral support; (2) using the media to discredit his opponents; (3) stirring up the situation to create the conditions for violence; (4) hiding himself away; (5) preparing to install an interim government and prime minister; (6) and drafting a constitution containing the basis for dictatorial power. Thailand, the writer of the article claimed, was now once again at stage three: the conditions for a violent crackdown were being created.

The cover of the February 2010 issue containing the first article shows a thief in disguise—bearing more than a passing resemblance to General Prem Tinsulanond—carrying away a bag containing billions of baht. A giant claw, perhaps the invisible foot mentioned in the article, follows the figure as if to grab hold of the bag. On the foot are written "Army," "Judiciary," "Democrat Party," "Assets Examination Committee," "National Anticorruption Commission," and "Election Commission."[47] Taken together, the article and the accompanying illustration offered an alternative organogram, a diagram of the monarchical network that stood in opposition to that of Thaksin. While the CRES organogram maps those supposedly engaged in overthrowing the monarchy (lom jao), *Voice of Taksin* instead sketched the forces allegedly dedicated to overthrowing Thaksin.

In certain respects, the two articles proved prescient: a violent crackdown on the redshirt protesters did indeed take place in April and May 2010, involving more than ninety deaths. Most of those who died were unarmed civilians, shot by soldiers. Among the fatalities was rogue major general Seh Daeng, mentioned in the first installment, who was apparently assassinated by a military marksman. But Somyot's lèse-majesté charges focused mainly on the alleged links between the monarchy and acts of violence in October 1976. The decision to charge Somyot was taken at a meeting of the DSI's special litigation committee on May 3, 2010: at the height of the Bangkok redshirt protests, and exactly a week after Colonel Sansern had revealed to the public the network treason organogram, which included both Somyot's name and that of *Voice of Taksin* magazine, not to mention those of Thaksin and Jakrapob.

Although Somyot was involved in some redshirt activities, including a protest at Privy Council president Prem Tinsulanond's house in July 2007,[48] he was very much his own man, as Jaran Ditapichai wrote: "Somyot is extremely independent-minded, he has consistently opposed military dictatorship, has never praised Dr Thaksin, and does not much care for the leadership of the UDD."[49] Somyot helped build up the redshirt movement in the years that followed, and his 24 June group took part in the April–May 2010 protests throughout; but he never went on stage. He became managing editor of the short-lived *Voice of Taksin* magazine, which appeared twice a month from May 2009 to early 2010. In 2011 Somyot was arrested when about to enter Cambodia, leading a tour group.[50] He insisted that at the time he was unaware of the lèse-majesté charges against him:[51]

> Prior to my arrest, it was not at all known to me that an arrest warrant had been issued on a charge of defaming, insulting and threatening the King, the Queen, the Heir Apparent or the Regent as per Section 112 of the Penal Code. Thus, I had been conducting my life normally, living from hand to mouth, working from dawn to dusk and participating in social and political activities.
>
> I am a professional journalist and run a tour business. On April 30, 2011, I was supposed to lead a group of 30 Thai tourists to visit Angkor Wat in Cambodia. A trip has been organized every month. On that day, I just walked to the checkpoint to get my documents inspected as usual without the slightest intention to run away.[52]

But Somyot's arrest on the border allowed the authorities to claim he had been planning to flee the country and provided a perfect excuse for them repeatedly to refuse his bail requests.

The two articles at the heart of the case were both written by "Jit Pollachan," identified by Somyot during his testimony as the pen name of former minister Jakrapob Penkair. Jakrapob had served under Thaksin as government spokesman from 2003 to 2005, and in 2008 was appointed a prime minister's office minister by Samak Sundaravej. But after he was accused of lèse-majesté based on an earlier talk at the Foreign Correspondents' Club, Jakarapob was forced to step down from his government post, becoming a member of Red Siam, a radical splinter group of the redshirt movement. Jakrapob fled Thailand after the failed redshirt protests of April 2009, while Red Siam's leader Surachai Danwattananusorn was arrested on lèse-majesté charges in early 2011, and later sentenced to a total of twelve and a half years in jail.[53]

Although Jakrapob was living in Cambodia when *Voice of Taksin* published the two contentious articles, the prosecution did not ask Somyot when he last met Jakrapob, whether the two had ever met in Cambodia, or whether he they had planned to meet in April or May 2011.[54] Jakrapob was a man of mystery, whom no witness ever acknowledged having met. Benja Homwan, a junior employee at the magazine, testified that she had heard Jakrapob was the writer using this pen name,[55] but in her two or three months at the magazine had never talked to him.[56] Her testimony was nervous, and she answered some of the prosecutor's questions simply with a nod of the head.[57] The court refused permission for the defense to ask Benja more questions about Jakrapob, "because this was not related to the issues in the case"—an extraordinary assertion, given that Jakarapob was the author of the articles in question.[58] Throughout the trial, it was apparent that the treasonous actions imputed to Somyot were in fact treasonous actions committed by Jakrapob; and arguably that Jakrapob's acts of treason were perpetrated on behalf of another unreachable figure, Thaksin himself. Somyot, the designated "voice of Thaksin," was being charged with lèse-majesté as a replacement for the absent former leader. Somyot was the fall guy, the stand-in's stand-in. All three men had been named and linked in the lom jao diagram.

What was the strategy of the defense? The short answer is either that his legal team had no clear strategy, or that their strategy was to engage in politically motivated moves that would prove unhelpful to the defendant. Somyot was a victim, not simply of an absurd law and an unsympathetic justice system, but also of a stubborn and confrontational defense team who arguably worked against their client's interests. Clashes between the defense lawyers and the bench were a regular feature of the trial. The senior judge, who invariably prepared the banthuek herself rather than delegating note taking to her junior colleague, reprimanded the defense team on at least seven occasions, mainly for asking improper questions which did not directly address the issues in the case.[59] The most bizarre reprimand, however, occurred on April 25, 2012, when the judge told off

Suwit Thongnuan (Somyot's second lawyer) for drinking water in the courtroom without her permission. Suwit was suffering from a cold and had asked her for permission to drink water the previous week. This time the judge launched into a tirade of irritation, even recording a critique of his water drinking in the official *banthuek*. Suwit's water drinking seemed to symbolize the disrespectful atmosphere of the courtroom, full of noisy, laughing people who were using their phones and generally violating order. Perhaps it also symbolized the disobedient and disloyal conduct of the defendant himself:

> It is noted that at this point the defendant's lawyer raised a bottle of water and drank it in the courtroom without requesting permission. When the court warned the defense lawyer about this, the lawyer stated that he had asked permission to do this on a previous day, and asked what he had done wrong. The court informed the lawyer that this was a form of disorderly conduct, and the court therefore had to advise him on how to conduct himself, that one permission did not guarantee all future permissions, and that he needed to ask permission to drink water.[60]

The judge's outburst about the water episode reflected badly on the court: if a warning was really necessary, she could have called Suwit over to the bench and delivered it discreetly. Her actions instead spoke to a deep insecurity at the heart of the case against Somyot, illustrating the judge's stance as a guardian of the monarchy.

One witness in the case was shaking visibly while giving testimony, finding the line of defense questions about Thai history ("Was Pridi involved in the death of Rama VIII"?) very stressful. Librarians who had been called by the prosecution simply to establish that *Voice of Taksin* was a legally registered publication found themselves ensnared in the provocative games of Somyot's lawyers. There were occasional moments of light relief, when the dark core of the case was occluded by levity and even playfulness. Karom's exchanges with prominent conservative royalist Boworn were at times richly comic. Boworn conspicuously wore a pink shirt to court: Karom, who usually wore a red tie, pointed this out and asked Boworn what TV station he watched:

> All of them, Boworn replied, and you don't know that I'm wearing red underwear.[61]
>
> "How many members does your organization have?" "10,000 on Facebook." "What is the Thai for "Facebook?" asks the judge. "Facebook" replies Boworn.[62]

Only in the exchange with Boworn did Karom really meet his match; his provocative manner served to cow numerous other witnesses, and consistently to infuriate the judges. Cross-examining one of the National Library staff, Karom asked her if she had ever seen a picture of a King wai-ing the people and proceeded to show her a photograph of the King of Bhutan doing just that.[63] Such party tricks were Karom's attempts to push the political envelope, taking advantage of the fact that nobody can be charged with *lèse-majesté* for statements made during court proceedings. Karom's cheeky-chappy courtroom persona and determination to be the undisputed star of the trial overshadowed the compelling facts of Somyot's case and did nothing to ingratiate his client with the bench.

Although military witnesses insisted they still believed the articles at the core of the case were connected to the monarchy, they could offer no evidence or sources in support of their views. The first witness, Colonel Wijan, explained that CRES had set up a special legal team in March 2010, at the time of the redshirt protests, which he has overseen. They had worked closely with the NSC, NIA, ISOC, army, and other security agencies to identify those suspected of engaging in lèse-majesté. They looked at print media and websites, as well as monitoring speeches made at protests, especially by the protest leadership.[64] In the process of doing this, they came across some problematic articles in *Voice of Taksin* and sent them off to the DSI. Asked by the judge what form of analysis they used, he explained that they first looked into whether articles dealt with the royal institution, and then whether or not they constituted lèse-majesté. Wijan was the official complainant in the case, but said he had not been involved in the initial scrutiny of the magazines, which was done by a working group.[65]

Opening his cross-examination of Wijan, Karom gratuitously declared to the court that he might ask some aggressive questions, but he was someone who was personally loyal to the royal institution. When Karom pressed Wijan for his views on the political role of the monarchy, he declined to answer the question. Karom demanded to know whether he had an answer in mind, or simply did not wish to answer. Wijan asked him not to press the subject and requested that Karom confine himself to short, clear questions. Was Wijan involved in the "working group" that created the 2010 antimonarchy organogram? No, insisted Wijan. At times his exchanges with Karom were testy, and earned them both a reprimand from the judge. Cross-examining DSI official Thawiwat Surasit, Karom tried to establish how the Somyot case had been classified as "special": Thawiwat explained that there was a special committee of the CRES, at the time chaired by deputy prime minister Suthep Thaugsuban, which was concerned with investigating insults to the monarchy.[66] The *Voice of Taksin* articles had been reported to the committee by an army officer: it started as a military investigation before being taken up by DSI.

Highlights of the witness testimony included Suwit's examination of Thongth-ong Chandrangsu, then secretary-general to the prime minister and a noted expert on the monarchy, who stated the penalties for violating the *lèse-majesté* law were excessive and should in his view be no different from those in ordinary defamation cases (covered by Article 326 of the Criminal Code). Thongthong affirmed that the law tended to be used as a political tool.[67] Another important exchange took place between Nirun Pitakwatchara of the National Human Rights Commission and the junior prosecutor, who persistently tried to discredit Nirun by branding him a communist sympathizer based on his student activism in the 1970s—a theme straight out of the ASTV lom jao playbook.[68]

Somyot's own testimony should have been a centerpiece of the trial, but in the end was rather anticlimactic.[69] Asked about his career history, Somyot did not directly mention his earlier opposition to Thaksin, just saying he was critical of whoever was in power: he did not see himself as yellow or red, but worked to support rights and democracy. Karom opened his initial questioning with a discussion of the events surrounding the April–May 2010 violence, which took place after the publication of the contentious articles and was a topic unlikely to present Somyot in a positive light to the judges. Karom went on to ask Somyot what was meant by the phrase "the King is above politics," and asked who was responsible for the political disorder of recent years in Thailand. Somyot stated that the disorder had been produced by protesters appropriating royalist symbols—such as the color yellow—and slogans. Somyot went on to explain that the redshirts had been created to oppose the yellowshirts and their use of the royal institution as a political tool. Incidents such as royal attendance at the funeral of a PAD supporter had led to confusion: after all, the King made a speech stating that he himself could be criticized.[70] However, Somyot had never made any such criticisms himself. Karom's line of questioning bore no relationship to the facts of the case, and surely served only to fuel any suspicions the judges may have harbored about the defendant's political stance.

According to the old 1941 Printing Act, the publisher was legally responsible for the content of newspapers and magazines; but this provision was not included in the 2007 Printing Records Act,[71] which had replaced the 1941 legislation.[72] Somyot insisted that he had never been the legal editor of *Voice of Taksin*, which was founded in 2009 and clearly came under the 2007 Act. The original managing editor had been Suthachai Yimprasert, while the editor was Prasaeng Mongkolsiri. From the ninth issue onwards, Somyot was listed inside the magazine as the publisher; he was not the magazine's owner, but an employee who was paid 25,000 baht per month.

In subsequent responses, Somyot admitted that the two offending articles were by Jakrapob, who used the pen name Jit Pollachan. Somyot himself always published only under his real name. The articles in question were mostly about "the ammart, the Democrat Party, the military and the Privy Council," he asserted.[73]

Pressed on who had the authority to edit submissions from Jakrapob, he declared that he "didn't dare" edit them and claimed that he did not believe the articles in question were really about the King.

Asked by his lawyer if he loved the King, he responded "like normal Thai people"—not a terribly convincing answer.[74] Did the article arouse any misgivings in him about the monarchy? No, he insisted. Responding to Karom's questions, Somyot asserted that the penalties for *lèse-majesté* were too severe, that the law contradicted people's human rights under the constitution, and that a truth defense should be permitted in such cases. The judge dutifully recorded his claim that the law "had become a political tool."[75] The sound of Somyot digging his own grave was practically audible in the courtroom: he had nothing to gain from criticizing the law under which he was charged, and Karom should surely never have led his defendant down such a dangerous path. But at no point did Somyot articulate an explicit rebuttal of the lèse-majesté law. Haberkorn argues that Somyot's criticisms of Article 112 constituted "public crimes against authority," which helped to explain his conviction and punishment.[76]

The prosecutor then asked Somyot a series of awkward questions that he struggled to answer convincingly. Isn't it the case that on page 3 of both of the issues containing the offending articles, you are listed as the "managing editor"? You have spent your career as an NGO activist campaigning on human rights. Was it true, that you had expressed support for the abolition of the *lèse-majesté* law? You believe this law is a political tool? You were a political activist between 1973 and 1976?[77] Were you the one who wrote all the magazine's one-sided editorials? Do you know whether there was a warrant out for Jakrapob's arrest? Do you know whether Jakrapob is living in Cambodia? The prosecutor also called attention to a cover illustration about justice, on one issue of *Voice of Taksin*—what did it mean? Does it mean there is no justice?[78] Don't you have to be extremely careful when reporting about news relating to the monarchy? Were you en route to Cambodia when you were arrested? Apart from engaging in tourism, were you doing any other business there? Were the publications you were printing in Cambodia legally registered? Did you have the final decision on whether articles in the magazine were published? After tussling for a while with Somyot's evasions on this last issue—Somyot finally claimed that Jakrapob himself was the one who decided whether his own articles appeared—the prosecutor ended his questioning abruptly by saying "I can't take any more, this is a waste of time."[79]

Karom was characteristically unrestrained when following up on the prosecutor's questions about the justice-themed cover illustration. The cover referred to the "double standards" used in political court cases, according to which the PAD did not face prosecution for their actions whereas redshirt groups did, Somyot unwisely elaborated.[80] It was significant that the person who had filed the complaint in this case was not an ordinary reader, but a military officer. Why did people agree to write for the magazine despite not receiving any payment, Karom asked? Because they wanted to be famous, Somyot explained. This was a very odd note on which to end his testimony: Somyot had apparently never wanted to be famous, and his recent fame had come at a terrible price.

As a defense lawyer for Somyot, Karom was not terribly effective. He traveled constantly and spent very little time preparing Somyot's case: he was primarily a courtroom performer. While his amiable but bumbling partner Suwit Thong-nuan was an old friend of Somyot's, Karom had been brought in by the UDD redshirt organization: his primary loyalty was arguably to Thaksin, and Somyot's family rued the day they had agreed to Karom's appointment. The lawyers' main strategy was to petition the Constitutional Court to have the *lèse-majesté* law declared unconstitutional, on the grounds that the penalties were excessively harsh (one of the points Somyot stressed in his testimony).[81] Given that the Constitutional Court was dominated by conservative ex-judges and bureaucrats whose main concern was not to rock Thailand's political boat, the chances of success seemed to me extremely bleak. Oddly, however, the lawyers appeared wildly optimistic that their gambit would succeed, and that a favorable Constitutional Court decision would lead to the immediate release not just of Somyot, but of other *lèse-majesté* defendants.[82]

In the event, the Constitutional Court failed to uphold Somyot's complaint, declaring that "The penalty designated for offenders is needed to maintain peace and order and the good morality of the people, in accordance with the rule of law, which is the morality or ethics of the law."[83] Although the vagueness of this language was rightly criticized by international commentators, the phrase "peace and order and good morality" derived from the wording of Article 45 of the 2007 Constitution. While the only English version circulated was a two page summary, the full fifty-three-page ruling in Thai, containing individual judgments by each of the court's nine judges, was much more detailed, if little more convincing. Echoing themes mentioned by Judge Jaran Phakdithanakun, the intellectual colossus of the court, the introduction noted tendentiously that King Bhumibol's rule had been especially beneficial to the Thai people,[84] as seen in the way that he had laid out the invaluable principles of the royally inspired sufficiency economy.[85] The most important individual judgment was that of Jaran himself. He opened his arguments by asserting that the Thai monarchy had headed the country since the Sukhothai period,[86] and went on to argue:

> An offensive act, be it physical or verbal, against His Majesty in his capacity as Head of State, whom the people esteem, as an institution that they worship as the heart, soul and embodiment of the unity of the Thai

people, causes widespread and intense psychological and emotional distress to the Thai people. Such severe distress is regarded as a threat to both national security and to peace and order among the people. It is imperative that these acts be prevented and suppressed in earnest. Thus although Article 112 of the Criminal Code is a law that limits freedom of expression to some degree, it is in accordance with the conditions and scope set forth by the Constitution's Paragraph 2 of Article 45, along with Article 29, regarding the enactment of laws to maintain the security of the state.[87]

The hostile Constitutional Court judgment meant that the sharpest arrow in the quiver of Somyot's defense team had missed its target. Following Jaran's lead, the court based its rejection of the petition on Article 112's national security functions, and glossed over whether long custodial sentences were proportionate for what amounted to crimes of defamation. Given the prevailing political context—in which the Yingluck government was in no position to push the envelope on Article 112—the decision was entirely predictable. Karom's petition to the Constitutional Court was a political move, rather than a serious attempt to fight Somyot's case.

Having apparently lost interest at this point, the two lawyers then failed to draft a closing statement for the defense; in the end Somyot wrote most of the closing statement himself, though Suwit added a few lines about how the case was essentially political, which were probably not well received by the judges. The closing statement was only submitted on December 28, 2012, a few days before the verdict was announced.[88] In a personal statement to the court that was never actually submitted, Somyot argued that his was a political case that arose from the intense social conflict following the September 2006 military coup.[89] Somyot declined, however, to present himself convincingly as a "good person," or to say anything positive about the monarchy. Whether or not they were technically guilty (and Somyot surely was not) most lèse-majesté defendants, like many of those listed on the network treason diagram, were not nice, normal people who had accidentally become embroiled in controversy. They were professional members of Thailand's awkward squad, given to provocative and even incendiary statements.

In the end, Somyot's case was decided not by the two female judges who had heard the trial testimony, but by a new pair of male judges who apparently relied solely on the official documents and the banthuek. The judgment by the lower court contained none of the curiously irrelevant references to the Sukhothai period or sufficiency economy theory that characterized the Constitutional Court judgment on the 112 law: instead, the judges stuck closely to the witness statements and the facts of the case. Nevertheless, their discussion of the witness testimony was strikingly disproportionate. While fourteen different prosecution witnesses were named and their testimony was summarized in some detail, each of six defense witnesses was mentioned by name only once, in a single three-line paragraph on page seven, which said they all "testified along the same lines" concerning the interpretation of the offending articles. Thus the testimonies of Somyot's star witnesses, a member of the National Human Rights Commission (Nirun) and prominent academics from Chulalongkorn and Thammasat universities (Suthachai and Piyabutr), were blended into a summary which merged their statements with those of two other witnesses, including that of a mechanic (Sanong). The prosecution had used an approach typical in such cases, trying to overwhelm the judges with a parade of hostile witnesses, mainly government officials. The defense had planned to call a wider range of nonmaterial witnesses, including sympathetic journalists and academics, but finally decided to drop some of these for fear they would not prove helpful to the outcome of the case. Prior to the main Bangkok hearings, provincial hearings had also been held all around Thailand—in Sa Kaeo, Petchabun, Nakhon Sawan, and Songkhla—but only a single provincial witness (one from Petchabun) was mentioned in the judgment. Forcing Somyot and his lawyers to traipse around the provinces amounted to a form of legal harassment.

Witness testimony left no serious doubt, argued the judges, that the articles in question did refer to the King and constituted a violation of Article 112. The judges did not concern themselves greatly with the technical questions of whether Somyot was the legal editor or publisher of *Voice of Taksin*: he was not being charged under either the 2007 or 1941 printing acts.[90] Instead, they focused on whether or not Somyot made final editorial decisions concerning the magazine's content. His claims to be a mere employee were contradicted by prosecution witnesses and lacked weight.[91] The argument that the articles had been submitted very late and the defendant had insufficient time to check them was not convincing, especially since articles along the same lines appeared in two consecutive issues.[92] Nor was it credible that Somyot did not realize the articles referred to the King. Concluding on the basis of witness testimony that Somyot determined what was published, the court decided to convict him:

> The articles defamed, insulted and threatened the King, and were wholly untrue, but the defendant still went ahead and chose to publish them, having them printed, distributed and widely disseminated. These actions by the defendant were those of someone who intended to defame, insult and threaten the King, under the provisions of Article 112 of the Criminal Code.[93]

The judges stated that Somyot's degree in political science and his long experience as an NGO activist and journalist meant that he should have been well aware of the need to be extremely careful about publishing such articles; his credentials counted against him, rather than for him. Neither the antimonarchy diagram nor the wider political context of the prosecution was mentioned anywhere in the judgment.

As Ferguson notes, the verdict is a central dramatic juncture in every American trial:

> Here defendants receive the right to speak within beyond the forms of the law. It is the final liminal moment for all concerned. . . . Asked at this point why sentence should not be imposed upon them, they enter a different realm of presumed candor and conscience without intermediaries and unimpeded by the intrusion of counsel.[94]

But in a Thai courtroom, there is no opportunity for such candor, let alone the potential for liminality. In the Thai verdict ritual, the defendant has no right to speak. The judge who reads aloud the verdict is often not the judge who presided at the original trial, and this was the case for Somyot. Decisions of the Court of Appeal or the Supreme Court are read not in the buildings where they originated, but back in the Court of First Instance: the judge—who is usually there primarily to try a different case—simply slits open an official envelope and reads aloud the contents. Any defendant who has been on bail prior to this point is immediately handcuffed when a custodial sentence is announced; the discreet arrival of a court security official at the back of the chamber signals what is to come. Rarely is there any sense of a circle being closed, or a resolution being achieved. A defendant who does not understand the verdict may ask a lawyer to seek clarification. Somyot's guilty verdict was announced to a packed room on January 23, 2013: he was sentenced to ten years in jail (he was also serving one year for another offence).

Somyot subsequently appointed a new lawyer, Vasant Panich, to handle his appeal. A former national human rights commissioner, Vasant was viewed with suspicion by many on the pro-Thaksin side for his "yellow" political sympathies. Karom resigned his own brief in disgust. Vasant took the appeal process extremely seriously, preparing a seventy-six-page submission full of meticulous technical arguments.[95] Unfortunately Vasant's submission, for the most part exhaustively rehearsing arguments previously discounted by the judges, again fell on deaf ears: in September 2014, Somyot was suddenly ordered back to court to hear that his appeal had been rejected. Neither the defendant nor his lawyer Vasant had even been informed that the judgment would be announced on that day—perhaps as a deliberate ploy to prevent hundreds of people from attending the judgment, as they had on the date of his original sentencing. The appeal judges did a much more thorough job than the lower court judges, locating the case within the context of Thailand's political conflict and paying proper attention to the testimony of individual defense witnesses, but their conclusions were essentially the same.[96]

In the end, Somyot was convicted on the basis of his allegedly criminal intentions. At best, he was a person who felt so comfortable with antimonarchical sentiments that he failed to spot them in Jakrapob's articles; at worst, he was actively conspiring with those seeking to bring down the monarchy, or lom jao. During his trial Somyot had unwisely criticized both the justice system and the lèse-majesté law itself. His lawyers had tried to humiliate prosecution witnesses and to provoke the bench at every opportunity. Somyot had made no attempt to ingratiate himself to the judges, offering no signs of deference towards the royal authority they doubtless believed they personified. While a more respectful approach and more convincing explanatory narrative by Somyot and his lawyers would probably not have secured an acquittal, they might have helped him gain a lighter sentence.

In February 2017, the Supreme Court reduced Somyot's jail term from ten years to six years.[97] He was finally released on April 30, 2018. The court reduced the sentences for each of his two charges from five years to three years, based on Somyot's age, the length of time he had already served, and the fact that he did not write the offending articles himself. The last of these three considerations should have formed the basis of a shorter sentence from the outset. In an analysis of the Supreme Court judgment, Thammasat law lecturer Sawatree Suksri argued that unless criminal intention could be demonstrated (as specified under Article 59 of the Criminal Code), Somyot was simply not guilty of lèse-majesté, since he was not the author of the articles in question.[98] The Supreme Court had dismissed the relevance of whether an editor could be held responsible for a publication's content, but proceed to convict Somyot precisely on the basis of his editorial role: the final judgment was highly inconsistent.

The important issues at stake in the Somyot case were often obscured, understandably, by intense emotions on both sides. When I talked to a prosecutor familiar with the case, his eyes welled up with tears at the thought of such insults to the King. Another explained to me that:

> If you can't accept it then it is not hard at all. You don't have to stay in Thailand and you can find somewhere else to stay . . . in Asian and Thai society, we uphold loyalty and treat it with the utmost importance. . . . As for those who really do it [defame the monarchy] intentionally, I'd say they are mentally and spiritually dysfunctional.[99]

He went on to explain that non-Thais would struggle to understand just how unacceptable these kind of critical statements about the monarchy really are. The prosecutor was concerned that when people heard about these lèse-majesté cases, they would get angry: frequent cases could lead to social disharmony, instability, and discord.

Prior to 2010, Thailand had contained certain zones of liminality, places were dissident thoughts could be expressed indirectly, but relatively freely. These zones included anonymous political columns and "independent" magazines, where almost anything could be written, so long as real names were not named. The arrest and trial of Somyot represented part of a larger attempt to crack down on thought crimes and on such maverick, even subversive "compassings." In theory, Somyot's trial might have been an opportunity to restore liminality, and achieve a moment of transcendence, outside the normal parameters of legal proceedings. Ideally, such a liminal moment might help to mute disagreements and achieve a degree of consensus on how to move forward. Episodes of levity and playfulness, as in the witty exchanges between Karom and Boworn, offered the possibility that the abyss awaiting those accused of thought crimes could be avoided. But ultimately the bitterness of the highly polarized courtroom exchanges and the harshness of Somyot's sentence precluded any such possibility: in short, his trial made matters worse, compounding the terrible darkness of the Daranee and Akong cases that preceded it. Karom's self-presentation during the trial—as an aggressive questioner who was never personally disloyal to the monarchy—failed to resonate with the bench. Similarly, there was no convincing story about Somyot that located him as an activist journalist who might have associated with those harboring treasonous thoughts, but who always believed he was acting in the national interest. For those who sat in judgment at the Court of First Instance, the Appeal Court, and the Supreme Court, Somyot's proximity to the words of Jakrapob was apparently enough: guilt by association.

In his criticisms of the 112 law, Somyot was certainly bold and outspoken, but not so bold as directly to confront the full apparatus of the Thai judicial system.[100] One foreign journalist argued that the unwillingness of lèse-majesté defendants to challenge the legitimacy of the law itself made it difficult for the international media to write compelling copy about their cases.[101]

The Somyot case abundantly illustrated the willingness of the Thai courts to punish a defendant harshly for his part in publishing articles that he had not himself written—a textbook case of guilt by association. While the two magazine articles at the core of the trial were undoubtedly highly offensive to royalists, they were not Somyot's own handiwork: everyone involved in the trial accepted that they had been authored by Jakrapob Penkair, a Thaksin loyalist and former minister living in exile in Cambodia. As the Supreme Court finally acknowledged, the ten-year jail term dished out to Somyot by the lower courts was excessive. Somyot's trial illustrated a collective judicial failure of empathy and imagination. Lèse-majesté was a symbolic crime, and one that King Bhumibol himself had directly criticized in his 2005 birthday speech. Given their professed dedication to acting on behalf of the King, judges could simply have dismissed 112 cases such as Somyot's, or handed down token punishments. Instead, they passed up the opportunity to exercise legal and moral leadership on a question of immense national importance.

FIGURE 2. Defendant bows before judges during a mock trial, 2012.

FIGURE 3. Commemoration of Prince Raphi Day, honoring the "founding father" of Thai justice.

FIGURE 4. The old Supreme Court Building adjacent to Sanam Luang, Bangkok.

FIGURE 5. A poster depicting four prominent figures in the anti-112 campaign (clockwise): Thammasat University law professor Worajet Pakeerat, defendants Somyot Prueksakasemsuk and Surachai Danwattananusorn, and Thammasat University historian Somsak Jeamteerasakul.

FIGURE 6. Anti-Nitirat demonstration in front of the Pridi Banomyong statue, Thammasat University, February 12, 2012.

FIGURE 7. Display of materials for campaign to reform the lèse-majesté law, 2012.

FIGURE 8. Political prisoner at Laksi special jail, 2012.

FIGURE 9. Posters of Pridi Banomyong and Thaksin Shinawatra at redshirt rally to celebrate eighty years of Thai democracy, 2012.

FIGURE 10. Redshirts celebrating the eightieth anniversary of the end of the absolute monarchy, 2012.

ศาลรัฐธรรมนูญ

THE CONSTITUTIONAL COURT OF THE KINGDOM OF THAILAND

FIGURE 11. Poster depicting the Constitutional Court of Thailand.

FIGURE 12. Democrat MP and petitioner Wirat Kalayasiri outside Constitutional Court, July 2012.

FIGURE 13. New Supreme Court building under construction, 2018.

COMPUTER COMPASSINGS

Not everyone accused of trying to bring down the monarchy—lom jao—ended up charged with lèse-majesté. This chapter examines another case brought under a different law that illustrates similar issues to the Somyot case. The national security provisions of the 2007 Computer Crime Act offer an alternative means of prosecuting the allegedly disloyal, another notch along the treason spectrum. An illustrative example is the case of former broker Katha Pajariyapong, who was accused of making two web-board postings critical of royalty on the web board of Fa Diao Kan, a critical journal that featured on the April 2010 antimonarchy organogram. The Katha case frequently resembled a theater of the absurd: laughable charges, inept lawyers who wanted to quit, bungling prosecution witnesses, and a presiding judge who claimed to be on the side of the defendant before sending him to jail. Yet the consequences of these farcical proceedings were very real: Katha ultimately served a couple of years behind bars for a meaningless "crime" that brought the law into disrepute. The chapter argues that judges again allowed their misguided understandings concerning how to show loyalty to the monarchy to take precedence over common sense. Katha's alleged actions had no effect on the country's national security, and no criminal intent was demonstrated during the trial.

In the Katha case, a purported computer crime involved lèse-majesté content; while the testimony was full of technical details, the case hinged on rumors about the King's health. Katha's case, also linked to the April 2010 network treason diagram, illustrated some of the structural contradictions of late Bhumibol Thailand. Again, it revealed a clash of cultures between the royalist, conservative dispositions of the judges, and the critical perspectives of the defendants and their lawyers.

Stock trader Katha Pachachirayapong was accused of having posted messages online that caused panic among the public and compromised national security. In his case, the panic—leading to a fall in the Bangkok stock exchange—was related to rumors that the King was in poor health.[1] In fact, the King's health woes were well known, since the monarch had spent several weeks staying at Siriraj Hospital. But the message in question suggested that he was close to death, and causing public panic was an offence under the 2007 Computer Crimes Act, Article 14 (2). The messages were alleged posted by Katha on the web board of *Fa Diao Kan* [Same Sky] a progressive bimonthly journal well known for critical discussions about the military, the monarchy, and modern political history. Later listed on the 2010 lom jao organogram, *Fao Diao Kan* was not much read by those working in the financial sector. The stock market dive was widely linked to a report from Bloomberg;[2] but although Theeranan Wiphuchanin, a former stockbroker with UBS who had translated the Bloomberg report into Thai for *Prachatai,* was also initially charged,[3] her case was later dropped.[4] At first, Katha appeared on a bizarre list of five alleged conspirators, along with Theeranan, a Chonburi snooker parlor owner, a medical doctor, and a Buddhist monk; but none of the others was ever put on trial. While the reasons for this were unclear, in comparison with the other alleged conspirators Katha conspicuously lacked wealth or connections. According to Katha, during the initial investigation he was accused of conspiring with these others to spread rumors, drive down share prices, and destabilize the country, a conspiracy that the authorities alleged had been orchestrated and funded by former premier Thaksin Shinawatra.[5] Such claims were made publicly on November 4 by then ICT minister Ranongrak Suwanchawee, who asserted that certain unnamed websites were hosting content "subversive to national security." Whereas Theeranan had apparently submitted just one message, according to Ranongrak, Katha had posted "inauspicious" messages on different websites and forwarded them to fellow traders.[6] In many legal systems, public statements by government ministers assigning guilt to named individuals would be considered prejudicial to a fair trial, but not in Thailand.

Originally the Department of Special Investigation (DSI) had planned to charge the suspects under finance-related legislation, but eventually Katha was left as the sole remaining defendant and was accused of violating the 2007 Computer Crime Act. Katha was then charged over two very short postings, one dating from the October 2009 stock market dip, and another unrelated April 2009 message, implying that Princess Sirindhorn was biased in favor of the yellowshirts. Just as the *Voice of Taksin* articles belonged to a certain genre of anonymous satirical political journalism, so Katha's messages belonged to the genre of the anonymous message, or *bai pliew*.[7] In earlier decades, anonymous defamatory messages were distributed in flyers around Bangkok's Sanam Luang, the royal field adjoining the Grand Palace, Thammasat University, and the Supreme Court. By the 1990s, they were pouring out of office fax machines; and by 2009 they took the form of anonymous electronic postings on web boards. In the past, such messages belonged to a murky nether realm of shadowy communiqués, largely ignored by the authorities. The 2007 Computer Crime Act made it possible to prosecute such message posters: the irony was that by doing so, the law gave a specious weight to otherwise ephemeral words. The inconsequential became a matter of grave consequence. Katha's case was not filed until mid-2011, and did not come to trial until June 2012.

Much of the testimony in his trial was of a technical nature: Was Katha really the person, using the ludicrous avatar "Wet Dream," who had posted the messages on the *Fa Diao Kan* bulletin board? A great deal of trial time was taken up examining whether the Ministry of Information and Communication Technology (ICT) had effectively demonstrated that Katha was responsible for the messages. Both the ICT Ministry and the DSI made a complete hash of the investigation, failing convincingly to link the messages with the defendant's computers. The testimony of Aree Jivorarak, the senior ICT Ministry official who took the lead on the case, was barely coherent. Through various lacunae in prosecution witness testimony, it became apparent that the investigators had illegally hacked into Katha's email account, something they were unable to admit. Katha was privately indignant about Aree's testimony, believing that he had repeatedly lied under oath: that the court eventually chose to believe these lies caused him to lose faith in Thai justice.[8]

On one level, Katha's trial was a de facto lèse-majesté trial: his "real" crime was making derogatory references to members of the royal family. Fortunately for Katha, he was not charged under Article 112, but under legislation that carried a much lighter sentence: unlike most lèse-majesté defendants, he was bailed out between his initial arrest in November 2009, and the day he lost his appeal in March 2014. As with lèse-majesté cases, questions of intention and character were always implicit: was Katha essentially a good person, or were his allegedly panic-provoking messages based on negative sentiments he harbored towards the monarchy?

The lead judge in the Katha case invariably paid respects to the photograph of the King behind the bench on entering the courtroom, something I did not observe in other criminal trials.[9] A strict disciplinarian, the judge forbade those attending the trial from making any written notes, saying that this was an important trial and problems would result if any incorrect records came out.[10] As Srimati Basu—who admits to "taking furtive notes when possible" during her trial observations in Kolkata—observes, "Courts are notoriously difficult to represent," while "Legal personages are lofty and stern, enforcers of discipline."[11] The Katha judges also banned observers from reading: one woman attending the proceedings muttered loudly, "Are we allowed to breathe?" But despite their draconian note-taking ban, the judges were relatively open towards the defense; most importantly, they carefully recorded all important points in the testimony.[12] A small group of regular observers attended the trial, mainly female and obviously redshirt supporters. The lead judge referred openly to them as Katha's "fanclub." On another occasion the same judge spoke to me directly, asking me if I could understand Thai.

The presiding judge shared the case with a junior colleague, whom he kept consulting on even the most basic technical questions. On July 6, a senior judge showed up to join the two regular judges on the bench. The senior judge liked waving his pencil at people, cutting off the defense lawyers, complaining to them about their questions and finding fault with the way they behaved. He said nothing at all when the prosecutor was speaking, instead playing *Angry Birds* on his iPad and sometimes even answering his phone, at one point turning his chair around to take a call without leaving the chamber. But the senior judge did ask numerous questions of witnesses, complaining that they had not explained themselves clearly enough. His presence seemed to dampen the ardor of the defense lawyers: Thiraphon Khumsap (hereafter, Art), the junior lawyer conducting his very first court case, was quite thrown off his stride by the judge's caustic interventions. A couple of times he paced around the courtroom in apparent stupefaction.[13] Matters improved after Art confessed his inexperience to the senior judge, who gave him some advice on how to examine witnesses.[14]

The opening day of the trial was something of a debacle: Katha had wanted to change his original lawyer, the provocative Anon Numpa, for the more senior Akom Ratanapojanart. However, Katha's request was disallowed by the judge, who insisted that Anon continue pleading the case. From day one, Katha's lawyer was someone he had tried to fire, with whom he had little rapport, and who strongly disagreed with him about how to fight the case. Anon wanted Katha to admit posting the messages and to argue that he had done nothing wrong: but Katha, who had acknowledged his guilt during the investigation process, now insisted that he was innocent. Anon had been a lawyer for a number of prominent defendants facing lèse-majesté or computer crime charges, including Akong and *Prachatai* editor Chiranuch Premchaiporn.[15] Chiranuch, the editor of Thailand's best-known alternative news website, received a suspended jail sentence in 2012 after failing to take down critical comments relating to the monarchy quickly enough. A young firebrand with a growing reputation as a wonderful poet, Anon was completely fearless and was always willing to accept, usually pro bono, troublesome cases that more senior (and more sensible) lawyers had turned down. At the same time, Anon had a short attention span and was not known for extensive case preparation: he relied on his quick wits and verbal facility to get him through difficult trials.[16] Following the 2014 military coup, Anon took part in some high-profile antigovernment protests and soon became a defendant himself. As of 2019, he had not won a single major trial, partly because he took on such challenging cases, and partly because his manner and approach often seemed calculated to irritate the bench.

Anon epitomized the "let's-annoy-the-hell-out-of-the-judges" approach to defending politically sensitive legal cases. He explained that his role models were Saengchai Rattanaseriwong and Ratsada Manuratsada, senior human rights lawyers with rather different political orientations, but quite similar courtroom styles.[17] At one point, after asking an important witness to give short answers so that they could finish early, Anon kept the same witness on the stand until 6.35 p.m., taunting him with questions that were both baffling and exasperating: "Is the King a member of the board of the Stock Exchange of Thailand?" "Did you ever submit a formal letter to the palace authorities requesting clarification concerning the King's health?"[18] When I spoke to a senior trial official the next day in the elevator, he told me he found Anon's questions very odd: they were probably undermining the defense case. Anon himself was unable to offer a logical explanation for the stock exchange question.[19]

Katha's legal team was very concerned to demonstrate that the messages at the core of the case were justified, on the basis that they were factually correct. This was the terrain on which Anon wanted to fight the case, but it was an uphill struggle: one of the messages crudely stated that the King was blind, seriously ill, and on the verge of death. Anon asked numerous questions of police officers and other prosecution witnesses in an attempt to validate these three "facts," though none was in any way qualified to answer. At times Anon seemed to be parodying the court proceedings, countering the ludicrous charges against Katha with even more absurd cross-examinations. While the trial may not have attained liminality, it frequently bordered on farce. At one point the senior judge reprimanded Anon for his line of questioning, telling him not to try using prosecution witnesses to elucidate issues such as the King's purported blindness:[20] the reference to blindness was itself "inappropriate,"[21] not an issue that could be proved true or false.[22] This was a highly telling statement: Katha's real crime was not panicking the stock market, but making inappropriate comments about the monarchy. At one point the judge asked Anon whether he could present any evidence that the King was blind—if not, he should not have raised this point:

> The judge then asked the defense lawyer to come close to the bench and explained that it should suffice it for the defendant to defend that he had

not committed the offence. It was too difficult to debate the meaning of the phrases since it would be very difficult to obtain any supporting evidence. An emphasis should be placed on some other issues. . . . But whether the King was blind or not was not the essential point of the case since the term sounds impolite. And it did not convey any meaning.[23]

The judge made clear that a truth defense—for example, that the message could not have caused panic, because people already knew that the King was seriously ill—would be inadmissible. But Anon was arguably less interested in making such a defense, than in exploiting the immunity afforded him by the Katha case to raise awkward questions about the human frailty of the monarch. By emphasizing the inappropriate and impolite content of the original message, Anon was repeating and indeed compounding his client's alleged offence.

Katha's position was complicated by the fact that his lead lawyer Anon was intent on treating the trial as a lèse-majesté case. Law lecturer and Nitirat member Sawatree Suksiri described an exchange she had with Anon about the case:[24]

> SAWATREE: Did you not have a chance to look at the case files? The case isn't related to 112.
> ANON: I know it's not about 112 but I have to talk about it in case the judge interprets it that way.[25]
> SAWATREE: You don't have to do it just in case. It's not an issue and you shouldn't bring it up.

Since 112 cases were notoriously hard to win, Katha's lawyers had no incentive to emphasize the lèse-majesté aspects of the charges he faced. Sawatree believed Katha's case failed to meet the criteria for prosecution under Article 14 of the Computer Crime Act, which concerns those who spread false information that may adversely affect national security: Katha's charge sheet referred simply to the spreading of a rumor—something very different from a demonstrated intention to undermine national security. She argued that the case should have been fought primarily on the basis of Katha's lack of criminal intent.

In response to Anon's bizarre line of cross-examination, the prosecutor began asking some very odd questions of his own: "You said the King has been in hospital, but didn't he just come out and go to the fields in Ayutthaya? What was he wearing, not a patient's outfit?"[26] It was hard to see how the King's state of health in mid-2012 had a material bearing on his alleged condition in October 2009; the prosecutor wanted to point out that the King was still alive and somewhat well, almost three years after the health rumors had surfaced. Unlike Anon, the prosecutor was not reprimanded by the judges for inappropriate questioning.

Katha himself testified on June 8, 2012. Here are my field notes:

> The lawyers look like they have been up half the night preparing, rolling in at the last possible moment. Luckily, Katha's testimony is delayed because someone is being sentenced to 12 years for murder: he stabbed a guy ten times in a drunken fight. He claims the other guy hit him repeatedly with a stick, but witnesses insist he was not sober enough to have done that. The defendant is small, and unprepossessing. Nobody except the officials and those attending for Katha's case (and one other case) is present to see him sentenced. Here is a brief reminder that real crime exists—it's not all about defamation and the posting of inappropriate messages. At least 6 people are following the Katha case every day, including me, but nobody has been killed or even injured; the virtual seems more important than the actual.
>
> Katha is called to the witness stand. He was very nervous beforehand, and I smiled to try and calm him. He seems to be in a world of his own, and with one apparent exception, those attending the trial are not his friends or family, but people who follow such cases routinely, and would probably be here whoever he was.
>
> He does not do a particularly good job of giving his testimony. His main emphasis is on how confused he was when arrested and how he signed the confessions to ensure he was bailed out, not because he was admitting the crime. He lost his job at the securities company after the incident, with no reason given. He is 38, and now runs a small newspaper distribution business. The defense does not ask him about his political views or feelings about the king—a mistake, I feel, but Anon does not seem to see the point. He also argues that the internet traffic reports supposedly showing him online when the comments were posted are incorrect—they were supplied by Microsoft using Pacific time in the USA, not the time in Thailand, and this has not been taken into account. This seems to be something he worked out himself, not noticed by the lawyers.
>
> The prosecutor goes through the documents, making exactly the points they told him last night would come up: this is your signature on all the documents, isn't it? Nothing has been faked? You have a BA degree, so you know how to read and write very well? The prosecutor also makes a big show of satirizing his "analysis" of an article from the *Fa Diao Kan* website which seems to be about the Crown Property Bureau—seems not to have helped him understand the real state of the King's health, which the Royal Household Office said was not too seri-

ous. He can be quite mean when he feels like it, but none of it really added up to much in terms of the core of the case, proving that Katha was the one who posted the messages. A couple of times the judge tells the prosecutor off for asking hypothetical questions beginning with "Supposing . . ."

More interesting than the testimony itself was what the judge said afterwards in response to the request for a postponement of the defense witness testimony. He complained that the lawyers had not handled the request properly—at one point waving a thick yellow book of court procedures and citing chapter and verse from it. He addressed some comments directly to me, saying that foreigners should understand he was giving the defense every opportunity, but there was a real problem—where were their witnesses? What had happened to the Navy guy who comes every day, but the day he needs to be called as a witness fails to show up, saying he has a meeting? What meeting could be more important than testifying in court? He should have rearranged it. The fan club (referring to the women redshirt activists who come every day) know what he means. Given how disorganized the defense has been, he can't grant them permission to call four more witnesses. This has to be considered as a concession to the defense, not giving them all they ask for.

The judge queries the inclusion on the list of proposed witnesses of Ajarn Sawatree Suksri, one of the Nitirat law lecturers.[27] What will she provide? Opinions are of little importance to the case.[28] Actually, the defense witnesses will not help the case much anyway, they are less significant than you might think. If you are a real man, just concentrate on getting the truth out.[29] The substance has already been covered. Honestly, of what value are opinions if they are biased towards one side? The problem is there are no neutral people in this society, very hard to find. What matters is the truth or otherwise of the allegations. The only witnesses worth hearing from would be those who could offer real insights into the technical issues or the facts of the King's health.[30]

The judge also remarks that he himself is now leaning towards the redshirt side—people protest, and he says he means the *Fa Diao Kan* side. It is hard to know how to take this. In the end he allows the defense three more witnesses on July 2. Sawatree will be permitted to submit a written statement as evidence without being called.

The atmosphere in court is very good today—the senior judge is absent, thank God—and everyone seems relieved. Afterwards one prosecutor tells another observer and myself that he is just doing his job, he thought Aree was a terrible witness and wondered how Aree could sign his name as part of the case. He does not like this law but so long as it is still on the books he has to perform his duty by prosecuting these cases to the best of his ability. The prosecutor says his own personal sympathies are close to those of Ajarn Sawatree—in other words, with Nitirat![31]

Following Katha's testimony, both the judge and the prosecutor declared that they were really on the side of the defendant, despite all appearances to the contrary. The judge invoked my own presence in the courtroom in support of his claims: even foreigners (I was the only one who had attended) could see that he was bending over backwards to accommodate the defense. It was hard to interpret these statements, other than as attempts by the judge and the prosecutor to ease their consciences during a travesty of a case: two absurd messages, a procession of laughably inept official witnesses, and a defense team intend on exposing the proceedings to maximum ridicule. The absurdity came to a head once Katha had his day in court: here was a likeable, diffident, and ineffectual young man, impossible to see as an enemy of the state.

Because of the last minute refusal of the judge to allow a new legal team, Katha's lawyers had struggled to fight his case. Art admitted that they were only "1 percent" prepared, compared with their work on Chiranuch's Prachatai web board case the previous year. Kob, a senior lawyer, explained that the outcome was likely to hinge on the credibility of the defendant.[32] Judges were typically driven by a couple of guiding principles: you would not end up in court if you had done nothing wrong, and state officials are unbiased people whose testimony should in principle be believed.[33] Kob's argument was perfectly illustrated in the judgment for Katha's case, which contained an interesting passage reflecting the typical view taken by Thai courts of testimony by officials:

> and when it is considered that all of the prosecution witnesses were state employees performing their officially designated duties, without any suggestion that they held any anger or vexation which would make them malign the defendant, so causing him to be unduly punished and thus risk being accused of abusing their power, this gave the collective testimony of the prosecution witnesses both weight and credibility.[34]

Kob recounted one case in which a dignified defendant had been acquitted because the prosecution witnesses were deemed "not credible."[35] At a case conference the night before Katha testified, Lawyer Art had repeatedly raised the question of why the defendant was not charged until after the 2010 redshirt protests.[36] He saw the case as part of a crackdown on dissent, along the lines of the network treason diagram plot. But Kob kept asking Art how raising this issue would help undermine the strength of the prosecution case: it did not address the nub of the trial, which hinged on whether the defendant had sent the messages or not.[37] Katha had confessed on three separate occasions during the investigation, only to deny the charges once he faced trial, and this created a serious problem for his lawyers. Kob argued for casting maximum doubt on the quality of the investigation and especially the interrogation process, stressing that Katha had been extremely anxious and had signed confessions under duress, out of an overwhelming desire to go home. The exchanges between Art and Kob during the case conference mirrored the tensions in the Somyot trial: redshirt-aligned lawyers were so eager to present defendants as the victims of a political witch hunt that they failed to press for an acquittal on the legal facts of the case. Given Katha's mild and naïve demeanor, presenting him as the victim of mistaken identity should have been a more fruitful line of defense than linking him to a larger political game.

Why did the defense team not ask Katha his views on the monarchy: in short, did he love the King? When I asked him this question the night before his testimony, Katha responded quite convincingly that he did love the King. Art explained that Anon had tried this in other cases. Thantawut Taweewarodomkul had declared "I love and respect the King like everyone else,"[38] while Akong had responded "I love him from the bottom of my heart," but in neither case was this approach effective.[39] Art argued that even if professing love for the King might achieve a positive outcome for the defendant, if you were an activist you should stick to your principles and discuss constitutional matters without asking whether your client loves the King or not. The self-administered loyalty oath strategy was unlikely to work with activists (such as Somyot) but might be helpful for ordinary defendants such as Akong or Katha. Such matters could always be left to the prosecution to bring up, Art argued, and Katha was indeed asked about his loyalty by the prosecution.[40] But the prosecutor asked this question not to present Katha in a positive light, but in order to show that as a loyal Thai, he should have been familiar with the real state of the King's health. A hostile loyalty question from a prosecutor had an entirely different import than a friendly invitation by a defense lawyer. In other words, the lawyers' reluctance to have Katha make declarations of loyalty, though it could be justified by reference to previous verdicts, was essentially an ideological position. Anon and Art were undertaking to defend Katha for ideological reasons, and not primarily in order to secure the most favorable outcome.

Asked why he took on cases like Akong or Katha's, Anon explained that they aligned with his politics and his desire to open up more space for free expression, and that he did not find them difficult or scary.[41] Since such cases were notoriously difficult, his statement smacked of hubris: did he lack the ability or experience to imagine what might be necessary to win them? Anon believed that all people were equal and had the right to insult one another. Having said the cases were not difficult, he promptly went on to argue that it was also "cool" to do something difficult.[42] Not entirely flippantly, Anon also claimed that he took on well-known cases to boost his chances of dating women. Asked whether it was effective to bring up the issue of the monarchy to very conservative judges, he argued that the lawyers had to do 100 percent from their side: the rest was a matter of how the judges interpreted it. He told a story about another case in which he had filed a complaint, after the judge demanded that he reduce the number of witnesses he could call from seventeen to five. The judge threatened to have him arrested, but eventually he was able to call the witnesses he wanted following intervention from above. Judges, he explained, were very wary of formal complaints filed against them. Anon was certainly not afraid of using brinksmanship to get his way: but whether such tactics were in the interests of his clients was another matter.

The detailed closing statement issued by the defense in the Katha case was another example of Anon's confrontational style. The statement not only elaborated the extensive shortcomings in the technical case against Katha, but also declared that the 2007 Computer Crime Act was unconstitutional,[43] that Katha had been illegally arrested, and finally that his arrest was an abuse of power arising from his holding divergent political views.[44] After the proclamation of an emergency decree in 2010, the government had cracked down on freedom of speech and assembly. These last points echoed the line pushed by Art at the June 7 case conference; but it was difficult to see how raising them was at all helpful to Katha. Katha's political views had not been discussed during any of the court testimony, and the prosecutor had not once referred to the alleged Thaksin-inspired conspiracy: his defense team had stressed the absence of material evidence to convict him, implying that the messages must have been sent by someone else. The defendant had no track record of political activity on the side of pro-Thaksin parties or the redshirt movement, but the closing statement had the implicit effect of "outing" Katha as a redshirt sympathizer. Far from corroborating Katha's self-presentation as the hapless victim of circumstances, the legal team was now incorporating him into a very different narrative about the clash of pro- and anti-Thaksin power networks. The prosecution, by contrast, argued that as a well-educated Thai national, Katha should have known better than to post these defamatory messages relating to the monarchy online. Katha's claims to be a respectable citizen thus formed part of the case against him.

As a matter of principle, courts believed the testimony of prosecution witnesses, especially when they were government officials: the assumption was always that government officials performed their duties honestly and without prejudice. In effect, defendants were deemed to be guilty unless proven innocent: the burden was on the defense to discredit prosecution evidence, not on the prosecution to demonstrate guilt beyond all reasonable doubt. The judgment also epitomized royalist views typical of those held by the Thai judiciary:

> Because it is widely known among Thai subjects including the defendant himself, who is also Thai, the defendant must have learned from the press release by the Bureau of the Royal Household that His Majesty's illness was not serious and that his condition improved steadily.[45]
>
> Because it is widely known that the King and all members of the royal family show love and loving kindness equally without dividing people according to which side they are on at all, and the King and all members of the royal family stand above political conflicts and are beloved and respected by all Thai people. Since the defendant is a Thai himself, he must know this well. The messages contained false information. Thus the people who read these messages were led to understand that the King and Somdej Prathep (Princess Sirindhorn) were not politically neutral, and loved the people unequally. This could cause both greater political conflict and violence, which could have an impact on national security, as well as the peace and order of the people and the wider society.[46]

Katha's Thai-ness was invoked twice in the judgment: as a Thai he had no excuse for not knowing either the real condition of the King's health, or the truth about the King's political neutrality. But the logic behind the judgment was opaque: if all Thai people knew perfectly well that the King was not in a serious health condition and was above politics, why would they have believed a couple of baseless messages posted anonymously online, and how could such messages have impacted on national security and order? Katha's crime was at core a violation of his own Thai-ness—could the author of such messages really be Thai? Not only had Katha made inappropriate statements about the King: he had also defamed the very popular Princess Sirindhorn, who was not covered by the lèse-majesté law.[47] In the eyes of the court, the actions of the defendant constituted an act of betrayal, located somewhere along the treason spectrum.

But to the neutral observer, Katha, like Darnton's eighteenth-century Parisian poets, posed no obvious threat to national security. He was nerdy and hesitant in his self-presentation, and had never been a political activist. Whether or not Katha sent them, the "Wet Dream" messages were posted from a jokey alias to an obscure web board, where they had zero impact either on the stock market or on popular faith in the royal institution. Objectively, the court case was a travesty from beginning to end.

While he always expressed gratitude to his original legal team, Katha had never felt full confidence in them, lamenting that only high-end, top-dollar law firms worked to a really professional standard.[48] Like Somyot, Katha decided to switch to a new lawyer to work on his appeal. This time he appointed Thitipongse Srisaen, who had a good grasp of the technical issues and had won an acquittal on appeal for Surapak Puchaisaeng, who had earlier been convicted in a similar case. Thitipongse expressed regret that he had not been the lawyer for Katha's original trial. In an impressive judgment, the Court of Appeal had written concerning Surapak:

> The fact that the defendant has a political attitude differing from a political group which explicitly expresses their loyalty to the King cannot be a reason to generalize that the defendant committed defamation against the King or the monarchical institution as the plaintiff complained. Otherwise, prosecution of the law in possible breach of the rule of law may create the opposite effect, namely ruining faith and respect in the monarch. People who are loyal to the King in the right way will not wish to see this kind of effect.
>
> Since this case is related to defamation of the King, social sanctions and social stigma toward the defendant would be as severe as a criminal prosecution. There is a need to be even more careful in examining the evidence than in general criminal cases.[49]

Thitipongse's forty-four-page appeal for Katha focused almost entirely on the factual shortcomings of the case against him, and the failure of the prosecution conclusively to link Katha with the messages. The appeal ended with a bold and direct statement of Katha's innocence:

> Based on the reasoning that the defendant has laid out to your honors from the outset, the defendant has not done anything wrong. The defendant is not the person who used the pen name "Wet Dream." The defendant therefore requests the Appeal Court to restore justice in his case by overturning the judgment of the Court of First Instance and dismissing the charges against him.[50]

But while the prosecution had failed to prove the technical case against Katha, Katha had also failed to substantiate his claims of innocence by presenting himself as someone unlikely to post such messages. Despite the worthy sentiments of the Surapak Appeal Court verdict, Thai judges were usually inclined to give any benefit of the doubt to the prosecution rather than to the defense.[51]

At 9:50 a.m. on March 5, 2014, a uniformed guard entered a ninth floor room at the Bangkok Criminal Court, holding a pair of handcuffs. A few minutes later, the presiding judge cut open a sealed envelope and read aloud the Appeal Court verdict. Katha's conviction was upheld, but his jail term was cut from four years to two years and eight months.[52] Like the Court of First Instance, the Appeal Court had reduced Katha's jail term by a third on the basis of his original confession, despite the fact that he had later retracted it: his harsh punishment was ameliorated by a certain benevolence. None of Katha's family was in court to hear the verdict. As always, the defendant was not invited to speak, and there was no sense of drama, climax, or catharsis. Shortly afterwards, Katha was led away to the cells. The Supreme Court promptly declined to bail him out pending a further appeal. In the event, Katha was released on September 22, 2015, having served just over eighteen months in jail.[53]

This chapter has illustrated the problems that follow from an overly broad interpretation of national security, from vague and hastily drafted computer crime legislation, and from a neurotic fixation with protecting the monarchy from criticism. The Katha case elevated a couple of obnoxious, idiotic Internet posts—best quickly deleted and forgotten—into weighty matters of state. Nobody associated with this sad, pointless case came out of it very well; indeed, everyone involved should have known better. King Bhumibol had stated in his 2005 birthday speech that he had never ordered people like Katha to be sent to jail. In any case, the relevant section of the 2007 Computer Crime Act made no mention of the monarchy. Katha's main crime was to repeat rumors that the King was seriously ill: but everyone knew these rumors, and everyone was already talking about them. Katha's offences lay not in violating national security, but in raising "inappropriate" topics: the King's blindness in one eye, and the possibility of his impending death. In many ways, the Somyot case was similar: raising questions about the role of the monarchy during the events of October 6, 1976, was inappropriate to the point of being deemed criminal. In the context of early twenty-first century Thailand, inappropriate utterances were potentially treasonous. The next chapter examines a case that at least focused on the defendants' allegedly inappropriate actions, rather than their alleged words.

AGAINST THE STATE

Like Somyot and Katha, Jon Ungpakorn and his nine codefendants were accused of violating national security. Their crime was having entered the compound of the junta-appointed National Legislative Assembly (the NLA: in effect, a puppet parliament) in December 2007 to stage a peaceful protest that briefly halted proceedings. The NLA had been rushing through some very ill-considered legislation—including the Computer Crime Act under which Katha was later convicted. A group of prominent NGO leaders and civil society activists involved in the protest were later charged with trespass and sedition. Unlike most of the freedom of expression defendants during this period, these defendants were not aligned with the pro-Thaksin redshirt movement: many were in fact well known for their anti-Thaksin views. But the authorities seemed confused about the aims of the NLA protests, mixing up Jon Ungpakorn with his more radical younger brother Giles Ji Ungpakorn, who had been named on the military's 2010 lom jao organogram.

On December 12, 2007, around a hundred protesters—mainly affiliated with various NGOs—climbed the walls of the Thai Parliament complex to protest against the alarming speed with which the military-appointed National Legislative Assembly was passing controversial bills in the final days before the scheduled December 23 election, sometimes at the rate of one every twenty minutes. The protesters were part of a larger group of about five hundred who had been demonstrating outside Parliament. This was the second of three such protests.[1] After negotiating briefly with the protesters, Meechai

Ruchupan, president of the NLA, agreed to suspend parliamentary proceedings for the day.

Parliamentary sessions resumed thereafter, and the token "NLA Sit-in" might well have been forgotten, but for a decision by the Office of the Attorney General to proceed with prosecutions against ten alleged "instigators" of the occupation:[2] prominent NGO activist Jon Ungpakorn; union leaders Sawit Kaewwan, Amnat Palamee, and Sirichai Mai-ngam; Pichit Chaimongkol of Rangsit University; Anirut Khaosanit, coordinator of the People Organization Network Council; Nasser Yeemha of Green Politics; leading human rights campaigner Phairoj Pholpet; consumer activist Saree Aongsomwang; and Supinya Klangnarong, a member of the National Broadcast and Telecommunications Commission.[3] Jon was a former elected member of the Senate; along with Phairoj and Saree, he was among the most senior figures in the Thai NGO community. Supinya was a household name for her work on media issues: in 2006, she had been famously acquitted in a high-profile defamation case brought against her by Thaksin's Shin Corporation. The ten faced a range of charges under Articles 116, 215, and 365 of the Criminal Code. In the Jon case, a large group of protesters had disrupted the military-appointed National Assembly. However, the selection of ten parliamentary protesters who were arrested was extremely arbitrary, while the charge of "rebellion" turned peaceful demonstrators into supposed subversives. Like the Somyot and Katha cases, the Jon case illustrated the contradictions surrounding the Thai state's use of legal processes to manage and control the expression of dissent. And like these two cases, it was linked—at least in the minds of the authorities—with a supposed plot to subvert authority, or lom jao.

A close reading of the Criminal Code sheds light on many issues that featured prominently during the "NLA Sit-In" trial. Article 116 is one of the code's national security clauses, along with the better-known Article 112: it is in effect a sedition law, somewhere along the treason spectrum. The vaguely worded paragraph 3 made it an offence to exhort the people to transgress the laws of the country, unless this was done "within the purposes of the Constitution," or to express an honest opinion or criticism.[4] Charging peaceful protesters with sedition was extremely provocative; the Article 116 charge had apparently been added only at a later stage, on orders from above. Article 215, which criminalized large gatherings that breached the peace, was the most obviously relevant law, and made specific reference to "ten persons upwards"—apparently explaining the decision to prosecute ten defendants.[5] But the provision distinguished sharply between ordinary assemblers, and those who could be viewed as "the manager or person having the duty to give orders." Penalties for the latter could include a five-year jail sentence. Finally, Article 365 provided for a draconian five-year jail term where a trespass was committed by just two or more people.[6]

The charges brought against Jon and his fellow defendants arose from a very specific political context. Like many of Thailand's leading NGO and human rights activists, most of the defendants (seven out of ten) had previously been associated with anti-Thaksin groups such as the People's Alliance for Democracy (PAD), or later aligned themselves with the People's Democratic Reform Committee (PDRC), the conservative grouping whose 2014 "Shutdown Bangkok" protest helped topple the Yingluck Shinawatra government. Saree and Supinya had spoken on the PAD stage in 2006,[7] while Suwit and Sirichai were among the "second wave" of PAD leaders.[8] Although Jon, Phairoj, and the two female defendants were highly respectable figures,[9] three of the men were at the more thuggish end of the anti-Thaksin movement. In 2013–14, Pichit became one of the leaders of the Kor Phor Thor (Network for Students and People for Reform of Thailand),[10] a hardline group associated with the PDRC that advocated using violence to bring down the Yingluck government; Masae, a former PAD activist, headed the Kor Phor Thor's security guard unit;[11] and Amnat was an activist in both the PAD and later the Kor Phor Thor.[12] Pichit and Amnat were among those who expected to face trial for the seizure of Suvannabhumi Airport in late 2008. Sirichai was one of thirteen PAD leaders later fined a total of US $16 million for his role in the airport occupations.[13] Some defendants found attending the protracted trial very burdensome, given their other responsibilities. The judge was unwilling to give them blanket permission to skip attending, and on the opening day threatened to issue arrest warrants for any defendant who failed to show up.[14]

Some of the defendants had joined the NLA occupation at least partly to assuage their guilt about having supported, actively or tacitly, the September 2006 military coup. Even among themselves, the defendants debated whether climbing over the parliament wall was a legal action or a transgression of the boundaries of free expression. As the original trial prosecutor explained to me, holding the trial served to counter allegations of double standards: "yellow" activists who had resisted the 2006–7 coup government would be treated in the same way as pro-Thaksin "red" protesters.[15] Thai justice officials tended to view NGO activists as an undifferentiated lumpen category of reheated leftists whose ideologies were firmly stuck in the 1970s. But these defendants were largely a bunch of anti-Thaksin activists, whose opposition to the coup was in some cases only skin-deep; many were primarily unhappy with particular bills passed by the NLA, such as the Water Resources Act, rather than deeply opposed to the ruling junta itself.

Part of the prosecution's confusion about the political orientation of the defendants seems to have arisen because they conflated two siblings: Jon Ungpakorn and Giles "Ji" Ungpakorn. Both men were Anglo-Thai sons of the distinguished former governor of the Bank of Thailand and rector of Thammasat

University, Puey Ungpakorn (1916–99), who was forced into exile following the bloody crackdown on the student movement in October 1976. Whereas Jon had devoted most of his career to working in Thailand for various social causes, Giles spent his early adult life as a leftist political activist in the UK, before moving to Thailand in 1997 to take up an academic post at Chulalongkorn University. Giles became well known for his criticisms of the military and the monarchy, and later as an outspoken figure on the radical fringes of the redshirt movement. Giles left Thailand for Britain in February 2009 to avoid possible prosecution for lèse-majesté. He was among those later named on the April 2010 network treason diagram, accused of being part of an antimonarchy plot. During the first phase of the NLA sit-in trial in 2012, defense lawyers observed that the prosecutor was referring to a file about Giles Ungpakorn,[16] who had taken part in at least one anti-NLA protest, but who never entered the parliament compound, and was not among those arrested or charged.[17] Saengchai pointed out later that this "confusion" by the prosecution should have been viewed as a serious breach of professionalism by the court, but no action was taken.[18] The mixing up of Giles and Jon, along with the addition of the Article 116 charges on the orders of the director-general, because the defendants were "stars," reflected the "yellow" mentality of prosecutors during the Abhisit premiership, when the defendants were charged: they viewed the ten protesters as part of a dark plot to undermine the Thai nation.[19]

The charges against the defendants were tendentious, to say the least, and could have been rebutted broadly by a defense that demonstrated that there was no big antiestablishment plot, pointing out the impeccable anti-Thaksin credentials of the defendants, and their lack of any seriously subversive intent. This line of argument could have been supported by a series of technical arguments to undermine central elements in the prosecution case. The defense could also have tried to win over the judges, who probably held quite similar political views to most of the defendants, much as the defense did in the 2006 Supinya defamation case brought by Thaksin. The aim of such a strategy would have been either to secure acquittals all round, or perhaps just token convictions on trespass charges.

For better or worse, the defendants, and especially their lawyers, had something entirely different in mind. Article 116 is the only article in the Criminal Code that cites the constitution as a possible defense. This detail excited the interest of an extensive legal team that included some of Thailand's leading human rights lawyers. Here was an historic opportunity to define the constitutional parameters of freedom of expression and assembly, and to demonstrate that under certain conditions trespass at important government locations could be justified. Jon explained to me that his aim in fighting the case was to set a precedent that would shore up such rights.[20]

It is easy to see why a defense strategy based on asserting the right to "honest criticism and expression of opinions," "within the purpose of the Constitution," put the defendants on a collision course with Thailand's legal and judicial authorities. During 2008, the year following the defendants' parliamentary sit-in, the PAD had briefly seized a government television station and then occupied Government House (the office of the prime minister) for almost three months, as well as later taking over Bangkok's two airports for more than a week. In 2010, pro-Thaksin redshirt protesters had occupied key locations in the capital, notably the major Rachaprasong retail and commercial area, between March 14 and May 19. Mass rallies in central Bangkok had long been a feature of Thailand's turbulent politics, but in recent years such rallies had become larger, more broad based, better funded, and longer in duration than ever before. No Thai court would be enthusiastic about endorsing the legality of mass occupations, which were increasingly becoming a standard playbook item for groups on both sides of the country's major political divide. Indeed, few countries in the world would readily permit demonstrators to occupy a national parliament or state assembly: the violation of legislatures is widely outlawed.[21]

In short, by seeking to establish a legal precedent that would support their right to occupy a major government building, the defendants were already pushing their luck. But the situation was even worse than that. Court of the First Instance do not set precedents in Thailand; their decisions are not even available for other judges to consult. The same applies to decisions of the Appeal Courts. Only Supreme Court decisions constitute precedents and enter case lore. Thus in order to achieve the larger—and extremely improbable—goal of setting a legal precedent that Thais had a right to occupy parliament, the defendants needed to lose the NLA case not just once, but twice. In normal court cases, the defense teams were trying to win; in the Jon case, they were trying to the best of their ability to lose. Or that is how the case appeared to this observer.

An easier line of argument would have been to point out certain salient facts: as a former senator, Jon had a pass to enter the parliament, and so charging him with trespass was nonsense (a point he deliberately chose not to raise). The defense could easily have argued that Jon had invited some friends and colleagues to enter parliament with him. This position was supported by Akhom Wattanaphan, then head of the parliamentary police, who testified that he recognized Jon as a former parliamentarian, helped him down from the ladder,[22] and then opened the gates for some other protesters to enter.[23] He did not arrest Jon, he told the court, because he assumed this was a matter involving politics.[24] Akhom's highly sympathetic testimony suggested a significant degree of collusion between the protesters and the parliamentary authorities, but this was not a line that either the prosecution or the defense wished to pursue.

Given the sensitivity of the charges, the prominent standing of certain defendants (especially Jon himself, as well as Supinya, whose position as an NBTC commissioner was technically equivalent in status to that of a cabinet minister), and the sheer number of people in the dock, this was a case demanding special attention from the courts. But the presiding judge had come fresh from handing down tough sentences in two controversial 112 cases, those of Akong and Surachai Danwattananusorn. Akong was soon to die in jail from cancer and would be hailed as a martyr to the harsh lèse-majesté law and the callousness of the courts. Thailand's most notorious judge was now face to face with a whole entourage of the country's most experienced, most dedicated, and most exasperating human rights lawyers. The ten defendants had one lawyer each, some of whom brought assistants; extra chairs were needed for the defense team. Lamenting that he was outnumbered ten to one, the original prosecutor went constantly on the offensive, trying to undermine the credibility of the defendants at every opportunity.[25] Just as judges were socialized to see themselves as occupants of the moral high ground, so human rights lawyers, often working pro bono, believed that they were invariably in the right. As Frank Munger has noted, "cause lawyers" in the Thai human rights field are an embattled, but dedicated and tightly networked minority.[26] Numerous court cases played themselves out as struggles between two obstinately self-regarding Thai legal cultures and dispositions.

The first weeks of the trial were thus extremely fraught: an incendiary clash of strong personalities. At every step, the defense lawyers tried to establish that their clients were not trying to incite "the people" to break any laws (the crux of Article 116); that their actions were "constitutional" (so invoking the defense offered by Article 116); were not "leaders" (and thus not liable for lengthy jail terms under Article 215); and that they had never "seized" all or part of the parliament compound or interfered with its "peaceable possession" (Article 362). At times defense lawyers literally read aloud from their copies of the Criminal Code. The approach of the defense lawyers might be characterized as a form of courtroom civil disobedience. The prosecution witnesses were all serving or recently retired government officials, mostly police officers. Some had not even been around during the occupation itself: even those who were present were ill-qualified to opine on whether or not the sit-in fell within the boundaries permitted by the constitution. But the operating maxim of the defense team could be summarized as: "No horse is too dead to be flogged." Every prosecution witness was grilled about the constitutionality of the protest, often by a whole series of defense lawyers, and despite the judge's constant interventions begging the lawyers to stop asking highly repetitive leading questions with no bearing on the knowledge or expertise of the witness. At the same time, the judge also forbade Saengchai from asking Meechai Ruchupan, the architect of several Thai constitutions, anything about the constitution: by no means all of the judge's strictures were reasonable.[27]

In the words of one former defendant, "Human rights lawyers in Thailand are not very good lawyers: they believe their job is to teach judges about the constitution and people's rights, rather than to win cases."[28] The defense team was informally led by two lawyers, Saengchai Rattanaseriwong (Jon's counsel) and Ratsada Manuratsada (Phairoj's counsel) who traced their professional "lineage" back to the legendary pioneering lawyer Thongbai Tongpao, via Somchai Homlaor, the dominant figure in the Thai human rights community.[29] Saengchai specialized in long philosophical soliloquies about the rights of the people, often only tangentially related to witness testimony, a style that the lead judge in the Jon case aptly dubbed "extravagant and windy";[30] while Ratsada, whose father Pradap Manuratsada had also been a very distinguished lawyer, was a master of the repeatedly reworded leading question. Both lawyers were centrally involved in the 2002 Songkla Thai-Malaysian gas pipeline case,[31] which had secured a landmark judgment in the Administrative Court concerning the right to protest.[32]

Saengchai argued that prosecutors epitomized those "higher class individuals" who feel superior to normal people and believe themselves entitled to bestow justice.[33] Similarly, judges were institutionally biased against defendants because of a belief that it was important to defend the homeland by supporting state officials; even in cases where the police had tortured or abused defendants, this was justified by the need to "protect the system."[34] In the Jon case, Saengchai saw the judge as troublesome: insulting both the defendants (including questioning their masculinity) and their lawyers, and failing to note important points. But Saengchai himself acknowledged that too many lawyers were used in the case, though he blamed this on the wishes of the defendants. Saengchai was also critical of tactics such as the "stupid" use of leading questions, or trying to get unqualified witnesses to give their views on the constitution—both techniques favored by Ratsada.[35] The two lawyers were on the same side, but did not always see eye-to-eye.

Ratsada saw the presiding judge in the Jon case as "not open-minded" and believed that it was impossible to deal with such an egotistical character.[36] Clashes between the legal team and the judge would continue so long as this kind of person was assigned to the case. He believed that judges had a similar worldview to state officials: they preferred harmony to disorder, wanted the world to be well governed, and disliked both political protests and people climbing over walls. Ratsada also explained that "as a matter of policy, we have to train new lawyers"—so the Jon case, with multiple defendants, had offered a good opportunity for such training. Asked whether ten lawyers were really needed, Ratsada answered: "But the lawyers feel cozy like this."[37] In other words, defense strategies reflected the emotional and professional needs of the human rights legal community more than the interests of the defendants. At least once, Ratsada apparently tried to provoke the judge into ejecting him from the courtroom.[38] At one point, Jon asked me whether English barristers were permitted to ask so many leading questions: I did not believe they were.

A second set of tussles concerned attempts by the lawyers to ensure that witness responses on issues such as constitutionality were duly recorded in the banthuek. The judges were often reluctant to record points of testimony that had been extracted through the use of leading questions, or which fell outside the expertise of witnesses—but they were constantly badgered to do so. A combination of lawyers putting words into the mouths of prosecution witnesses and then insisting that these words were duly noted led to considerable tensions between the defense team, the prosecutor, and the judges from the very outset of the trial:

> A typical leading question would be along the lines of: "Although the witness has long experience of police work including observing and overseeing numerous political demonstrations over many years in the vicinity of the Parliament and other official buildings, as far as the witness saw, nothing that any of the defendants was doing or saying on that day in any way contravened the law, or went beyond the limits of what is permitted within the framework of the constitution, is that right?" The witness would then answer "yes,"[39] and the lawyer would look at the judges imploring them to banthuek the leading question as a statement by the witness, which for the sake of an easy life they would quite often do. Sometimes they declined, saying "We already have that noted," or words to that effect. Often 5 or 6 defense lawyers would stand up in succession and try to get the witness to assent to a series of similar statements with the aim of creating a favorable banthuek.
>
> Ratsada gives a lengthy spiel about the meaning of the word *kaen nam* (leader)—is Meechai Ruchaphan a kaen nam, for example, in the view of the policeman?[40] The presiding judge tells the other judge there is no need to banthuek this. Judge asks him to stop asking questions in this vein. Jon insists this is important—he himself is the prathan of an organisation but not a kaen nam, which has a negative connotation.[41] Ratsada insists that people like Jon do not have the power to order their followers in the sense implied by the term *kaen nam*. Ratsada has a point, but I am unclear why the witness testimony of a police sergeant-major is being invoked in support of it—this witness simply has no nam nak (weight, standing) for his view of what does or not constitute a kaen nam to begin with.[42]

Given the frequent rotation of judges and the probability of future appeals, it was highly likely that the defendants' fates would at some point be decided by judges who had not attended any of the proceedings. In the longer term, what was written down in the banthuek could prove much more important than the courtroom strife that went into crafting the official record. But in the short term, the disruptive tactics of the defense lawyers invited the bench to find the defendants guilty, emulating as they did the disruption of parliamentary business of which their clients were accused. The defense technique of bombarding witnesses with irrelevant questions slowed down the proceedings considerably. While the defense kept complaining that the judge was biased against them, for each prosecution witness the bulk of the banthuek comprised responses to defense cross-examination.

The beleaguered prosecutor then decided to adopt an extremely disruptive tactic of his own. He asked witnesses to view videos of the protests—which were shown on a laptop placed in front of the witness stand—and narrate what they saw. The origins of the videos were unclear; some were from progovernment TV news broadcasts complete with running commentaries, rather than recordings taken by police officers as evidence. At times, footage from different protests seemed to be mixed in with footage from the NLA occupation. Showing the videos was very time-consuming, sometimes lasting up to half an hour: the prosecutor kept asserting that he did not have sufficient budget to edit them down to the most relevant episodes.[43] The sound track on the videos was extremely loud, and it was impossible for most people in the courtroom to view the laptop screen properly: the main impression repeatedly created was of a rambunctious and disorderly gathering. Simply airing the videos allegedly showing the trespass and the rowdy occupation was an attempt by the prosecution to undermine the defense case. The prosecutor repeatedly stated that if the defendants would accept their guilt, there would be no need to show the videos.[44] When the defense protested that the judges could not even see the clips from the bench, one judge said he would watch them at home later. Eventually, the defense lawyers filed a letter of complaint on the basis that the recordings should not constitute evidence, while the banthuek summarizing witnesses recounting what they had just seen on the videos created the misleading impression that this was actual witness testimony concerning the events on the day of the protests. The judges should probably have halted the videos at an early stage in the proceedings, but apparently allowed their screening as a form of "fairness," to offset the heft of the extra-large defense team.

From the outset, the presiding judge seemed testy and given to outbursts of frustration. During the first couple of days he accused an apparently homosexual defendant of not being a "real man," for refusing to plead guilty as charged.[45]

On various occasions, Jon himself stood up and asked to speak, making critical comments about the conduct of proceedings. The judge permitted this in
apparent deference to Jon's seniority. Early in the trial Jon phoned me at home,
asking me to co-sign a letter criticizing the judge for bias against the defendants
and requesting that he be removed from the case.[46] I declined to sign, and this
particular letter was never sent. But matters came to a head on March 13, following another letter of complaint submitted by the defense team over the way
proceedings were being conducted:

> The judge speaks about the letter from the defendants (complaint about
> proceedings). There is a problem of the defense questions not being
> relevant to the point (trong praden). He needs to manage (khuapkhum)
> the proceedings to keep them under control. The defendants may mis-
> understand the image of judges. In quite an outburst, the judge com-
> plains that some defendants have a negative image of him, and begs the
> lawyers to stick to the point and not torment police witnesses on topics
> they know nothing about. He has never in 19 years as a judge punished a
> lawyer for contempt of court and does not intend to do so, but he really
> wants them to cooperate.
>
> Private information from a defendant—judge got complaints from
> his boss, not about his behavior but the fact that the trial is taking so
> long, and witnesses are being postponed. He has been too indulgent in
> allowing the defense lawyers to ask very lengthy questions but really
> needs to stop this. In order to defend himself against any possible criti-
> cism over the banthuek he is having everything noted, but he really
> wants to stick to the praden at issue.[47]

The presiding judge was in a very difficult position, stuck between a defense
team intent on drawing out the proceedings interminably, ten highly opinion-
ated and sometimes vocal defendants, a very aggressive prosecutor, a completely
unrealistic witness schedule, and judicial superiors who were watching his every
move. But instead of smoothing over difficulties and seeking compromise, he
tended to respond emotionally and so ratchet up tensions between the parties.
He regularly walked out of the courtroom in mid-testimony and could often
then be seen smoking furiously in the judges' private lobby, apparently trying to
calm his nerves.

On the basis of a number of hostile outbursts, the presiding judge was viewed
by the defense side as very conservative. At one point when Ratsada was pon-
tificating about the rights to protest, the judge declared: "You have the right to
express your opinion—write it on a placard and put it up outside the court."[48]
Phairoj told me he believed the judge planned to send them all to jail to teach

them a lesson, while Jon was convinced the judge was determined to convict them regardless of the evidence.[49] But at one point the same judge spoke politely to the defense lawyers, summoning them to the bench, and explaining that he had no bias against them, and did not plan to punish their clients heavily.[50] Another of the lawyers told me the judge was only human, and not that bad after all. On one occasion, when the singing of protest songs was mentioned during the testimony, the judge beamed and bizarrely invited Ratsada to sing such a song; perhaps unwisely, Ratsada declined to sing, passing up an opportunity to bond with the bench.[51]

The first phase of the trial came to an abrupt end on March 15, 2012, when the prosecutor announced at the end of the morning's proceedings that he had no witnesses to call in the afternoon; he was about to be transferred to a new post in Chonburi and would be handing the case over to his successor. The prosecutor later told me he was looking forward to his move to Chonburi, where he hoped to focus on nice straightforward murder cases with no political ramifications. In the event, hearings did not resume until early in 2013, with a new prosecutor but—to the undisguised frustration of the defense team—the same presiding judge.

During their 2013 testimony, defendants were asked about the claim that their protest had violated a "royal zone."[52] The plot on which the Thai parliament complex was built adjoined the Dusit Palace and remained Crown property; thus while parliament itself constituted the legislature, the legislature was situated on royal land, and occupying the legislature could be seen as a violation of royal prerogatives.[53] Jon argued that: "Even if this space is granted by the King, the parliament is the people's space where people are allowed to enter."[54] In earlier testimony, the secretary-general of the Senate had confirmed in response to the defense question that the Royal Household had never "delegated authority" to parliament to bring prosecutions against trespassers[55]—an argument which could have been useful in arguing for an acquittal on technical grounds.[56] But the legal team was strangely reluctant to point out the incongruity of pressing trespass charges without any authority from the landowner in question.

Jon disputed the prosecution's characterization of the protests as a "united front," a loaded term in Thai, also used by his brother Giles; Giles was only part of a larger rally comprising groups with different orientations.[57] Jon insisted that although they had climbed over the wall of the parliament—using a ladder—they had not "invaded" the compound.[58] Asked by the prosecutor whom he meant when he used the term "we," Jon insisted that he meant only the protesters themselves—he was not invoking a larger notion of the Thai people, or the country.[59] Similarly, Supinya argued that although the protesters were a network of the people's sector, they did not claim to represent "the people." Supinya later asserted that she had not originally intended to climb over the wall, but did so only in order to take responsibility as a "good citizen"; and that she did not join any subsequent rallies "as she thought she had already done her best."[60] Cross-examining Phairoj, the prosecutor brought up a 1992 Supreme Court judgment concerning the right to protest; Phairoj responded that 1992 precedents had surely been invalidated by the much more liberal 1997 and 2007 constitutions. The final defense witness, Thammasat University assistant law professor Kittisak Prokati (himself a student leader at the time of October 6, 1976), argued that whether it was legal to climb over the wall of the parliament depended on whether it was necessary, and whether it was intended to protect what the law ultimately wants to protect or not.[61] Drawing an emotive but overly ingenious parallel with a Supreme Court judgment stating that it was not illegal for a son-in-law to enter a private home to save his wife from being sexually abused by her father, Kittisak argued that by forcing through ill-considered legislation, the junta was "raping" the NLA, and so the protesters could be justified in coming to the rescue.

But the defense arguments were not always clear. In the early days, responding to a statement by Jon in open court that the defendants could not be expected to control their lawyers, a junior judge urged the legal team not to fight on all fronts, but to focus their arguments more directly.[62] In a closing statement submitted to the court, the defense emphasized the exceptional conditions that obtained in December 2007 and which justified the NLA occupation: Thailand was still under a military junta, but a new constitution had already been approved, and the country was just weeks away from an election.[63] Yet some of the vague but idealistic language of the submission was not likely to sit well with the judges.[64] The thirty-six-page defense closing statement argued the protesters had simply wanted to bring their concerns to the NLA's attention,[65] which they claimed was permitted under the 2007 Constitution—though under what article was not specified.[66]

The final judgment contained a detailed discussion of the NLA sit-in, the evidence against the defendants, and an examination of their public interest defense. As with the Somyot case, witness testimony was summarized rather cursorily, and there were no detailed quotations from individuals: the evidence given by seven important defense witnesses, including two law professors and several prominent figures in Thai society, was bundled together as all "along the same lines."[67] The courts ascribed little weight to the kind of "commentary testimony" favored by human rights lawyers, the wheeling-in of leading academics and other prominent figures to express their support for the defendants. The occupation of the parliament was a particularly serious matter, declared the judgment, since parliament was an important location as one of the three branches of state sovereignty.[68] Although no serious violence had occurred, disorder had taken place, and the protesters had forced open a door in one of the buildings.[69] Parliament was not a public place where people could simply act on a whim.[70] The court then turned the arguments about the right to protest upside down: the defendants' actions were a "clear violation of the right to protect the territory of the parliamentary authorities."[71] While the early stages of the protest were peaceful and constitutional, later on the protesters committed acts of violence and inappropriately violated the rights of others; they could not reasonably cite article 63 of the 2007 Constitution in defense of their actions.[72] They had collectively violated the peace of the country (*banmuang*). Jon's leadership was demonstrated by several of his actions, including giving a press conference to the media at the scene of the protest.

All of the defendants were given suspended jail terms by the Court of First Instance: the "leaders," Jon, Sawit, Sirichai, Phichit, Amnat and Phairoj received sixteen months (reduced by a third from two years), while the remaining defendants were given eight months (reduced from one year); additionally, all of the defendants were fined. The convictions were based only on Article 215 (assembling to breach the peace) and Articles 362 to 365 (trespass): nobody was convicted for the more serious offence of sedition (Article 116). Indeed, the judgment concluded by observing that suspended sentences were merited because "all ten defendants violated the law with the important intention of defending the national interest," something that was apparently enough to merit a lighter sentence, though not an acquittal.[73] A critical article on the case argued that the judgment failed to give proper weight to the defendants' lack of criminal intent.[74]

According to inside sources, the then chief justice of the Criminal Court had been eager to see the ten behind bars; it was the presiding judge and the deputy chief justice who had persuaded him to agree to the suspended sentences.[75] The very same judge who had been demonized by the defense team eventually spared the defendants from incarceration, despite the extensive provocations to which he was subjected. The presiding judge apparently saw himself as a moderate figure in a Thai judiciary containing many diehard royalists, and denied rumors that he and his family had any special connection with the palace. As I had written in my field notes on the first day of the trial proceedings: "I actually suspect the judge would like to find a way of letting them off, but the line of questioning is not helpful."[76]

The Jon story had a fake happy ending: in August 2014, the Court of Appeal dismissed all the charges against the defendants, on the basis that they had never meant to violate disorder, had engaged in peaceful negotiations with parliamentary officials, and had left the compound promptly once an agreement had been reached.[77] Since the defendants had acted purely to express their principles and their opposition to the actions of the NLA, they had lacked any intent to commit a criminal trespass.[78] The case that the defendants had failed to win before the original presiding judge was successfully won on appeal—perhaps partly because the appeal judges had not experienced the infuriating behavior of the defense lawyers at first hand. But their victory reflected the turbulent politics of the 2013–14 PDRC protests, and perhaps a growing consensus on the royalist side that the occupation of government buildings was a legitimate tactic for concerned citizens in times of crisis. Had Kittisak's conservative arguments in favor of civil disobedience become mainstreamed?

Unfortunately for the defendants, the Court of Appeal did not have the last word. In March 2017, the Supreme Court rejected the Appeal Court's ruling and restored the verdict of the Court of First Instance: the defendants were found guilty of trespass and assembling to breach the peace (Articles 215 and 365).[79] Times had again changed: peace and order was now firmly in vogue, and the authority of military juntas was not to be challenged. Unlike in August 2014, another military-appointed National Legislative Assembly was now in place, which was churning out legislation in a similar way to the 2007 NLA. All ten defendants were given two-year jail terms, which were not enforced: they were all classed as "awaiting sentence" on the grounds that they were knowledgeable and capable people who were working in the national interest and had acted with good intentions—while some of them were also elderly. According to Article 56 of the Penal Code, the courts can either use a suspended jail sentence or order the defendants to "await sentence." The legal effect is exactly the same, but the latter allows defendants to assert that they have not in fact been punished. Almost never used, the "awaiting sentence" provision has a less serious connotation than a suspended sentence. Although the "awaiting sentence" provision may have been invoked by the Supreme Court for all of the defendants purely in an attempt to allow Supinya to retain her high-profile position as a national broadcasting commissioner, in the end she was forced out anyway.

While Jon insisted he had no regrets,[80] he ruefully acknowledged that his generation had done their best to advance the struggle against injustice, and it was for the coming generation to continue these struggles.[81] Yet arguably Jon and his fellow defendants in the 2007 NLA sit-in case had achieved precisely the opposite of what they had hoped for: the Supreme Court had established a clear precedent that the occupation of public buildings for the purpose of political protest was illegal.

The Jon Ungpakorn trespass trial represented a perplexing clash of cultures: defendants whose core political values were rather conservative tried to use the NLA case to establish a landmark right to hold protests in public buildings. To this end, they mobilized a large team of prominent human rights lawyers whose incendiary tactics provoked the ire of the prosecution and infuriated the judges. The various courts made strikingly divergent rulings on the case: ultimately, the defendants were found guilty, and their chosen mode of protest was declared illegal by the Supreme Court, in a binding precedent that had major negative ramifications. Nevertheless, the case demonstrated that by no means all judges were biased against all protesters: the original judge, who struggled to maintain order and to curb the excesses of the defense team, was more sympathetic than he appeared. The NLA case illustrated the need for nuance: criminal trials in political cases often involve messy attempts to manage intractable proceedings—for which judges may be mainly, but never solely, to blame.

The April 2010 antimonarchy organogram, depicting a vast conspiracy to overthrow the Thai monarchy, was a military fabrication. But the production of the diagram testified to profound levels of national anxiety, and to an appetite for overarching explanations for intense political polarization. Charges of treason, however implausible, easily took on a judicial life of their own. In different ways, the three cases examined here have illustrated the parameters of Thai treason. Somyot, despite the fact that he had not committed lèse-majesté himself, was designated the "voice" of archtraitor Thaksin Shinawatra, and became a fall guy for the self-exiled ex-premier. Katha, the hapless former broker, took the rap for the "crime" of posting online about the King's failing health—a topic that most Thais discussed endlessly in private. Katha was the Thai Everyman, jailed simply for mentioning (and satirizing) the unmentionable on the disreputable *Fa Diao Kan* bulletin board. The case of Jon and his nine codefendants was messier still: the authorities had apparently confused Jon with his more radical brother Giles. The sedition charges brought against them were entirely misdirected: most of the defendants were conservative "yellows," whose politics had nothing in common with the redshirts named in the organogram.

In different ways, all three of these trials were cases of (deliberately) mistaken identity. These defendants had not committed acts that lay anywhere on the treason spectrum. Instead, Somyot, Katha, and Jon were singled out for symbolic and theatrical purposes: in Voltairean terms, "to encourage the others." The trials sought to crack down on the possibilities of liminality in Thai society: ambiguities about the right to publish satirical articles, the right to engage in acts of anonymous defamation, and the right to stage token protests against the authorities were all challenged. Courts found themselves engaged in the judicialization of public and indeed private life, charged with closing off opportunities for critical expression, with redesignating grey areas as black or white spaces. In the Somyot and Katha cases, the judges proved all too willing to suppress liminality, so exacerbating social and political tensions. Steam was bottled in, rather than released.

In the more ambiguous NLA case, the Appeal Court found a way to fudge the issue, though quite possibly for all the wrong reasons, but the Supreme Court overturned that ruling.

In all three trials, the proceedings intermittently verged on farce: yet the judges were not the only ones to blame. Somyot, Katha, Jon, and their lawyers failed to present these cases in the best possible light, often preferring instead to bait the bench with a series of exasperating and counterproductive tactics. None of these trials produced any possibility of liminality: far from helping resolve the wider societal conflicts underlying the charges, these and similar political trials in the wake of May 2010 fueled popular discord and laid the foundations for future rounds of protest, upheaval, violence, and military intervention.

Nevertheless, the judges hearing these cases had much to answer for. All too often, they sought to deal with desperate defendants and loquacious lawyers by trying to impose their own versions of peace and order in the court, banning note taking, berating annoying observers, and communicating their own anger and frustrations to those involved in the trials. At times they insisted on treating as common criminals defendants whose only possible crimes were illicit thoughts or improper compassings that in no way threatened national security or public safety. The Somyot, Katha, and Jon cases all exemplified colossal failures of judicial empathy and imagination. Trained to try ordinary criminals, the judges overseeing these cases struggled to accommodate the complex realities of Thai society to their own dispositions, attitudes, and prejudices. Criticized by elements of the media and under intense pressure from their own superiors, the judges failed to create a safe space in which the facts of the cases could be established. They consistently deferred to official witnesses, even when those witnesses lacked all credibility, and they assumed a kneejerk adversarial relationship with defense lawyers. Rarely was it possible to see the judges as neutral arbiters seeking to dispense justice, rather than to firm up the status quo. The system was not, however, uniformly punitive: the Court of First Instance treated Jon with kid gloves, and the Appeal Court acquitted him (though the Supreme Court disagreed); the Supreme Court reduced Somyot's sentence; and Katha was released early. Like the monarchs they admired and sought to emulate, Thai judges were by turns draconian and benevolent.

CRIMES OF THAKSIN

Discussions of judicialization, politicization of the judiciary, judicial activism, or juristocracy in the Thai case often led back to a simple question: how could the malign influence of Thaksin Shinawatra be removed from politics? The problem that King Bhumibol called on the courts to solve in April 2006 was essentially the Thaksin problem. But Thaksin could only be dealt with by the courts if he had committed a crime, or had violated the constitution. This chapter examines some of the legal cases brought against Thaksin, his political parties, and his sister Yingluck. Did they form part of a coherent plan to expunge the Shinawatras from political office? Or was the relationship between pro-Thaksin forces and the courts much messier and more ambiguous than a few headlines have suggested? This chapter examines how Thaksin's legal cases illustrated the dilemmas experienced by Thai judges, as they struggled to negotiate their own standing within the network monarchy.

At the core of Thai attempts to use the judicial system to manage and control the political order was the controversial figure of Thaksin Shinawatra.[1] A Sino-Thai hailing from Chiang Mai, and a former police officer who had married the daughter of a deputy police chief, Thaksin had grown extremely wealthy by securing a series of government concessions from the late 1980s onwards, including a contract to supply IBM computers to the Thai government, and later some of the first satellite and mobile phone concessions. After gaining a Texan doctorate in criminal justice studies, he quit the police force to concentrate on his business empire, Shin Corporation, and diversified into a range of activities, including advertising and broadcasting. Following four false starts in the 1990s (brief spells as foreign minister, deputy prime minister, and party leader), Thaksin launched his own political party, Thai Rak Thai, which swept to power in the 2001 general election. Pro-Thaksin parties have won the largest number of seats in every Thai general election since, fueled by a powerful appeal to the have-nots.

Thaksin was a troubling figure in many respects. Arrogant and self-centered, he was ruthless in the pursuit of money and power, refusing to take no for an answer. While a master of electioneering, his instincts were authoritarian: he showed no interest in decentralizing power to his many supporters in the provinces. He eventually alienated the military, who removed him in the September 2006 coup. Thaksin, his associates, and his political parties then found themselves embroiled in numerous court cases, and he went into self-imposed exile in 2008. But Thaksin's biggest supposed crimes were ones for which he was not actually charged until 2017: disloyalty to the monarchy, and failing to show due respect to King Bhumibol.[2] These allegations formed the basis of the mass street protests against Thaksin and his associates by the People's Alliance for Democracy (PAD) in 2006 and 2008.

The history of Thaksin's court cases was thus a shadow history: formal proceedings on charges of corruption, abuse of power, and violations of election and assets declaration laws matter less than underlying allegations that the former premier was guilty of crimes on the treason spectrum ranging from lèse-majesté to sedition and outright insurrection. The irony of Thaksin's supposed crimes was that they turned him from perpetrator to victim, allowing him to rebrand himself as a champion of democracy and human rights, when he was never anything of the kind.

Thaksin faced legal challenges from the very beginning of his political career. He was forced to resign as foreign minister in 1995, because of a conflict of interest between his business activities and his role as the nation's chief diplomat: a conflict he did nothing to play down. In the years that followed the promulgation of the 1997 Constitution, Thaksin fell afoul of a number of newly created independent agencies: the Constitutional Court, the Counter-Corruption Commission, and the Election Commission.

Thaksin's first major brush with the law took place in 2001, immediately following the Thai Rak Thai election victory that had made him prime minister. He was accused of failing properly to complete his assets declaration during a brief spell as deputy prime minister in 1997. Between March 2000 and October 2002, the Constitutional Court issued nineteen verdicts in cases falling under Article 295, the assets declaration clause.[3] Defendants were convicted in eighteen similar cases, normally unanimously, or by a clear majority of the fifteen judges. The only exception was the Thaksin case, in which the serving prime minister was acquitted on an 8–7 vote. The eight justices who had acquitted Thaksin could be divided into two groups. Four of them argued that Thaksin had left office before the 1997 Constitution came into force and was no longer deputy prime minister: offences committed during previous terms of office should no longer be punishable. Another four justices offered different arguments: article 295 did apply, but Thaksin's actions or omissions did not amount to a deliberate offence. Amara and Klein criticize the bundling together of these two "minority" opinions to form an acquittal, which they describe as a "procedural quirk."[4] Since seven other defendants had already been convicted for offences committed during previous terms, the first set of arguments was terribly problematic. One judge who had acquitted Thaksin on other grounds argued that if the Constitutional Court went on like this, it would collapse—this was a case of "every man for himself."[5]

The rights and wrongs of this August 2001 verdict have been extensively debated ever since.[6] The four justices who had argued that Article 295 did not apply to Thaksin were later charged with malfeasance by the National Counter-Corruption Commission, though they were never convicted. In retrospect, the 2000–2002 period was the high-water mark of the assets declaration regime, which saw large numbers of politicians banned from office for five years for essentially technical violations that did not entail any real corruption or abuse of power—in other words, this was a draconian punishment for the crime in question, which the Constitutional Court itself termed a "severe political sanction."[7] But pragmatic arguments—critiques of legalism as politically troublesome and unworkable—were not those advanced in court to support Thaksin's case.

In 2001, Thaksin was acquitted not on the basis of the law, nor on the basis of criticisms of the law. The already controversial premier, just shy of six months in office, was acquitted for entirely political reasons. At the time, Thaksin was backed by an alliance of liberal royalists who saw him as their best hope for firming up the political system and ensuring stability. Royalist monk Luangta Maha Bua and ninety-year-old former health minister Dr. Sem Pringpuangkeo, with support from a wide range of conservative elite figures, gathered 1.4 million signatures in support of Thaksin.[8] Even members of the Privy Council were implicated: it was widely believed that Privy Council president Prem Tinsulanond had himself phoned a couple of the Constitutional Court judges and asked them to change their votes to not guilty, just before the verdict was issued. One judge declared, "I was forced to swallow my blood while writing this."[9] Thaksin himself—in what was to become a familiar refrain—invoked the 11 million people who had voted for him, arguing that they constituted a more legitimate power than the fifteen constitutional court judges.[10] The dangers inherent in Thaksin's majoritarian argument became increasingly evident over time, but during this period the monarchical network not only tolerated Thaksin, but actively embraced him.

Judge Jaran argued that the 2001 Thaksin acquittal was the single biggest reason behind the court's lack of public faith and trust. How could eight judges have voted to let the defendant off? "People know but we don't speak about it."[11] The verdict helped create the popular belief that the Constitutional Court was not a real court, but a political entity: as a result, the court "bankrupted itself." The worst point was that it confirmed the belief of ruling politicians that they were able to manipulate the functions of the court: "That is why they could not accept the decisions of this court, and I don't blame them, because they believed that this court could be manipulated. And if they cannot do it, it means the opposite party has done so." Jaran believed that restoring the reputation of the Constitutional Court would need ten or twenty years of continuity. The problem, of course, was that the outcome of the 2001 case had not been manipulated simply by Thaksin and his allies, a bunch of bad politicians: it had also been subverted by the royalist establishment, those at the core of virtuous rule. Royalists' lobbying for Thaksin's acquittal was testament to their lack of respect for constitutionalism. Neither bad politicians nor good royalists really believed in the rule of law, though for different reasons. The real lesson of the 2001 acquittal was not "politicians are bad and must be controlled," but "the arbiters of virtuous rule are no better than the politicians they tell us to despise."

If the royalists believed that the prime minister now owed them a debt of gratitude for saving his premiership, this was not a view shared by Thaksin himself. Thaksin saw the acquittal as a green light to pursue his agendas, rather than an amber light warning him that he could be removed from office at any moment. The 2001 Constitutional Court decision illustrated that despite the supposed shift to a rules-based political game ushered in by the promulgation of the 1997 Constitution, the Thai establishment remained deeply ambivalent about applying fixed principles and was willing to give precedence to pragmatic political considerations.

For Thaksin, a criminal justice expert who held the law largely in contempt, this was a very welcome message. But as Thaksin grew more and more powerful, his royalist opponents frequently rued the day that they had abetted his rise by balking at the prospect of removing him from office in 2001. Kramol Tongdhamachart, one of the four justices who had acquitted Thaksin on a questionable technicality, assumed the presidency of the Constitutional Court in 2003: a move that was widely criticized as reflecting Thaksin's attempts to neutralize the power of independent agencies.[12] Thaksin's approach to the 1997 Constitution and the subsidiary legislation and new agencies it has spawned was highly pragmatic: he wasted no time on legal or constitutional changes, focusing entirely on neutralizing the effectiveness of the independent agencies by lobbying, bullying, and co-opting them. Thaksin showed a consistent disdain for legalism, preferring to deploy political means to manage and delimit the effectiveness of laws and institutions.

The first peak of Thai constitutionalism occurred between the promulgation of the 1997 Constitution, and Thaksin's de facto capture of the Constitutional Court in 2003. The nineteen assets declaration cases heard by the court during this period were just one example of the enthusiastic embrace of punitive measures by independent agencies. The period of these assets cases coincided with an immense enthusiasm on the part of the Election Commission for issuing football-style "red" and "yellow" cards to candidates accused of election law violations, resulting in numerous poll reruns. This was most clearly seen in the March 2000 elections for the two-hundred-member senate, for which the EC ordered no less than six reruns, covering seventy-eight candidates from thirty-five provinces.[13] The final rerun for ten seats was not held until April 2001 and resulted in the ousting of the newly appointed president. As a result, the Senate was not properly seated until more than a year after the original elections. Similar shenanigans took place following the lower house elections in January 2001, the outcomes of which were formally challenged in 337 out of 400 constituencies. There were four rounds of voting in total, the last of which took place on August 18, 2001, two weeks after Thaksin's acquittal. Many of the complaints brought against candidates for alleged vote buying and other abuses of election laws were brought maliciously by political opponents, or even by gambling syndicates with a substantial stake in manipulating the outcome. As a result, election results were now "inherently provisional, rather than essentially authoritative."[14] The overall effect of the draconian election laws was to make Thailand virtually ungovernable, undermining the collective fictions that allow politics to function everywhere: the willingness of the populace to accept inherently unsatisfactory election outcomes in order to permit the country to operate. Thaksin's 2001 acquittal marked a moment when Thais collectively rejected the idea that legalism should be given free rein. On some level, people recognized that this way madness lay—although few were able to articulate the point so succinctly. At the same time, the acquittal also marked a moment when a central principle behind the 1997 Constitution, the introduction of "rules of the game" to regulate political behavior, was effectively abandoned. Temporarily at least, Thaksin was able to suspend the operation of legalism. As a result, after August 2001 the salience of legalism and constitutionalism waned dramatically, before reemerging during Thaksin's more troubled second premiership from 2005 onwards. The zeal of both the Election Commission and the Constitutional Court was greatly tempered during this period. Indeed, the Constitutional Court consistently favored the Thaksin administration. This was seen in cases such as the Constitutional Court's rejecting a February 2006 petition that Thaksin's premiership be terminated on the grounds that he had been guilty of a conflict of interest over the controversial sale of his Shin Corp telecommunications empire to the Singaporean holding company Temasek.[15] The court rejected the petition on technical grounds, arguing that the petitioners had failed to make a clear case that Thaksin should be removed from office.

However, the co-optation and domestication of independent agencies under Thaksin was just as troubling and politicized a development as their hypervigilance in the immediate post-1997 period, or their renewed activism following the September 2006 coup. As Thaksin's grip on power began to falter in early 2006, there was no easy path available to a moderate, reflexive, and judicious legalism. Instead, Thailand reverted to hyperlegalism mark two, an even more virulent and aggressive mode of legalism than the version Thaksin had vanquished after 2001. Faced with protests against his government and the defection of some former lieutenants, Thaksin declared on his weekly radio show: "The only person who can tell me to quit is His Majesty the King. If His Majesty whispers to me, 'Thaksin, please leave,' I'll go."[16]

Three weeks later Thaksin called a snap election for April 2, 2006, which was boycotted by the main opposition party, the Democrats. In many seats the only competitors were Thaksin's TRT and various no-name parties that had entered the fray simply to validate TRT victories. If a parliamentary candidate stood unopposed and was unable to gain 20 percent of the vote, the election in that constituency was voided—hence the value of token opposition candidacies. Immediately after the election, Thaksin was summoned to a meeting with the King and emerged declaring that for an interim period he would not perform the duties of the prime minister, handing them over instead to one of his deputies.[17] This unsatisfactory arrangement—which had no constitutional basis—lasted for a few weeks, convincing nobody. The King had apparently wanted the Supreme Court (one of his favorite institutions) to resolve the April 2006 election crisis, not the Constitutional Court—but the Supreme Court had no power to deal with such issues. This was a further illustration of what Hewison terms King Bhumibol's "ambivalence towards constitutionalism."[18]

Coups and the Courts

Thaksin Shinawatra was finally removed from power not by the courts, but by a different mode of extraconstitutional action: the *coup d'état* of September 19, 2006. The military power seizure was justified by claims that Thaksin had been disloyal to the monarchy and had sought to undermine the 1997 Constitution. Three of the nine justifications advanced by the military for seizing power referred to Thaksin's attacks on the constitution: but ironically the incoming military junta struck down the very same constitution overnight. In a clear illustration of the schizophrenia afflicting Thailand's royalist elite, the sanctity of constitutionalism was invoked to justify arbitrarily abrogating the constitution. More serious were Thaksin's alleged transgressions of royal prerogatives and acts of disloyalty. These were also highlighted in the list of justifications offered for the coup. The official coup announcements in English stated:

> The administration is also usually bordering on 'lest majest' [sic] actions against the revered king.[19]
>
> Frequently, the dignity of the Thai people's king was affected.

These assertions apparently referenced a couple of statements by Thaksin: his February 4 ear-whispering comment, and his accusing "an organization beyond the constitution, not the constitution, that is an individual that appears to have charismatic power outside the constitution" of trying to create turmoil.[20] Later on, these accusations of insulting the monarchy were quietly dropped, while the name of the 2006 junta was discreetly changed from the initial Council for Democratic Reform under Constitutional Monarchy to the more anodyne Council for National Security. This name change reflected the kind of footwork often practiced by Thailand's rulers: the monarchy may serve as the pretext behind moves to manage or suppress certain forms of political activity, but these connections are rarely spelled out in public.

The 2006 military coup saw the temporary replacement of the Constitutional Court by the Constitutional Tribunal, a smaller nine-member body that provided the template for the slimmed-down charter body ushered in by the 2007 Constitution. Members of the tribunal were drawn from the Supreme Court and the Supreme Administrative Court: by no means all of them had much enthusiasm for the task.[21] The literal shrinking of the new court, reconvened in 2008, reflected both a reduced prestige and a lowering of expectations. The drafting of the 1997 Constitution, the high point of collective faith that independent agencies could restrain the excesses of politicians, had become a dark episode in Thai political history. To return to the 1997 principles—also seen in innovations such as a wholly elected Senate—would be to walk backwards into a canal. For many observers, the Constitutional Court had lost its way, and needed cutting down to size.

The pressure was on to emulate the tough anti-Thaksin stance of the 2006–7 Constitutional Tribunal: in its first few months the new Constitutional Court ruled that the foreign minister and cabinet had acted unconstitutionally by endorsing the proposal for Preah Vihear to be registered as a World Heritage Site without parliamentary approval;[22] removed Samak Sundaravej from the prime ministership;[23] and then banned the People Power Party, whose predecessor Thai Rak Thai had been dissolved by the Tribunal eighteen months earlier.[24] The Constitutional Court seemed to be positioning itself as the legal arm of the yellow-shirt movement. But after the draconian interventions of 2008, hostile moves against pro-Thaksin parties by the Constitutional Court petered out. Perhaps predictably, the court rejected two petitions for the dissolution of the Democrat Party in late 2010, when the party was in power.[25] But while UDD leader Jatuporn Prompan was stripped of his MP status on a technicality in May 2012,[26] early in 2013 the court upheld the right of government minister Varathep Rattanakorn to remain in office, despite his holding a two-year suspended jail term.[27] As late as October 4, 2013, the Constitutional Court rejected a petition asserting that the 2014 budget bill was unconstitutional.

It was not until November 20, 2013, that the Constitutional Court upheld a substantive petition against the Yingluck government. The court found 5–4 that a proposed charter amendment to reintroduce an elected Senate was unconstitutional. This was the first conclusively "anti-Thaksin" verdict to be issued by the court in almost five years, reflecting both changes in the composition of the bench and elite fissures seen in the mobilization of the fledgling PDRC to bring down Yingluck's administration, through mass demonstrations that began on November 4.[28] When the Yingluck government declared in the days that followed that it did not accept the authority of the Constitutional Court to rule on the elected Senate issue, the political temperature rose dramatically, and protester numbers increased accordingly. From then on, the gloves came off: the Constitutional Court proceeded to rule that another draft constitutional amendment was illegal,[29] as were 2 trillion baht's worth of government loans for infrastructure development.[30] This latter decision was unanimous, a worrying sign for Yingluck that the Constitutional Court justices were closing ranks. On March 15, 2014, the Constitutional Court invalidated the February 2 general election, which had been boycotted by the Democrats; finally, on May 7, the court removed Yingluck and seven other cabinet ministers from office for abuse of power. It is striking that the Constitutional Court only began to take down the Yingluck government almost two and a half years after the 2011 elections: hostile judgments followed from the unraveling of the elite pact that had allowed her to assume office. They reflected an ugly mood among much of the Thai capital's public, who had actively or tacitly supported the PDRC's "Bangkok shutdown" and the associated antielection campaign.

The lengthy preamble to the 2014 Interim Constitution, announced by the junta in the wake of the May 22 coup, contained an implicit indictment of the failings of the Constitutional Court:

> Economic development, politics, and governance came to a halt. [The conflicts] affected the use of legislative, executive, and the judicial powers. Law enforcement became ineffective. This sort of intense crisis had never occurred before. Though the state tried to solve the problems through existing legal mechanisms and measures, such as applying laws relating to the maintenance of public peace and order; dissolving the House of Representatives and holding a general election; and using such third parties as business groups, constitutional organizations, political parties, the armed forces and the Senate tried to resolve the conflict by means of peaceful negotiations, these attempts did not succeed. In addition, new legal and political conflicts unfolded and made the problems more complicated. Divergent conflicting views broadened greatly and grew more serious until unrest became likely.[31]

The preamble suggested that in the eyes of the National Council for Peace and Order (NCPO), the Constitutional Court was part of the problem: constitutionalism had not alleviated the unfolding crisis, but had indeed compounded it. Yet the junta stopped short of abolishing the Constitutional Court; indeed, Article 45 of the interim charter specifically charged the court with adjudicating cases in accordance with the constitution's opening paragraph—in other words, the rambling preamble itself. Legalism was dead: long live legalism.

Crimes

What was the real nature of Thaksin's crimes? Were they violations of laws and constitutions, or were they insults to the monarchy, acts of disloyalty, or simply an improper impulse to be as popular as the King? While the 2006 military coup was successful in ensuring that Thaksin was removed from office, the crime of disloyalty in high officials was typically punishable by banishment. Pridi Banomyong and Phibun Songkram, two former prime ministers who had played leading roles in the overthrow of the absolute monarchy in 1932, both ended their days abroad after being vanquished by rivals. Pridi spent more than thirty years in exile after 1949: first in China, then in Paris, where he died in 1983. After fleeing Thailand in 1958, Phibun lived out his final years in Japan, passing away in 1964. A whole series of lesser Thaksin-aligned figures went into exile following the 2010 crackdown and the 2014 military coup. In 2017, former prime minister

Yingluck Shinawatra was also banished, opting to flee Thailand rather than face a jail term over her alleged mishandling of the rice subsidy policy. Whatever the exact nature of Thaksin's crimes, he was expected to accept his banishment meekly and not to agitate for the right to return. His refusal to live quietly was one of the major triggers of the political upheavals experienced in Thailand during the years after 2006 and helps explain the series of legal cases brought against him and his political associates from then onwards.

In the years that followed, Thaksin and his allies faced an extraordinary barrage of charges in both the Constitutional Court and the Courts of Justice. These included the dissolutions of several political parties by the Constitutional Tribunal and Constitutional Court, notably Thaksin's own Thai Rak Thai in May 2007, and its successor People Power Party in December 2008, along with former Thaksin coalition partners the Chart Thai Party and Matchima Thippatai Party. The Thai Rak Thai ban was accompanied by the banning from politics for five years of all 111 members of the party executive, while the People Power Party dissolution saw another 109 members banned.[32] As a result, by December 2008, 220 politicians, including virtually everyone who had served in a pro-Thaksin cabinet, had been banned from office for an extended period.

Thaksin himself faced a variety of personal legal problems. His assets had been seized at the time of the 2006 coup, and a Supreme Court ruling in February 2010 confirmed that two-thirds of these assets, worth some $1.4 billion would be retained by the state, since they were deemed "unusual wealth" gained during his time in office.[33] Around $900 million in assets were returned to him. The Assets Examination Committee sued Thaksin, with forty-six other defendants, for abuse of power and graft when introducing two and three digit lotteries in 2003. He and his wife also faced assets concealment charges for disguising their ownership of two shell companies, Ample Rich and Win Mark. Thaksin's defamation suit against former senator Kaewsan Atibhoti for asserting that he had sought to evade tax in the Temasek deal was thrown out by the Appeal Court in 2013. Most seriously for him, Thaksin was convicted in September 2008 of violating conflict of interest rules, by helping his wife to buy land from a state agency at a reduced price.[34] The Supreme Court's Criminal Division for Holders of Political Positions sentenced him to two years in jail. Unwilling to be incarcerated, Thaksin declined to return to Thailand in the years that followed. Ironically, the same court had just a few weeks earlier permitted him to leave Thailand, ostensibly to attend the opening ceremony for the Beijing Olympics: he never returned. It seemed highly likely that the Supreme Court deliberately gave Thaksin the opportunity to slip out of the country in the hope that he would prefer not to come back. This "generous" decision, coupled with a harsh sentence for a rather technical crime, illustrated the schizophrenic operation of royal banishment in modern Thailand.

As well as cases involving Thaksin himself, a series of other cases focused on his associates. Samak Sundaravej, the right-wing royalist who served as Thaksin's stand-in for the 2007 elections, was ousted from prime ministerial office by the Constitutional Court in September 2008 for illegally hosting a television cooking show—an episode that made global headlines because of its sheer absurdity. The decision hinged on the argument that Samak was improperly serving as an "employee" of Face Media, the company that produced his show "Tasting While Grumbling." He thus fell afoul of constitutional provisions designed to prevent conflicts of interest between politicians and the private sector. The verdict was quite curious: in 2001, the Constitutional Court had dismissed similar charges against ten former or serving ministers who held positions as company directors.[35] A crucial passage in the summary of the Samak court decision read as follows:

> Concerning whether or not the defendant was an employee of Face Media Co. Limited, the court concluded that article 267 of the constitution, forbids the prime minister and other ministers from being employees of anyone, to ensure that they perform their duties legitimately, and to prevent anything from happening that violates the interests of the kingdom and violates ethics, by making it difficult for them to choose between personal interest and public interest. When an officeholder thinks in terms of personal benefit more than public interest, there is a conflict between their personal interests and the power they exercise in their position, such that their personal interests take priority over the public interest.[36]

Using this logic, the Constitutional Court airily dismissed the question of whether Samak was legally an "employee" in the same sense as laid down in commercial or employment law: the issue at stake was simply one of ethics and potential conflicts of interest, though no actual conflict was specified.[37] Arguably, Samak and other politicians were subject to a supralegal ethical standard concerning conflicts of interests, one that went beyond the letter of the constitution. Jaran's decision on the Samak case contained an interesting passage: "Thus we gathered that the explanation of the defendant and the testimony of the two witnesses was untrue, and their behavior suggested some dubious practices. Some facts were probably concealed and distorted."[38] Jaran was rightly incensed by the evasions and downright lies of Samak and his legal team about the pattern of payments made to him by the media company concerned. But did any of this amount to a real conflict of interest? Did the judges' disapproval of the defendant's behavior lead the court to convict Samak improperly, and counter to the February 2001 precedent? How far was Samak's most serious misbehavior in fact the selling of his conservative, royalist credentials to Thaksin? Ironically, Jaran himself was subsequently accused of a conflict of interest under the same clause of the constitution, on the grounds that he served as a paid visiting lecturer at various law faculties in addition to his duties as a Constitutional Court judge. In the end, the National Anticorruption Commission decided that there was no case to answer, though Jaran insisted he had been fully prepared to resign his judgeship if the decision went against him.[39]

The Constitutional Court ruled in July 2008 that Foreign Minister Noppadon Pattama and the whole cabinet acted unconstitutionally by supporting the Cambodian bid to register Preah Vihear as a UNESCO world heritage site without parliamentary approval. In late 2008, former house speaker and Thaksin stalwart Yongyuth Tiyapairat was indicted by the Election Commission and then convicted by the Supreme Court for electoral fraud, in moves that led to the dissolution of the People Power Party. Jatuporn Prompan, one of the leaders of the pro-Thaksin UDD redshirt movement, had his MP status removed in May 2012 on essentially technical grounds.[40] In April 2014, Samak Sundaravej, who had died in 2009, was convicted of malfeasance over the purchase of fire trucks during his time as Bangkok governor in 2004: the heirs to his estate were ordered to pay back the equivalent of US $18 million.[41] Finally, Thaksin's sister Yingluck Shinawatra was removed from office as prime minister in May 2014 for abusing her power by illegally transferring the head of the National Security Council.[42]

"Anti-Thaksin" decisions by the Constitutional Court received considerable media attention. But equally striking were a series of more ambiguous Constitutional Court decisions, some of which could be construed as pro-Thaksin. Given the short-lived premierships of Samak and Somchai, many analysts initially assumed that Yingluck would not survive more than a few months in office: but in the event, she lasted nearly three years, largely because the Constitutional Court repeatedly refrained from taking her down. In July 2012 the court rejected petitions arguing that attempts by the Yingluck government to amend the charter were unconstitutional—but advised that future changes should be backed by a popular referendum. Similarly, in October 2013 the court rejected arguments that the 2014 budget bill was unconstitutional because it reduced financial allocations to the courts and the National Anticorruption Commission.

Matters changed after the debacle of the Pheu Thai Party trying to push through parliament an amnesty bill that would have allowed Thaksin to return to Thailand. The amnesty bill triggered massive antigovernment protests and marked the beginning of the end of the deal that had allowed Yingluck to assume office. In November 2013, the Constitutional Court found by 5 votes to 4 that a proposed charter amendment seeking to alter the composition of the senate violated the constitution. In January 2014, the court found that another proposed amendment to modify the clause on international agreements (Article 190) was unconstitutional; while in March the court decreed that the government's planned program of 2 trillion baht infrastructure loans was unconstitutional. Later in March, the Constitutional Court annulled the February 2, 2014, election on the grounds that it failed to meet the constitutional requirement for elections to be completed on a single day—a direct result of protest action by those who were intent on disrupting the polls.

A series of important legal decisions from November 2013 onwards went against the pro-Thaksin side, so lending credence to the idea that the courts in general—and the Constitutional Court in particular—favored the conservative establishment. Yet these anti-Thaksin judgments need to be seen in the context of a series of pro-Thaksin (or at least pro-Yingluck) judgments issued during the period from mid-2011 to late 2013, when an elite pact was in operation to allow Yingluck Shinawatra to serve as prime minister. As Jaran himself acknowledged, the national interest was an overriding concern of the Constitutional Court. During the periods when the conservative establishment was aligned with pro-Thaksin forces, the Constitutional Court was more likely to issue pro-Thaksin judgments—since these judgments could be viewed as in the national interest. At times when the conservative establishment was at loggerheads with pro-Thaksin forces, the Constitutional Court was more likely to issue anti-Thaksin judgments.

Ultimately, Thailand's Constitutional Court was a political court. Precedents counted for little, especially since the country's constitutions were constantly changing: the decisive factor shaping the court's judgments was the judges' view of the national interest. When Thaksin was in, judgments went in his favor; when Thaksin was out, judgments went against him. The Constitutional Court was a bellwether—albeit an unreliable one—of Thailand's prevailing political winds.

A series of Thaksin-related cases illustrated the profound ambiguity of legal responses to Thailand's most troublesome ex-premier. Thaksin's parties were shut down by the courts twice, but were allowed to reconstitute themselves under new names and near-identical logos. This was in sharp contrast to the judicial closure of the Cambodian National Rescue Party in 2017: the neighboring Hun Sen regime did not permit its political opponents to return in a rebranded format. Viewed in this light, the Constitutional Tribunal's 2007 treatment of Thai Rak Thai was a fake closure. Similarly, the Constitutional Court's removal of Samak Sundaravej from the premiership in 2008 was a piece of sound and fury that signified nothing: Thaksin, not the courts, prevented Samak's immediate reinstatement as prime minister.

The legal cases that led to the departures of Thaksin and later Yingluck Shinawatra from Thailand were also fraught with ambiguity: the Supreme Court allowed Thaksin to leave Thailand in August 2008, ostensibly to attend the opening ceremony of the Beijing Olympics. In retrospect, this decision reflected a deliberate attempt to convert his impending jail term into an extended—perhaps lifelong—period of banishment from the kingdom. Much the same applied to Yingluck's rice scheme case nine years later: the authorities whisked her out of the country just before her jail sentence could be pronounced, so avoiding the adverse political consequences of imprisoning the popular ex-premier, and effectively banishing her from the kingdom. The outcomes of all these cases reflected hesitancy and confusion on the part of the judiciary, rather than the actions of a coherent and unified deep state. Such judicial dilemmas arose partly because the monarchical network had a deeply conflicted relationship with the Shinawatras, one that was alternately antagonistic and collaborative. Simply put: since King Bhumibol did not know what to do about Thaksin, and because those around the King could not agree on what to do about Thaksin either, judges also found themselves far from sure about how to deal with the maverick former prime minister.

COURTING CONSTITUTIONALISM

Thailand's Constitutional Court has been characterized as the chosen instrument of a "Deep State" intent on enforcing the political stance of King Bhumibol. But the close examination of the Constitutional Court offered in this chapter suggests a more complex and messy picture. As already seen in a series of Thaksin-related cases across different courts, Thai judges have struggled to implement the royal will—not least because it was often unclear what exactly the King wanted them to do. While there is significant evidence of anti-Thaksin bias in recent Constitutional Court decisions, examination of a pivotal 2012 constitutional amendment case illustrates the ways in which the judges sought to avoid making difficult decisions—which included trying to recuse themselves from hearing the case. During the final decade of the Ninth Reign, the Constitutional Court was frequently wavering, tentative, and downright evasive in its decisions, again reflecting the ambiguous stance adopted by the network monarchy. This was especially the case during the 2011–14 Yingluck government, which enjoyed significant royal favor until its final tumultuous months.

On the outskirts of Bangkok, lines of riot police surrounded the Chaeng Wattana Government Complex containing the Constitution Court, in anticipation of possible trouble.[1] The nine judges had all slipped into the building early, and a line of people waited in eager anticipation of attending the proceedings. Thailand's Constitutional Court holds most of its meetings in camera: the well-appointed public chamber, with galleries seating over a hundred observers, is rarely opened. After convincing the officials I am a genuine researcher and undergoing two separate searches, I find a seat near the front. There are some obvious People's Alliance for Democracy (PAD) supporters in the public area: I later see one wearing a "Save the Nation" headband during lunch, but he takes it off for the hearings, perhaps at the request of the security guards.[2]

The court had accepted a petition concerning the legality of the Yingluck Shinawatra government's attempts to amend the constitution. If the court endorsed the arguments of the petitioners, Yingluck's Pheu Thai Party would have been dissolved, and her government might have collapsed. Pro-Thaksin groups hailed the very acceptance of the petition as the beginning of a judicial coup.[3] For a few days, Thais were transfixed by a court case that seemed on the verge of upending the country's politics—the latest in a series of such cases that stretched back to 2001.

How to prevent public disorder without resorting to a military coup? How to maintain virtuous rule without regular monarchical interventions? How to firm up Thailand's political institutions in the face of growing popular demands, vocal populist leaders, and a ready recourse to street rallies? Above all, how to prevent outbreaks of mass violence that could delegitimize not just the Thai state, but the nation, religion, and the King? These were the questions that had inspired royalist liberals to promote an agenda of constitutionalism in the mid-1990s. By establishing a new flotilla of independent agencies under the 1997 Constitution to check and balance the power of elected politicians, major figures in the network monarchy hoped to avert future crises, or at least to prevent them from degenerating into chaos. The creation of new bodies such as the National Counter-Corruption Commission, the Election Commission, and the National Human Rights Commission formed part of a global trend of "new constitutionalism" that was widespread during the 1980s and 1990s. Countries around the world revised their constitutions to create similar new agencies.[4]

At the core of the post-1997 reform project was the Constitutional Court,[5] inspired by European models such as the German Bundesverfassungsgericht.[6] Like its German counterpart, the Thai Constitutional Court has the power to review legislation and declare it unconstitutional. Borwornsak Uwanno, one of the architects of the 1997 Constitution, described the new court's functions as follows: "A Constitutional Court is to be established which is empowered to deal with all laws challenged as unconstitutional and to decide issues involving overlapping authority."[7] But for most Thais, the Constitutional Court is best known for adjudicating petitions related to topical political issues—including dissolving political parties and removing politicians from office—performing a classic role of judicial "referee." Rarely did the court declare any laws unconstitutional.[8]

When King Bhumibol asked the judiciary to help solve the country's political crisis in 2006, he directed his remarks to the judges of the Supreme Court and the Administrative Court. The content of the speeches suggested that the King saw the Constitutional Court as politicized and unreliable—but in the end, most of the judicial action undertaken in 2006 was carried out by the Constitutional Court. Nevertheless, in the wake of the military coup that same September that ousted premier Thaksin Shinawatra, Thailand remained bitterly divided. When Thaksin's sister Yingluck Shinawatra became prime minister in 2011, the opposition tried every possible means to destabilize her rule, including petitioning the Constitution Court on various questionable grounds.

One particular Constitutional Court case in 2012 epitomized the strengths and weaknesses of the court's refereeing role. A group of petitioners alleged that proposals by the Yingluck government to amend the 2007 Constitution were themselves unconstitutional. At the core of the case lay the question of whether an elected sitting government was entitled to initiate proceedings for constitutional revision or redrafting. The bitter infighting generated by this case was a harbinger of things to come; by late 2013, protesters were back on the streets of Bangkok, and by May 2014 Yingluck was removed from office by the Constitutional Court, shortly before her government was ousted by yet another military coup.

Understandably, many scholars have been highly critical of the Thai Constitutional Court. In an influential article, Eugénie Mérieau claims that the Constitutional Court forms part of an invisible framework of unaccountable power that she terms the "Deep State."[9] Not only is the court dedicated to advancing the agendas of the military and the monarchy, but according to Mérieau "the Deep State organized for the Constitutional Court to take on the 'king's role' as defined by McCargo."[10] Citing a passage from my 2005 network monarchy article, she thus suggests that the Constitutional Court has assumed the role of "ultimate arbiter of political decisions," a role formerly exercised by King Bhumibol himself. While acknowledging that the "Deep State" is "not monolithic," Mérieau asserts that it is "organized, autonomous and possesses its own hierarchy and rules."[11]

The notion of an ominously capitalized Deep State is naturally attractive to many critics of the Thai monarchy, military, bureaucratic elite, and indeed the judiciary. However, to describe Mérieau's explanation as undertheorized would be generous. Nor does she offer any particular evidence for her claims that the Deep State sought to transfer its powers from the monarch to the Constitutional Court.[12] One of the cases Mérieau cites—the Constitutional Court's July 2012 dismissal of a challenge to the Yingluck government's attempts to revise the 2007 Constitution—is examined in detail below. Mérieau's puzzling claim that "this dismissal did not alter the strong signal sent by the acceptance of the case" needs to be carefully unpacked in the light of the facts.[13] This chapter argues that both the court's acceptance and subsequent dismissal of the 2012 constitutional amendment case are typical examples of the muddled, inept workings of network monarchy in the final years of Bhumibol's reign and cannot be explained by a reductionist reading that assumes the existence of a Deep State.

Under King Bhumibol, the question of agency was highly opaque. The late King usually declined to make his wishes explicitly clear, instead allowing a wide range of individuals and organizations to assert that they were acting on his behalf. The result was often a muddle: despite its generally booming economy and dynamic society, Thailand had one of the world's most unstable political orders. During Bhumibol's final decades, the guiding principle of Thai politics was "anything goes"—military coups, elections, election boycotts, election annulments, new constitutions, party dissolutions, street protests, airport occupations, and even mass killings of unarmed demonstrators. Network monarchy is a nuanced concept that tries to capture the ambiguity, confusion, and sheer messiness that afflicted a political order in which a revered monarch persistently neither made his wishes clear, nor sought to enforce his will. This chapter will argue that the Constitutional Court modeled itself on the palace, which meant doing its best to avoid difficult decisions and to postpone the day of reckoning whenever possible.

Dressel and Khemthong have raised important concerns about the political bias of the Constitutional Court, both in terms of important decisions since 2006 and "increasingly partisan nominations."[14] Khemthong has also argued that the court's "aggressive exercise of judicial review is a dangerous tactic," weakening both electoral democracy and the legitimacy of the judiciary.[15] Piyabutr has argued that the Constitutional Court has consistently confronted elected governments while coddling military regimes.[16] While concurring that the Constitutional Court is a terribly flawed institution, this chapter argues that the court has also often sought to avoid difficult choices, preferring to issue judgments that fudge sensitive issues and promote compromise. While the criminal courts have struggled to achieve liminality in their handling of political cases, the Constitutional Court has at times come closer to doing so, by creating a safe space where the performative venting of intense emotions were permitted—arguably an example of Turner's "normative communitas." Turner defines normative communitas as "the attempt to capture and preserve spontaneous communitas in a system of ethical precepts and legal rules."[17] The Constitutional Court could support such communitas by permitting the airing of strongly opposing political views in a carefully managed realm of shared "Thai-ness." This was decidedly so in July 2012. Though too brief to count as a great trial, the 2012 Thai constitutional amendment case included all three of Ferguson's larger-than-life elements: spread of conflict, a dramatic twist, and the use of iconography.

Wider Questions

On July 5, 2012, the first of two days of scheduled testimony, the dark-paneled formality of the long, windowless courtroom gave the proceedings a weighty feel as the nine male judges, clad in black robes adorned with red velvet, belatedly slipped in through a concealed door before taking their seats on the bench together at 10:10.[18] The first petitioner, retired general Somjed Boonthanom, swore a brief affidavit ("I pledge to testify the truth in all that I say"). In principle, testimony was supposed to be short and to the point: petitioners were meant to limit themselves to responding to defense criticisms raised by their petitions (which had already been supplied to them) and adding any supplementary arguments. Sporting some fairly implausible hair, Somjed spoke initially for just a couple of minutes, excitedly accusing the government of planning a coup to change the constitution in the name of democracy. Even though the ruling party might claim they did not plan to change the system of government, could they be trusted? Everything rested in the hands of the president of parliament. Could we leave the future of the country under the direction of this one man (Pheu Thai MP Somsak Kiatsuranont), who had already shown he was not trustworthy? Somjed was cross-examined by a lawyer for the ruling Pheu Thai Party (PTP), whose calm demeanor made the petitioner sound borderline hysterical by comparison.

During this 2012 case, Somjed gave media interviews claiming that the government was attempting to stage a coup d'état by revising the constitution, a curious criticism given his own prominent role in the actual 2006 coup. He was a former head of the secretariat for the Council for National Security—the 2006–7 military junta. Not one to hold back, in August 2009 Somjed had publicly called for redshirt leaders campaigning for Thaksin to be pardoned by the King to be tried and executed;[19] he later organized against Pheu Thai during the 2011 elections.[20] Following the May 2014 coup, Somjed was again appointed to the National Legislative Assembly.

The other petitioners were Wanthongchay Chamnankit, the personal lawyer of former Democrat minister Thaworn Senneam, who specialized in preparing anti-Thaksin lawsuits;[21] Wirat Kalayasiri, a fourth-term Democrat MP from Songkla who constantly harassed pro-Thaksin forces through the courts, usually in a "personal capacity";[22] Warin Thiemjarat, a lawyer and appointed senator with close ties to the military;[23] and self-styled businessman and social activist Boworn Yasintorn, who was involved in numerous anti-Thaksin campaigns.[24] In 2015, Boworn became the focus of controversy when he was briefly nominated to become a member of the National Human Rights Commission, and faced accusations of links to rightist vigilante groups.[25]

This professional awkward squad was camped out in the space formerly occupied by prominent PAD leaders such as Sondhi Limthongkul: although the petitioners articulated the real views of many in the monarchical network, they had to be kept at a distance because their rabble-rousing and emotionalism were suspect, and their real loyalties and connections to the royal institution were rather questionable. In effect, Somjed represented the military, Wirat and Wanthongchay worked for the Democrats, and Boworn stood for royalist "civil society" groups. On one hand the petitioners were opportunists, exploiting a difficult political climate; at the same time, they were also being used by members of the royalist network who preferred to remain in the background, to remind the Yingluck government that there were limits on what would be tolerated. Piyabutr has noted that institutions such as the Constitutional Court were dependent on a regular cast of conservative petitioners to supply cases against elected politicians.[26] For periods of time, the network monarchy had been willing to accept Thaksin and Yingluck heading their governments as prime ministers, so long as they operated within a set of implicit rules that included not challenging the autonomy or perks of the military and defending both royal prerogatives and the lèse-majesté law.

Yet prior to 2012, constitutional revision had never been initiated by anyone other than the military or elite civilian royalists. For many close to the palace, the PTP's moves to redraft a constitution were quite simply a form of treason, shifting the definition of "the people" away from reliable agents of the establishment and towards politicians who claimed to be acting on behalf of the mass of voters. This chapter argues that the function of the Constitutional Court was not to adjudicate the theatrical "dispute" between the petitioners and the government, but to create a surrogate political space in which this standoff could be aired and mediated in such a way that the finely balanced "deal" between the monarchical network and the government could be reblessed and emerge intact. The Constitutional Court was engaged in an exercise in buying time, justified by the court's overriding concern with the national interest. The petitioners in the case were not the real prime movers in any serious attempts to oust the Yingluck government, but rather a warm-up act, a bunch of placeholders. When serious anti-Yingluck moves began in late 2013, none of the July 2012 petitioners were more than bit players. Although their 2012 petition did not succeed in the short term, their goal of ousting Pheu Thai from power was accomplished within two years.

The respondents in the case were also a slightly curious list: the president of Parliament (not by name, but by virtue of his position), the cabinet, the Pheu Thai Party, the Chart Thai Pattana Party, "Sunai Chulapongsathorn and team," and "Paradorn Prissanananthakul and team."[27] Sunai, who served as deputy government spokesman during the ill-fated 1996–97 Chavalit government, was a veteran MP and political bruiser who had played a leading role in pushing the proposed new constitution in early 2012.[28] In the wake of the 2014 coup, Sunai fled Thailand, and later had his passport revoked for failure to report to the military authorities. Paradorn, just thirty-two at the time, had led a constitution-drafting team for the Chart Thai Pattana Party, a junior coalition party with nineteen parliamentary seats.

The names of both the petitioners and the respondents clearly showed that the constitutional amendment case was a proxy battle. Major politicians such as Abhisit, Suthep, Yingluck, or Thaksin, and even leading redshirts like Jatuporn Prompan or Nattawut Saikua, went unmentioned.[29] None of those named—either as petitioner or respondent—had ever held ministerial office, led a political party, or spearheaded a big protest. Nor were they especially prominent for other reasons. Thais who did not follow politics closely had probably never heard the names of any of the protagonists. This was not the first team taking on an opposing top team, but the B team warming up against another bunch of reserves.[30] The secondary identities of both the petitioners and respondents were an indication that the Constitutional Court action was more shadow play than serious political showdown.

At the heart of this confusing and highly technical case lay an apparently simple question: Did parliament have the right to propose drafting a new constitution? The petitioners were adamant that this was a profoundly subversive act, but why? Under Article 291, the cabinet could propose a revision of the constitution. The question was whether that extended to the creation of a new constitution-drafting assembly. The cabinet, testified Yingluck's critics, was not a person or a juridical person. The petitioners asserted that the government intended to change the system of administration and to reduce the powers and privileges of the monarchy during any such revision—in effect, that the proposal was a prelude to treason. During his testimony Somjed highlighted a quote from pro-Thaksin politician Adisorn Piengkes saying that he dreamed of "our institution" (the monarchy) being a symbol. A lawyer protested that Adisorn was not an executive member of the Pheu Thai Party: he did not speak for it. More importantly, Somjed's arguments would have applied with equal force to the 1997 Constitution, which was drafted during a period of parliamentary rule: was he seriously saying that no elected government has the right to propose a new constitution? Somjed responded that the political atmosphere and Thai society were very different in 1997.

Recusal

At this point, the proceedings take a curious turn, a Fergusonian movement of dramatic shift and surprise. A question from a defense lawyer is answered by one of the judges, and the whole case shifts course.

Pheu Thai lawyer Chusak Sirinil claimed that one of the Constitutional Court judges, Judge Jaran Phakdithanakun, had stated back in 2007 that it would be best to accept the draft constitution first and amend it later. Does Jaran admit that he said this? Jaran speaks directly from the bench in response to the question, saying that amending articles individually would be perfectly acceptable, but rewriting the constitution completely would be a different matter: he had never suggested such a process.[31] Chusak responds that he has a copy of the original interview and will file it with the court—indicating that there was a discrepancy between Jaran's answer and his original statement.[32]

Jaran Phakdithanakun is literally the eminence grise of the Constitutional Court. Boasting boyish good looks well into his sixties, and crowned by a fine head of grey hair, Jaran is a Cambridge law graduate who, like his mentor, the former premier Thanin Kraivichien, was called to the English bar before pursuing a distinguished judicial career. After holding the important post of secretary-general to the Supreme Court, Jaran served as permanent secretary of the Ministry of Justice before becoming a Constitutional Court judge. Jaran was one of a new team of judges appointed in the wake of the 2007 Constitution he had helped draft. Their mission was to improve the image and standing of an institution that had been tarnished first by the 2001 Thaksin acquittal, then by persistent acquiescence to the government during Thaksin's premiership, and finally by the Constitutional Tribunal's harsh dissolution of Thai Rak Thai in the immediate aftermath of the 2006 coup.

Soft-spoken, silver-tongued, and unfailingly polite, Jaran deployed his considerable legal knowledge and his immense charisma in his efforts to redeem the discredited Constitutional Court and restore its authority. While Jaran liked to pooh-pooh the idea that he was the real president of the court, repeatedly claiming that he was the youngest of the nine judges, in practice he towered above his more lackluster colleagues, both intellectually and personally.[33] Chai-Anan Samudavanija observed that Jaran could have been a progressive, reforming leader of the judiciary, but had instead moved sideways to the Constitutional Court.[34] Jaran was too outspoken and too high profile for some of his fellow Supreme Court judges, who were happy to see him move on. Nitirat member Teera Suteewarangkurn argued that Jaran's assignment to the Constitutional Court may have been a deliberate move: he was a trusted enforcer of royalist orthodoxies.[35] As the only well-known Constitutional Court judge—any of the others could have strolled through Bangkok's Siam Square unrecognized—Jaran was frequently interviewed in the media: he was not simply the legal powerhouse of the court, but also its public face. A master image maker, Jaran was often praised for his modest demeanor, famously spending his free time visiting Buddhist temples.

When the judges belatedly return for the afternoon's proceedings at 2:05, there is a surprise: Jaran is missing. The president of the court, Wasant Soypisut, explains that Jaran decided to withdraw from the case because the question this morning about his previously expressed views on the 2007 Constitution made him feel uneasy: he was seen as being biased. Chusak swiftly objects that he was not questioning Jaran's suitability—but Jaran has already stepped down, and the case proceeds with only eight judges. According to Wasant, Jaran withdrew because he had expressed an opinion in advance and was therefore not able to decide on the case without being exposed to criticism. I suspected Wasant may have wanted Jaran to step down after expressing his views in open court.

By Jaran's own later admission, he was caught out by Chusak's question. He remembered having said that the constitution could always be amended clause by clause, but claimed he had forgotten once suggesting that it could also be amended by creating a new constitution drafting assembly, as was done prior to 1997. During the lunch break on the day of the hearing, his secretary tracked down a video clip of him speaking at a public debate on whether to support the draft constitution, organized by an NGO in 2007.[36] In the clip, he began by stating that the 2007 charter had numerous glaring deficiencies, but approving it was a necessary step to move on from the coup period. Jaran went on to say:

> There are some points, lots of points that you have suggested here—we have started a revision process. I would like us to do this like we did in 1997, we can have just 50,000 people support a proposal, and then just a quarter of the MPs in parliament. We can propose revising just one article, like we began to do in 1997, and have that lead to a process of drafting a whole new people's constitution. This way will be smoother than if we just complain—let's do it.[37]

Watching the video clip, Jaran immediately realized he was in trouble: he had stated, on national television, an unambiguous opinion about a central issue in the case he was now hearing. He went to speak to his colleagues and informed them that he needed to recuse himself from the proceedings, since he had previously expressed a predisposition; even if he had since changed his mind, nobody would believe he could pass judgment fairly on the matter.

The military junta had staged a referendum on the new draft constitution in August 2007, securing a narrow "yes" vote. Interviewed in 2015, Jaran argued that in 2007 he had really wanted the constitutional referendum to pass so that democracy could be restored—but meanwhile the situation had moved on. During the 2012 case, his fellow judges were very reluctant to permit him to withdraw and tried to talk him out of it. When Jaran insisted he wished to recuse himself, he was asked to wait outside the conference room for fifteen minutes while they discussed his request: a Constitutional Court judge may only be recused from a case by the agreement of the court. Eventually an official came out and told him a majority of the judges had agreed he could withdraw. Jaran claimed that he never asked what happened during the meeting and was never told. But his insistence on withdrawing had profound consequences for the case, since it left open the possibility that the court could be deadlocked if the judges were split 4–4. This was indeed what happened. Jaran's withdrawal did not prevent him from giving media interviews both explaining his reasons for recusing himself[38] and expressing his views on the judgment.[39]

At the beginning of the second day's proceedings on Friday, July 6, Wasant emerged to explain that three other judges had also wanted to recuse themselves from the case: Supot and Nurak, plus Wasant himself.[40] Supot and Nurak tendentiously asserted that they ought to be recused because they had been involved in the drafting of the 2007 Constitution; while Wasant had also publicly suggested that a new drafting assembly could be formed. After deliberation, the remaining five judges had decided to reject these three requests for recusal. Jaran later insisted that his own situation was very different: Supot and Nurak had expressed views in an academic context as legal experts, while there was no rule in Thailand or elsewhere that a person who had taken part in the drafting of a constitution could not sit in judgment in constitutional cases.[41] By contrast, Jaran had offered a specific opinion in an official capacity to the wider public—a very different matter.[42] Curiously, the radio interviewer who brought up Nurak and Supot did not ask Jaran about Wasant's position, which appeared strikingly similar to Jaran's, although Wasant's remarks were made during a television interview and not a formal public meeting.

Nobody commented on another significant problem: Jaran's misrepresentation of his own earlier position when he responded from the bench to Chusak's point. Jaran's overconfident rebuttal of the Pheu Thai lawyer's challenge seemed curious, given that his speech at the August 2007 seminar was not a random utterance but apparently reflected his considered view during this period. What he had said on television was totally consistent with his conversation with officials from the US Embassy in February 2007, in which he expressed doubts that the new constitution would last long: "For these reasons, the new constitution might not be 'sustainable.' A possible outcome, he said, was to get an 'OK' constitution, get through the referendum, get a "government of the people" and start again (on constitutional reform)."[43] Had Jaran genuinely forgotten his earlier view that a more sustainable constitution was needed, an opinion he apparently held for at least six months between February and August 2007? A more skeptical reading is that Jaran responded to Chusak's point very deliberately, seizing the opportunity to recuse himself from an extremely tricky case. According to one version of this argument, Jaran hoped to shape the outcome of the judgment without having his own fingerprints on the court's decision.

What Jaran meant by a "people's constitution" or a "government of the people" was never made explicit.[44] It is unlikely that he meant a new constitution drafted by a Shinawatra-led government. More probably, he had in mind an administration led by trusted royalist liberals: the "we" invoked in his seminar comments. In this sense, the situation in 2012 with the Pheu Thai Party in charge was indeed very different: but this was not something Jaran could directly acknowledge.

Justices

The post-2007 Constitutional Court had four categories of justices: three nominees of the Supreme Court, two nominees of the Supreme Administrative Court, two legal experts, and two experts in political science. In Thai, Constitutional Court judges are "justices" (*tulakan*) rather than judges. The legal and political science representatives were appointed by a five-member committee made up of the president of the Supreme Court, the president of the Supreme Administrative Court, the president of Parliament, the leader of the opposition, and an elected representative from among the chairs of the independent agencies. In 2008, the two slots assigned to "legal experts" were given to high-profile former Supreme Court judges—Wasant and Jaran—who were not actually nominated by the Supreme Court. Wasant had enjoyed an important but second-tier judicial career: the highest position he reached was president of the Supreme Court's juvenile division. He applied to become an election commissioner in 2006, but his candidacy was rejected when he made some bold criticisms during the Senate selection process. Wasant was one of the judges who convicted Thaksin in the 2008 land case, and he later gained notoriety for commenting that the real "ammat" (aristocrat) in Thailand was Yingluck, the most powerful person in the country.[45] Wasant had strong credentials as an outspoken legal conservative, but did not hold a master's degree and had never studied abroad: his credibility as a "law expert" was questionable.

The political science experts on the Constitutional Court were also somewhat surprising choices. While in the early days of the court, these positions were held by some of the country's most prominent political science professors—Chai-Anan Samudavanija, Suchit Bunbongkarn, and Kramol Tongdhamachart—the two experts appointed in 2008 were both former ambassadors to second-tier countries. Chalermpon Ake-uru (1945–2016) had served as ambassador to both Vietnam and Hungary, and gained a master's degree from Columbia University— but held no degree in political science. Supot Khaimuk had been ambassador to

Poland and Iran; he held a BA in international relations and a French doctorate in law and political science. The only obvious logic behind including former diplomats was that occasional constitutional cases—notably the 2008 Preah Vihear dispute between Thailand and Cambodia—concerned international treaties. Yet appointing two mid-ranking former ambassadors to the Constitutional Court slots assigned for political science experts suggested an aversion to anyone with a serious academic understanding of Thailand's domestic politics, partly reflecting establishment unease at the role Kramol Tongdhamachart had played as president of the court during the Thaksin era. In terms of voting, Chalermpon often wrote "pro-Thaksin" judgments, while Supot was a royalist stalwart: the two ex-diplomat political science experts generally cancelled one another out.

The other Constitutional Court justices had more predictable backgrounds. Former Constitutional Court president Chat Chonlavorn, like Wasant, had served as president of the Supreme Juvenile Court; like Jaran, he had served as secretary-general to the Office of the Judiciary. Boonsong Kulbubpar had only served in the Supreme Court for a year before being nominated to the Constitutional Court. Nurak Mapraneet was the great survivor: he was the only member of the 2006–8 military-appointed Constitutional Tribunal to be reappointed to the Constitutional Court in 2008, eventually becoming president after Wasant stepped down.

Chai-Anan Samudavanija, a political science professor who served as a Constitutional Court judge from 1998 to 2000, argued that the professional judges appointed to the bench were often ill-qualified for the task: "They are so conservative and have such long experience with the courts that their thinking is so narrow. If you look at my rulings, in many cases they are different, and they think that I am not doing my job in the right way."[46] According to Chai-Anan, these professional judges did not refer to the constitution, but to judgments of the Supreme Court: the procedures they used were not constitutional procedures. They failed to take into account the role of the state and the wider political context. The Constitutional Court was also full of second-rate judges: the best people, those with overseas degrees or who had been called to the English bar, for example, did not usually put themselves forward. Instead, the Courts of Justice nominated less-qualified judges who did not want to remain in the regular courts.

Wasant

Court president Wasant Soypisut's own published account of the 2012 constitutional amendment case makes interesting reading. Wasant had enjoyed a difficult relationship with pro-Thaksin politicians: in 2015, a former MP and a former government spokesman were given jail terms after he sued them for criminal defamation. They had accused him of favoritism towards the Democrats in a party dissolution case.[47] In his subsequent memoirs, Wasant began by explaining that there were genuine reasons for believing that the Yingluck government might be seeking to upend the existing political order and to reduce the powers and privileges of the monarchy. Wasant based this claim on having seen pro-red posters displayed during the 2009 and 2010 redshirt demonstrations that declared "New Thai State: President Thaksin Shinawatra."[48] But his concerns grew stronger when the court agreed to consider the petition: he was shocked by the outpouring of hostility from the progovernment side: an array of critical media commentators on TV channels 9 and 11,[49] including various "independent scholars" and pundits who had apparently never studied law at all.[50] Wasant lamented that critics of the petition has chosen to direct their ire, not at the antigovernment petitioners, but at the Constitutional Court itself.[51] An intense dislike of pro-Thaksin lawyers and their aggressive tactics is a recurrent theme of the book: he appeared to take attacks on him by the pro-Thaksin side very personally.[52] Why didn't the government take the opportunity to clarify its position, demonstrate its sincerity, and explain the reasoning behind the constitutional reform proposals? Did the administration's failure to explain itself mean that the petitioners might be right about the Yingluck government's sinister intentions to subvert Thailand political order?

Wasant had a reasonable point: Yingluck was already becoming notorious for failing to explain publicly the reasons behind her administration's policies and parliamentary maneuvers, a problem that became even more acute during the amnesty bill debacle in late 2013.[53] Wasant does not directly state that the government side was in serious danger of alienating sympathetic judges, but he implies as much. He observes that the testimony of parliament president Somsak and deputy prime minister Yongyuth was eminently satisfactory: both promised to the court and to all parties to the case that they had no intention at all of changing either the political structure of the country, or royal powers and privileges.[54] A similar point was made by Chat, the most pro-Yingluck-government judge on the bench, who had opposed accepting the petition in the first place.[55] Following Somsak and Yongyuth's pledges, Wasant's concerns were assuaged. Despite his apparent sympathies for the petitioners, Wasant went on to state that he could see no reason why the government should not be entitled to make constitutional amendments that did not undermine the political system or the monarchy. In the end, the president of the court did not allow his anti-Thaksin leanings to sway his judgment. He was one of the four judges who rejected the petition on all counts. Arguably, however, Wasant was in much the same situation as Jaran. He had given a television interview on August 18, 2011, in which he expressed support for establishing a new constitution drafting assembly, a view he had repeated in a newspaper interview as recently as February 2012.[56] Had he supported the petitioners, he could have faced strong criticism.

Testimony

During the afternoon of July 5, petitioner and Democrat MP Wirat Kalayasiri was refused permission to show twenty minutes of video clips from speeches by people associated with the redshirt movement, including Giles Ungpakorn, Jatuporn Prompan, and Jakrapob Penkair, in support of his claim that there was a plot to overthrow the political order. Sporting a "senior justice system administrator" jacket that proclaimed his own personal ties to the judiciary, Wirat argued that Giles Ji Ungpakorn, speaking in Sweden, had claimed that a certain person had ordered the killings of redshirts in 2010.[57] Wirat also asserted that "bright eyes," a phrase used by Nattawut and Jatuporn, was being invoked by the redshirts to make inappropriate insinuations.[58] Wirat's apparently irrelevant assertions were criticized by the defense lawyers who argued that they undermined the petitioner's own credibility. But although the case against Pheu Thai was technically about the right of the government to amend the constitution, Wirat and his fellow petitioners sought to raise accusations of disloyalty towards the crown against Thaksin and his close associates. Constitutionalism served simply as a cover for much darker allegations on the treason spectrum.

In a sop to the petitioners, the president overruled the objections of the Pheu Thai lawyers, declaring that all of Wirat's arguments were relevant to the case. Pheu Thai lawyers baited Wirat, who floundered when asked awkward questions: more than once, President Wasant declared: "Don't start fighting."[59] The premise that this was a nonadversarial legal forum was hard to sustain, given that the petitioner on the witness stand was a Democrat MP, while defense lawyer Chusak Sirinil was a former Thaksin-aligned minister. As in many other Constitutional Court cases, the lines between the legal and the political were completely blurred.

The businesslike mode of the morning's proceedings had given way to an atmosphere more reminiscent of a parliamentary no-confidence debate. The president directed the Pheu Thai lawyers not to ask too many questions concerning the opinion of the witnesses, which would become a waste of time. They took the president at his word: the final witness, arch-royalist Boworn Yasinthorn, made relatively short remarks, and the Pheu Thai lawyers declared themselves very happy with his statement and announced they had no questions for him. In that case, asked Boworn, could he use the remaining time to make some additional points? No, declared the president—you have said enough.

Explanations

The short shrift given to Boworn could be read in more than one way. The day's proceedings had a tokenistic quality: the judges allowed the two sides to air their arguments, but had little intention of allowing either the petitioners or the lawyers to sway their views.[60] But the curt dismissal of Boworn, and the palpable bemusement of the judges when they called time on the proceedings, also suggested that the decision was a foregone conclusion.[61] The court had accepted the case and agreed to hear the petitioners in order to assuage the critics of the Yingluck government, but had no real intention of finding in their favor. Far from a judicial coup, this was a judicial holding operation.

The 2012 constitutional amendment case was one of a series of legal challenges brought against Thaksin and his proxies in the wake of two important royal speeches given on April 25, 2006, which marked the formal outbreak of judicial hostilities. Some other political court cases may loom larger in the public imagination, notably the 2008 criminal charges that resulted in a two-year jail sentence (issued in absentia) for Thaksin himself, the 2008 removal of Samak Sundaravej as prime minister, the confiscation of the bulk of Thaksin's assets in 2010, and the judicial ousting of his sister Yingluck from the office of prime minister in May 2014. But a distinctive feature of the 2012 case was the treason allegation at its core: the petitioners argued that pro-Thaksin forces were seeking to overthrow the system of government and modify the status and privileges of the monarchy. This central accusation against Thaksin—his disloyalty to the crown—was not made explicit in any of these better-known cases, even though it may have underpinned them. When pro-Thaksin forces were explicitly charged with disloyalty in 2012, the allegations would not stick and an elaborate fudge was required to obfuscate the Constitutional Court's painful predicament.

On Saturday, July 7, the day after the two-day hearings, King Bhumibol—who had spent most of the past four years in Siriraj Hospital—made a rare public excursion, donning a naval uniform to travel up the Chao Phraya River on the royal vessel *Angsana*.[62] This was his second major outing that year; in May, he had visited an agricultural project in Ayutthaya Province, to great fanfare. As with the May trip, his visit was broadcast live on all Thai national television stations, this time from 4:00 to 8:00 p.m. As in May, Prime Minister Yingluck played an important presiding role in the associated ceremonies.[63] Yingluck's proximity to the monarchy during a highly unusual event conspicuously staged on the weekend between the Constitutional Court hearings and the judgment, suggested that striking a heavy blow against her party's rule, let alone removing Yingluck from office, was unthinkable.

Yingluck may have owed her position as prime minister to a deal done between the palace, the military, and her party in the run-up to the general election a year earlier.[64] According to this theory, the powers-that-be agreed to accept the election results, so long as Yingluck did not rock the boat: in short, she agreed to protect the monarchy (which included not seeking to roll back the lèse-majesté laws), not to curtail the privileges of the military, and not to agitate for her brother's return from Dubai. Whether or not such accounts of an explicit preelection deal between Yingluck, the military, and the palace were entirely accurate, developments during her premiership were broadly consistent with a tacit alliance between the network monarchy and the ruling party. While previously Thaksin's allies had pushed for him to be pardoned, during the Yingluck government no such moves were made.[65] Yingluck received three different royal decorations in 2011 and 2012 and was widely believed to enjoy good relations both with the King himself, and with General Prem.[66] While third-string members of the royalist and Thaksin networks argued their cases before the Constitutional Court during the 2012 amendment case, the palace and the prime minister appeared to be on excellent terms.

Judgment

The judgment, issued a week later, confirmed these suspicions. The judges took their arguments almost verbatim from the testimony of law professor Suraphon Nitikraipot, the former rector of Thammasat University, who argued that since the 2007 Constitution had been ratified by a popular referendum, another referendum would be desirable in order to amend it.[67] Suraphon's submissions provided the court with a convenient way out, allowing the judges to throw a sop to the petitioners without acceding to any of their substantive claims. The court cleared Pheu Thai of all charges: there was nothing illegal in what the ruling party proposed. Yet as Khemthong Tonsakulrungruang points out, the Constitution Court's referendum proposal was not legally binding, but merely a suggestion.[68] By making a half-baked proposal, the Constitutional Court was arguably not acting as a court: courts are obliged to issue legal judgments, not expressions of opinion.

As Wasant explains in his memoir, Jaran's withdrawal had been a very unwelcome complication. Had Chusak not challenged Jaran about his views in open court, Jaran would have been unable to recuse himself. Chusak might have released the transcript of Jaran's earlier comments after the hearings were finished, but before the judgment was announced: Jaran would then have felt obliged to support the government against the petitioners, resulting in the rejection of the petition by 5 votes to 4 and a green light for the government to press ahead with the constitutional amendments. That this did not happen was the achievement of a Pheu Thai lawyer, wrote Wasant sarcastically. As a law professor rather than a practicing trial lawyer, Chusak did not think through the implications of his challenge, apparently not realizing that he would give Jaran an opening to recuse himself.

Curiously, Wasant makes no direct reference in the chapter either to his previous media comments on the amendment issue, or his own request to recuse himself from the case—which was rejected by his fellow judges. But his comments on Jaran's case could be seen as a description of his own situation: did he find against the petitioners because this represented his real view of the case, or was he boxed in by his previous statements? If Wasant only voted against the plaintiff out of sheer necessity, the case might otherwise have turned out very differently. Chusak's challenge to Jaran may have neutralized not just one but two potential votes against the ruling party. Wasant noted in his book that he was criticized by various judges from the Courts of Justice for being pro-Thaksin. Citing the words of the oath sworn by judges to the King, he stated that judges cannot make their rulings on the basis of personal likes or dislikes. Those who felt otherwise should not be judges: "We may dislike someone, but we can't make an adverse judgment against them if they are not wrong: if someone is on the right side, they have to win the case."[69] His rather defensive comments illustrated the pressures Wasant faced, and the difficulties he experienced trying to negotiate his position.

In this July 2012 decision, the Constitutional Court followed the political winds, reflecting rather than shaping the course of events. This was not a case of the judicialization of politics, but of an already thoroughly politicized judiciary. Jaran's decision to recuse himself, the attempts of three other judges to follow suit, the president's hollow humoring of the self-parodying petitioners, the court's issuing an advisory statement in lieu of a proper judgment, and its appropriation of Suraphon's testimony to form the basis of that statement were all examples of the court's pragmatism and evasions, testifying to a deep reluctance to rock the ship of state at a time when the monarchy and the Yingluck government were literally in the same boat. Borwornsak Uwanno had rightly argued that a central duty of the Constitutional Court was not to take sides politically: ironically, one way to avoid overt partisanship was simply to fudge important issues.[70]

Iconography

Between 2006 and 2008, Thailand's politics had many parallels with a reality television show.[71] A TV host, ousted from his show, began a movement to displace from power the TV channel-owning prime minister who had just removed him.

When the TV channel owner sold his station to a foreign country, the ousted TV host was able to mobilize huge crowds to mass rallies at which he sold them subscriptions to his own television channel. Later, the ousted TV host sent his supporters to take over a government television station, in a failed attempt to broadcast his own channel through government transmitters. The following month, the Constitutional Court removed a prime minister from office for illegally hosting his own television show.[72]

In the aftermath of 2008, YouTube "clips," easily viewed video fragments, began to loom larger than real-time television as instruments of political change and struggle. In a society where accountability was elusive and collective memories were unreliable, forces on both sides of the deeply polarized political divide sought to deploy video clips to undermine their opponents (or, less commonly, to shore up their own position). The 2012 constitutional amendment case was not the first time that video clips had been deployed to challenge the authority of the Constitutional Court, which was dogged by allegations of corruption and improprieties during this period,[73] but it was the first time such a clip triggered a constitutional crisis on which the future political direction of Thailand hinged.[74] The 2012 constitutional amendment case did not hinge on an iconic object—such as the gloves in the O. J. Simpson trial—but on the iconic use of video footage. This was not footage of a defendant, but of one of the judges.

The deliberations of a constitutional court should be based on the prevailing constitution, as well as on relevant laws and precedents. But the notion of precedents is problematic in Thailand, since after the annulment of the 1997 Constitution in 2006, all previous decisions of the Constitutional Court were no longer directly applicable. Not only were they based on a different constitution, but the credibility and legitimacy of all those decisions had been retrospectively called into question, owing to a widespread view that under Thaksin the Constitutional Court became politicized. Nor could the decisions of the military-appointed 2006–7 Constitutional Tribunal, based on the 2006 interim charter, necessarily inform those of the reestablished post-2008 Constitutional Court. Given the unreliability of precedents, Constitutional Court judges were obliged to base their decisions on the prevailing constitution itself, and their own understandings of the intentions behind it. For at least three of the judges in office in 2012, these understandings were closely shaped by their direct involvement in the drafting of the 2007 charter.

In the 2012 charter amendment case, YouTube videos replaced case lore and precedents as a means of disciplining judges to adhere to consistent positions. Instead of passing judgment based on legal principles or precedents, Constitutional Court judges were expected to remain consistent to the positions they had expressed in earlier video clips. Jaran, who was confronted during case hearings over his YouTube stances, was permitted to recuse himself; while Wasant, who was not challenged in open court, was not allowed to withdraw.

Thailand's Constitutional Court had pursued pragmatic accommodations with power holders throughout its history, during a series of incarnations. The court had variously operated as the post-1997 large court of fifteen justices, both before and during Thaksin's premiership; as the military-appointed Constitutional Tribunal, 2006–7; and after being reborn as a smaller, more royalist-inclined nine-judge court from 2008 onwards.[75] The political complexion of the court changed over time, but its modus operandi remained broadly similar. Just as before making any political intervention the monarchy had to consider the preservation of royal standing, so the Constitutional Court was primarily concerned to defend its collective interests—and above all, to avert its own abolition. Even senior figures in the Courts of Justice claimed they were afraid to challenge the legitimacy of a military coup for fear of being abolished; the Constitutional Court was on far shakier ground, having already been shut down after the 2006 coup.

For much of its history, the Constitutional Court has had few friends. The court has been viewed with grave mistrust by most judges from the Courts of Justice, who argued that it was a political institution and not a real court of law. Sarawut Benjakul, a senior figure in the judiciary who had held a number of important posts—including secretary to the president of the Constitutional Court—argued that it would be possible to organize the body as a constitutional tribunal rather than a court.[76] One progressively oriented judge argued that most of the judges on the Constitutional Court had no obvious qualifications, including the representatives from the Supreme Court, who were very conservative and lacked understanding of public law.[77] The Constitutional Court was criticized by the King in 2006 as unreliable, given to shirking its responsibilities, and much inferior to the Supreme Court.

Yet the Constitutional Court was equally unpopular with the entire political class, who were wary of its extensive powers to thwart parliamentary and executive authority. It was similarly unpopular with progressive-minded scholars and media pundits. Former Chiang Mai University law faculty dean Somchai Preechasinlapakul argued that the majority of Constitutional Court judgments did more to defend the government of the day than to uphold either the constitution, or citizens' rights.[78] In the days following the 2012 decision, the Nitirat group of critical legal scholars called for the Constitutional Court to be abolished in its current form.[79] While the Nitirat abolition proposal was rather hastily conceived, similar arguments had been made from various political perspectives during the drafting of the 2007 Constitution and were to resurface during the debates surrounding a new constitution following the May 2014 coup. During 2014, the court tried to institutionalize its existence by drafting a Constitutional Court Act, which could be ratified by parliament and thus could not easily be abrogated in the event of another coup.[80] Thailand was in the curious situation that it was easier to abolish a constitution than to revise a statute. The Constitutional Court could not rest easy under the protection of the highest law of the land, and so sought to defend itself with a lower order of legislation. Lack of respect for the Constitutional Court was a symptom of the lack of regard in which existing constitutions were held, despite the immense effort that always went into creating new ones. The Constitutional Court was the unloved child of Thai legalism, combining enormous authority with terrible vulnerability, and viewed almost universally with intense suspicion. As a result, the court was generally eager to please and very reluctant to antagonize those with power over its future.

Principles

Jaran explained that the Constitutional Court had to base its decisions on three questions: the constitution, the intentions of the drafters, and the interests of the nation. Herein lay the rub, since the constitution was often ambiguous and the intentions of the drafters were at best unclear, and arguably even contradictory. As a drafter himself, Jaran could be forgiven for assuming that his own intentions and his personal view of the 2007 Constitution could serve him as a good guide in his judgments (an argument which applied with lesser force to a couple of the other judges). Hence the remaining core concern was one of national interest, and how to adjudge it. National interest could trump legal niceties, and regularly did. When Thaksin was acquitted in 2001, it was on the basis of national interest and not law. Similarly, when the Constitutional Court fudged the constitutional amendment case in 2012, this was because Thailand was experiencing bitterly divided politics, and fudging the case was the most pragmatic response to the prevailing conditions. Over the next two years, the Constitutional Court struggled to keep sitting on the fence, trying to shift the burden for important decisions back to the Election Commission, the NACC, or the Senate. Precisely the same reluctance to act with which the King had reproached the Constitutional Court back in 2006 characterized its moves between mid-2012 and early 2014, though for different reasons. In 2006 the Constitutional Court had been broadly aligned with Thaksin, whereas in 2012–14 the Constitutional Court mirrored the agonies of the monarchical network, which was torn between trying to work through Yingluck and at the same time very much wishing her gone. The removal of Yingluck from office in May 2014, when it finally came, was an example of the court's attempts to address what they it saw as the national interest. But again, as in 2006 or 2008, annulling an election or removing a premier from office was insufficient to "restart" Thailand's political order. Interventions by the Constitutional Court proved nothing more than a palliative, or even exacerbated ongoing political crises. In the end, the Constitutional Court was exactly what Jaran asserted it should not become: a quasi-political court, or a political court. It exercised not constitutional power but extraconstitutional power. Its decisions often reflected the ambivalent status of the establishment: in the end, the court generally served as an instrument by which the network monarchy could promote notions of virtuous rule—and defend its own interests. Constitutional Court judges swore an oath of loyalty to the King, following exactly the same wording as new judges in the Courts of Justice.[81]

The guiding principle of the court was a quest to advance the "good of the nation," a project which was largely political rather than legal. A quest to locate the public interest was therefore a theme of Constitutional Court decisions. In 2012, Chat Chonlawon wrote that there was a public "consensus" for revising the constitution—hence his decision to find against the petitioners.[82] While Chat's judgment was more explicit than those of his peers, it illustrated the ways in which judges were constantly aware of the prevailing political winds. Explaining his 2007 statements in support of the idea that the new charter could be rewritten later, Jaran argued that at the time he simply wanted to get through the referendum so that they could bring the period of military rule to an end. In other words, his reasons were entirely political. In the changed circumstances of 2012, this reasoning had become a liability: the end of military rule had brought a return to pro-Thaksin rule: as Wasant argued in his book, there were reasons to believe that the Pheu Thai Party could not really be trusted to revise the constitution.[83] But scholars who have portrayed the Constitutional Court as a mere tool of the monarchical network, bent on removing pro-Thaksin forces, are glossing over the nuances of the story. If the network monarchy had opposed the Yingluck government, it could have withdrawn cooperation much earlier. Just as the network broadly facilitated Thaksin's rule from 2001 until 2005, so the network was largely on side with Yingluck between 2011 and at least mid-2013. Under these circumstances, the role of the Constitutional Court was actually to restrain the vulgar excesses of the anti-Thaksin movement, as epitomized by bumptious figures such as General Somjed, Wirat, and Boworn.

By giving the petitioners a hearing, the court hoped to reduce political tensions. But the hearing itself was largely theatrical, as Wasant acknowledged: "In truth, the hearing of testimony from the petitioners was simply in order to have a means of assessing the level of national anxiety. In any event, on the first day there was an incident which created problems for our judgment, and remains a problem until the present time."[84]

In other words, the role of the Constitutional Court was not to address intense political problems by assigning winners and losers, but to neutralize ongoing conflicts.[85] Repeating this steam-letting exercise grew more difficult in the rapid succession of cases that followed, as anti-Thaksin forces ramped up both their rhetoric and their actions on the streets. The Constitutional Court was caught in a cleft stick: act weakly and appear irrelevant (and face calls for abolition), or act strongly and provoke intense enmity (and face calls for abolition). In many respects, the Constitutional Court's dilemma resembled both that of the monarchy in 1992 (only intervene if you are sure you have identified the winning side) and the military in the wake of the failed 1991 and 2006 coup processes (only stage a coup d'état if you believe you can really deliver the coup de grace). Put simply: the new constitutionalism, drawing on European models and normative assumptions about representative government and the rule of law, was not a fit for Thailand's deeply polarized politics. A constitutional court was of very little use to a country such as Thailand: for a country moving towards anocracy, legalism could promote a slide towards polarization and extremism, opening up new realms of contestation.

An alternative view is that the political trials of the Constitutional Court offered a way towards liminality, a means of shifting deep-rooted conflicts off the streets and into the courtroom, of creating rituals and performances that could help Thais deal more constructively with their profound disagreements. But this is not an argument for legalism or new constitutionalism in the strict sense, merely a way of creatively deploying such institutional mechanisms as an alternative and less destructive form of mass engagement in politics, in the same way that elections meet political needs that go well beyond representation and the narrow forms of participation enshrined in voting itself.

The 2012 constitutional amendment case was a piece of pure political theater. Ostensibly, a bunch of third-tier politicians stood accused of violating the provisions of the constitution. In reality, former premier Thaksin Shinawatra stood accused of disloyalty to the monarchy: legalism and constitutionalism offered a means of "indicting" a man who was not named as a respondent, and who had not set foot in Thailand for four years, on charges that were never spelled out. Virtually nothing in this case was what it seemed.

Many of the themes of the 2012 case were revisited in another case decided by the Constitutional Court in November 2013. This time, the petitioners—once again headed by Somjed Boonthanom and including Wirat Kalayasiri—focused on Pheu Thai proposals to abolish the appointed component of the Senate and marshaled evidence that the ruling party had abused parliamentary voting procedures to get its way. By sticking to these more clearly defined legal issues, the petitioners were on firmer ground, and the court ruled 5–4 that the Pheu Thai plan to reform the Senate was unconstitutional:

> The constitutional amendment pursuant to the petitions is a return to the former defects, which are perilous and likely to bring an end to the faith and harmony of the majority of the Thai people. It is an attempt to draw the Nation back in the canal, as it would bring the Senate back to the state of being an assembly of relatives, assembly of family members and assembly of husbands and wives. In consequence, the Senate would lose its status and vigour as the source of wisdom for the House of Representatives, but would merely be an echo for the people from the same group. The principles of the bicameral system would be debased, leading to the monopoly of state powers and the exclusion of the participation of the members of various sectors and professions. The amendment is thus an effort of its initiators to regain the national government power by the means not recognized by the Constitution—the 2007 Constitution approved by the majority of the people of Thailand at a referendum.[86]

Nevertheless, the actions of the court still spoke larger than these words: despite this damning criticism, the Constitutional Court did not dissolve the ruling Pheu Thai Party. The judgment simply stated, without a word of explanation, that the conditions for party dissolution were not met. The result was another fudge: the Yingluck government was barred from reforming the Senate and was reprimanded for manipulating parliamentary procedures; but the government could remain in office and was not prevented from pursuing other constitutional amendments. This was a stronger reprimand than the previous year's, but still not a judicial coup.

What happened between July 2012 and November 2013 to produce this shift in tone? Wasant had now left the Constitutional Court bench, replaced as president by the more conservative Nurak Mapraneet, and as a judge by Taweekiat Meenakanit. The change had an immediate impact on voting outcomes.[87] Taweekiat was a Thammasat University law professor with an American degree and a French doctorate, known for his outspoken conservative views on issues such as Article 112.[88] He had been a member of the committee that drafted the controversial 2007 Computer Crime Act. Thai PBS reported that he was aligned with an ultra-royalist group of more than twenty law and political science lecturers known as Siam Prachapiwat.[89] This grouping emerged in January 2012, aiming to discredit Nitirat's calls for reform of the lèse-majesté law.[90] Siam Prachapiwat was closely linked to the "Twenty-Three Lecturers," a group of legal academics established in October 2011 to counter Nitirat calls for the "nullification" of the 2006 coup, but Siam Prachapiwat included political scientists as well as lawyers.[91] While only a handful of academics were formally part of both groups, in practice there was a significant overlap between the two, which were unified by a shared ideological position.[92] Members of these groups also engaged in legal harassment of Thaksin-aligned politicians: Komsan Pokhong was one of the petitioners who took a case to the Constitutional Court in 2013, accusing Thaksin of engaging in unconstitutional attempts to undermine the political order by using Skype and video links to participate in both private and public meetings, despite being a fugitive from justice.[93]

The appointment of Taweekiat was highly significant. Selected after eight rounds of voting, he was one of nine candidates, comprising four judges, a senior prosecutor, the head of the military court, and three academics. His main rival was Banjerd Singkaneti, a law professor at NIDA and a leading figure in Siam Prachapiwat.[94] Banjerd was a more prominent controversialist than Taweekiat, but their political views were very similar.[95] In the tense political conditions of late 2013, professional judges were not sufficiently reliable: outspoken academics were preferred for the bench. Prior to Taweekiat's appointment, the Constitutional Court received petitions from anti-Thaksin activists; after Taweekiat's appointment, the Constitutional Court had its own in-house anti-Thaksin activist.

As the late Chai-Anan Samudavanija put it, by the time of the 2006 coup "everything had failed . . . the judges are the only thing left, but they don't want to do it."[96] In practice, the (un)willingness of the Constitutional Court to check the power of politicians was selective. When the government of the day clearly lacked royal approval (Thaksin after April 26, 2006; Samak Sundaravej and Somchai Wongsawat throughout their brief 2008 terms) the Constitutional Court was willing to nullify elections, oust serving premiers, and dissolve ruling parties. But the ambiguous role played by the court was seen most clearly during the Yingluck administration, which governed for more than two years with the tacit blessing of the palace, and stumbled on for seven months between November 2013 and May 2014, during which time the network monarchy seemed unable to come up with any solution. Under these conditions, the judges of the Constitutional Court were at times quite unsure what to do.

The 2012 constitutional amendment case, which failed to produce a legally binding judgment, epitomized the judges' dilemmas. No less than four of the nine judges—including the president of the court—tried to recuse themselves from the case. Only one, leading royalist jurist Jaran Phakdithanakun, succeeded in doing so. The 2012 case had echoes of the 2001 Thaksin acquittal: for the Constitutional Court to find against the administration of the day would have precipitated an unprecedented political crisis. In both cases, the way out was a fudge that allowed the government to remain in office. In other words, both the 2001 and 2012 cases were messy, troubling triumphs of common sense over legalism. The Constitutional Court was at its most politically effective when behaving badly in legal terms. An important function of the Constitutional Court was arguably to find ways of circumventing the overscripted legalism of successive constitutions.

Most criticism of the Constitutional Court since 2006 has concerned the harsh treatment it meted out to pro-Thaksin parties and premiers. The 2008 Samak case—in which a serving prime minister was removed from office for having hosted a television cooking show—symbolizes the crass expediency of such interventions. At the same time, the Thai parliament could have convened immediately to reappoint Samak as prime minister. That parliament failed to do so, instead replacing him with Thaksin's brother-in-law Somchai Wongsawat, indicates that by then Samak had outlived his usefulness to the exiled power broker. Ultimately, Samak was removed from office not by the Constitutional Court, but by Thaksin Shinawatra. Thaksin took advantage of the court's action to rid himself of a figure who had done a sterling job of winning the December 2007 election but had subsequently become a serious political liability. In this sense, Thaksin and the Constitutional Court were in alliance over Samak's removal— something the judges may have understood perfectly well.

The role of the Constitutional Court in the extended political crisis that culminated in the May 2014 ouster of Yingluck and the subsequent military coup was still more murky and ambiguous. The court could have dissolved Pheu Thai and removed Yingluck from office as early as July 2012, but ducked numerous opportunities to do so—notably over the November 2013 constitutional amendment case. Instead, the court passed the buck to the Senate, which in turn failed to impeach the prime minister during the months that followed. On crucial questions such as whether the government or the Election Commission was responsible for deciding the election date, the Constitutional Court declined to take a stance. Some analysts argued that a "judicial coup" against Yingluck might offer a means of avoiding a military seizure of power.[97] But ultimately, the events of 2006 repeated themselves: a judicial coup failed to forestall a military one. The Constitutional Court's May 2014 ouster of Yingluck was either too little, too late—or simply a warm-up exercise that helped legitimate the real intervention two weeks later, that of the military.

But the procrastinations of both the courts and the army between November 2013 and May 2014 suggest that the monarchical network was trying to maintain the Yingluck government in office, or at least to avoid a potentially damaging showdown. Again, Thaksin himself must bear some responsibility. While the

Yingluck government apparently came to power on the basis of a deal between the monarchy and the military, over time Thaksin chafed at one crucial element in the tacit understanding: his own continued banishment from Thailand. Jealous of Yingluck's superior diplomatic skills and growing popularity, Thaksin deliberately sabotaged her government by making repeated moves to seek constitutional amendments and secure an amnesty for himself. Yingluck lacked sufficient authority over Pheu Thai MPs to prevent them from launching the disastrous parliamentary moves for an amnesty bill.[98]

In truth, Thailand's Constitutional Court was always a political court: judicialization was integral to its founding principles. The court's mission to act on behalf of the national interest overrode purely legal considerations, especially given the limited relevance of precedents in a country where constitutions kept being rewritten, and where previous court judgments were tainted by their association with earlier political regimes. Constitutional Court decisions consistently sought to accommodate power holders: Thaksin during his heyday (2001–6); the monarchical network once Thaksin fell from grace (2006–11); Yingluck during her first two-plus years as a compromise premier (2011–13); and the military in the weeks leading up to the May 2014 coup (2014). The King's speeches of April 2006 were explicitly critical of the Thaksin-era Constitution Court and sought to shift the burden of responsibility to the Supreme Court. But in practice, the dirty work of political interventions was confined largely to the Constitutional Court. The main contribution of the Courts of Justice was to permit Thaksin to leave Thailand in July 2008, and then to punish him, in absentia, with jail time: in effect, a sentence of exile. The Courts of Justice performed a parallel role in the rice scheme case that forced Yingluck into exile in August 2017.

Accordingly, to see the Constitutional Court as the primary instrument of royal power during the final decade of Bhumibol's rule would be a real stretch. Tempting though it may be to rail, Donald Trump-like, about the perfidies of the supposed Deep State, such crude interpretations do little to capture the confusion, complexity, and uncertainty that reigned inside Thailand's Constitutional Court. Both in 2006 and in 2014, it was not the country's judges or legalists who took decisive action to oust Shinawatra-led governments: it was the military. Like King Bhumibol himself, the justices of the Constitutional Court were deeply conflicted about how to deal with the Shinawatras and were very reluctant to take assume responsibility or blame for moves that contradicted the will of the majority of the country's citizens and voters. When the Constitutional Court took action, it was usually too little and too late. Despite the prevailing discourse of judicialization, cautious and conservative Constitutional Court judges were rarely the lead actors in Thailand's political turmoil.

This chapter illustrates that reductionist explanations viewing the late Bhumibol Constitutional Court through a single, anti-Thaksin lens do not bear close scrutiny. The court was against Thaksin overall, but its judges were extremely cautious about taking the lead on troublesome political issues, preferring to let other actors—including the military—call the shots. The hesitancy of the Constitutional Court reflected the intermittently collaborative relationship that existed between the network monarchy and the Thaksin network, seen most clearly during the 2011–14 Yingluck government. But it also reflected a recognition that heavy-handed judicial interventions in Thailand's turbulent politics always came at a price: a price paid not simply by the political class, but also by the judiciary and by the courts themselves.

While judges certainly merit serious criticism for many of their actions and decisions concerning political trials, it would be simply impossible for the courts to restore national happiness (to borrow the language of the post-2014 military junta). Nor can they be held principally responsible for exacerbating the country's already entrenched political woes. For all the talk of judicial coups, the Thaksin and Yingluck governments were ultimately removed from office not by judges, but by generals.

Conclusion

THE TROUBLE IS POLITICS

This book has demonstrated that Thailand is suffering from a surfeit of legalism: revolving-door constitutions, politicized independent agencies—including a problematic Constitutional Court—and a judiciary that works on behalf of an imagined monarchy, rather than in the public interest. The results are plain to see: a profound degree of political instability, high levels of social polarization, very high conviction rates, the abuse of punitive treason spectrum laws, and a prison population that is rising uncontrollably. Far from easing tensions through reflexive and moderating decisions, the courts have aggravated matters and fueled growing levels of crisis.

The book raises important questions about the extent to which solutions grounded in legalism—ranging from new courts to draconian legislation—fail to address substantive political problems. In many respects, Thailand's travails are simply an extreme illustration of the shortcomings of legalistic fixes in many parts of the world. I argue that courts should strive for what Judith Shklar terms "tribunality": the pragmatic and judicious resolution of complex political problems. If this means fudging legal niceties to achieve a workable outcome, so be it. I also hope that trials may provide for moments of what Victor Turner calls "liminality," when the use of legal ritual and formality creates episodes of catharsis. A judiciously conducted trial can move conflict into the realm of ritual, moderating disagreements and producing a solution that captures nuance and maintains ambiguity. Such liminality prepares the way for tribunality: practical judicial solutions that are grounded in political and social realities rather than in rigid attachment to the letter of very imperfect laws.

However, the more Thai judges see themselves as enforcing loyalty to the crown, the more unattainable even brief glimpses of tribunality and liminality become. Thailand has a justice problem: an "injustice cascade" seen in a culture of impunity, excessive incarceration, and far too many people accused and convicted of crimes of compassings—in other words, thought crimes. Ironically, closely related to this injustice cascade has been a troubling rise in legalism. Rule of law and the need for peace and order have been invoked to justify a judicial call to arms. In 2006, King Bhumibol himself called on Thailand's judges to solve its intractable political problems. These pressures put the judiciary—already suffering from a dangerous combination of overconfidence and lack of imagination—in a near impossible situation.

Thai judges are at the core of this book. In many ways these judges seem rather admirable: after passing an extremely difficult entrance examination at an early age, they are socialized into a professional world somewhat removed from normal society, an organizational culture that rewards caution and reserve, in which promotion based on standing and seniority is highly predictable. Judges command high social status and public regard, and are generally the most honest and incorruptible officers of the Thai state. Yet the disposition of Thai judges has its darker, self-satisfied, and self-regarding side. Because they are inclined to see themselves as epitomizing virtuous rule, they are reluctant to reflect critically on their own culture and practices. Since 1997, Thai judges have been insulated from political oversight; while a positive step in some respects, this shift to greater self-regulation has also fostered a greater sense of entitlement.

In particular, Thai judges tend to equate serving the King with performing justice, despite the fact that the absolute monarchy was abolished close to a century ago. King Bhumibol actually assumed the bench on a number of occasions to judge cases, despite his lack of legal training. Thai kings retain their traditional status as "lords of life" by deciding whether death sentences are carried out. Royal pardons have regularly seen thirty thousand prisoners released at once. Wide-ranging royal prerogatives to hear court cases, to reprieve those on death row, and to pardon so many prisoners are anomalies and anachronisms. Punitive laws that criminalize criticism or even open discussion of the monarchy have no place in a democratic society, but many judges believe their highest loyalty is to the crown rather than the public interest. Their belief that they are literally—rather than just figuratively—judging "in the name of the King" creates confusion and ambiguity about the nature of justice.

As Thailand's politics became more polarized after the political ascent of former prime minister Thaksin Shinawatra, so the contradictions implicit in the country's monarchy-aligned judicial system grew more apparent. Critics of the judiciary argued that the courts were practicing double standards, punishing those on the pro-Thaksin side while handling royalists and anti-Thaksin activists with kid gloves. The death in prison of *lèse-majesté* defendant Akong highlighted the cruelty of a system that routinely denied bail and medical help to those accused of political crimes. Judges found themselves on the defensive, but they lacked spokespeople who could take on critics such as the outstanding Thammasat University legal scholar Worajet Pakeerat and his Nitirat group. For all their supposed brilliance, Thai judges often appeared inarticulate and leaderless, and proved unable to give a decent account of themselves when faced with growing challenges.

Close examination of three representative political courts cases illustrates the problems of Thailand's legal system. Using ethnographic trial observations coupled with an analysis of case documents and interviews with protagonists, the book examines how iconic court cases can shed light on wider social and political questions. All three cases were connected with an organogram issued by the Thai military in April 2010, which purports to depict a plot to overthrow the monarchy (lom jao) by people, publications and organizations liked to Thaksin Shinawatra. But there was no evidence for this antimonarchist conspiracy; Pramote Nakhonthap, an anti-Thaksin activist who made similar allegations in a series of newspaper articles about the so-called "Finland plot" was convicted of defamation for his claims in 2009. Network treason was a bad dream, a dark imaginary constructed by conservative activists and later taken up by the Thai state. Despite this lack of evidence, most of those named on the 2010 diagram were charged with a variety of offences shortly afterwards. These cases illustrated that crimes of compassings— thought crimes on the treason spectrum—remained extremely salient in the Thai context. Judges proved all too ready to send people to jail for symbolic crimes such as *lèse-majesté*, computer crime, or purportedly seditious peaceful protest.

Although King Bhumibol himself had expressed his concerns about abuse of the *lèse-majesté* laws in his 2005 birthday speech, the number of charges brought under Article 112 of the Thai criminal code increased exponentially during the final decade of his reign. One of those charged was journalist Somyot Prueksakasemsuk, who had worked on a provocative, short-lived magazine known as *Voice of Taksin*. Somyot spent six years in jail over two satirical articles that he did not write, published in a magazine of which he was not the legal editor. The articles concerned did not even refer directly to the monarchy. But Somyot had been an outspoken critic of the *lèse-majesté* law and had run an important mouthpiece of the redshirt movement. While matters were made worse by his legal team, who spent much of the trial baiting prosecution witnesses and antagonizing the bench, Somyot should never have been punished so harshly. His treatment was a direct result of the judiciary's failures of empathy and imagination, and inability to understand the role of the courts in a democratic order. As confirmed in a landmark Constitutional Court decision arising from the Somyot case, Thai judges believed that protecting the monarchy was a matter of national security that took precedence not only over questions of freedom of expression, but over matters of punitive proportionality. Readily offended by criticism of the monarchy, Thai judges were rarely similarly offended by acts of tyranny, or acts of violence committed by the military.

Less well known are the provisions of Thailand's computer crime legislation, contained in a draconian 2007 coup-era law that was revised and strengthened in 2017. The Computer Crime Act allows for the prosecution of those whose online postings threaten national security, a term that is never explicitly defined. Katha Pachachirayapong was convicted in 2012 of violating the law by posting two messages on a political web board, one message critical of Princess Sirindhorn, and another repeating a rumor that the King was on his deathbed. The prosecution tried to claim that Katha's second posting had contributed to a run on the stock market. Despite the fact that officials from the IT ministry were unable convincingly to demonstrate that Katha had actually posted either of the messages, he was found guilty and sentenced to four years in jail—although he ended up serving just over eighteen months. Again, Katha's lawyers had made matters worse by turning a ridiculous case into a complete circus of a trial, in a deliberate attempt to satirize the proceedings and infuriate the judges. Katha's crimes were trivial and ludicrous: his messages could not possibly have undermined national security, weakened popular faith in the monarchy, or influenced the stock market. This was just one of many politically related cases where the courts should have thrown out the charges, or given the defendant a token slap on the wrist. Again, it illustrated a terrible failure of judicial imagination.

The "NLA sit-in" case of Jon Ungpakorn and nine other defendants was yet another example of a trial that should never have taken place. Proceedings in the military-backed National Legislative Assembly were briefly disrupted by a peaceful NGO protest in December 2007. More than four years later, ten of the alleged leaders of the protest found themselves in court facing charges of trespass and sedition. An irony of this case was that most of the defendants were anti-Thaksin activists whose political views were not very different from those of most judges. Despite facing an essentially sympathetic judge, the large team of human rights lawyers working on the case engaged in aggressive, counterproductive tactics that did little to help their cause, subjecting witnesses to endless leading questions and engaging in lengthy philosophical diatribes. It soon became clear that some of the defendants—and most of their lawyers—actually hoped to lose the case in the lower courts only to be vindicated by the Supreme Court, thereby establishing a precedent that occupying public buildings could be legally justifiable. In the end, the defendants accomplished precisely the opposite, when their freedom to occupy arguments were dismissed by the Supreme Court, and they were all given deferred custodial sentences. The trial proved a great waste of energy and resources, a clash between unimaginative judges and lawyers whose idealism bordered on the delusional. As in the Somyot and Katha cases, the interests of the defendants were tangential to the courtroom dramas that unfolded.

Lurking behind the various post-2010 " antimonarchy" court cases was the ever-present but physically absent Thaksin Shinawatra, who laid constant siege to the royalist polity online and by satellite link-up from his main base in Dubai. A number of court cases involved Thaksin himself, his political parties, and his lieutenants. The treatment of Thaksin was at times curious; while he and his associates attracted a disproportionate amount of legal attack, his banned political parties were permitted to reopen under new names, while he and his sister Yingluck were allowed to slip out of Thailand and avoid actual jail time. In this respect the Thai establishment was rather kinder to its bête noire than the Hun Sen regime in nearby Cambodia—whose courts permanently shut down the opposition Cambodian National Rescue Party in 2017—or Malaysia's UMNO, which twice had opposition leader Anwar Ibrahim jailed for extended periods on trumped up charges. Despite headline anti-Thaksin cases, the stance of the courts towards the former premier and his associates was rather ambivalent. The judiciary was well aware that Thaksin remained popular with large swathes of the Thai public and was reluctant to move against him too harshly. This reluctance echoed the stance of the monarchy—which was deeply conflicted about Thaksin, and later about Yingluck—and indeed that of the military.

Military distrust of the civilian courts was seen in the NCPO's extensive use of the military court system to try political offenders in the aftermath of the 2014 coup. The failure of civilian judges to object to these legally questionable incursions into their sphere of authority was extremely disappointing, if unsurprising. The NCPO's lack of regard for legal niceties was seen in the junta's initial failure to appoint a cabinet or a prime minister, and its willingness to govern the country for two months without the benefit even of an interim constitution. When the military's own hand-picked body drafted a constitution that failed to satisfy the junta, the generals simply instructed their appointed legislators to strike the 2015 charter down, and proceeded to start the whole process again under a different chair. In similar fashion, General Prayud seemed very uneasy about holding a referendum on the 2016 draft, and the junta took a range of measures to suppress popular debate about its contents. Even so, the privileging of Buddhism contained in the draft led to its overwhelming rejection in the country's Muslim-majority southern border provinces.

The Constitutional Court has been the focus of intense criticism, and even dubbed an agent of a monarchy-aligned Deep State dedicated to countering the influence of Thaksin. But a careful scrutiny of actual cases reveals a more nuanced picture. While there is evidence of anti-Thaksin bias in court decisions, close examination of the pivotal 2012 constitutional amendment case demonstrates that not only were leading judges reluctant to find against the Yingluck government: they were falling over themselves to try and avoid hearing the case at all. Four of the nine judges sought to recuse themselves, including the court president—though only one succeeded. Given that Prime Minister Yingluck Shinawatra was in the good graces of the palace at the time, the Constitutional Court's reluctance to find against her Pheu Thai Party was already very understandable. And when Yingluck appeared on a royal boat, sailing down the Chao Phraya River and presiding over ceremonies in the presence of the King, the Queen, and Princess Sirindhorn, right in the middle of the constitutional amendment case, the outcome of that case was a foregone conclusion. Precedents counted for little, since Thai constitutions change so frequently. The Constitutional Court, primarily concerned with the protecting the national interest, was a highly adaptive institution that blew with the changing political winds.

Since the King's April 2006 speeches, Thailand's courts have been viewed through a lens of judicialization or judicial activism. On one level this is not surprising: the courts subsequently annulled a couple of elections, banned two major political parties, removed two election-winning prime ministers from office, and convicted two former premiers on corruption-related charges. But judicial activism is not a helpful notion in this context. By international standards, Thai judges are nonactivist: even the Constitutional Court is firmly in response mood, judges do not initiate proceedings, and they are generally uncomfortable performing inquisitorial roles. For the most part, judges only acted against pro-Thaksin defendants when cases were submitted to the Constitutional Court or the Supreme Court's division for political offenders via anticorruption agencies, usually at the instigation of petitioners linked to the anti-Thaksin movement. Thai discourse about the supposed judicialization trend has often been pretty incoherent. Royalists have praised judges for cracking down on Thaksin and his allies; while progressives have hoped that judicial activism would lead to important precedents on issues such as land rights and environmental protection; and democrats have portrayed judicialization simply as a cover for authoritarianism.

Srimati Basu ends her wonderfully written and researched book *The Trouble with Marriage*, an ethnographic study of family law in India, with a short concluding chapter entitled "The Trouble is Marriage." Criticizing the widespread idea that law has "weaponized" marriage in India, Basu argues that legal changes can only go so far: broader social transformations are urgently needed.[1] Much the same could be said about law and politics in Thailand. Thailand's legal systems, courts, judges, and constitutions all reflect wider issues in the state and society. Changes since 1997 have weaponized Thailand's courts, but to no great avail. In the Thai case, the trouble is politics: weaponized judges engage in politics by other means, usually both ineptly and reluctantly.

This book has been concerned with the peculiar political and legal conditions that obtained during the final decade of the Ninth Reign. The passing of King Bhumibol in October 2016 was an opportune moment to draw a line under the decade-long era of "judicialization." The ultimate rationale for weaponizing the Thai judiciary to bring down pro-Thaksin politicians was that judges were acting on behalf of an essentially benevolent monarchy, and thus serving the greater good. But the ascent to the throne of King Vajiralongkorn—who had previously been seen as closely linked with Thaksin—upset this Manichean dichotomy between good and evil. If the Emperor has no clothes, and virtuous rule is no longer virtuous, what are well-meaning judges meant to do?

Two important election-related Constitutional Court judgments of 2019 illustrate the changing role of the court in the new reign. On February 8, former princess Ubolratana Mahidol, the oldest child of King Bhumibol, was nominated for the position of prime minister by the pro-Thaksin Thai Raksa Chart Party. That night, King Vajiralongkorn issued an unprecedented statement, declaring her nomination to be inappropriate.[2] A month later, the Constitutional Court unanimously dissolved the party for illegally nominating the princess—a decision widely seen as echoing the King's declaration. Then, the very night before the election, the King issued a second declaration urging voters to select "good people"—generally read as code for promilitary parties—at the ballot box. On May 8, another Constitutional Court ruling permitted the Election Commission in effect to change the rules by which party list seats were calculated, making the formation of a promilitary government much more likely.[3] In both cases, these rulings had no obvious basis in law, nor were they clearly made in the national interest. Rather, the Constitutional Court was acting in line with the express wishes of the palace.

Judicialization in the Thai context has now peaked. It thrived during the final Bhumibol decade from 2006 to 2016, when the monarchy was not greatly engaged in political oversight, and had delegated much of its authority to other actors, notably the military and judiciary. The Tenth Reign is seeing a reassertion of royal authority. No longer does the monarchical network have extensive latitude to take the initiatives: power now emanates from a single center, and the function of courtiers is to listen and to obey royal instructions. While network monarchy still exists, the character of the monarch and the nature of royal power have changed profoundly since October 2016.

Political polarization of the kind that afflicts twenty-first century Thailand reflects a deep-rooted set of conflicts that cannot be legislated or wished away by creating new institutions, by banning bothersome politicians from office, by abolishing political parties, by banishing troublesome leaders from the country, or by locking up obnoxious critics. Such moves serve only to deepen polarization, aggravating divisions, and so rationalizing further military coups and authoritarian interventions. They also turn people who are trying to work within the system into outcasts and rebels. Legalism becomes part of the problem, not the solution.

Possible answers are not hard to see. If Thai judges paid more attention to delivering justice, did not see themselves as obliged to defend and protect the status quo, and were more willing to acquit those arbitrarily charged with political offences and crimes of compassing, then tribunality—a judicial politics based on moderation and common sense—might readily be attained. And if Thai judges were ready to hold the military to account, and even to question the legality of coups d'état, the balance of power could shift in a more democratic direction, one that fostered a creative and quizzical citizenry. In the post-Bhumibol era, clinging nostalgically to a chimeral monarchical afterlife will do nothing for the legitimacy of the courts. Thai judges are, for the most part, bright people. If these judges could cultivate powers of imagination and empathy to match their legal knowledge and acumen, Thailand could become a much better place for all who live there—and a force for good in the world.

In recent years, the judicialization of politics has been an important global trend. Many scholars appear to hope that a more activist judiciary will boost the salience of human rights and lead to more liberal judgments on a range of issues: in short, that law courts will rescue the citizenry from the shortcomings of much legislation and the failings of elected politicians. Much has been written about the new constitutionalism—involving the creating of constitutional courts and other independent agencies designed to balance the check the excesses of executive power. Like several other Southeast Asian countries, including Cambodia, Indonesia, Malaysia, and the Philippines, Thailand illustrates that judicialization is the handmaiden of politicization: the more courts (both old and new) try to manage politicians, the worse matters become.

This book argues for a radical anti-legalism. We now need less legalism, and not more: the time has come to roll back judicial power all over the world, and to abandon many of its recently constructed institutional outposts. Countries should be run by elected politicians and not by courts. Politicians who perform badly should be removed at the ballot box.

Notes

PREFACE

1. Birthday speech of King Bhumibol, December 4, 2005, http://kanchanapisek. or.th/speeches/2005/1204.th.html. In places, this and other royal speeches are almost untranslatable.

2. http://kanchanapisek.or.th/speeches/2003/1204.th.html. My translation; for a discussion, see Michael K. Connors, *Democracy and National Identity in Thailand* (Copenhagen: NIAS Press, 2007), 259–60.

INTRODUCTION: LEGALISM AND REVIVAL OF TREASON

1. Scholars of Thai kingship owe an important debt to Gray's pioneering work on these issues. See Christine Gray, "Thailand: The Soteriological State in the 1970s" (Ph.D. diss., University of Chicago, 1986).

2. On virtuous rule, see Duncan McCargo, *Tearing Apart the Land: Islam and Legitimacy in Southern Thailand* (Ithaca, NY: Cornell University Press, 2008), 15–16; and Michael K. Connors, "Article of Faith: The Failure of Royal Liberalism in Thailand," *Journal of Contemporary Asia* 38, no. 1 (2008): 148–51.

3. Benedict Anderson, "The State of Thai Studies: Studies of the Thai State," in *The Study of Thailand*, ed. Eliezer B. Ayal (Athens: Ohio University Center for International Studies, Southeast Asia Program, 1978), 209. Emphasis in original.

4. Patrick Jory, *Thailand's Theory of the Monarchy: The Vessantara Jataka and the Ideal of the Perfect Man* (Albany: SUNY Press, 2016), 22; see also 180–85.

5. See Duncan McCargo, "Network Monarchy and Legitimacy Crises in Thailand," *Pacific Review* 18, no. 4 (2005): 499–519.

6. Andrew Harding and Peter Leyland, *The Constitutional System of Thailand* (Oxford: Hart, 2011), 255.

7. See Duncan McCargo, "Thaksin and the Resurgence of Violence in the Thai South: Network Monarchy Strikes Back?" *Critical Asian Studies* 38, no. 1 (2006): 58–61.

8. For a discussion, see Duncan McCargo, "Thai Politics as Reality TV," *Journal of Asian Studies* 68, no. 1 (2009): 15.

9. ตาสว่าง. This near-untranslatable phrase, popular among redshirts, refers to the "enlightened," those whose eyes have been opened or brightened about the realities of power in Thailand, especially concerning the role of the monarchy. For a discussion, see Serhat Ünaldi, *Working Towards the Monarchy: The Politics of Space in Downtown Bangkok* (Honolulu: University of Hawai'i Press, 2016), 197, 215–17.

10. Author field notes, Prawase Wasi speech at Siam Intercontinental Hotel, Bangkok, November 2, 1995.

11. On this process, see various chapters in Duncan McCargo, ed., *Reforming Thai Politics* (Copenhagen: NIAS, 2002).

12. For relevant discussions, see Andrew Harding and Penelope Nicholson, eds., *New Courts in Asia* (Abingdon, UK: Routledge, 2010).

13. See Duncan McCargo and Ukrist Pathamanand, *The Thaksinization of Thailand* (Copenhagen: NIAS, 2005), 70–120.

220   **NOTES TO PAGES 7–12**

14. Richard Lloyd Parry, "Ousted Thai leader Thaksin Shinawatra Calls For 'Shining' New Age After King's Death," *The Times*, November 9, 2009.

15. Tom Plate, *Conversations with Thaksin* (Singapore: Marshall Cavendish, 2011), 33–38.

16. Personal communication, December 2016.

17. See "ธีรยุทธ บุญมี ชู 'ตุลาการภิวัฒน์' แก้วิกฤต-ปฏิรูปการเมือง," [Thirayudh Boonmi Pushes Judicialization to Solve Crisis and Reform Politics], *Matichon*, June 1, 2006; and Thirayudh Boonmi, *ตุลาการภิวัฒน์* [Judicial Review] (Bangkok: Winyachon, 2006).

18. For detailed discussions, see Duncan McCargo, "Readings on Thai Justice: A Review Essay," *Asian Studies Review* 39, no. 1 (2015): 23–37; and Duncan McCargo "Competing Notions of Judicialization in Thailand," *Contemporary Southeast Asia* 36, no. 3 (2014): 417–41.

19. Pichet Maolanond et al., *ตุลาการภิวัฒน์ (คันฉ่องส่องตุลาการไทย)* ฉบับ "ตุลาการตีความข้ามตัวบท & ตุลาการวางนโยบายสาธารณะ [Judicialization: Judges Offering Non-standard Decisions and Judges Setting Public Policy] (Bangkok: National Public Health Foundation, 2007).

20. Interview, Jarun Kaonanun, March 19, 2008.

21. For a discussion of this group of seven critical scholars from the Thammasat University Faculty of Law, see Duncan McCargo and Peeradej Tanruangporn, "Branding Dissent: *Nitirat*, Thailand's Enlightened Jurists," *Journal of Contemporary Asia* 45, no. 3 (2015): 419–42.

22. Piyabutr Saengkanokkul, *ศาลรัฐประหาร* [Coup Court] (Bangkok: Fa Diao Kan, 2017), 18.

23. Ibid., 21.

24. Ibid., 56–57.

25. Thongchai Winichakul, "The Monarchy and Anti-Monarchy: Two Elephants in the Room of Thai Politics and the State of Denial," in *Good Coup Gone Bad*, ed. Pavin Chachavalpongpun (Singapore: ISEAS, 2014), 91–92.

26. For a detailed discussion, see Chris Baker and Pasuk Phongpaichit, *Thaksin* (Chiang Mai: Silkworm 2009), 260–69.

27. Later changed to "Council for National Security" (CNS), to counter any impression that the monarchy was implicated in the coup.

28. For contrasting accounts and analyses of these events, see People's Information Committee, *Truth for Justice: A Fact-Finding Report on the April–May 2010 Crackdowns in Thailand* [English] (Bangkok: PIC, 2012) at http://www.pic2010.org/en-report/; and Truth for Reconciliation Commission of Thailand, *Final Report of the Truth for Reconciliation Commission of Thailand (TRCT), July 2010–July 2012* [English] (Bangkok: TRCT 2012) at http://library.nhrc.or.th/ulib/document/Fulltext/F07939.pdf.

29. Constitutional Court Judgment 9-2557, May 7, 2014, 46.

30. Richard Paddock and Ryn Jirenunwataug, "Former Thai Leader Yingluck Said to Have Fled Country After Failing to Appear for Verdict," *New York Times*, August 24, 2017.

31. Chris Baker and Pasuk Phongpaichit, *The Palace Law of Ayutthaya and The Thammasat: Law and Kingship in Siam* (Ithaca NY: Cornell University Southeast Asia Program, 2016), 49.

32. Ibid., 48–49.

33. David M. Engel, *Law and Kingship in Thailand During the Reign of King Chulalongkorn* (Ann Arbor: University of Michigan Center for South and Southeast Asian Studies, 1975), 123.

34. Baker and Pasuk, *Palace Law*, 7.

35. Ibid., 11–12.

36. Ibid., 131.

37. Chris Baker, email communication, January 26, 2018.

38. Somchai Preechasilapakul, ความยอกย้อนในประวัติศาสตร์ของบิดาแห่งกฎหมายไทย [Complications in the History of the Father of Thai Law] (Bangkok: Winyuchon, 2003), 27–35.

39. Neil A. Englehardt, *Culture and Power in Traditional Siamese Government* (Ithaca NY: Cornell Southeast Asia Program, 2001), 33.

40. Engel, *Law and Kingship*, 78.

41. Somchai, ความยอกย้อน, 15–20, 39–45; Walter J. Tips, *Gustave Rolin-Jaequemyns and the Making of Modern Siam* (Bangkok: White Lotus, 1996), 247–84.

42. Walter E. J. Tips, *Crime and Punishment in King Chulalongkorn's Kingdom* (Bangkok: White Lotus, 1998), 13.

43. Mr. and Mrs. Émile Jottrand, *In Siam: The Diary of a Legal Adviser of King Chulalongkorn's Government*, trans. and ed. Walter E. J. Tips (Bangkok: White Lotus, 1996), 73.

44. Jottrand, *In Siam*, 84.

45. Tips, *Crime and Punishment*, 28.

46. Engel, *Law and Kingship*, 78.

47. Ibid., 103–9.

48. Ibid., 124.

49. David M. Engel, "Rights as Wrongs: Legality and Sacrality in Thailand," *Asian Studies Review* 39, no. 1 (2015): 38–52.

50. Fred W. Riggs, *Thailand: The Modernization of a Bureaucratic Polity* (Honolulu: University of Hawai'i Press, 1966), 131.

51. See Naris Charaschanyawong, อนุสรณ์งานศพ สมาชิกคณะราษฎร [Cremation Volumes of People's Party Members], *Silpawattanatham* 6 (2017): 70–113.

52. On the Bowaradej Rebellion and its judicial aftermath, see M. R. Nimitmongkol Navarat, *The Dreams of An Idealist, The Victim of Two Political Purges and The Emerald's Cleavage*, ed. and trans. David Smyth (Chiang Mai: Silkworm 2009), 214–18.

53. Federico Ferrara, *The Political Development of Modern Thailand* (Cambridge: Cambridge University Press, 2015), 109.

54. David Streckfuss, *Truth on Trial: Defamation, Treason, and Lèse-Majesté* (Abingdon: Routledge, 2011), 118–21.

55. See Pong Santi, ed. บันทึกลับวิกฤตการณ์ตุลาการ [Secret Notes on the Judicial Crisis] (n.p., 1992), especially 514–18.

56. "Dispute Over Senior Judicial Posts Settled," *Straits Times*, November 13, 1992.

57. Rangsan was eventually convicted of Pramarn's attempted murder in 2008 and given a twenty-five year jail sentence, but the verdict was overturned by the Court of Appeal in 2010.

58. See undated document apparently titled "The Supreme Court of Thailand," 1, at http://www.supremecourt.or.th/file/dika_eng.pdf.

59. Walter F. Vella, *Chaiyo! King Vajiravudh and the Development of Thai Nationalism* (Honolulu: University of Hawai'i Press, 1978), 60.

60. See Kathryn Sikkink, *The Justice Cascade: How Human Rights Prosecutions are Changing World Politics* (New York: Norton, 2011).

61. For such arguments, see Ellen L. Lutz and Caitlin Reiger, eds., *Prosecuting Heads of State* (New York: Cambridge University Press, 2009).

62. See Duncan McCargo, "Transitional Justice and its Discontents," *Journal of Democracy* 26, no. 2 (2015): 5–20.

63. The 2005–6 National Reconciliation Commission to examine the southern insurgency, and the 2010–12 Truth for Reconciliation Commission on the April–May 2010 violent suppression of the redshirt protests.

64. Srimati Basu, *The Trouble with Marriage: Feminists Confront Law and Violence in India* (Oakland: University of California Press, 2015), 6.

65. Nick Cheesman, *Opposing the Rule of Law: How Myanmar's Courts Make Law and Order* (Cambridge: Cambridge University Press, 2015), 6–7.

66. Ibid., 29.

67. Peter A. Jackson, "The Thai Regime of Images," *SOJOURN* 19, no. 2 (2004): 184.

68. Cheesman, *Opposing the Rule of Law*, 36.

69. Kevin Hewison, "The Monarchy and Democratisation," in *Political Change in Thailand: Democracy and Participation,* ed. Kevin Hewison (London: Routledge 1997), 70.

70. Michael K. Connors, "Article of Faith: The Failure of Royal Liberalism in Thailand."

71. Roberto Mangabeira Unger, *The Critical Legal Studies Movement* (Cambridge, MA: Harvard University Press, 1983).

72. Ibid., 108.

73. Judith N. Shklar, *Legalism*, 2d ed. (Cambridge MA: Harvard, 1986), 11.

74. For a discussion of the issues raised by Shklar, see McCargo "Transitional Justice and Its Discontents."

75. Shklar, *Legalism,* viii–xi.

76. Ibid., 149.

77. On Nitirat's 112 proposal, see McCargo and Peeradej "Branding Dissent," 426–29.

78. See McCargo and Peeradej, "Branding Dissent," 434–36. Nitirat member Piyabutr later changed his stance, resigning his academic post and entering politics as secretary-general of the new Future Forward Party in 2018.

79. Similar arguments were famously advanced about Britain in J.A.G. Griffith's provocative article "The Political Constitution," *Modern Law Review* 42, no. 1 (1979): 1–21.

80. Cheesman, *Opposing the Rule of Law*, 260–61.

81. In a private conversation, a senior Thai judge asserted to me that Article 112 was in fact a defamation law. Conversation, August 2, 2015.

82. See Tyrell Haberkorn, *In Plain Sight: Impunity and Human Rights in Thailand* (Madison: University of Wisconsin Press, 2018), 201–3 and 282n49. For a related report cited by Haberkorn see "แท่งอัปลักษณ์ แสดงสถิติคดีหมิ่นฯ กลางถนนราชดำเนิน" [Ugly Bars: Display of Royal Defamation Statistics in the Middle of Rachadamnoen Avenue], *Prachatai*, December 17, 2011, https://prachatai.com/journal/2011/12/38371.

83. Little attention has been paid to Chapter 4 of the Criminal Code, concerning relations with friendly foreign states. Article 133 makes it an offence to defame the sovereign or head of such a state, while Article 134 applies the same principle to the defamation of an accredited ambassador.

84. See Sawatree Suksri, Siriphon Kusonsinwut, and Orapin Yingyongpathana, *Computer Crime? Impact of the Computer-related Crime Act 2007and State Policies on the Right to Freedom of Expression* (Bangkok: iLaw 2012), especially 580–95, at https://th.boell.org/en/2013/11/12/computercrime-impact-computer-related-crime-act-2007-and-state-policies-right-freedom.

85. See Sikkink, *The Justice Cascade*; and Haberkorn, *In Plain Sight*, 12–13.

86. See "Lords Halt Challenge to Treason Law," *The Guardian*, June 26, 2003, https://www.theguardian.com/media/2003/jun/26/pressandpublishing.themonarchy.

87. One case was brought in Australia in 1916.

88. Streckfuss, *Truth on Trial*, 197.

89. Thanyarat Doksone, "Thai Scholar May Face Jail for Insulting King Who Died in 1605," *The Independent*, October 19, 2014.

90. As usual, I find the Oxford English Dictionary definition less helpful than the wonderful Collins: "A devising, planning; a device, design, artifice, contrivance."

1. PRIVILEGED CASTE?

1. "Supreme Court" is the official translation of Thailand's highest court, and so has been used throughout this book. Nevertheless, the Thai Supreme Court bears little relation to its US counterpart, while the Thai name ศาลฎีกา alludes to an earlier tradition of royal petitions by those seeking justice.

2. See, for example, Howard S. Becker's classic article, "The Career of the Chicago Public Schoolteacher," *American Journal of Sociology* 57, no. 5 (1952): 470–77.

3. In 2012, the Judicial Commission declined a request to appoint Dol Bunnag, chief justice in the office of the President of the Supreme Court, to be a member of the Law Reform Committee. *Judicial Commission Minutes*, 7/2555, February 27, 2012. Dol Bunnag was later refused permission to join a ministry subcommittee on promoting women's rights; Judicial Commission members objected to the ministry requesting a specific person to act in this role. *Judicial Commission Minutes*, 14/2555, June 6, 2012.

4. Penny Darbyshire was told by one English judge she interviewed: "You can't be seen having a drink with lawyers." See Penny Darbyshire, *Sitting in Judgment: The Working Lives of Judges* (Oxford: Hart 2011), 134.

5. One former judge told me that judges should not sing in public (Judge C, March 18, 2008). But the ethics handbook does not mention a singing ban—and for chief judges in the provinces, karaoke skills may even be an asset.

6. According to Darbyshire, then Lord Chancellor Lord McKay insisted in 1994 that English judges had to conduct themselves professionally and privately in a way that would maintain "public confidence in the judiciary." *Sitting in Judgment*, 124.

7. Courts of Justice, ประมวลจริยธรรมข้าราชการตุลาการ [Judicial Code of Ethics] (Bangkok: Office of Courts of Justice, 2010).

8. Judge K, October 9, 2012.

9. Ibid.

10. Judge M, November 26, 2012.

11. Natthapakon Phitchayapanyatham, บันทึกลับฉบับคนอยากนั่งบัลลังก์ศาล [Secret Notes: For Those Who Want to Sit on the Court Bench] (Bangkok: Athataya Millennium, 2011), 32–33.

12. Judge R, August 20, 2012.

13. *Luk chao ban.* Judge Q, October 18, 2012.

14. Judge P, November 19, 2012.

15. Judge Q, October 18, 2012.

16. Many would-be judges ask practicing lawyers to add their names to existing open-and-shut cases (such as uncontested petitions to appoint a guardian), on which they do little or no real work, in order to meet these paper requirements. For an analogous discussion of Japanese prosecutors, see David T. Johnson, *The Japanese Way of Justice* (New York: Oxford University Press, 2002), especially 88–118.

17. This route is not limited, as some believe, only to those who hold two master's degrees from abroad—though since master's degrees in law are typically only one year in duration in the UK, prospective applicants often undertake two MA or LLM degrees.

18. Sarawut Benjakul, interview, August 18, 2014.

19. Judge O, November 27, 2012.

20. One judge, himself of very humble origins, told me his own daughter planned to apply by this route. Judge P, November 19, 2012. Another judge claimed he immediately recognized most of the surnames on the *sanam jiew* pass list (Judge R, August 29, 2012).

21. For selected English summary translations of these decisions, see http://www.thailawforum.com/supremecourtopinions.html.

22. Khemthong Tonsakulrungruang, former LLB program director at Chulalongkorn University, personal communication, January 21, 2018.

23. Thammasat's decision to move all undergraduate teaching to Rangsit (outside Bangkok proper) from 2006 arguably led to a loss of standing vis-à-vis the more centrally located single-campus Chulalongkorn University.

24. Natthapakon, บันทึกลับ, 23.

25. Ibid., 51–58.

26. Ibid., 11–16.

27. Some informants asserted that there was no difference in status between *sanam lek* and *sanam yai* entrants: although officially true, a number of informants confirmed that in practice the sanam yai generally took precedence.

28. For example, Judge N, November 20, 2012.

29. For example, Judge L, October 9, 2012.

30. Judge P, November 19, 2012.

31. Judge E, March 19, 2008.

32. มาตรฐาน.

33. Judge O, November 11, 2012.

34. On entrance examinations for the Chinese mandarinate, see Benjamin A. Elman, *Civil Examinations and Meritocracy in Late Imperial China* (Cambridge MA: Harvard University Press, 2000), especially 147–210.

35. See ibid., 176–78.

36. Previously it had been very common for judges assigned a particular case to skip many of the hearings, Judge Q, October 18, 2012. Article 236 of the 1997 Constitution stated: "The hearing of a case requires a full quorum of judges. Any judge not sitting at the hearing of a case shall not give judgment or a decision of such case, except for the case of *force majeure* or any other unavoidable necessity as provided by law." This provision was dropped in the 2007 Constitution, apparently after lobbying by the courts.

37. Judge R, August 30, 2012.

38. Judge E, March 19, 2008.

39. Thongbai Thongpao interview, March 20, 2008.

40. Nidhi Eeoseewong, "ศาล ในฐานะกลไกของระบอบ. . . ?" [The Courts as a Mechanism of a System?]. Presentation at Nitirat seminar on The Judiciary and Justice in Thai Society, Thammasat University, March 17, 2013.

41. Survey results show comparatively high levels of public respect for the courts in Thailand. See, for example, Yingyos Leechaianan et al., "Public Confidence in Thailand's Legal Authorities," *Journal of Police Science and Management* 14, no. 3 (2012): 1–18.

42. Judge E, June 25, 2015.

43. Judge N, November 12, 2012.

44. See Samson Lim, *Siam's New Detectives: Visualizing Crime and Conspiracy in Modern Thailand* (Honolulu: University of Hawai'i Press, 2016), 1–11.

45. Judge R, August 23, 2012.

46. See "Court of Protection Judge Hits Out at Expenses of Cases Costing £9000 a month," *Local Government Lawyer*, December 2, 2014, http://localgovernmentlawyer. co.uk/index.php?option=com_content&view=article&id=21037:court-of-protection-judge-hits-out-at-expense-of-cases-costing-p9000-a-month&catid=1:latest-stories.

47. Loic J.D. Wacquant, "Habitus," in *International Encyclopedia of Economic Sociology*, ed. Jens Beckert and Milan Zafirovski (Abingdon, UK: Routledge 2013), 317–20. For Bourdieu's own elaborations of habitus and disposition, both of which are notoriously slippery concepts, see Pierre Bourdieu and Loic J.D. Wacquant, *An Invitation to Reflexive Sociology* (Chicago: University of Chicago Press, 1992), especially 131–38. For a critique, see Rogers Brubaker, "Social Theory as Habitus," in *Bourdieu: Critical*

Perspectives, ed. Craig Calhoun, Edward LiPuma, and Moishe Postone (Cambridge: Polity, 1993), 212–34.

48. Judge J, November 19, 2012. For complaints about the evaluation system, see interview with Judge Chaiwat Suriwattanakul (conducted by Praphon Sahapattana) in *Trends in the Judiciary: Interviews with Judges across the Globe*, ed. David Lowe and Dilip K. Das, vol. 3 (Abingdon, UK: Routledge, 2018), 40.

49. Judge J, November 19, 2012.

50. Everett Hughes, *Men and Their Work* (Glencoe, IL: Free Press, 1958), 128.

51. H. H. Gerth and C. Wright Mills, *From Max Weber: Essays in Sociology* (New York: Oxford University Press, 1946), 240–44.

52. See Official Decree on Adjustment of Salaries of Judges, 2012; Regulations on Temporary Cost of Living Allowances for Judges, 2014.

53. Becker, *Chicago Public Schoolteacher*, 471, 476.

54. Judge E, March 19, 2008.

55. More than seven thousand people have been killed in an ongoing separatist insurgency in three of Thailand's Muslim-majority southern border provinces since 2007. On the southern insurgency, see McCargo, *Tearing Apart the Land*. On courts and justice in the region, see 89–98. A small number of so-called *datho yuthitham* serve as judges in the deep South, with responsibility for administering cases that involve Islamic family law.

56. Judge O, November 27, 2012.

57. *Annual Report 2015*, 31.

58. *Judicial Commission Minutes*, 8/2555, March 2, 2012, 23.

59. Under the Thai system, *san khwaeng* (district, or municipal courts) deal with minor civil cases, or criminal cases where the penalty does not exceed a three-year jail term. The Chiang Mai municipal court, with just eleven courtrooms, dealt with a remarkable 19,408 cases in 2011—many resolved without a formal hearing before a judge. See ศาลแขวงเชียงใหม่ [Chiang Mai District Court], undated informational DVD apparently produced in early 2012.

60. In 2012 there was a backlog of around 17,000 drug appeals, all dealt with by a unit in Bangkok to which only around twenty regular judges were assigned. They were processing around 7,000–8,000 cases annually.

61. Chaiwat Suriwattanakul, in Lowe and Das, eds., *Trends in the Judiciary*, 46.

62. See Article 219 of the 2007 Constitution, which was followed up a new 2008 Supreme Court regulation.

63. Judge M, October 19, 2012.

64. Judge R, August 23, 2012.

65. See Act Amending the Civil Procedure Code (No 27), BE 2558 (2015), September 1.

66. Darbyshire, *Sitting in Judgment*, 323.

67. Ibid., 378.

68. Judge P, November 19, 2012.

69. Chalermkiat Charnsilp, ปัจจัยที่มีผลกระทบต่อความล่าช้าในการพิจารณาพิพากษาคดีของศาลอุทธรณ์ภาค 1. [Factors Causing Delays in Judgments of the Regional Appeal Court 1], Paper prepared for the Senior Executives' Training Program [Bo Yo So] Class 10, College of Justice, Courts of Justice, 2007, 47–48.

70. Sirichai Watthanayothin, ศิริชัย วัฒนโยธิน. 2551. ข้อขัดข้องในการบริหารศาลยุติธรรม. รายงานนี้เป็นส่วน หนึ่งของการอบรมหลักสูตร ผู้บริหารกระบวนการยุติธรรมระดับสูง รุ่นที่ 11, วิทยาลัยการยุติธรรม, สำนักงานศาลยุติธรรม, [Difficulties in Administration of the Court of Justice] Paper prepared for the Senior Executives' Training Program [Bo Yo So] Class 11, College of Justice, Courts of Justice, 2008, 36. This problem was later addressed by moving regional appeal court offices to Bangkok, so that those overseeing them did not have to work in the provinces.

71. Judge J, November 19, 2012.

72. Judge Q, October 18, 2012.

73. Judge S, December 22, 2012.

74. Judge J, November 19, 2012.

75. Judge R, August 30, 2012.

76. Judge S, December 22, 2012.

77. Thongbai Thongpao interview, March 20, 2008.

78. See 2007 Constitution, Articles 220 and 221.

79. Judge E, March 19, 2008.

80. Amnat Chotichawaranont, ความคิดเห็นของผู้พิพากษาศาลยุติธรรมต่อระบบการสรรหา คณะกรรมการตุลาการ ศาลยุติธรรม (ก.ต.) ตามรัฐธรรมนูญฉบับปัจจุบัน พุทธศักราช 2550 [Judges' Opinions on the Selection System of the Judicial Commission According to the Current 2007 Constitution], Paper prepared for the Senior Executives' Training Program [Bo Yo So] Class 12, College of Justice, Courts of Justice, 2009, 61–65.

81. *Judicial Commission Minutes*, 8/2555, March 2, 2012, 24.

82. Judge A, March 20, 2008.

83. Judge J, November 19, 2012.

84. Copies of all the Judicial Commission minutes cited here were made by Supreme Court library staff at my request; I accessed these materials quite openly. But after the Supreme Court moved from its original Phra Nakhorn location to Chaeng Wattana in late 2012, Judicial Commission minutes were no longer placed on the open shelves.

85. Judge K, October 9, 2012.

86. ปลดออก or ไล่ออก.

87. Judge U interview, December 12, 2014.

88. http://www.isranews.org/isranews-news/item/32966-news06.html. The term *presiding judge* or *chief judge* here is misleading: it refers to the head of an *ongkhana* (team) of three supreme court judges, and not to the chief of the entire court.

89. See http://englishnews.thaipbs.or.th/four-senior-judges-fired-gross-disciplinary-violations/.

90. Veera Prateepchaikul, "Judge Sackings Send Shockwaves Across The Benches," *Bangkok Post*, August 11, 2014. Given Veera's well-known conservative and royalist views, the tenor of his commentary is quite extraordinary.

91. Judge K, October 9, 2012. This statement is known as "Blackstone's formulation," after the distinguished English jurist William Blackstone, who coined the point in the 1760s. None of the judges who cited the formulation to me attributed it to anyone.

92. The rolls of past NDC graduates list the great and the good of the Thai bureaucratic polity. See http://web.archive.org/web/20051221044849/www.thaindc.org/name_student. html.

93. For a discussion of these and similar training programs, see Nualnoi Treerat and Parkphume Vanichaka, "Elite Networking through Special Executive Courses," in *Unequal Thailand*, ed. Pasuk Phongpaichit and Chris Baker (Singapore: NUS Press, 2016), 73–96.

94. Judge O, November 27, 2012.

95. Judge A, March 20, 2008.

96. Judge E, June 25, 2015.

97. The grounds on which Chaiyan was acquitted did not directly validate peaceful civil disobedience, but rested on the Constitutional Court's subsequent decision that the elections were illegal. See *Prachatai*, October 31, 2010, http://www.prachatai3.info/journal/2010/10/31684.

98. Judge E, June 25, 2015.

99. For the legal arrangements post-1997, see Act on Judicial Administration of the Courts of Justice, 2543 (2000), at http://www.jla.coj.go.th/doc/data/jla/jla_1499072147.pdf (Thai) and http://www.coj.go.th/en/pdf/law_act_on_judicial_administration.

pdf (English); and the amendments introduced in 2014, http://webcache.googleuser content.com/search?q=cache:http://library2.parliament.go.th/giventake/content_ nla2557/law120-141258-5.pdf.

100. Act on Judicial Administration 2000, Section 8.

101. Judge E, June 25, 2015.

102. Sirichai, ข้อขัดข้องในการบริหารศาลยุติธรรม, 2–3.

103. Article 258 ค (2), 2017 Constitution.

104. Judge R, August 23, 2012.

105. Judge K, October 9, 2012.

106. Field notes, July 23, 2009.

107. Judge K October 9, 2012.

108. Informant interview, July 26, 2009.

109. Informant interview, March 18, 2008.

110. Lawyer interview, March 21, 2008.

111. Judge K, October 9, 2012.

112. Kasem Suppasit, ความเป็นอิสระของผู้พิพากษาในการพิจารณาคดี, เอกสารวิชาการส่วนบุคคล, อนุมัติให้เป็นส่วน หนึ่งของ การอบรมหลักสูตรผู้พิพากษาศาลชั้นต้น รุ่นที่ 2 [Independence of Judges in Judging Cases], Paper for Training Course for Judges from Courts of the First Instance, Class 2, College of Justice, Courts of Justice, 2004, 10.

113. Kasem, ความเป็นอิสระของผู้พิพากษา, 11.

114. In Appeal and Supreme Court cases, defendants do not know the names of the judges reviewing their cases until the judgments are issued. See Wicha Mahakhun et al., จริยธรรมในวิชาชีพกฎหมาย [The Code of Conduct of Legal Professions] (Salaya: Faculty of Social Sciences and Humanities, Mahidol University, 2013).

115. ปรึกษา.

116. Judge N, November 20, 2012.

117. His real name is Thanat Thanawatcharanon.

118. "Tom Dundee Gets 7 Years," *Bangkok Post*, June 2, 2016.

119. This special division was originally established under the provisions of the 1997 Constitution.

120. The frequency of these en banc meetings is not fixed, but is determined by the current president of the Supreme Court. In 2018, a new law was passed granting generous meeting allowances to all judges who took part in such meetings.

2. BENCH AND THRONE

1. This episode is described in a poster displayed at the Museum of the Courts of Justice in Bangkok.

2. Richard A. Posner, *How Judges Think* (Cambridge, MA: Harvard University Press, 2008).

3. Around a sixth of Thailand's twenty-nine premiers have been former judges.

4. Somchai rose through the judicial ranks before heading an appeal court division, and then becoming permanent secretary of the Ministry of Justice, later transferring to the Labor Ministry.

5. See Streckfuss, *Truth on Trial*, 118–21.

6. เจ้าชีวิต. Worajet interview, December 22, 2012.

7. See Interim Constitution of June 27, 1932, Articles 1 and 2, original at http:// www.ratchakitcha.soc.go.th/DATA/PDF/2475/A/166.PDF; and Thawatt Mokarapong, *History of the Thai Revolution: A Study in Political Behaviour* (Bangkok: Chalermnit, 1972), 111.

8. See Article 58 of the December 1932 Constitution, original at http://www. ratchakitcha.soc.go.th/DATA/PDF/2475/A/529.PDF.

9. See Thawatt, *History of the Thai Revolution*, 120–22.

10. 2007 Constitution, Article 197; c.f. 2017 Constitution, Article 188.

11. The King's brief stints as a judge included Civil Court and Courts of Justice, Bangkok (1952); Central Children's and Juvenile Court, Bangkok (1952), Chiang Mai (1958), Songkhla (1959), Pattani (1959), and Chiang Mai (1984). The Crown Prince assumed the bench at Fang, Chiang Mai (1977), and at the Civil Courts and Courts of Justice, Bangkok (1987, 1992). This may not be an exhaustive list.

12. เนติบัณฑิต. In Thailand, lawyers obtain a license to practise law by taking a special examination. But to appear in court they need to pass a separate bar examination involving at least a year's postgraduate study, and often longer.

13. The *wai* is a two-handed salute, used as a greeting or sign of respect.

14. See Hikari Hori, *Promiscuous Media: Film and Visual Culture in Imperial Japan, 1926–1945* (Ithaca, NY: Cornell University Press, 2017), 31–35.

15. "I offer my oath that I shall be loyal to the King and shall perform my duty in the name of the King with honesty, removed from all biases, in order to create justice for the people and peace for the Kingdom. I shall preserve and adhere to the democratic regime with the King as the head, the constitution of the Thai Kingdom, and the law." 1997 Constitution, Article 252; 2007 Constitution Article 201; 2017 Constitution, Article 191. English and Welsh judges also take a personal oath of loyalty to the Queen, which may sound distinctly feudal, but plays little part in their understandings of their role. According to Penny Darbyshire, an expert on the English judiciary: "I honestly don't think the monarch ever enters their heads. They don't mention the monarch any more than ordinary people do. I expect they don't see themselves as in any relationship with the monarchy." Penny Darbyshire, email communication, September 22, 2014.

16. Michel Foucault, *Wrong-Doing, Truth-Telling: The Function of Avowal in Justice* (Chicago: University of Chicago Press, 2014), 48.

17. Judge M, October 10, 2012.

18. Constitution of the Kingdom of Thailand 2560 (2017), compare articles 24 and 191.

19. Thanin Kraivichien, in พระบารมีปกเกล้าฯ ชาวศาลยุติธรรม [Royal Charisma Protects the People of the Courts of Justice (literally, "Covers the Heads of the People of the Courts of Justice")] (Bangkok: Office of the Supreme Court, 2006), 148–49.

20. See Elliot Kulick and Dick Wilson, *Thailand's Turn: Profile of a New Dragon* (Basingstoke: Macmillan, 1992), 31.

21. On Thanin's ideology, see Michael K. Connors, *Democracy and National Identity* (Copenhagen: Nordic Institute of Asian Studies Press, 2007), 92–93, 136–37.

22. Interview with Thongthong Chandrangsu, FM 92.5, broadcast June 22, 1996. Transcribed and published in Ministry of Justice, พระพิทักษ์ยุติธรรม์ ถ่องแท้ [His Majesty Who Truly Protects Justice] (Bangkok: Ministry of Justice 2006), 57–58. Thongthong later became permanent secretary in the Office of the Prime Minister in the Yingluck Shinawatra government.

23. Later on, public prosecutors began swearing a similar oath—a "right" for which they had long lobbied.

24. This ideological project is a major theme of Connors, *Democracy and National Identity*, especially, 128–52.

25. See Nikon Thatsoro, "ศาลยุติธรรมกับสถาบันพระมหากษัตริย์ 'บรรพตุลาการศาลฎีกาใกล้เบื้องพระยุคลบาท'" [The Courts of Justice and the Monarchy: "Biographies of Judges of the Supreme Court Who Worked Closely Under the King"], in การดำเนินความยุติธรรมตามรอย พระยุคลบาท [Processing Justice: Following the Royal Footprints] (Bangkok: Courts of Justice, 2007), 183.

26. See Connors, *Democracy and National Identity*, 132–33.

27. Paul Handley, *The King Never Smiles: A Biography of Thailand's King Bhumibol Adulyadej* (New Haven, CT: Yale, 2006), 375, 441.

28. See, for example, Jarunee Thanaratapon, "สถาบันพระมหากษัตริย์กับศาลยุติธรรม," [The Monarchy and the Courts of Justice], in การดำเนินความยุติธรรมตามรอยพระยุคลบาท, 301.

29. ข้าราชการตุลาการ.

30. ข้าราชบริพาร.

31. Judge E, March 19, 2008.

32. The 1987 and 1992 cases are detailed in binders at the Museum of the Court Archives in Bangkok; the original sources for the documents are not indicated. Unfortunately, there is no information about how the 1992 case was decided.

33. "ศาลเตรียมถวายการต้อนรับสมเด็จพระบรม" [Courts Preparing To Welcome the Crown Prince], *Siam Rath*, May 28, 1987; "พระบรมฯ เสด็จพิจารณาคดี" [Crown Prince To Decide Cases], *Thai Rath*, May 20, 1987.

34. การดำเนินความยุติธรรมตามรอยพระยุคลบาท [Processing Justice: Following the Royal Footprints].

35. Phuttipong Ponganekgul, ความชอบด้วยกฎหมายวิธีพิจารณาความ: กรณี ร.๙ พิพากษาคดีในศาล? [Legality of the Criminal Procedure Code: The Case of King Rama IX Deciding Cases In Court?], 2013, http://blogazine.in.th/blogs/phuttipong/post/4356.

36. Jarunee Thanaratapon, "สถาบันพระมหากษัตริย์กับศาลยุติธรรม," 301.

37. See Pramual Rujanaseri, พระราชอำนาจ [Royal Powers] (Bangkok: Sumet Rujanaseri, 2005).

38. For an excellent discussion, see Connors: "Article of Faith," 153–56.

39. An original shirt from this period is in the author's possession, bearing the Thai slogan เราจะสู้เพื่อในหลวง—"We will fight for the King."

40. Pramual, พระราชอำนาจ. On the monarchy and the courts, see 80–88.

41. Article 2, Section II.

42. Details of all US pardons and commutations since 1989 may be found at http://www.justice.gov/pardon/clemencyrecipients. Barack Obama was rather restrained in issuing pardons and commutations; during his first year of office, Donald Trump dispensed just one of each.

43. Chachapon Jayaphorn, "The Pardoning Power of Kings Before the Reform of the Legal and Judicial Systems," *Thailand Law Journal* 14, no. 2 (2011): 1–25.

44. See ibid.

45. Quoted in ibid., 21.

46. Thongthong interview in Ministry of Justice 2007, 58.

47. See Ministry of Justice 2007, 18, พระบรมเดชานุภาพคุ้มครองแผ่นดินคนละอย่างกัน และยิ่งใหญ่กว่าอำนาจศาล.

48. For example, the proclamation of a general pardon for the Queen's eightieth birthday in 2012 explicitly covered Articles 107 to 135 of the Criminal Code. See Royal Decree on Royal Pardons 2012, Appendix, 1.

49. Richard Barrow, http://www.thaiprisonlife.com/blogs/12000-prisoners-released-on-first-day-of-royal-pardon/.

50. See Tyrell Haberkorn, "A Thai Freedom Diary: Thanthawut on His Release from Prison," *Prachatai*, July 14, 2013, http://prachatai.org/english/node/3644.

51. Thanin Kraivichien, "พระราชอำนาจในการพระราชทานอภัยโทษของพระบาทสมเด็จพระเจ้าอยู่หัวภูมิพลอดุลย เดช" [HM King Bhumibol Adulyadej's Royal Power to Grant A Royal Pardon], in [title unknown] (Department of Corrections, Ministry of Justice, Bangkok: 2007), 11.

52. Thanin Kraivichien, "พระราชอำนาจ," 7.

53. See "นิสิตวิศวะฯ ถวายฎีกาขอพระราชทานอภัยโทษพ่อหลวง" [Engineering Students Appeal for Royal Pardon from King Father], *Campus Star*, November 14, 2016, https://campus.campus-star.com/variety/22734.html.

54. Thongthong interview in Ministry of Justice 2007, 58.

55. For detailed results, see http://www.prisonstudies.org/ and search for Thailand under "Highest to lowest" Prison Population Totals and Prison Population Rates. In May 2019, only the USA, China, Brazil, Russia, and India had more people in jail than Thailand. Thailand had a higher proportion of its population behind bars than any of these countries apart from the United States and El Salvador; and also ranked number 9 in the world for the proportion of female prisoners.

56. In terms of prison population rate, in May 2019 Thailand ranked third in the world with 553 incarcerations per 100,000; in ASEAN, Singapore ranked next with 199, Cambodia had 189 and the Philippines 179.

57. See Chairat Charoensin-o-larn, "Thailand in 2009: Unusual Politics Becomes Usual," *Southeast Asian Affairs* (Singapore: ISEAS, 2010), 303–31.

58. See Borwornsak Uwanno, "การใช้สิทธิทูลเกล้า ฯ ถวายฎีกาตามกฎหมายและประเพณี" [The Right to Royal Petition According to Law and Custom], August 8, 2009, http://m.prachachat.net/news_detail.php?newsid=1249609269.

59. Prince Chula Chakrabongse, *Lords of Life: A History of the Kings of Thailand* (London: Alvin Redman, 1960), 16.

60. Engel, *Law and Kingship*, 87.

61. ศรีสมบัติ โชคประจักษ์ชัด และคณะ, รายงานฉบับสมบูรณ์โครงการศึกษาความเป็นไปได้ของการยกเลิกโทษประหารชีวิตตามแผนสิทธิมนุษยชนแห่งชาติฉบับที่ 2 [Srisombat Chokprajakchat et al., Final Research Report into the Possibility of Abolishing the Death Penalty According to the National Human Rights Plan, 2d ed.] (Bangkok: Faculty of Social Science and Humanities, Mahidol University, 2014), 91–97.

62. Peaks of 16 executions were reached in 1986 and 1998, while total executions during the Ninth Reign were 237. The average annual number was 3.34. See data collated by David T. Johnson and Franklin E. Zimring, *The Next Frontier: National Development, Political Change, and the Death Penalty in Asia* (New York: Oxford University Press, 2009), 403. Vastly more people were sentenced to death—around 93 a year between 2008 and 2012—than were ever executed. See Srisombat et al., โทษประหารชีวิต [Death Penalty], 122.

63. Handley, *The King Never Smiles*, 375.

64. Johnson and Zimring, *The Next Frontier*, 405.

65. There were no executions from 1945 to 1950, 1988 to 1995, 2004 to 2006, and 2010 to 2017.

66. International Federation on Human Rights (FIDH), *The Death Penalty in Thailand* (Paris: FIDH, March 2005), https://www.fidh.org/IMG/pdf/Thailand411-2.pdf.

67. Johnson and Zimring, *The Next Frontier*, 22.

68. Handley, *The King Never Smiles*, 425, 441.

69. Two in 2009 and one in 2018.

70. Johnson and Zimring, *The Next Frontier*, 403.

71. FIDH, *Death Penalty in Thailand*, 12.

72. See Srisombat et al., โทษประหารชีวิต [Death Penalty], summarized in Ministry of Justice, Department of Rights and Liberties Protection, เอกสารทางวิชาการรณรงค์เปลี่ยนแปลงโทษประหารชีวิตตามหลักสิทธิมนุษยชนสากล [Academic Materials Advocating the Reform of the Death Penalty Based on Principles of Human Rights] (Nonthaburi: Ministry of Justice, 2014), 41–42. http://www.rlpd.go.th/rlpdnew/images/rlpd_1/HRC/CampaignDeathPenalty_57.pdf.

73. FIDH, *Death Penalty in Thailand*, 13.

74. Johnson and Zimring, *The Next Frontier*, 406.

75. Srisombat et al., โทษประหารชีวิต [Death Penalty], 156.

76. Ibid., 158.

77. "Amnesty Calls for Death Penalty Axe," *The Nation*, April 13, 2018.

78. "Thailand: Country's First Execution Since 2009 a Deplorable Move," Amnesty International, June 19, 2018, https://www.amnesty.org/en/latest/news/2018/06/thailand-countrys-first-execution-since-2009-a-deplorable-move/.

79. See https://www.facebook.com/dhammaandlaw/.

80. รายการเจาะใจ: กว่าจะเป็นผู้พิพากษา [Jojai: Before Becoming a Judge], broadcast July 25, 2013, TV Channel 5: https://www.youtube.com/watch?v=hKUJI5vcwH4.

81. This quote, dated August 2, 2014, seems to come originally from the judge's own Facebook page (which I was not able to locate) and was reposted on Marudi's page: https://www.facebook.com/marudikaka?fref=ts.

82. For newspaper coverage see ชาวเน็ตสดุดี "ปัญจพล เสน่ห์สังคม" "ผมเป็นผู้พิพากษาของพระเจ้าอยู่หัว" [Internet Users Praise "Panjapol Sanehsangkhom" "I Am a Judge of the King"]: http://www.matichon.co.th/news_detail.php?newsid=1407318989: August 6, 2014.

83. See "Thai Princess becomes UNODC Goodwill Ambassador on the Rule of Law for Southeast Asia," UNODC, February 14, 2017, https://www.unodc.org/southeastasiaand pacific/en/2017/02/goodwill-ambassador-hrh-princess-bajrakitiyabha-mahidol/story. html.

84. Http://www.tijbangkokrules.org/upload/filematerials2/11/Bangkok%20Rules_ English_ORIGINAL.pdf.

85. Kittipong Kittayarak interview, July 20, 2012.

86. Most Thai judges are Buddhist, but even non-Buddhists are expected to join the meditation course.

87. For an English translation of Buddhadasa's earliest lectures to judges, first given in 1956 [originally คู่มือมนุษย์], see Buddhadasa Bhikkhu *Handbook for Mankind*, http://sys.dra. go.th/module/attach_media/sheet2320090714122239.pdf.

88. For a discussion, see Tomomi Ito, *Modern Thai Buddhism and Buddhadasa Bhikkhu: A Social History* (Singapore: NUS Press, 2012), 60–62.

89. Sulak Sivarak interview, July 26, 2012. Sulak argued that Buddhada's willingness to lecture judges reflected his naivety about society and politics; but also reminded me that no monk can decline to teach the dharma when invited.

90. Prosecutor interview, May 4, 2012.

91. กฎหมาย and กฎแห่งกรรม.

92. Field notes, May 30, 2012.

93. แผ่นดิน.

94. Field notes, July 23, 2009.

95. Field notes, July 22, 2009.

3. CHALLENGES TO THE JUDICIARY

1. For a summary, see Lisa Gardner, "A Chronology of Uncle SMS's Imprisonment and Death," *Asian Correspondent*, May 8, 2012, https://asiancorrespondent.com/2012/05/ uncle-sms-akong-jailed-for-lese-majeste-dies-a-chronology/.

2. On Akong's death, see Tyrell Haberkorn, "Tanthawut Mourns Ah Kong: An Account of Injustice," *Prachatai*, June 12, 2012, http://www.prachatai3.info/english/node/3258.

3. See Pavin Chachavalpongpun, *Thailand's Fearlessness: Free Akong* (n.d. or place of publication, probably Bangkok, ca. 2011).

4. Judge N, November 20, 2012—as summarized in field notes.

5. Judge S, December 23, 2012.

6. Most English sources have relied on *The Nation*'s April 27, 2006, translations of the speeches—but *Phujatkan*'s Thai transcription contains some important variations.

7. See http://www.manager.co.th/Home/ViewNews.aspx?NewsID=9490000054995.

8. ขอบเขต.

9. His statement that the court "stopped working" suggested a dim view of the Thaksin era Constitutional Court.

10. มีคนเขาก็อาจจะมามาบอกว่าพระมหากษัตริย์รัชกาลที่ 9 เนี่ยทำตามใจชอบ ไม่เคยทำอะไร ตามใจชอบ.

11. The nature of the "claims" referred to here is rather unclear and ambiguous.

12. Chai-Anan Samudavanij Interview, March 19, 2008. Chai-Anan became a full professor at just thirty-one and was widely viewed in the 1980s and early 1990s as Thailand's most intellectually distinguished political scientist.

13. He did not mention more controversial royal moves, notably his appointment of the arch-conservative Supreme Court judge Thanin Kraivichien as prime minister in 1976.

14. For a more sympathetic analysis of Democrat reasoning in 2006, see Connors, "Article of Faith," 157–58.

15. See Constitutional Court, Judgment 9/2006, May 8, 2006.

16. Summary of Constitutional Court Ruling 9/2549, May 8, 2006, 5.

17. Jaran Phakdithanakun interview, July 21, 2015. He also insisted the three courts never sat down together and always worked separately. This claim was contradicted by media sources, quoting Jaran himself as announcing just such a meeting on April 26, 2006: http://news.bbc.co.uk/2/hi/asia-pacific/4945196.stm.

18. In 2013, their convictions were finally quashed by the Supreme Court. See *Khom Chat Luk*, June 14, 2013.

19. For the text of Thaksin's letter (dated June 23) and Bush's reply (July 3), see "Letters between Thai Prime Minister and US President," *The Nation*, July 12, 2006.

20. Summary of Constitutional Court Ruling 9/2549, May 8, 2006. Bangkok: Constitutional Court, 6. The 1997 constitution stipulated that polls must be held within sixty days of the house dissolution, but set no minimum number of days. Since the April 2006 election took place thirty-seven days after the dissolution, this objection was quite curious.

21. US Embassy discussion with Vishnu Varunyou, then deputy chief justice of the Central Administrative Court on May 1, 2006, summarized in 06BANGKOK2567 COURTS LEAN TOWARD NULLIFICATION; TRT FIGHTS BACK, State Department "Wikileaks" cable, May 2, 2006.

22. Chai-Anan interview, March 19, 2008.

23. Sarawut Benjakul interview, August 18, 2014. Sarawut had also served on the Judicial Commission, and on the committee that prepared the entrance exam for judges: he was the consummate judicial insider.

24. Judge K, October 9, 2012.

25. Judge N, November 20, 2012.

26. Judge P, November 19, 2012.

27. Judge Q, October 18, 2012.

28. Ibid.

29. Prapan Sapsaeng, ประพันธ์ ทรัพย์แสง, การค้นหาความจริงของศาลฎีกา แผนกคดีอาญา ของผู้ดำรงตำแหน่งทางการเมือง: แนวทางปัญหาสู่ความเป็นระบบไต่สวนเต็มรูปแบบ รายงานนี้เป็นส่วนหนึ่งของการอบรมหลักสูตร ผู้บริหารกระบวนการยุติธรรมระดับสูง รุ่นที่ 8, วิทยาลัยการยุติธรรม, สำนักงานศาลยุติธรรม [Accessing the Truth in the Supreme Court's Criminal Division for Persons Holding Political Positions: Ways to Conduct a Systematic Inquiry], Paper submitted in partial fulfillment of the requirements for the program of Senior Executives [Bo Yo So], 2005, 50–56.

30. Judge M, November 26, 2012.

31. Judge R, August 30, 2012.

32. Judge N, November 20, 2012.

33. Judge Q, October 18, 2012.

34. Judge C, March 18, 2008.

35. *Judicial Commission Minutes*, 8/2555, March 2, 2012, 14–15.

36. Judge M, November 26, 2012.

37. Sarawut interview, August 18, 2014.

38. While Article 28 does place tight limits on how judges may express their opinions to the public, electronic media is only briefly mentioned; the main focus of the article concerns judges speaking about court cases or other related matters, rather than expressing

views on a wide range of political issues. Courts of Justice, ประมวลจริยธรรมข้าราชการตุลาการ [The Code of Judicial Conduct] (Bangkok: Office of Courts of Justice, 2010), 66–70. For a 2013 dual-language version, see http://www.coj.go.th/en/pdf/CodeofConducts.pdf.

39. The English courts issued the following, equally ambiguous, guidance to judges in 2013: "Blogging by members of the judiciary is not prohibited. However, judicial officeholders who blog (or who post comments on other people's blogs) must not identify themselves as members of the judiciary. They must also avoid expressing opinions which, were it to become known that they hold judicial office, could damage public confidence in their own impartiality or in the judiciary in general." *Guide to Judicial Conduct*, 2013, Appendix 4.

40. Judge K, October 9, 2012.

41. Judge E, June 25, 2015.

42. Judge L, October 9, 2012.

43. According to official statistics, conviction rates in Thailand for 1997, 2003, and 2004 averaged around 98.5 percent. See Streckfuss, *Truth on Trial*, 198n38.

44. Judge J, November 19, 2012.

45. Judge K, October 9, 2012.

46. Judge R, October 8, 2012.

47. Judge R, August 20, 2012.

48. See http://buddhismlaw.blogspot.com/2012/01/blog-post_3190.html.

49. แสดงอำนาจ.

50. Judge J, November 19, 2012.

51. Judge N, November 20, 2012.

52. This is a conservative estimate of coup totals: cases can be made for including at least a couple of others.

53. Sarawut interview, August 18, 2014.

54. See Piyabutr Saengkanokkul, พระราชอำนาจ องคมนตรี และผู้มีบารมีนอกรัฐธรรมนูญ [Royal Powers, The Privy Council, and Extraconstitutional "Charismatic" Persons] (Bangkok: Openbooks, 2007), 101.

55. Piyabutr, พระราชอำนาจ, 104.

56. นิติกร.

57. "Embattled *Lèse Majesté* Suspect Accused of Disrespecting Military Court," *Prachatai*, September 29, 2016, https://prachatai.com/english/node/6604; his full comments may be accessed via http://www.tlhr2014.com/th/?p=2273.

58. Judge E, June 25, 2015.

59. NCPO Order 37/2557, May 25, 2014.

60. NCPO Order 43/2557, May 27, 2014.

61. On Nitirat, see McCargo and Peeradej, "Branding Dissent."

62. Worajet interview, December 22, 2012.

63. Piyabutr interview, December 14, 2012.

64. Perhaps surprisingly, Worajet was promoted to full professor in 2014. He is also listed on his faculty's website as among its most distinguished alumni.

65. Piyabutr interview, December 14, 2012.

66. มือสังหาร.

67. Interview, August 18, 2014.

68. Jantajira Eiamayura, Teera Suteewarangkurn, Piyabutr Saengkanokkul et al., การพัฒนาระบบการจัดการคดีการเมืองในศาลยุติธรรม [Developing the System for Managing Political Cases in the Courts of Justice] (Bangkok: Institute of Research Development, Office of the Judiciary, 2012), 195–99. Worajet was listed as the project's academic adviser.

69. This was quite different from the existing system under which the Supreme Court had a special division for hearing parliamentary election-related cases, while the Appeals Court had jurisdiction over local elections (Article 219 of the 2007 Constitution).

70. Judge Sathit Phairo interview, June 22, 2015.

71. Judge Q interview, June 25, 2015.

72. Both arch-royalist Borwornsak Uwanno and critical legal academic Worajet Pakeerat were in rare agreement that the Administrative Court had no standing in the Preah Vihear case. See Puangthong Pawakapan, *State and Uncivil Society At The Temple of Preah Vihear* (Singapore: ISEAS, 2013), 68–70; and "'วรเจตน์' ยันหลักวิชาศาลปกครอง ไม่มีเขตอำนาจเหนือคดีเขาพระวิหาร" ["Worajet" Insists Administrative Court Has No Standing In Khao Phra Viharn Case], *Prachatai*, July 17, 2008, https://prachatai.com/journal/2008/07/17229.

73. Teera Suteewarangkurn made the same point, interview, December 12, 2012.

74. ขึ้นบัลลังค์ศาล.

75. ผีบัลลังค์เข้าสิง.

76. Jantajira Eiamayura interview, December 14, 2012.

77. ยึดโยง.

78. โอวาท.

79. Teera Suteewarangkurn interview, December 12, 2012.

80. Worajet Pakeerat interview, December 22, 2012.

81. Sawatree interview, November 14, 2012.

82. In Thai, ปฏิญญาหน้าศาล ปลดปล่อยนักโทษการเมือง [literally: Declaration Before the Court: Free Political Prisoners]. Suda Rangkupan, personal interview, February 4, 2013; email communication, March 17, 2016.

83. For a selection of related videos, mainly from Speedhorse TV and Asia Update, see https://www.youtube.com/watch?v=djfDaKBg-5Y&list=PLdkMomyS_vjzwktC8-v8ZvmpMrU89wsmO&index=46.

84. Sathit interview, June 22, 2015.

85. "For among [times of] arms, the laws fall mute," attributed to Cicero.

86. Judge H, July 23, 2015.

87. Sawatree interview, November 14, 2012.

88. Judge C, March 18, 2008.

89. Judge H, July 23, 2015.

90. สองมาตรฐาน.

91. Claudio Sopranzetti, *Owners of the Map: Motorcycle Taxi Drivers, Mobility, and Politics in Bangkok* (Berkeley: University of California Press, 2017), 167.

92. Judge N, November 20, 2012.

93. Judge M., November 26, 2012.

94. นักประท้วง.

95. Judge P., November 19, 2012.

96. กมธ. ต่างประเทศถกคดี ม. 112 เปรียบสนธิ-อากง มาตรฐานต่างกัน [House Committee on Foreign Affairs Discusses Article 112 Cases, Comparing Different Standards Applied to Sondhi, Akong], *Thai Rath*, May 17, 2012, http://www.thairath.co.th/content/260954.

97. Judge H, July 23, 2015.

98. Nidhi has argued that the idea of a benevolent and sacred judiciary, modeled on that of the monarchy, is extremely problematic. See Nidhi Eoseewong, พิพากษ์ศาล [Judging the judges] (Bangkok: Matichon 2012), 19–20.

4. AGAINST THE CROWN?

1. For the best explanation of the fabrication, see Boonrot Sisombat, "บทเรียนการปฏิบัติการข่าวสาร: กรณี ปปส. ในเมือง (มีนาคม–พฤษภาคม 2553)" [Lessons from Information Operations (IO): The Case of Prevention and Suppression of Insurgency in Bangkok (March–May 2010)], *Senathipat* 60, no. 1 (2011): 69–81.

2. Robert A. Ferguson, *The Trial in American Life* (Chicago: Chicago University Press, 2007), 24.

3. Victor W. Turner, *From Ritual to Theatre: The Human Seriousness of Play* (New York: Performing Arts Journal Publications, 1982), 84.

4. Haberkorn, *In Plain Sight*, 17.

5. Ferguson, *The Trial*, 13.

6. Ibid., 12–13.

7. Ibid., xi.

8. Ibid., 2–3. Ferguson uses the Greek term *peripeteia* for the unsettling element of surprise, his second element. In Greek drama, following the moment of *peripeteia* the play moves rapidly towards a denouement.

9. "ยุทธศาสตร์ฟินแลนด์: แผนเปลี่ยนการปกครองไทย?" *Phujatkan Daily*, May 18, 19, 22, 23 and 24, 2006. The first article is at http://www.manager.co.th/Daily/ViewNews.aspx?NewsID=9490000065158.

10. On the "October generation" of 1970s student leaders and activists, see Kanokrat Lertchoosakul, *The Rise of the Octobrists in Contemporary Thailand* (New Haven, CT: Yale University Council on Southeast Asia Studies, 2016). The election of provincial governors has long been opposed by senior Thai bureaucrats who fear a substantial decline in their power and prestige would follow.

11. Those named by Pramote were Kriengkamon Laohapirot, Chaturon Chaisaeng, Surapong Suebwonglee, Adisorn Piengkes, Sutham Saengprathum, Amnuaychai Patiphat-phaophong, Varit Mongolsiri, and Phumtham Wechayachai.

12. "Criminal Court Rejects Thaksin's Suit against Sondhi," *The Nation*, March 25, 2009.

13. ASTV-Manager, ขบวนการล้มเจ้า [The Movement to Overthrow the Monarchy], Bang-kok: ASTV–Phujatkan. For an alternative discussion of this book, see Ünaldi, *Working Towards The Monarchy*, 78–82.

14. ข้าราชการ, literally servants of the King.

15. T-News Editor, เปิดโปงขบวนการแดงล้มเจ้า [Exposing the Red Anti-Monarchy Movement] (Nonthaburi: Green Panyayan Publishing, 2010). The online broadcasts were entitled เจาะ ข่าวร้อน ล้วงข่าวลึก [Delving into Hot News, Dipping Deeply into the News]. For a sample 2009 clip, see https://www.youtube.com/watch?v=CuKjqekNGyo.

16. Democrat Party, "เชื่อมั่นประเทศไทยกับนายกฯ อภิสิทธิ์ 26. เม.ย. 53" [Trusting in Thailand with PM Abhisit (April 26, 2010)], http://www.democrat.or.th/th/news-activity/media/detail.php?ID=4507&phrase_id=684638. Seh Daeng was a maverick cavalry officer whose "guards" provided an armed militia to defend and support the redshirt movement. He was assassinated in May 2010. Chavalit Yongchaiyudh, a former army commander who had briefly served as prime minister (1996–97), had long been accused of disloyalty to the crown.

17. "'สรรเสริญ' อัดเสื้อแดงทำตามกันเป็นลัทธิ ยกระดับสู่การก่อการร้าย-มุ่งโจมตีสถาบัน" ["Sansern" Attacks Cult-Like Redshirts, Designates Them Terrorists, Aiming at Attacking the Monar-chy], *Prachatai*, April 29, 2010, http://www.prachatai.com/journal/2010/04/29151. For additional discussions, see Bangkok Pundit, "Conspiracy to Overthrow the Monarchy," April 27, 2010, https://asiancorrespondent.com/2010/04/conspiracy-against-the-monarchy/; and "Thai Army Backtracks on Conspiracy to Overthrow the Monarchy Chart," May 26, 2011, https://asiancorrespondent.com/2011/05/thai-army-backtracks-on-the-conspiracy-to-overthrow-the-monarchy-chart/.

18. Thailand Democracy Watch. "มาร์ค" รับเครือข่ายล้มสถาบันเคลื่อนไหวตลอด ช่วงนี้เห็นภาพมากขึ้น ศอฉ. แจกแผนผังขบวนการล้มเจ้า ["Mark" Accepts Overthrowing Monarchy Movement Constantly Active. The Picture (of the Movement) is Currently Clearer. CRES Distributes Anti-Mon-archy Plot Diagram], April 27, 2010, http://www.tdw.polsci.chula.ac.th.

19. "ไม่มก ศอฉ. ยอมรับแต่ง 'ผังล้มเจ้า' เพื่อตอบโต้การใส่ร้ายท่านผู้หญิงจรุงจิตต์" [CRES Spokesperson Admits "Overthrowing-Monarchy Diagram" Was Created to Respond to A Slander on Lady Jarungjit], *Prachatai*, May 26, 2011, http://www.prachatai.com/journal/2011/05/34974.

20. "'ธาริต' ปูด 'รบ.มาร์ค' ใช้ผังล้มเจ้าทำเกมจบ" ["Tharit" Reveals "Mark's Government" Using Overthrowing-Monarchy Diagram to End Game], Kom Chad Luek, May 25, 2012, http://www.komchadluek.net/news/politic/131151.

21. See Boonrot Sisombat, บทเรียนการปฏิบัติการข่าวสาร [Lessons from Information Operations]: 69–81.

22. Kasian Tejapira, "ชันสูตรพลิกศพ 'ผังล้มเจ้า' " [Performing An Autopsy on the "Overthrowing-Monarchy Diagram"], April 27, 2012, http://www.matichon.co.th/news_detail.php?newsid=1335488423.

23. For a parallel diagram, see Robert Darnton, *Poetry and the Police: Communication Networks in Eighteenth-Century Paris* (Cambridge, MA: Belknap Press, 2010), 16.

24. Darnton, *Poetry and the Police*, 22.

25. See Voice TV, "ข้อสังเกตบางประการต่อคำสารภาพเรื่องแผนผังล้มเจ้า" [Some Remarks on the Confession Concerning the Overthrowing-Monarchy Diagram], http://news.voicetv.co.th/thailand/11541.html.

26. The crime of compassings is specified under English law in the 1848 Treason Felonies Act: "If any person whatsoever shall, within the United Kingdom or without, *compass,* imagine, invent, devise, or intend to deprive or depose our Most Gracious Lady the Queen, from the style, honour, or royal name of the imperial crown of the United Kingdom, or of any other of her Majesty's dominions and countries, or to levy war against her Majesty, within any part of the United Kingdom, in order by force or constraint to compel her to change her measures or counsels, or in order to put any force or constraint upon or in order to intimidate or overawe both Houses or either House of Parliament, or to move or stir any foreigner or stranger with force to invade the United Kingdom or any other of her Majesty's dominions or countries under the obeisance of her Majesty, and such *compassings,* imaginations, inventions, devices, or intentions, or any of them, shall express, utter, or declare, by publishing any printing or writing . . . or by any overt act or deed, every person so offending shall be guilty of felony." Treason Felonies Act 1848, italics added.

27. David Streckfuss, *Truth on Trial*, 83.

28. เรียบร้อย สงบ มีน้ำใจ.

29. King Bhumibol interview, Soul of the Nation, BBC documentary, 1979. See https://www.youtube.com/watch?v=5ih9cgmYY5M, starting at 22.25.

30. Field notes, January 19 and 24, 2012.

31. For details of the Somyot case, see https://freedom.ilaw.or.th/case/61.

32. See Duncan McCargo, *Politics and the Press in Thailand: Media Machinations* (London: Routledge, 2000), 136–57. While Somyot did not write the articles over which he was charged, he did author other very critical articles during this period that may have offended the military.

33. On these *libelles*, see Robert Darnton, *The Great Cat Massacre and Other Episodes in French Cultural History* (New York: Vintage, 1984), 176–81.

34. In Thai แนวร่วมประชาธิปไตยต่อต้านเผด็จการแห่งชาติ, abbreviated to นปช. The movement was originally established in 2007 to counter the anti-Thaksin yellowshirts.

35. For an example of such thinking, see Saksith Saiyasombut, "'Black Khmer Magic' a Threat to the Thai Army?!" first published at *Siam Voices*, February 20, 2011, https://saiyasombut.wordpress.com/2011/02/20/black-khmer-magic-a-threat-to-the-thai-army/.

36. Arisman was a former entertainer and MP, Suphorn (nicknamed Rambo Isan) an ex-MP for Nakhon Ratchasima, and Darunee a well-known TV personality. A new wave of Thai dissidents fled to Cambodia in the immediate aftermath of the May 22, 2014, military coup.

37. For a discussion of the Thaksin/Taksin connection, see Ünaldi, *Working Towards The Monarchy*, 55; and in relation to the Somyot case, 82–83.

38. These two words are spelled differently in Thai. The *banthuek* consistently used the Thai symbol for "Th" followed by a long "a," as in Thaksin, not "T" for "Taksin" followed by a short "a" (ทักษิณ with tho-thahan, not ตากสิน, with to-tao). In fairness, the ทักษิณ spelling did appear—albeit in small letters—on the cover of the magazine itself.

39. See Naruemon Thabchumpon and Duncan McCargo, "Urbanized Villagers in the 2010 Thai Redshirt Protests: Not Just Poor Farmers?" *Asian Survey* 51, no. 6 (2011): 993–1018.

40. Somyot Prueksakasemsuk, กะเทาะเปลือกทักษิโณมิคส์: ความเป็นจริงอีกมุมหนึ่งของ สังคมที่ถูกปิดบัง ซ่อนเร้นในช่วง 4 ปีของระบอบทักษิณ [Broken Shell of Thaksinomics: Another True Perspective on a Closed Society, Concealed during Four Years of the Thaksin Regime] (Bangkok: Puthuchon, 2004).

41. Jit Pollachan, "แผนนองเลือด" [Bloodbath Plan], *Voice of Taksin* 15 (February 2010): 45–47.

42. In his 2013 appeal, Somyot's new lawyer Vasant Panich referred to the articles as นิยาย, stories or fables. To their credit, neither Somyot nor his original lawyers used this euphemism in their final submissions to the lower court.

43. See Thomas Fuller, "Thai Leader Narrowly Escapes Jet Explosion," *New York Times*, March 5, 2001. The cause of the explosion has never been conclusively resolved.

44. Seh Daeng "predicted" attacks on PAD demonstrators in October 2008, and grenades were indeed hurled into the protests shortly afterwards. Judges were understandably concerned about threats concerning their own safety made by Seh Daeng in January 2010.

45. Jit Pollachan, "6 ตุลา แห่ง พ.ศ. 2553" [October 6, 2010], *Voice of Taksin* 16 (March 2010): 45–47.

46. All three were army commanders who later became prime minister.

47. This body was set up in the wake of the 2006 coup to investigate the assets and alleged wrongdoings of former prime minister Thaksin Shinawatra.

48. For a discussion of these protests and the media coverage of the incident, see http:// asiancorrespondent.com/20356/media-coverage-of-the-anti-prem-protests/.

49. Jaran Ditapichai, "สมยศที่ผมรู้จัก" [The Somyot I know] in วารสาร 24 มิถุนาประชาธิปไตย: สมยศ พฤกษาเกษมสุข [Journal of 24 June for Democracy: Somyot Prueksakasemsuk] 1 (2012): 54.

50. วารสาร 24 มิถุนาประชาธิปไตย [Journal of 24 June for Democracy], 9.

51. วารสาร 24 มิถุนาประชาธิปไตย [Journal of 24 June for Democracy], 8.

52. See "Letter from Somyot," May 3, 2011, http://freesomyot.wordpress.com/letter-from-somyot/, and the Thai original at http://www.prachatai3.info/journal/2011/05/34347.

53. Surachai was granted a royal pardon and released in October 2013; in the wake of the May 2014 military coup he went into exile in Laos.

54. The prosecutor did ask Somyot whether Jakrapob was living in Cambodia; Somyot simply replied that he did not know—but said nothing about Jakrapob's whereabouts in 2010 or 2011.

55. I-law, Somyot Trial Notes, Petchaboon, 5–6.

56. Since Jakarapob was living in Cambodia throughout the period when the magazine was published, Benja's not having met him at the office was unsurprising. I-law, Somyot Trial Notes, Petchaboon, 5.

57. Ibid., 3.

58. Ibid., 6.

59. For six such warnings, see I-law, Somyot Trial Notes, Bangkok, April 18 (13, 20, 23), April 24 (53), May 1 (60), and May 2 (67).

60. Official court record, Somyot trial, April 25, 2012, 5.

61. This witty riposte was noted neither in the official *banthuek* or by I-law.

62. Field notes, Somyot trial, April 24, 2012.

63. Ibid., April 25, 2012.

64. I-law, Somyot Trial Notes, Bangkok, 10–14.

65. ผู้กล่าวไทย.

66. Field notes, Somyot trial, April 26, 2012.

67. I-law, Somyot Trial Notes, Bangkok, 50–51; Court Banthuek, Somyot case, April 24, 2012, 5–8.

68. I-law, Somyot Trial Notes, Bangkok, 77–78.

69. Field notes, Somyot trial May 1, 2012; I-law, Somyot Trial Notes, Bangkok, 54–59; Court Banthuek, Somyot Trial, May 1, 2012.

70. Somyot appeared to be referring to the 2005 royal birthday speech; see "The King Can Do Wrong," *The Nation*, December 5, 2005, http://www.nationmultimedia.com/2005/12/05/headlines/data/headlines_19334288.html.

71. See Printing Records Act, 2007.

72. The 2007 Act does not explicitly state that the author, editor, or publisher is legally liable—or not liable—for press content. The vaguely worded Act was another of the hastily drafted 2007 coup-era laws prompting the protests behind the Jon Ungpakorn case. See Wad Rawee, "The Case of Somyot Prueksakasemsuk: Guilty of Lèse Majesté for Reaching a Different Interpretation," Pen International, April 2016, http://www.pen-international.org/04/2016/the-case-of-somyot-prueksakasemsuk-guilty-of-lese-majeste-for-reaching-a-different-interpretation/?print=print.

73. Court Banthuek, Somyot Trial, May 1, 2012, 8.

74. "เหมือน [ประชาชน] คนไทย [โดย] ทั่วไป;" Field notes, Somyot trial, May 1, 2012; I-law, Somyot Trial Notes, Bangkok, 58; Court Banthuek, Somyot Trial, May 1, 2012, 11.

75. Court Banthuek, Somyot Trial, May 1, 2012, 11.

76. Haberkorn, *In Plain Sight*, 213.

77. Somyot was only twelve in 1973 and fifteen in 1976; this was not the first time the prosecution had tried to insinuate that he was very radical in his youth.

78. The judge recorded that the picture "was about political cases at that time concerning which there was no justice." Court Banthuek, Somyot case, May 1, 2012, 14.

79. "ไม่เอาแล้ว เสียเวลา," I-law, Somyot Trial Notes, Bangkok, 58.

80. Court Banthuek, Somyot Case, May 1, 2012, 16.

81. In their petition, Somyot's lawyers argued that the 112 law violated Article 3 paragraph 2; Article 8; Article 29; and Article 45 paragraphs 1 and 2 of the 2007 Constitution.

82. Lunch conversation with Somyot's defense lawyers, April 24, 2012.

83. Constitutional Court Judgment, "Evaluating Article 112 of the Criminal Code: Is it Compatible with Articles 3, 29 and 45 or Not?" October 10, 2012, 1.

84. Constitutional Court on 112, 10.

85. Ibid., 27.

86. Ibid., 19.

87. Ibid., 22–23.

88. Somyot Defense Closing Statement, December 28, 2012.

89. คำแถลงการณ์ปิดคดี [Closing statement as drafted by Somyot, not submitted], December 28, 2012.

90. Somyot Court of First Instance Verdict, as retyped by I-law, January 23, 2013, 2–3.

91. Ibid., 4.

92. Ibid., 9.

93. Ibid., 9.

94. Ferguson, *The Trial*, 145.

95. Appeal, Somyot Prueksakasemsuk, April 1, 2013, 72.

96. Court of Appeal Verdict, Somyot Prueksakasemsuk, July 28, 2014. The appeal judgment ran to sixty-six pages, in contrast with the twenty-eight-page lower court judgment. Why it took nearly two months for the appeal verdict to be announced after it was written was unclear.

97. "ศาลฎีกาลดโทษ เหลือจำคุก 6 ปี คดี 112 สมยศ พฤกษาเกษมสุข" [Supreme Court Reduces Somyot Prueksakasemsuk's 112 Case Jail Sentence to 6 Years], *Prachatai*, February 23, 2017, https://prachatai.com/journal/2017/02/70228.

98. See Sawatree Suksri, "ข้อสังเกตบางประการต่อคำพิพากษาคดีสมยศ พฤกษาเกษมสุข นับแต่ศาลชั้นต้นถึงชั้น ฎีกา" [Some Observations on Judgments in the Somyot Prueksakasemsuk Case from Court of the First Instance to the Supreme Court], *Prachatai*, February 24, 2017, https://prachatai.com/journal/2017/02/70247.

99. Interview, May 4, 2013.

100. According to one informant, Somyot had contemplated saying some of these things, but had finally decided against it. Interview, October 13, 2013.

101. Nick Nostitz interview, June 19, 2012.

5. COMPUTER COMPASSINGS

1. For details of Katha's case, see https://freedom.ilaw.or.th/case/83.

2. "Thai Stocks, Baht Slump on King's Health Speculation" (Update 3), *Bloomberg*, October 14, 2009, http://www.bloomberg.com/apps/news?pid=newsarchive&sid=aWSL mdQccvyo. ICT Minister Ranongrak Suwanchawee was cited in *Thai Rath* as saying that the royal health stories had been spread by a "rumor mongering gang." See http://www.prachatai.com/english/node/1481.

3. http://www.komchadluek.net/news/crime/35639; http://www.manager.co.th/Crime/ViewNews.aspx?NewsID=9520000130815; http://www.manager.co.th/Crime/ViewNews.aspx?NewsID=9520000131061. The Thai translation of the Bloomberg article did not appear until after the stock market had closed.

4. For details, see http://www.prachatai.com/english/node/1478 and http://www.prachatai.com/english/node/1474.

5. Katha interview, February 12, 2014.

6. http://www.prachatai.com/journal/2009/11/26439. The minister's claims about Katha's multiple postings were never substantiated, and he was only charged in connection with a single posting relating to the October 2009 stock price fall.

7. For related discussion, see Duncan McCargo, "Patani Militant Leaflets and the Use of History," in *Ghosts of the Past in Southern Thailand: Essays on the History and Historiography of Patani*, ed. Patrick Jory (Singapore: National University of Singapore Press, 2013), 277–97.

8. Katha interview, February 12, 2014.

9. This took the form of a *wai*, or two-handed salute—a traditional Thai greeting and sign of respect.

10. For this reason, my own notes on the Katha trial are much briefer than for other trials I attended; I was obliged to write up what had taken place during breaks in the trial. Fortunately, I-law was able to make use of notes taken by Katha's legal team to prepare fuller summaries of the proceedings.

11. Basu, *The Trouble with Marriage*, 21, 6.

12. Art interview, October 28, 2012.

13. Art had become involved in the case by chance, after meeting Katha at the offices of *Prachatai*, and because he had a fairly good understanding of the IT issues. I-law staff interview, October 28, 2012; Art interview, October 28, 2012.

14. Art interview, October 28, 2012.

15. For a summary, see https://globalfreedomofexpression.columbia.edu/cases/chiranuch-premchaiporn-v-thailand/.

16. I-law staff interview October 28, 2012.

17. Anon interview, December 5, 2012.

18. Katha notes, June 5, 2012.

19. Anon interview, December 5, 2012. He claimed that when a company director died this could affect the value of that company's shares; but Anon's answer had no obvious relevance to how royal succession might affect Thai share values as a whole.

20. On the 1948 car accident that impaired the eighteen-year-old King's vision in one eye, see Handley, *The King Never Smiles*, 103–4.

21. ไม่เหมาะสม.

22. Field notes, Katha trial, June 6, 2012.

23. "Mr. Katha P. Case," [Undated I-Law notes], 12.

24. Sawatree Suksiri interview, November 14, 2012.

25. แต่ต้องพูดเผื่อๆไว้ กันศาลตีไปด้านนั้น.

26. Field notes, Katha trial, June 6, 2012. On May 25, 2012, King Bhumibol made a day trip to nearby Ayutthaya Province, apparently his first excursion outside Bangkok since entering Siriraj Hospital in 2009. He wore a military uniform.

27. On Nitirat, see McCargo and Peeradej, "Branding Dissent."

28. The judge pointedly used the word ความเห็น, rather than the more substantive ความคิดเห็น.

29. ลูกผู้ชาย.

30. This statement contradicted the senior judge's advice that the facts of the King's health were not relevant to the case.

31. Field notes, Katha trial, June 8, 2012, slightly edited for language.

32. Pseudonym. Field notes, Katha case conference June 7, 2012.

33. Thai prosecutors always end their examination by asking witnesses if they knew the defendant before. The implication is that anyone (usually a police officer or government official) who did not know defendants personally could not harbor any bias against them. A similar point was made by Saengchai Rattanaseriwong, interview, December 3, 2012.

34. Katha Court of First Instance Verdict, December 25, 2012,15.

35. ไม่น่าเชื่อถือ.

36. Field notes, Katha case conference June 7, 2012.

37. ทำลาย หักล้าง.

38. The former webmaster of the "Redshirt USA" site, Thantawut was convicted of lèse-majesté in 2011 and granted a royal pardon in 2013. He left Thailand following the May 2014 coup.

39. Art interview, October 28, 2012.

40. ข้าฯ มีความจงรักภักดีต่อพระมหากษัตริย์, Court Banthuek, Katha case, June 8, 2012, 11.

41. Anon interview.

42. มันแท่นะเวลาทำอะไรยากๆ.

43. On July 2, 2012, the defense team separately filed a five-page appeal to the Constitutional Court asserting that the 2007 Computer Crime Act was unconstitutional, on the grounds that it failed clearly to define the kind of acts that could undermine national security or generate public panic. This appeared to be a copycat move, emulating the appeal by Somyot's lawyers over Article 112. Unsurprisingly, on September 12, 2012, the appeal was rejected; Anon later claimed that it was not a serious defense strategy.

44. Katha Defense Closing Statement, August 17, 2012, 20.

45. Katha Court of First Instance Verdict, 16.

46. Katha Court of First Instance Verdict, 15–16.

47. Katha may have been charged under the Computer Crime Act partly so that he could be convicted over the less-discussed April 2009 derogatory message about Sirindhorn.

48. Katha interview, June 12, 2012.

49. Court of Appeal Judgment, Surapak Phuchaisaeng case, at "ยกฟ้อง! คดีโปรแกรมเมอร์ถูกกล่าวหาโพสต์เฟซบุ๊กหมิ่นสถาบัน" [Charges Dropped! Case of Programmer Accused Over *Lèse-Majesté* FacebookPost],*Prachatai*,October31,2012,https://prachatai.com/journal/2012/10/43413. More details of the case at https://freedom.ilaw.or.th/th/case/176#detail#.

50. อุทธรณ์ [Katha Appeal], April 2013, 44.

51. Surapak's acquittal was upheld by the Supreme Court on August 13, 2015.

52. Field notes, March 5, 2014. In the interests of full disclosure, I should declare that in the absence of Katha's lawyers, I assisted a reporter in her attempts to have him bailed out.

53. Nat Sattayaphornpisut, Facebook, September 26, 2015.

6. AGAINST THE STATE

1. The others were on November 29 and December 19.

2. แกนนำ.

3. For details of the NLA case, see https://freedom.ilaw.or.th/case/468.

4. Article 116: Whoever makes an appearance to the public by words, writings or any other means which is not an act within the purpose of the Constitution or for expressing an honest opinion or criticism in order:

1. To bring about a change in the Laws of the Country or the Government by the use of force or violence;
2. To raise unrest and disaffection among the people in a manner likely to cause disturbance in the country; or
3. To cause the people to transgress the laws of the Country, shall be punished with imprisonment not exceeding seven years.

5. Article 215 Whenever ten persons upwards being assembled together do or threaten to do an act of violence, or do anything to cause a breach of the peace, every such person shall be punished with imprisonment not exceeding six months or fined not exceeding one thousand Baht, or both.

If any of the offenders carries an arm, all the offenders shall be punished with imprisonment not exceeding two years or fined not exceeding four thousand Baht, or both. If the offender be the manager or person having the duty to give orders for the commission of the offence, such offender shall be punished with imprisonment not exceeding five years or fined not exceeding ten thousand Baht, or both.

6. Article 362: Whoever, entering into the immovable property belonging to the other person so as to take possession of such property in whole or in any part or entering into such property to do any act disturbing the peaceful possession of such person, shall be imprisoned not more than one year or fined not more than of two thousand Baht, or both.

Section 365 If the offence under Article 362, Article 363 or Article 364 be committed:

1. By an act of violence or threat to commit an act of violence;
2. By a person carrying arms or by two persons upwards participating; or
3. By night, the offender shall be punished with imprisonment not exceeding five years or fined not exceeding ten thousand Baht, or both.

7. http://www.prachatai.com/journal/2006/03/7653.

8. See "ศาลอุทธรณ์ยกฟ้องคดี 10 เอ็นจีโอบุกบินสภา สนช. 2550" [Court of Appeal Clears 10 NGO Leaders of 2007 CNS NLA Occupation] *Prachatai*, November 26, 2014, http://www.prachatai.com/journal/2014/11/56691.

9. In his testimony, Jon acknowledged being close to Phairoj, Saree, and Supinya. The defendants could be divided into two main groups: the "Jon group" of human rights activists, and a more hardline anti-Thaksin element. Field notes, NLA Trial (PT), February 18, 2013.

10. See https://www.youtube.com/watch?v=4PCS9Wt0OaU.

11. On Pichit's PAD role see, for example, *Matichon*, August 27, 2008, http://www.matichon.co.th/news_detail.php?newsid=1219763698.

12. For Amnat's PDRC Kor Phor Thor role, see this clip of him on stage in October 2013: https://www.youtube.com/watch?v=PlQFzNM3Eb0; for more details on Kor Phor Thor see *Phujatkan*, March 18, 2014, http://www.manager.co.th/Politics/ViewNews.aspx?NewsID=9570000030971&Html=1&TabID=3&.

13. Saiwan Mokkhasen, "Yellowshirt Leaders Fined 522M for 2008 Airport Shutdown," *Khao Sod English*, September 22, 2017, http://www.khaosodenglish.com/politics/2017/09/22/yellowshirt-leaders-fined-522m-seizing-airports/.

14. Community Resource Center (CRC) Trial Observations, February 21, 2012.

15. Field notes from conversation with prosecutor, March 15, 2012.

16. CRC Trial Observations, February 21, 2012. The official case document จ.๑๒, purportedly the history of defendant number 1 (Jon), included materials about Giles on page 16 (CRC, testimony of Police Lt Col Saphum Chomphutwachasathit, March 1, 2012). Another incorrect file confusing Jon with Giles, จ.๔๒, was identified the following day (testimony of Police Senior Sergeant Major Surakrit Kertnidetchakron). The same issue came up again on March 15, 2012 (testimony of Police Colonel Surapong Chaijan). Jon referred to this problem in his own testimony: see I-law, Trial Observation Report NLA Occupation Case, January 22, 2013.

17. Email communication from Giles Ungpakorn, October 4, 2015.

18. Saengchai interview, December 3, 2012.

19. Field notes from conversation with prosecutor, March 15, 2012.

20. Field notes, March 1, 2012.

21. Rare examples of such occupations include the Taiwan parliament, April 2014; and the Wisconsin state legislature, February–June 2011.

22. Field notes, Jon trial, February 23, 2012; CRC, Trial Observation Report, February 23, 2012. This crucial point was omitted from the official court banthuek.

23. Court Banthuek, Akhom Wattanaphan, February 23, 2012, 11.

24. Court Banthuek, Akhom Wattanaphan, February 23, 2012, "มีความเห็นว่าเป็นเรื่องทางการเมือง," 12.

25. Field notes, NLA trial, February 23, 2012.

26. Frank W. Munger, "Trafficking in Law: Cause Lawyer, Bureaucratic State, and Rights of Human Trafficking Victims in Thailand," *Asian Studies Review* 39, no. 1 (2015): 69–87.

27. CRC Trial Observations, February 21, 2012.

28. Former defendant interview, February 29, 2012; Saengchai interview, December 3, 2012.

29. "จารีต," Saengchai interview, December 3, 2012.

30. "เยิ่นเย้อฟุ่มเฟือย," CRC Trial Observations, February 21, 2012.

31. For a detailed discussion of the case, see *The Struggle of Villagers in Chana District, Southern Thailand in Defense of Community, Land and Religion against the Trans Thai-Malaysia Pipeline and Industrial Project (TTM), 2002–2008* (Sturminster Newton, UK: The Corner House, 2008), http://www.thecornerhouse.org.uk/sites/thecornerhouse.org.uk/files/TTM2002-2007.pdf.

32. Ratsada Manuratsada interview, June 17, 2006. Alas, Administrative Court decisions were not recognized by the Courts of Justice.

33. "บุคคลชั้นสูง," Saengchai interview, December 3, 2012.

34. "เค้าก็ยังมีหน้าที่ที่จะต้องรักษาระบบเอาไว้," Saengchai interview, December 3, 2012

35. However, Saengchai was not above asking leading questions himself.

36. "ไม่ใจกว้าง," Ratsada Manuratsada interview, October 28, 2012.

37. "แต่ทนายความคนทำงานเค้ารู้สึกอบอุ่นดี," Ratsada interview, October 28, 2012.

38. Field notes, NLA case, March 13, 2012.

39. Krap, or chai—the former is a particle, more an acknowledgment than an active statement of assent.

40. The Thai legal term *kaen nam* has a pejorative connotation, suggesting a rabble-rouser or agitator.

41. ประธาน—president or chair.

42. Field notes, NLA trial, March 2, 2012.

43. Ibid.

44. Ibid.

45. He used the phrase ลูกผู้ชาย on more than one occasion; it was also picked up by the prosecutor. Field notes February 23, 2012; February 28, 2012.

46. Field notes, NLA trial, March 1, 2012.

47. Field notes March 13, 2012.

48. During this period there were regular protests and banners displayed outside the Bangkok Criminal Court, some proclaiming "Free Akong," referring to one of the 112 cases over which the same judge had presided.

49. Phairoj, field notes, February 28, 2012; Jon, field notes March 1, 2012.

50. Field notes, NLA trial, March 2, 2012; this reportedly occurred on February 29.

51. Field notes, NLA trial, March 2, 2012.

52. เขตพระราชฐาน.

53. Following the royal succession in late 2016, King Vajiralongkorn took up residence immediately behind the parliament compound and announced his wish to reclaim the whole area as grounds for his palace. See Duncan McCargo, "Lights Out On a Parliamentary Era in Thailand," *Asia Times*, December 14, 2018, http://www.atimes.com/article/lights-out-on-a-parliamentary-era-in-thailand/.

54. Jon testimony, NLA trial notes (PT), February 18, 2013.

55. มอบอำนาจ.

56. Field notes, NLA trial, February 23, 2012.

57. I-law, คดีปืนสภาสนช. [NLA Occupation Case], January 22, 2013.

58. Jon testimony, NLA trial notes (PT), February 18, 2013.

59. Ibid.

60. Supinya testimony, NLA trial notes (PT), February 18, 2013.

61. "เป็นการคุ้มครองสิ่งที่กฎหมายคุ้มครองยิ่งกว่าหรือไม่," Kittisak testimony, NLA trial notes (PT), March 7, 2013. In late 2013, Kittisak himself became closely involved with the PDRC and was among the PDRC leaders for whom arrest warrants were issued on May 14, 2014 on insurrection charges. See "ศาลออกหมายจับ 30 แกนนำ กปปส." [Court issued arrest warrants for 30 PDRC leaders] *Phujatkan*, May 14, 2014, http://www.manager.co.th/Crime/ViewNews.aspx?NewsID=9570000053501. He continued to advance similar arguments justifying the seizure of public buildings. "กิตติศักดิ์อ้างชัยวัฒน์ยึดสถานที่ราชการเป็นสันติวิธีเชิงรุก" *Prachatai*, November 29, 2013, http://prachatai.com/journal/2013/11/50059.

62. "อย่าเล่นทุกเรื่อง," field notes, NLA trial, February 29, 2012.

63. NLA Defense Closing Statement, 5–6.

64. For example, "These were conditions that made the people's sector anxious," NLA Defense Closing Statement, 6.

65. NLA Defense Closing Statement, 7.

66. Ibid., 35–36.

67. NLA Judgment, Court of First Instance, 18.

68. Ibid., 23.

69. Ibid., 24.

70. อำเภอใจ.

71. NLA Judgment, Court of First Instance, 24.

72. Ibid., 25.

73. "จำเลยทั้งสิบกระทำความผิดโดยมีเจตนาปกป้องผลประโยชน์ของชาติบ้านเมืองเป็นสำคัญ" NLA Judgment, Court of First Instance, 32. See also http://www.prachatai.com/english/node/4538.

74. iLaw: จาก "ชุมนุม" สู่ "มั่วสุม-ก่อความวุ่นวาย-ใช้กำลังประทุษร้าย," *Prachatai* June 4, 2013, http://www.prachatai.com/journal/2013/06/47032.

75. Interview, June 2014.

76. Field notes, NLA case, February 21, 2012.

77. NLA Case Appeal Court Judgment, 13.

78. NLA Appeal Judgment, 21–22.

79. See "ศาลฎีกาพิพากษาคดี 'ปืนสภาต้าน กม.สนช. ปี 50' มีความผิด แต่สั่งรอกำหนดโทษ 2 ปี," [Supreme Court Judgment in 2007 Parliament Occupation Case: Guilty But Sentences Deferred for 2 Years], *Prachatai*, March 15, 2017, https://prachatai.com/journal/2017/03/70576.

80. "Jon Has 'No Regrets' over 2007 Protest," *The Nation*, March 17, 2017.

81. *Prachatai*, March 15, 2017.

7. CRIMES OF THAKSIN

1. On Thaksin, see Duncan McCargo and Ukrist Pathmanand, *The Thaksinization of Thailand* (Copenhagen: NIAS, 2005); Baker and Pasuk, *Thaksin*.

2. In October 2017, the attorney general announced plans to prosecute Thaksin for *lèse-majesté* on the basis of a 2015 South Korean media interview—finally making concrete a longstanding belief among the traditional elite that Thaksin was trying to discredit the monarchy. See Teeranai Charuvastra, "New AG Vows to Try Thaksin for Insulting Monarchy," *Khao Sod English*, October 9, 2017, http://www.khaosodenglish.com/politics/2017/10/09/new-ag-vows-try-thaksin-insulting-monarchy/.

3. See Article 295: "Any person holding a political position who intentionally fails to submit the account showing assets and liabilities and the supporting documents as provided in this Constitution or intentionally submits the same with false statements or conceals the facts which should be revealed shall vacate office as from the date of the expiration of the time limit for the submission under section 292 or as from the date such act is discovered, as the case may be, and such person shall be prohibited from holding any political position for five years as from the date of the vacation of office."

4. Amara Raksasataya and James R. Klein, *The Constitutional Court of Thailand: The Provisions and the Workings of the Court* (Bangkok: Constitution for the People Society, 2003), 71. Amara was himself a judge of the Constitutional Court from 2000 to 2003, losing the presidency to Kramol Tongdhamachart by a 6–8 vote in March 2003.

5. Preecha Chalermvanit, quoted in *Matichon*, August 4, 2001.

6. For a useful summary of the legal issues in question, see Amara and Klein, *The Constitutional Court*, 71–78.

7. Thaksin verdict English summary, 4.

8. For a discussion of the petition movement and a list of elite backers, see John Funston, "Thailand: Thaksin Fever," in *Southeast Asian Affairs 2002* (Singapore: ISEAS 2002), 315–16 and 325n4.

9. *Bangkok Post*, August 4, 2001.

10. Thaksin made this argument the following day at a meal with reporters—see *Bangkok Post*, August 5, 2001.

11. Jaran interview July 8, 2015.

12. "Constitutional Court: Kramol Grabs Presidency," *The Nation*, March 21, 2003. http://www.nationmultimedia.com/headlines/CONSTITUTION-COURT-Kramol-grabs-presidency-75406.html. Amara, Kramol's main rival for the job, was in any case just months from retirement.

13. Duncan McCargo, "Balancing the Checks: Thailand's Paralyzed Politics Post-1997," *Journal of East Asian Studies* 3, no. 1 (2003): 139.

14. McCargo, "Balancing the Checks," 139.

15. For the full decision, see Constitutional Court Judgment 4/2006, February 16, 2006.

16. "From The Royal Plaza," *The Nation*, February 4, 2006, http://www.nationmultimedia.com/specials/sondhirally/.

17. Chitchai Wannasathit notionally served as acting prime minister from April 5 to May 23, 2006.

18. Kevin Hewison, "The Monarchy and Democratisation," 70.

19. http://news.bbc.co.uk/2/hi/asia-pacific/5361756.stm, from the initial statement and second communiqué respectively.

20. See Michael Montesano, "Thailand: A Reckoning with History Begins," *Southeast Asian Affairs 2007* (Singapore: ISEAS, 2007), 319. Thaksin later told the US Embassy he was referring to Prem, but at the time many assumed he meant the King himself.

21. According to Sarawut Benjakul, one president of the Supreme Court seriously considered resigning from the judiciary rather than accept military instructions to join the Constitutional Tribunal. Interview, August 18, 2014.

22. Constitutional Court Judgment 6-7/2551: 23/2551, 24/2551, July 8, 2008.

23. Constitutional Court Judgment 12-13/2551: 19/2551, 29/2551, September 9, 2008.

24. Constitutional Court Judgment 20/2551: 45/2551, December 2, 2008.

25. These related to alleged abuses of funds and donations by the party. See "มติศาลรธน. 4:2 ให้ยกคำร้องยุบปชป" [Court Verdict Rejects Petition for Democrat Party Dissolution 4: 2], *Khom Chat Luk*, November 29, 2013, http://www.komchadluek.net/news/politic/81189.

26. The court's reasoning may have been legally sound, if somewhat troubling: Jatuporn had failed to vote in the 2011 general election (because he was in jail at the time), and so was not qualified to run as a candidate.

27. Constitutional Court judgment 1/2556: 56/2555, February 1, 2013.

28. Conservative law professor Taweekiat Menakanist became a Constitutional Court judge on October 21, 2013.

29. Constitutional Court judgment 1/2557: 55/2556, January 8, 2014.

30. Constitutional Court judgment 3–4/2557: 67/2556, 68/2556, March 12, 2014.

31. Interim Constitution of the Kingdom of Thailand 2014, preamble.

32. See Aim Sinpeng, "Party Banning and the Impact on Party System Institutionalization in Thailand," *Contemporary Southeast Asia*, 36, no. 3 (2014): 442–66.

33. The Supreme Court's Criminal Division for Person Holding Political Positions Verdict Red Case Number 1/2553, *Royal Thai Government Gazette*, Issue 127 Section 21 Ko, March 24, 2010, http://www.ratchakitcha.soc.go.th/DATA/PDF/2553/A/021/1.PDF.

34. For a discussion, see Pasuk and Baker, *Thaksin*, 327–31.

35. For a brief summary of the case concerning the ten ministers, see http://www.kodmhai.com/vinit/2544/4-1.html.

36. Samak Constitutional Court Verdict Summary, 12-13/2551, September 9, 2008, 3.

37. Samak Summary, 4.

38. Constitutional Court, Full Judgment Samak Case, Jaran decision, 24.

39. Jaran interview, July 8, 2015. At the time, a Constitutional Court judge could only be removed by an impeachment procedure under Article 274 of the 2007 Constitution, requiring a vote by three-fifths of the whole senate, which was unlikely to pass. However, Jaran said he would have resigned before such a vote could be held.

40. Jatuporn had been in jail at the time of the July 2011 election; although elected to parliament, he was retrospectively disqualified by the Election Commission. While removing Jatuporn from office might appear to be a blow against Pheu Thai, Yingluck also stood to gain from the move, which reduced the bargaining power of the redshirt movement vis-à-vis her government; it was arguably in keeping with the terms of the "deal" under which she operated. Whereas Jatuporn had his parliamentary status removed, in February 2013 the Constitutional Court refused to debar then minister Varathep Ratanakorn from office after he was given a suspended jail sentence on corruption charges—illustrating the willingness of the court to be supportive of the Yingluck administration. See Joe Jaturavith, "Reluctance and Hesitancy: An Analysis of the Constitutional Court's Rulings Between 2012–2014," Independent Study Research Paper, NYU Gallatin, May 2016.

41. This was a decision of the Central Administrative Court.

42. Constitutional Court Judgment 9/2557, 34/2557, May 3, 2014.

8. COURTING CONSTITUTIONALISM

1. Field notes, July 5, 2012.

2. กู้ชาติ, a well-known slogan of the PAD, or yellowshirts.

3. Some analysts continued to assert that the Constitutional Court's decisions comprised a judicial coup, despite the fact that no such coup had taken place.

4. See Lisa Hilbink, "Assessing the New Constitutionalism," *Comparative Politics* 40, no. 2 (2008): 227–45.

5. For background on the Constitutional Court, see ความรู้เบื้องต้นศาลรัฐธรรมนูญ [Basic Information on the Constitutional Court], Bangkok: Constitutional Court, 2007, at http://dl.parliament.go.th/bitstream/handle/lirt/302988/50372.pdf?sequence=1; and สิบปี ศาลรัฐธรรมนูญ: สู่ศตวรรษใหม่ของนิติรัฐไทย [Ten Years of the Constitutional Court: Entering a New Century of Law-Abiding Thai State], Bangkok: Constitutional Court, 2008, at http://dl.parliament.go.th/bitstream/handle/lirt/301276/55294.pdf?sequence=1.

6. On the importance of German models for the Thai Constitutional Court, see Borwornsak Uwanno, "ศาลรัฐธรรมนูญตามรัฐธรรมนูญแห่งราชอาณาจักรไทย พ.ศ. 2540" [The Constitutional Court According to the 1997 Constitution of the Kingdom of Thailand], วารสารสถาบัน ประชาธิปก [King Prajadhipok Institute Journal] 1, no. 1 (2003): 10.

7. See Borwornsak Uwanno and Wayne D. Burns, "The Thai Constitution of 1997: Sources and Process," *University of British Columbia Law Review* 227 (1998): 248.

8. For the most detailed study of the workings of the Constitutional Court to date, see Kla Samudavanija, ขอบเขตอำนาจหน้าที่ศาลรัฐธรรมนูญ เพื่อการส่งเสริมการปกครอง ในระบอบประชาธิปไตยและคุ้มครอง สิทธิเสรีภาพของประชาชน, [The Scope of Power and Responsibilities of the Constitutional Court to Support Governance under the Democratic System and Protect the Rights and Liberties of the People] (Nonthaburi: King Prachadipok Institute, 2016).

9. See Eugénie Mérieau, "Thailand's Deep State, Royal Power and the Constitutional Court (1997–2015)," *Journal of Contemporary Asia* 46, no. 3 (2016): 445–66.

10. Ibid., 447.

11. Ibid., 446.

12. Ibid., 462.

13. Ibid., 460.

14. See Bjorn Dressel and Khemthong Tonsakulrungruang, "Coloured Judgements? The Work of the Thai Constitutional Court, 1998–2016," *Journal of Contemporary Asia* 49, no. 1 (2018): 1–23.

15. Khemthong Tonsakulrungruang, "Thailand: An Abuse of Judicial Review," in *Judicial Review of Elections in Asia*, ed. Po Jen Yap (Abingdon, UK: Routledge 2016), 186.

16. Piyabutr, ศาลรัฐประหาร [Coup Court], 56–57.

17. Victor Turner, "Variations on a Theme of Liminality," in *Secular Ritual*, ed. Sally F. Moore and Barbara G. Myerhoff (Amsterdam: Van Gorcum, 1977), 42.

18. To date, all Thai Constitutional Court judges have been men.

19. See "Death Penalty Offence," *Bangkok Pundit*, August 10, 2009, citing *Matichon*: http://www2.asiancorrespondent.com/2009/08/death-penalty-offence/.

20. Before the 2011 election, Somjed orchestrated a billboard campaign, urging voters not to support candidates linked to the 2010 redshirt protests that had culminated in a series of arson attacks. See "Senators Ask Voters to Reject Riot Instigators," *Pattaya Today*, n.d. http://pattayatoday.net/news/senators-ask-voters-to-reject-riot-instigators/.

21. Wanthongchay later became one of the leaders of the PDRC. In December 2015 he sued former deputy prime minister Chalerm Yubamrung for abuse of power.

22. A sympathetic *Matichon* profile portrayed Wirat as one the Democrat Party's top legal specialists. See *Matichon*, July 15, 2012, http://www.matichon.co.th/news_detail. php?newsid=1342330920; and Marc Askew, *Performing Political Identity: The Democrat Party in Southern Thailand* (Bangkok: Silkworm, 2008), 335–36.

23. Warin later became a member of the NCPO's National Reform Council. Warin was a personal adviser to Admiral Surin Rerng-Arom, who had been chief of staff of the navy at the time of the 2006 coup.

24. For a clip of Boworn explaining why he became a petitioner, see his comments given at a meeting in the Senate building on July 3, 2012: https://www.youtube.com/watch?v=e7nQTPydSCw. He was called as a witness in the Somyot 112 case, when he was described as president of the People's Network to Protect the Institution [เครือข่ายราษฎรอาสา ปกป้องสถาบัน], I-law notes, 51–54.

25. For reports on these allegations and Boworn's responses, see "กระทิงแดง รีเทิร์น เปิดตัว 'แนวร่วมกอบกู้วิกฤติชาติ' เน้นป้องสถาบัน," *Prachatai*, February 20, 2013, http://www.prachatai.com/journal/2013/02/45401; and Jitsiree Thongnoi, "The Ultra-royalist Who Wants to Defend Your Human Rights," *Bangkok Post*, August 2, 2015, http://www.bangkokpost.com/print/640764/.

26. Piyabutr, *ศาลรัฐประหาร* [Coup Court], 31–32.

27. "และคณะ."

28. At the time Sunai served as chair of the house foreign relations committee.

29. Jatuporn Prompan and Nattawut Saikua were the best known of the redshirt UDD movement's leadership triumvirate, both of them notorious for aggressive, rabble-rousing public speeches and television appearances.

30. This was reminiscent of the way leading Thai politicians would often instruct their aides to sue their rivals' subordinates for defamation, rather than signing the lawsuits themselves.

31. For footage of the exchange and its later outcome, see this clip from Matichon TV, July 5, 2012: https://www.youtube.com/watch?v=4mPTsE9usAw.

32. Jaran gave an interview in the run-up to the court decision, suggesting that Article 68 of the 2007 Constitution (which made it illegal to overthrow democratic rule with the King as head of state) could be used to curb the power of the executive and legislature, an argument that led some analysts to believe he sympathized with the petitioners. See Voice TV, June 8, 2012, http://news.voicetv.co.th/thailand/41282.html.

33. Jaran interviews, July 8 and 21, 2015. He was never actually the youngest judge: according to the court's website, Boonsong was born the day after Jaran.

34. Interview, March 19, 2008.

35. Teera Suteewarangkurn interview, December 12, 2012.

36. See, for example, NBT TV news report from August 3, 2007 (uploaded in 2008), https://youtu.be/rjZSXZdbPdo. For a July 2012 Thai PBS clip putting the story in context,

including a phone interview with Jaran explaining his decision, see https://www.youtube.com/watch?v=ivo8VVFtIWQ.

37. A full transcript of Jaran's remarks appears as "จรัญ ภักดีธนากุล (5 ปีที่แล้ว) เสนอให้รับ รธน. 50 แล้วค่อยแก้มาตราเดียวเพื่อยกร่างใหม่," *Prachatai* July 5, 2012. http://www.prachatai.com/journal/2012/07/41395.

38. See, for example this lengthy MCOT radio interview Jaran gave the day after he withdrew from the case: https://www.youtube.com/watch?v=4n12PxDRQDo.

39. See for example T-News, July 14, 2012 https://www.youtube.com/watch?v=5mSH3155SVk.

40. See *Thai Rath*, "ที่ประชุมศาลรธน. ไม่อนุญาต 3 ตุลาการถอนตัว" [Meeting of Constitutional Court denies permission for three judges to recuse themselves], July 6, 2012, http://203.151.20.61/content/273908. Nurak Mapraneet succeeded Wasant as court president in 2013.

41. Jaran was too diplomatic to suggest that according to this logic, neither Nurak nor Supot should have accepted appointments to the Constitutional Court in the first place.

42. MCOT interview, https://www.youtube.com/watch?v=4n12PxDRQDo (minute 3.00). The reference to his "official capacity" seemed to be a sop to Wasant, who was speaking to television reporters informally, in his shirtsleeves, prior to becoming the court president.

43. See "Constitution Drafter Reports Progress," US Embassy Cable 07BANGKOK1188, February 27, 2007, Wikileaks, http://cables.mrkva.eu/cable.php?id=98207.

44. For a relevant discussion about Thai meanings of "the people," see Duncan McCargo, "Peopling Thailand's 2015 Draft Constitution," *Contemporary Southeast Asia* 37, no. 3 (2015): 329–54.

45. See "Top Judge Has Led a Life Full of Achievements," *The Nation*, June 8, 2012, http://www.nationmultimedia.com/politics/Top-judge-has-led-a-life-full-of-achievements-30183716.html.

46. Chai-Anan interview, March 19, 2008. After 2006, Chai-Anan was closely associated with the anti-Thaksin movement.

47. See "Pheu Thai Spokesman Jailed for Defaming Former Constitutional Court President," *Bangkok Post*, July 24, 2015, http://www.nationmultimedia.com/breakingnews/Pheu-Thai-spokesman-jailed-for-defaming-former-Con-30265139.html.

48. Wasant Soypisut, เรื่อง(ไม่)สนุกในศาลรัฐธรรมนูญ [Unhappy Stories from the Constitutional Court] (Bangkok: Khlet Thai, 2014), 185.

49. Wasant เรื่อง(ไม่)สนุก, 186, 190–91.

50. For an example of a lengthy television program highly critical of the court's decision, see Matichon TV, "ศาลรัฐธรรมนูญ ... ศาลรัฐประหาร?" [Constitutional Court, *Coup d'état* Court?], broadcast in June 2012, https://www.youtube.com/watch?v=WdaaSnndlL4. The program opened by interviewing former minister Chaturon Chaisaeng, who declared that the court's action in accepting the petition was itself unconstitutional, before going on to feature extensive commentary from "independent scholar" Verapat Pariyawong and from Bangkok senator Rosana Tositrakul. Neither Chaturon nor Rosana held law degrees.

51. Wasant refrains from mentioning more alarming redshirt excesses, such as reading out judges' phone numbers and addresses on stage.

52. See, for example, Wasant เรื่อง(ไม่)สนุก, 77–89, 134.

53. Yingluck's role model for her smiling leadership style was not her loquacious brother, but Thaksin's arch-rival, Privy Council president General Prem Tinsulanond. See Duncan McCargo, "Thailand's Yingluck Shinawatra Turning From 'Stopgap' to a Lasting Presence," *Asia Blog*, September 25, 2012, http://asiasociety.org/blog/asia/thailands-yingluck-shinawatra-turning-stopgap-lasting-presence.

54. Wasant เรื่อง(ไม่)สนุก, 195.

55. See Judgment 18-22/2555, Petition for Constitutional Court Opinion, Article 68, July 13, 2012, judgment of Chat Chonlawan, 58–59.

56. See more details in this YouTube clip from Voice TV, July 6, 2012. Wasant's original interview was given on August 18, 2011. https://www.youtube.com/watch?v=hbDohcjxbKA.

57. บยส [การอบรมหลักสูตรผู้บริหารกระบวนการยุติธรรมระดับสูง[[Training Program For Senior Justice System Administrators] is a course for senior judges, in which nonjudges are also permitted to enroll. It is unclear whether Wirat graduated from the program.

58. For a related discussion see Ünaldi, *Working Towards the Monarchy*, 197, 215–17.

59. "อย่าทะเลาะกัน" See ไต่สวนผู้ถูกร้องล้ม รธน. "โภคิน" ปะทะเดือด "วิรัตน์" รับไม่ปกปิดทาสรับใช้ "แม้ว" [Investigating Respondents for Overthrowing the Constitution. Phokin's Heated Battle with Wirat. Admits Being a Slave of "Maew" (Thaksin)], *Phujatkan Online*, July 6, 2012, http://www.manager.co.th/Politics/ViewNews.aspx?NewsID=9550000082958.

60. On the brisk proceedings, smooth other than the recusal of Jaran, see Wasant เรื่อง (ไม่)สนุก, especially 192–96.

61. A similar view was expressed by ML Nattakorn Devakula, aka Mom Pluem, a prominent commentator on a pro-Thaksin channel: to his surprise, during the two-day hearing the judges had shown no bias towards the petitioners throughout their lightweight and sometimes over-emotional testimony. On the contrary, the judges had tried to "break" the petitioners from rambling off topic and to maintain the focus on substantive issues. See VOICE TV, July 6, 2012, https://www.youtube.com/watch?v=hbDohcjxbKA.

62. The King visited Koh Kret and the Irrigation Department, where he presided over the inauguration of five flood prevention projects. For news footage of the event see https://www.youtube.com/watch?v=DHOYqcZkoZc.

63. Yingluck's role as master of ceremonies was shown at length on national television, as seen in this clip which shows her apparently aboard the royal boat: https://www.youtube.com/watch?v=gg2oEkjvkhg.

64. The deal argument was first advanced in Shawn Crispin, "The Deal Behind Thailand's Polls," Asia Times, June 30, 2011, http://www.atimes.com/atimes/Southeast_Asia/MF30Ae01.html. Some of Crispin's details have been disputed, but the survival of the Yingluck government for nearly three years can best be explained by an elite pact along these lines. Off-the-record key informant conversations support the existence of such a pact.

65. Wasant, เรื่อง(ไม่)สนุก, 22.

66. Yingluck's three royal decorations ranked numbers eight to ten in the order of precedence, and were more or less standard issue for senior politicians. They were issued in markedly quick succession between November 2011 and April 2012. Abhisit, Samak, Surayuth, and Prayut were not given any additional decorations during their terms as prime minister. Thaksin was promoted to an unusually high rank in 2002, giving his then wife, Potjaman, the title of "Khunying" (roughly equivalent to "Lady"). This elevation, never given to Chuan or Abhisit, and yet to be granted to Prayut either, implied that Thaksin was in special favor with the palace during the early years of his premiership.

67. Constitutional Court Judgment 22-2555, July 13, 2012, 23.

68. Khemthong Tonsakulrungruang, "Entrenching the Minority: The Constitutional Court in Thailand's Political Conflict," *Washington International Law Journal* 26, no. 2 (2017): 259–60.

69. Wasant, เรื่อง(ไม่)สนุก,199.

70. "ความไม่เป็นฝักเป็นฝ่ายทางการเมือง" [not taking one side or another politically], Borwornsak, ศาลรัฐธรรมนูญ [The Constitution Court], 28.

71. See Duncan McCargo, "Thai Politics as Reality TV," *Journal of Asian Studies* 68, no. 1 (2009): 7–19.

72. In this paragraph, the ousted host was Sondhi Limthongkul, the main founder of the PAD; the TV channel owner was Thaksin Shinawatra, whose Shin Corp, which owned iTV, was sold to Singapore's Temasek at the beginning of 2006; Sondhi touted subscriptions to his ASTV channel at PAD rallies; the PAD briefly seized control of NBT (formerly Channel 11) in August 2008; and prime minister Samak Sundaravej was removed from office in September 2008 for illegally hosting a television cooking show.

73. See Khemthong, "Entrenching the Minority," 253.

74. Video clips alleging corruption in Constitutional Court hiring practices led to the departure of the secretary to the court president in 2010. None of the judges implicated resigned. See the series of three videos entitled พฤติกรรมศาลรัฐธรรมนูญไทย ตอนที่ 1 2 3 [Behavior of the Thai Constitutional Court: Parts 1 2 3], at https://www.youtube.com/watch?v=iP4r-1isXJs, https://www.youtube.com/watch?v=4mDnFau3UUQ, https://www.youtube.com/watch?v=bWQ9xT71sSU.

75. This was the first coup in Thai history to abolish a judicial entity, the Constitutional Court. Jaran explained in a television interview that the 2006 abolition reflected a widespread perception that politicians had managed to place enough of their people in all of the independent agencies to neutralize their effectiveness—what became known as the block vote—hence the need for a complete revamp of the Constitutional Court after the 2006 coup. ITV, November 28, 2013, https://www.youtube.com/watch?v=wHcXsoDZjoQ.

76. "คณะตุลาการ รัฐธรรมนูญ," Interview, Sarawut Benjakul, August 18, 2014.

77. Judge E, June 25, 2015.

78. Interview, March 17, 2008. Somchai's arguments were based on a research project he had conducted into Constitutional Court judgments.

79. Field notes, Nitirat seminar, Thammasat University, July 15, 2012. For Nitirat's proposal, see ข้อเสนอแก้ไขเพิ่มเติมรัฐธรรมนูญแห่งราชอาณาจักรไทยเพื่อยกเลิกศาลรัฐธรรมนูญและจัดตั้งคณะตุลาการพิทักษ์ระบอบรัฐธรรมนูญ [Proposal to Amend the Constitution of the Kingdom of Thailand to Abolish the Constitutional Court and to Establish the Judicial Commission to Defend the Constitutional System], July 15, 2012, http://www.enlightened-jurists.com/download/76.

80. Interview with Constitutional Court official, August 30, 2014.

81. Wasant, เรื่อง(ไม่)สนุก, 32. The wording is specified in Article 201 of the 2007 Constitution.

82. On Chat's views, see http://www.siamintelligence.com/1-to11-law/, August 11, 2012. The importance of consensus, spelled out in the preamble to the 2007 Constitution, is also mentioned by Boonsong in his judgment. See Judgment 18–22, 2555, Petition for Constitutional Court Opinion, Article 68, July 13, 2012, 67–68.

83. Wasant, เรื่อง(ไม่)สนุก, 191.

84. Wasant, เรื่อง(ไม่)สนุก, 192.

85. Jaran came quite close to saying this in the final minutes of an MCOT interview, July 6, 2012, https://www.youtube.com/watch?v=4n12PxDRQDo.

86. Constitutional Court Decision No. 15–18/2556, https://en.wikisource.org/wiki/Constitutional_Court_Decision_No_15%E2%80%9318/2556?oldid=4884183. A footnote states that the Thai phrase นำประเทศชาติให้ถอยหลังเข้าคลอง ["draw the nation back into the canal"] has been variously translated by the international media.

87. On the first question—whether the procedures and resolutions used by Pheu Thai were unconstitutional—Nurak, Jaran, Jarun, Supot, Boonsong, and Taweekiat found for the petitioners, while Chalermpon, Chat and Udomsak found against them (a 6:3 vote). On the more substantive issue of whether the draft itself was unconstitutional, Boonsong rejected the petition, resulting in a 5–4 vote. See http://www.bangkokbiznews.com/mobile/view/news/544641.

88. See, for example, Taweekiat's very aggressive column in response to Nitirat's 2011 call for the 2006 coup to be "nullified" in *Matichon*, October 2, 2011. There was nothing

tempered or judicious about his tone, and no reference to the fact that the Nitirat lecturers were his academic colleagues at Thammasat, http://www.matichon.co.th/news_detail.php?newsid=1317534718&grpid&catid=02&subcatid=0200.

89. "เปิดประวัติ 9 ตุลาการศาลรัฐธรรมนูญ" [Revealing the Backgrounds of 9 Constitutional Court Judges], Thai PBS, November 20, 2013 http://news.thaipbs.or.th/content/ เปิดประวัติ 9 ตุลาการศาลรัฐธรรมนูญ.

90. For a brief overview, see Siam Intelligence profile, which gives seventeen members, http://politicalbase.in.th/index.php/กลุ่มสยามประชาภิวัฒน์. A longer list of twenty-six members may be found at http://www.prasong.com/การเมือง/5-8/. For a January 2012 Voice TV news clip introducing Siam Prachapiwat, see https://www.youtube.com/watch?v=gwuahmRmrss.

91. See "23 คณาจารย์นิติศาสตร์ เห็นต่าง 'นิติราษฎร์' ต้องกล้าวิพากษ์วิจารณ์เผด็จการทุกรูปแบบ ไม่ใช่แค่เผด็จการทหาร" [23 Legal Academics Disagree with Nitirat, Must Dare to Criticise All Forms of Dictatorship, Not Just Military Dictatorship], *Matichon*, October 2, 2011, http://prachatai.com/journal/2011/10/37192.

92. Interview with Komsan Pokhong, law lecturer at Sukhothai Thammathirat University, and member of both the "23 lecturers" and Siam Prachapiwat, June 5, 2013. Between ten and fifteen academics formed the core of Siam Prachapiwat. Komsan described their main ideological stance as opposition to monopoly capitalism.

93. This case was filed with the Constitutional Court on May 1, 2013. The other petitioners were Paiboon Nitiwan and Chermsak Pinthong. See "เจิมศักดิ์-คมสันต์-ไพบูลย์ร้องศาลรธน." [Chermsak, Komsan, and Paiboon File a Petition to Constitutional Court], *Khom Chat Luk*, May 2, 2013, http://www.komchadluek.net/news/politic/157457.

94. See "'ทวีเกียรติ'กลุ่ม'สยามประชาภิวัฒน์'นั่งตุลาการศาลรธน.คนใหม่" [Thaweekiat "Siam Prachapiwat" Appointed As New Constitutional Court Judge], *Thai Rath*, August 29, 2013, http://www.thairath.co.th/content/366617. Banjerd was a member of both the 2007 and 2014–15 Constitution Drafting Committees.

95. Back in 2003, Thailand's academic legal community had not been so ideologically divided: Banjerd had coauthored a book on the Constitutional Court not just with Suraphon Nitikraiphot (later the rector of Thammasat), but also with future Nitirat members Worajet and Teera. See Suraphon Nitikraiphot et al., ศาลรัฐธรรมนูญกับการปฏิบัติพันธกิจตามรัฐธรรมนูญ [The Constitutional Court and the Implementation of Its Constitutional Mission] (Bangkok: Winyuchon, 2003).

96. Interview, March 19, 2008.

97. For example, see comments by Paul Chambers in Cameron McKinley, "Thai Coup Threat: Voting Gaffe Least of Problems for Prime Minister Yingluck," *Epoch Times*, February 4, 2014, http://www.theepochtimes.com/n3/488333-thai-prime-minister-faces-judicial-and-military-coup/.

98. The argument in this paragraph reflects nonattributable conversations with well-placed individuals familiar with these developments.

CONCLUSION. THE TROUBLE IS POLITICS

1. Srimati Basu, *The Trouble with Marriage*, 212–17.

2. See เล่ม ๑๓๖ ตอนพิเศษ ๓๗ ง ราชกิจจานุเบกษา, February 8, 2019, http://www.ratchakitcha.soc.go.th/DATA/PDF/2562/E/037/T_0001.PDF.

3. "List-MP Calculation Method is Constitutional, Court Rules," *Bangkok Post*, May 8, 2019, https://www.bangkokpost.com/news/politics/1674040/list-mp-calculation-method-is-constitutional-court-rules.

Index

Studies of the Weatherhead East Asian Institute Columbia University

Selected Titles
(Complete list at: http://weai.columbia.edu/publications/studies-weai/)

Residual Futures: The Urban Ecologies of Literary and Visual Media of 1960s and 1970s Japan, by Franz Prichard. Columbia University Press, 2019.

Down and Out in Saigon: Stories of the Poor in a Colonial City, by Haydon Cherry. Yale University Press, 2019.

The Power of Print in Modern China: Intellectuals and Industrial Publishing from the End of Empire to Maoist State Socialism, by Robert Culp. Columbia University Press, 2019.

Beyond the Asylum: Mental Illness in French Colonial Vietnam, by Claire E. Edington. Cornell University Press, 2019.

Borderland Memories: Searching for Historical Identity in Post-Mao China, by Martin Thomas Fromm. Cambridge University Press, 2019.

Sovereignty Experiments: Korean Migrants and the Building of Borders in Northeast Asia, 1860–1949, by Alyssa M. Park. Cornell University Press, 2019.

The Greater East Asia Co-Prosperity Sphere: When Total Empire Met Total War, by Jeremy A. Yellen. Cornell University Press, 2019.

Thought Crime: Ideology and State Power in Interwar Japan, by Max Ward. Duke University Press, 2019.

Statebuilding by Imposition: Resistance and Control in Colonial Taiwan and the Philippines, by Reo Matsuzaki. Cornell University Press, 2019.

Nation-Empire: Ideology and Rural Youth Mobilization in Japan and Its Colonies, by Sayaka Chatani. Cornell University Press, 2019.

Fixing Landscape: A Techno-Poetic History of China's Three Gorges, by Corey Byrnes. Columbia University Press, 2019.

The Invention of Madness: State, Society, and the Insane in Modern China, by Emily Baum. University of Chicago Press, 2018.

Japan's Imperial Underworlds: Intimate Encounters at the Borders of Empire, by David Ambaras. Cambridge University Press, 2018.

Heroes and Toilers: Work as Life in Postwar North Korea, 1953–1961, by Cheehyung Harrison Kim. Columbia University Press, 2018.

Electrified Voices: How the Telephone, Phonograph, and Radio Shaped Modern Japan, 1868–1945, by Kerim Yasar. Columbia University Press, 2018.

Making Two Vietnams: War and Youth Identities, 1965–1975, by Olga Dror. Cambridge University Press, 2018.

A Misunderstood Friendship: Mao Zedong, Kim Il-sung, and Sino–North Korean Relations, 1949–1976, by Zhihua Shen and Yafeng Xia. Columbia University Press, 2018.

Playing by the Informal Rules: Why the Chinese Regime Remains Stable Despite Rising Protests, by Yao Li. Cambridge University Press, 2018.

Raising China's Revolutionaries: Modernizing Childhood for Cosmopolitan Nationalists and Liberated Comrades, by Margaret Mih Tillman. Columbia University Press, 2018.

Buddhas and Ancestors: Religion and Wealth in Fourteenth-Century Korea, by Juhn Y. Ahn. University of Washington Press, 2018.

Idly Scribbling Rhymers: Poetry, Print, and Community in Nineteenth Century Japan, by Robert Tuck. Columbia University Press, 2018.

China's War on Smuggling: Law, Economic Life, and the Making of the Modern State, 1842–1965, by Philip Thai. Columbia University Press, 2018.

Forging the Golden Urn: The Qing Empire and the Politics of Reincarnation in Tibet, by Max Oidtmann. Columbia University Press, 2018.

The Battle for Fortune: State-Led Development, Personhood, and Power among Tibetans in China, by Charlene Makley. Cornell University Press, 2018.

Aesthetic Life: Beauty and Art in Modern Japan, by Miya Elise Mizuta Lippit. Harvard University Asia Center, 2018.

Where the Party Rules: The Rank and File of China's Communist State, by Daniel Koss. Cambridge University Press, 2018.

Resurrecting Nagasaki: Reconstruction and the Formation of Atomic Narratives, by Chad R. Diehl. Cornell University Press, 2018.

China's Philological Turn: Scholars, Textualism, and the Dao in the Eighteenth Century, by Ori Sela. Columbia University Press, 2018.

Making Time: Astronomical Time Measurement in Tokugawa Japan, by Yulia Frumer. University of Chicago Press, 2018.

Mobilizing without the Masses: Control and Contention in China, by Diana Fu. Cambridge University Press, 2018.

Post-Fascist Japan: Political Culture in Kamakura after the Second World War, by Laura Hein. Bloomsbury, 2018.

China's Conservative Revolution: The Quest for a New Order, 1927–1949, by Brian Tsui. Cambridge University Press, 2018.

Promiscuous Media: Film and Visual Culture in Imperial Japan, 1926–1945, by Hikari Hori. Cornell University Press, 2018.

The End of Japanese Cinema: Industrial Genres, National Times, and Media Ecologies, by Alexander Zahlten. Duke University Press, 2017.

The Chinese Typewriter: A History, by Thomas S. Mullaney. The MIT Press, 2017.

Forgotten Disease: Illnesses Transformed in Chinese Medicine, by Hilary A. Smith. Stanford University Press, 2017.

Borrowing Together: Microfinance and Cultivating Social Ties, by Becky Yang Hsu. Cambridge University Press, 2017.

Food of Sinful Demons: Meat, Vegetarianism, and the Limits of Buddhism in Tibet, by Geoffrey Barstow. Columbia University Press, 2017.

Youth For Nation: Culture and Protest in Cold War South Korea, by Charles R. Kim. University of Hawaii Press, 2017.

Socialist Cosmopolitanism: The Chinese Literary Universe, 1945–1965, by Nicolai Volland. Columbia University Press, 2017.

The Social Life of Inkstones: Artisans and Scholars in Early Qing China, by Dorothy Ko. University of Washington Press, 2017.

Darwin, Dharma, and the Divine: Evolutionary Theory and Religion in Modern Japan, by G. Clinton Godart. University of Hawaii Press, 2017.

Dictators and Their Secret Police: Coercive Institutions and State Violence, by Sheena Chestnut Greitens. Cambridge University Press, 2016.

The Cultural Revolution on Trial: Mao and the Gang of Four, by Alexander C. Cook. Cambridge University Press, 2016.

Inheritance of Loss: China, Japan, and the Political Economy of Redemption After Empire, by Yukiko Koga. University of Chicago Press, 2016.

Homecomings: The Belated Return of Japan's Lost Soldiers, by Yoshikuni Igarashi. Columbia University Press, 2016.

Samurai to Soldier: Remaking Military Service in Nineteenth-Century Japan, by D. Colin Jaundrill. Cornell University Press, 2016.

CPSIA information can be obtained
at www.ICGtesting.com
Printed in the USA
BVHW032356011219
565338BV00003B/39/P